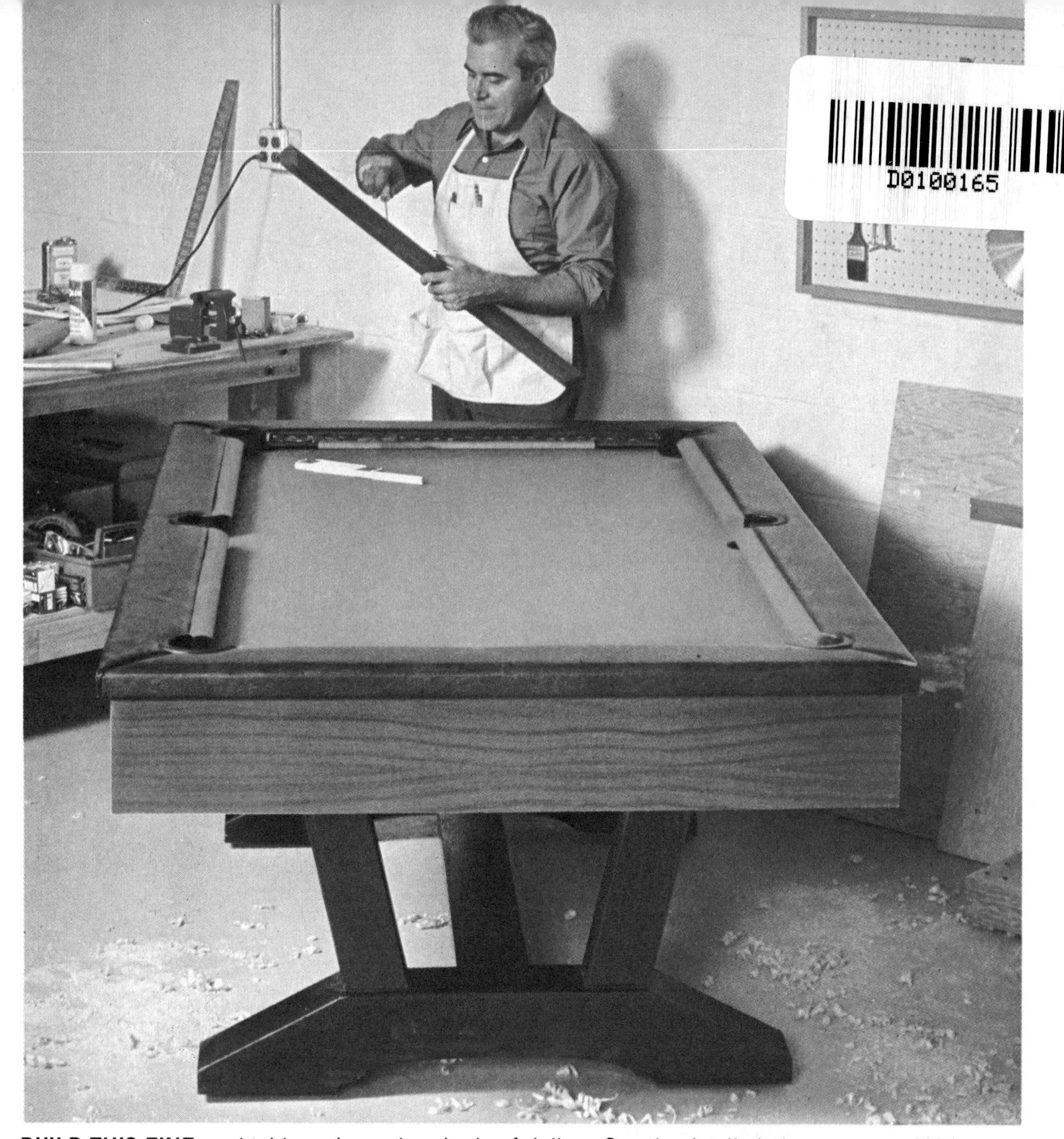

BUILD THIS FINE pool table and save hundreds of dollars. See the detailed plans on page 2384.

In this volume . . .

CHOOSE THE PROP that's right in diameter and pitch, and you'll add knots. See page 2445.

KEEP THAT BEAUTIFUL electric range in topnotch condition. Actually, it's one of the simplest appliances in your home to service. See the troubleshooting charts on page 2491.

HERE ARE SOME IDEAS for attractive privacy screens that will add pleasure and value to your home. You'll find others—and construction details—on page 2440.

PLYWOOD IS THE MOST VERSATILE of building materials. You can even use it as a ceiling material, indoors or out. Learn to buy the grade that will save money on page 2364.

YOU CAN BUILD this handsome platform boat in a surprisingly short time. Foam pontoons are available, and the rest of the construction is simple. See the article on page 2378.

BUILD THESE exciting projects from Plexiglas. This cutting board is durable, sanitary and nonabsorbent.

THIS NOVEL stepladder displays favored plants in fine style. It's easy to build, and can be moved to follow the sun.

COFFEE TABLE is easily made by combining your favorite wood with a pair of U-shaped legs fashioned from clear plastic. The result is an airy, floating effect. You'll find instructions for making these and other projects on page 2339.

Popular Mechanics do-it-yourself encyclopedia

in 18 volumes

a complete how-to guide for the homeowner, the hobbyist—and anyone who enjoys working with mind and hands!

All about:

- home maintenance
- home-improvement projects
- wall paneling
- burglary and fire protection
- furniture projects
- finishing and refinishing furniture
- outdoor living
- home remodeling
- solutions to home problems
- challenging woodworking projects
- hobbies and handicrafts
- model making
- weekend projects
- workshop shortcuts and techniques
- hand-tool skills
- power-tool know-how
- shop-made tools
- car repairs
- car maintenance
- appliance repair
- boating
- hunting
- fishing
- camping
- photography projects
- radio, TV and electronics know-how
- clever hints and tips
- projects just for fun

volume 13

Popular Mechanics, 250 W. 55th St., New York, NY 10019

The Hearst Corporation cannot assume responsibility for proper application of techniques, implementations or proper and safe functioning of any of the manufactured or reader-built items, products or projects resulting in whole or in part from all or any part of any plans, prints, projects or instructional materials published in this volume.

ISBN 0-910990-68-9
Library of Congress Catalog Number 77 84920

Printed in the United States of America

Contents

You can stow away this picnic table

By WAYNE C. LECKEY

It looks complex, but this handsome picnic table is easy to build. It's designed to fold up to a compact 2 x 5 feet for convenient storage

IT'S GREAT TO HAVE a big table out on your deck or patio for those pleasant summer-evening meals. But finding a place to store it is something else. Often it simply stays outdoors all year.

We tossed the storage problem at designer Tom Fung, well known for his unique designs, who came up with the ingenious folding table you see here. Eighteen pivot points make it possible to fold the table into an incredibly small space of 2x5 feet, which means you can park it in a garage or basement with room to spare.

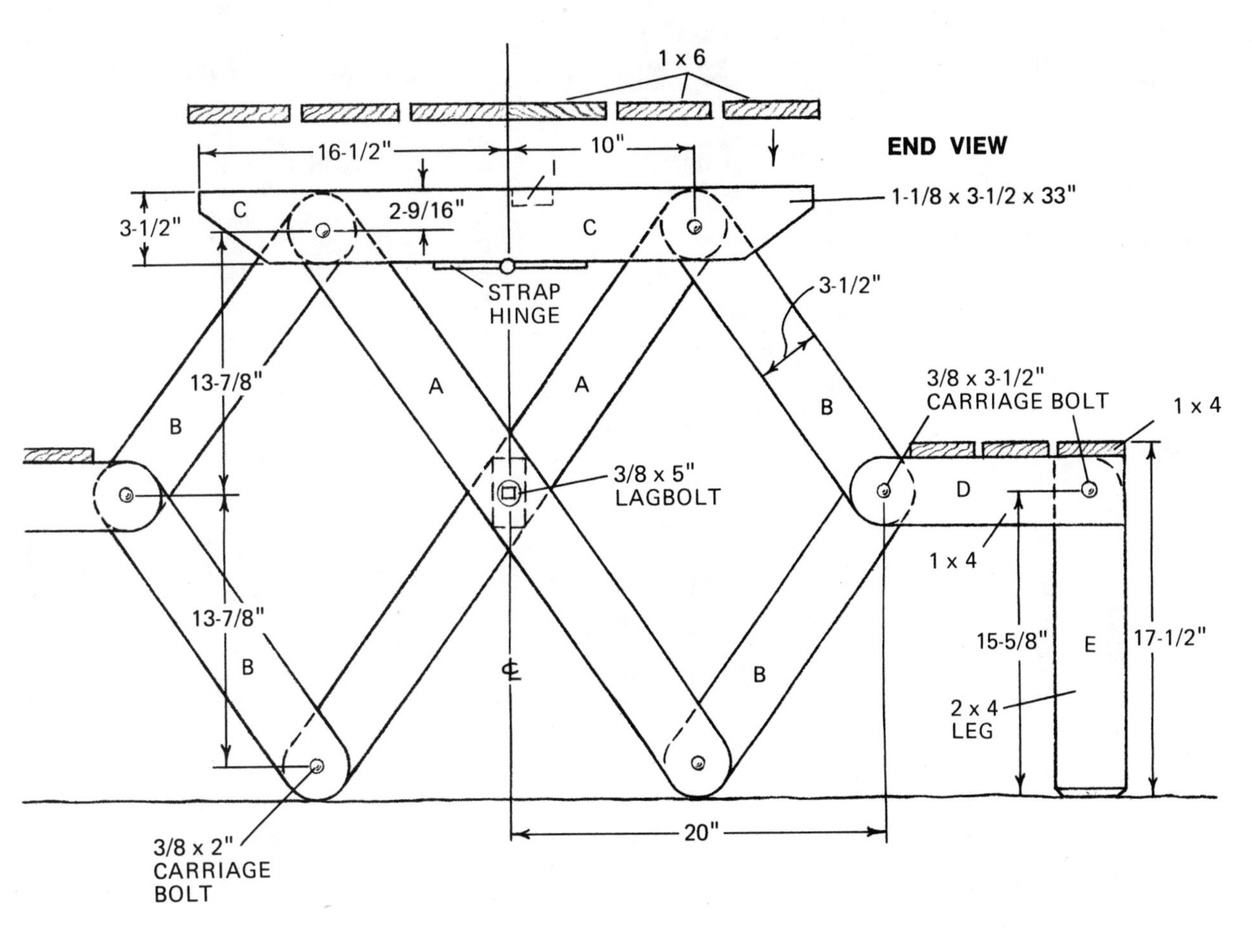

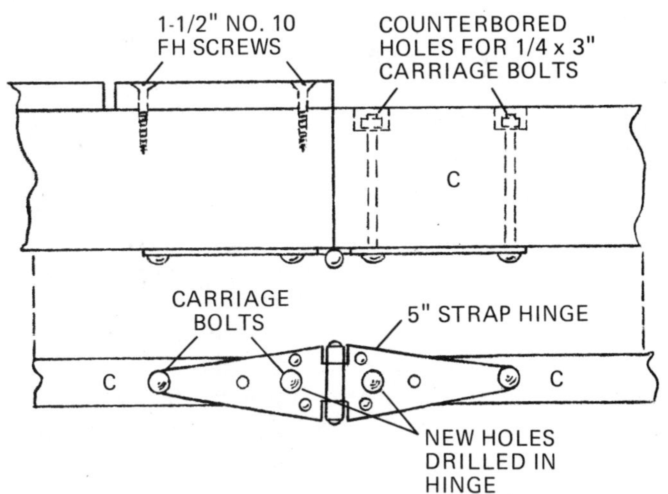

HINGE JOINT

SEE ALSO

Benches, deck . . . Bolts . . . Cookout bars . . . Dining tables . . . Garden shelters . . . Gazebos . . . Grill houses . . . Hinges . . . Patios . . . Stowaway furniture

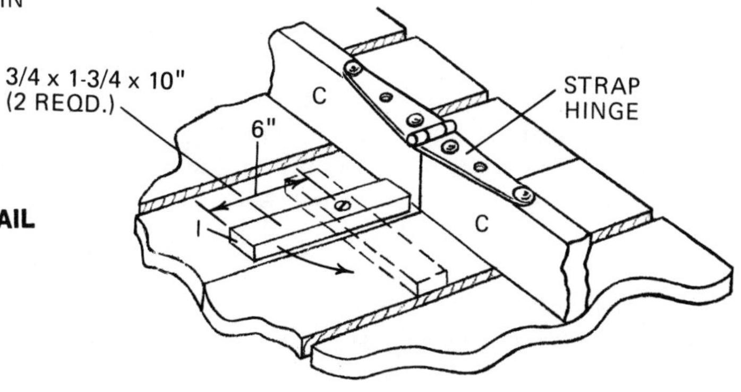

TURNBUTTON DETAIL

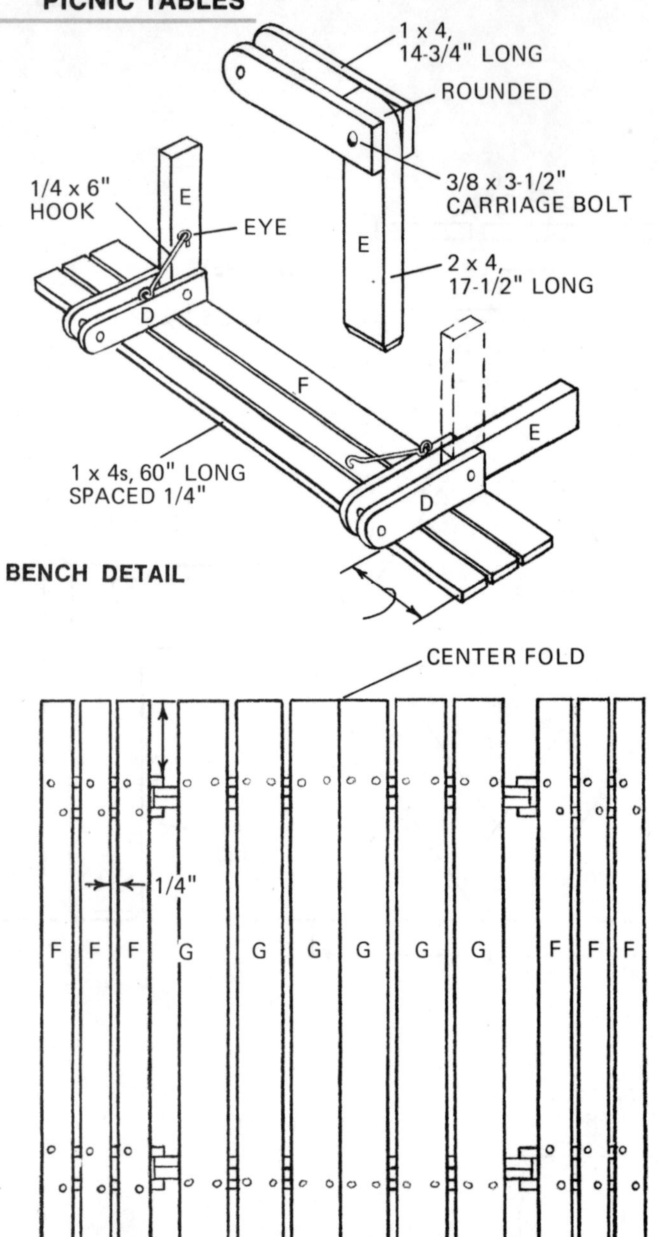

MATERIALS NEEDED (Redwood)

Key	Size	Amt.
A	¾ x 3½ x 38″	4
B	¾ x 3½ x 20¾″	8
C	1⅛ x 3½ x 16½″	4
D	¾ x 3½ x 14¾″	8
E	1½ x 3½ x 17½″	4
F	¾ x 3½ x 60″	6
G	¾ x 5½ x 60″	6
H	1½ x 3½ x 34¾″	1
I	¾ x 1¾ x 10″	2

Hardware

Item	Amt.
¼ x 3″ carriage bolts	8
¼ x 3½″ carriage bolts	4
¼ x 2″ carriage bolts	4
1¼″ No. 10 FH wood screws	2
1½″ No. 10 FH wood screws	48
¼ x 6″ hooks and eyes	4
5″ strap hinges	2
Cadmium-plated washers	34

We built the prototype, from long-lasting redwood, for a material cost well under $100. If you use No. 2 pine and paint it, you can make it for less. While it may look difficult, it's actually an easy table to build, mainly because all the parts are of lumberyard size. You just cut them to length.

The table is identical each side of a centerline. Each bench is alike, as is each scissor-folding leg. Spotting the seven pivot holes for each leg is done best by marking their locations on a sheet of plywood or wrapping paper and drilling the holes in the leg members to correspond. Round the ends of the members to a 1¾-in. radius and drill holes at the compass points. A good stunt to follow when rounding the ends and drilling the holes is to do two or more ends at one time by clamping the members together. This assures perfect alignment of the holes and makes for a neater job.

Cut parts C, to which the six tabletop members are attached, from 1⅛-in.-thick stock and join them endwise with 5-in. strap hinges. Drill an additional hole in each hinge leaf for a second carriage bolt. Use wood turnbuttons to lock the tabletop in the open position; place them on the underside near the hinges, on opposite sides of the centerline. You can keep the bench legs from being kicked outward accidentally by use of king-size hooks and eyes, and drawing up the carriage bolts holding the legs snugly so the legs do not swing freely. Place three large washers between leg members at each point where the benches attach, elsewhere, just one washer. Place washers under all nuts, of course.

Two unique picnic-table plans

continued

PLENTY OF ELBOW ROOM and attached benches are two of the most obvious advantages offered by the two king-sized redwood tables shown here and detailed on the following pages.

The hexagon design can be framed with 1¼-in. tubing, 1-in. standard pipe or 1¼-in. square tubing. If you don't have access to bending equipment, use square tubing and cut V-notches at the bending points, then bend and weld each joint.

The octagon model is a simple, straight-forward carpentry project with no metal-working involved.

Since redwood has its own natural preservative, the only finishing required is a thorough sanding and a coat of redwood stain to ensure uniform color. Finish other woods with exterior enamel.

SEE ALSO

Barbecues . . . Benches, deck . . . Cookout bars . . . Garden shelters . . . Gazebos . . . Grill houses . . . Patios . . . Screened summer rooms . . . Tubing, metal

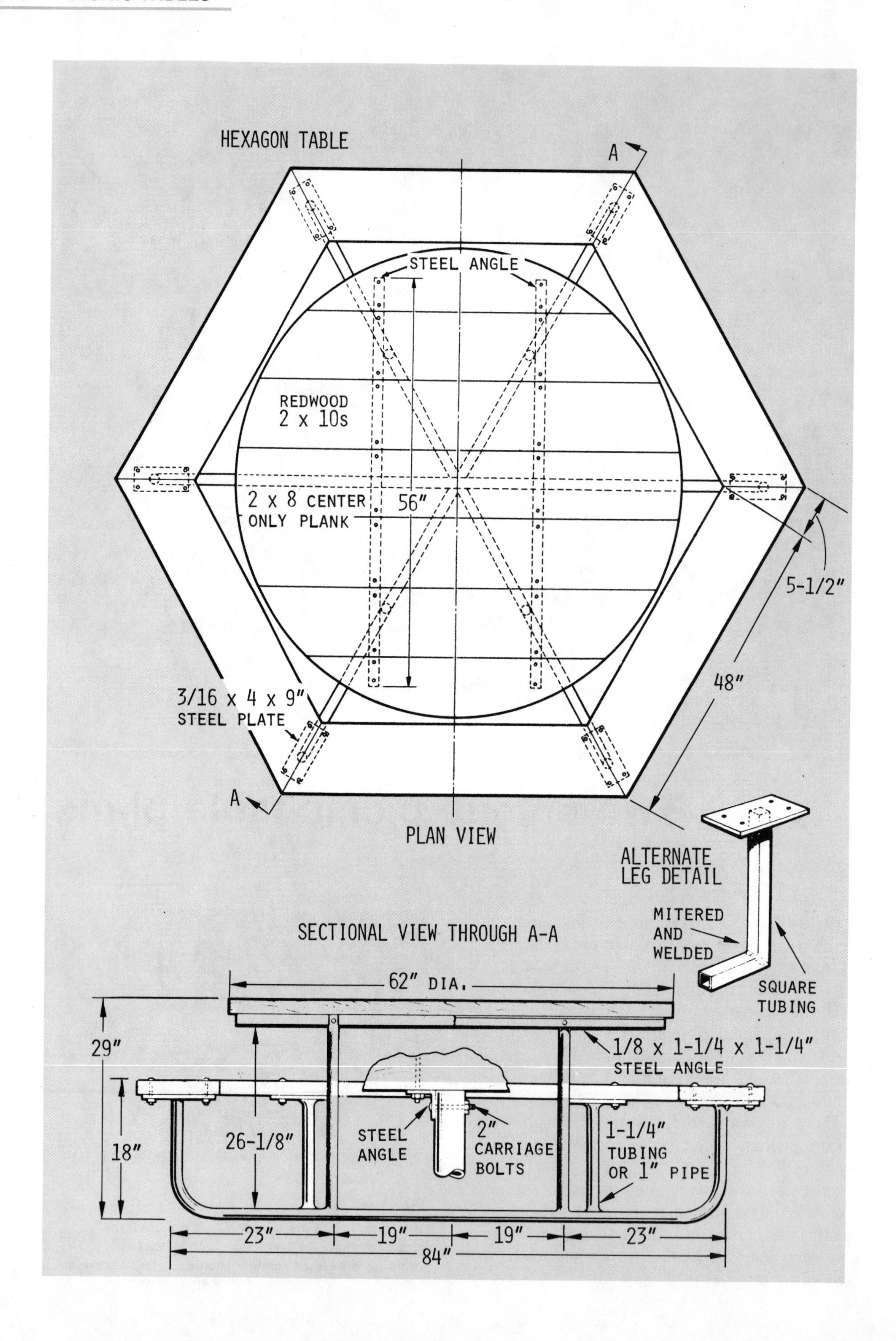
HEXAGON TABLE
A
STEEL ANGLE
REDWOOD
2 x 10s
2 x 8 CENTER
ONLY PLANK
56"
5-1/2"
48"
3/16 x 4 x 9"
STEEL PLATE
A
PLAN VIEW
ALTERNATE
LEG DETAIL
MITERED
AND
WELDED
SQUARE
TUBING
SECTIONAL VIEW THROUGH A-A
62" DIA.
29"
1/8 x 1-1/4 x 1-1/4"
STEEL ANGLE
18"
26-1/8"
STEEL
ANGLE
2"
CARRIAGE
BOLTS
1-1/4"
TUBING
OR 1" PIPE
23"
19"
19"
23"
84"

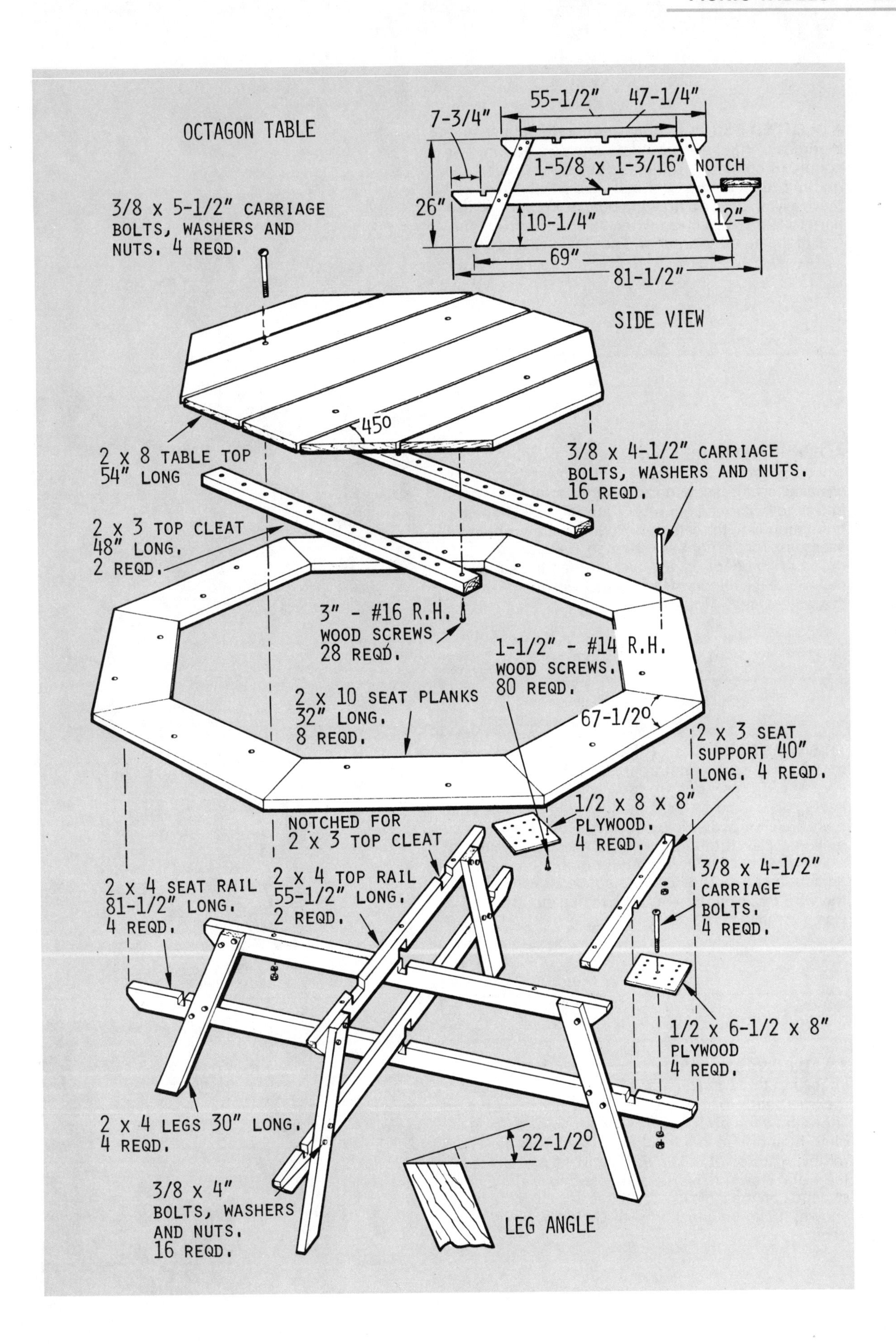
OCTAGON TABLE
55-1/2"
47-1/4"
7-3/4"
1-5/8 x 1-3/16" NOTCH
26"
10-1/4"
12"
69"
81-1/2"
SIDE VIEW
3/8 x 5-1/2" CARRIAGE BOLTS, WASHERS AND NUTS. 4 REQD.
45°
2 x 8 TABLE TOP 54" LONG
3/8 x 4-1/2" CARRIAGE BOLTS, WASHERS AND NUTS. 16 REQD.
2 x 3 TOP CLEAT 48" LONG. 2 REQD.
3" - #16 R.H. WOOD SCREWS 28 REQD.
1-1/2" - #14 R.H. WOOD SCREWS. 80 REQD.
2 x 10 SEAT PLANKS 32" LONG. 8 REQD.
67-1/2°
2 x 3 SEAT SUPPORT 40" LONG. 4 REQD.
1/2 x 8 x 8" PLYWOOD. 4 REQD.
NOTCHED FOR 2 x 3 TOP CLEAT
2 x 4 SEAT RAIL 81-1/2" LONG. 4 REQD.
2 x 4 TOP RAIL 55-1/2" LONG. 2 REQD.
3/8 x 4-1/2" CARRIAGE BOLTS. 4 REQD.
1/2 x 6-1/2 x 8" PLYWOOD 4 REQD.
2 x 4 LEGS 30" LONG. 4 REQD.
22-1/2°
3/8 x 4" BOLTS, WASHERS AND NUTS. 16 REQD.
LEG ANGLE

A SLOTTED BLOCK to hold drafting templates and triangles upright was one draftsman's solution to a couple of common problems. Picking up such drafting tools is often difficult—especially when they're lying flat on a drawing board or table. It's also hard to keep them clean when they're slid from one end of the board to another. The slots are simply saw kerfs.—*Victor J. Lamoy.*

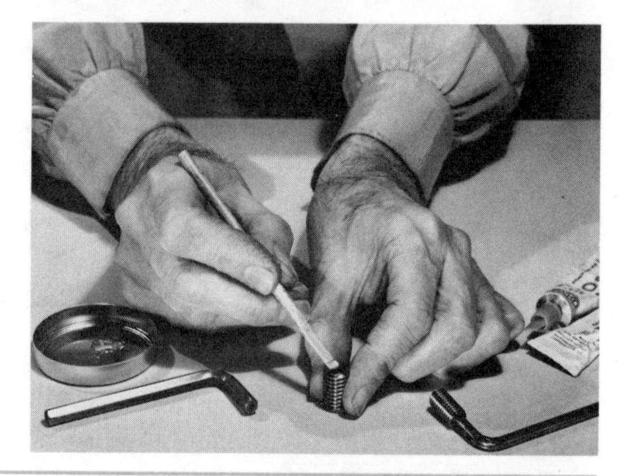

ALLEN SCREWS are often used as temporary adjusting screws or setscrews with power tools such as jigsaws, belt-disc sanders or Unimat lathes. I often find it advantageous to epoxy the Allen wrenches permanently to the setscrews to avoid the problem of searching for the right-size wrench. Before applying a drop or two of epoxy, however, tighten the screw to make sure the handle of the wrench will remain out of the way.—*Jay K. Wallace.*

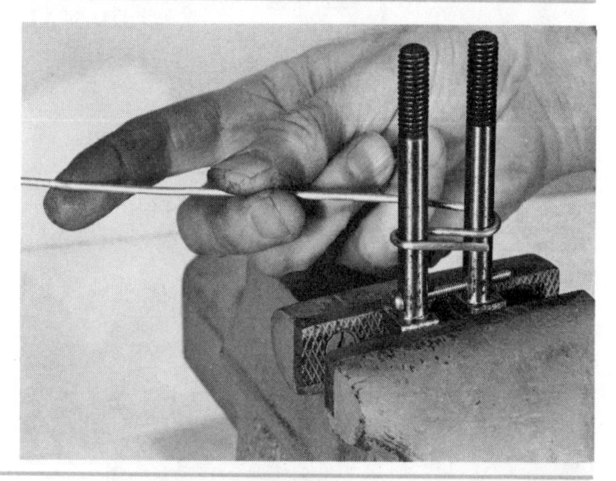

THIS WIRE BENDER is easily made and can be used for bending wires of different sizes when gripped in your vise. It consists of two square-headed bolts, each having one side of its head cut flush with its flank. The bolts are clamped with the cut sides together; then a hole is drilled through the shank's sides. One is reamed for a slide fit, the other tapped for the adjusting screw. The bolts are spaced for the size of the wire to be bent; then the jig is clamped in a vise.—*Peter Legon.*

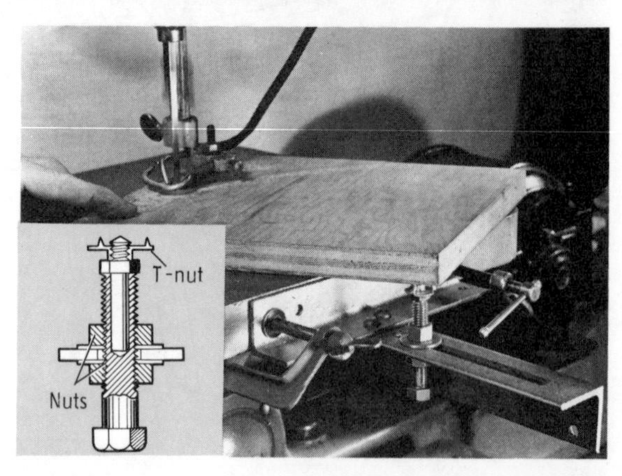

AN ADJUSTABLE PIVOT sliding in a slotted length of angle iron that's attached to the table of your jigsaw makes a handy fixture for cutting true discs. The detail shows how the pivot and its Tee-nut point rests in a blind hole drilled in a machine screw. This permits removing the pivot and driving it into the underside of the work. How the fixture is attached to the machine depends on the table itself. If it has a lip, like the one shown, it can be attached with C-clamps.—*Peter Legon.*

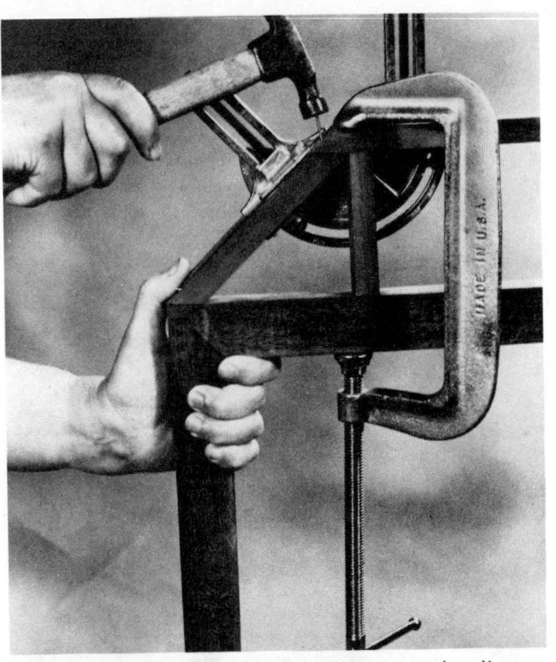

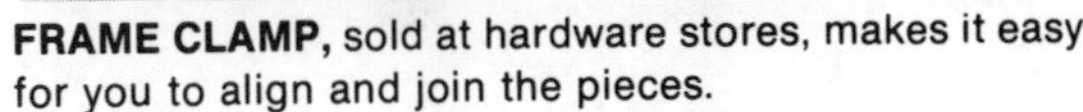

FRAME CLAMP, sold at hardware stores, makes it easy for you to align and join the pieces.

Optical-illusion picture frame

By ELMA and WILLARD WALTNER

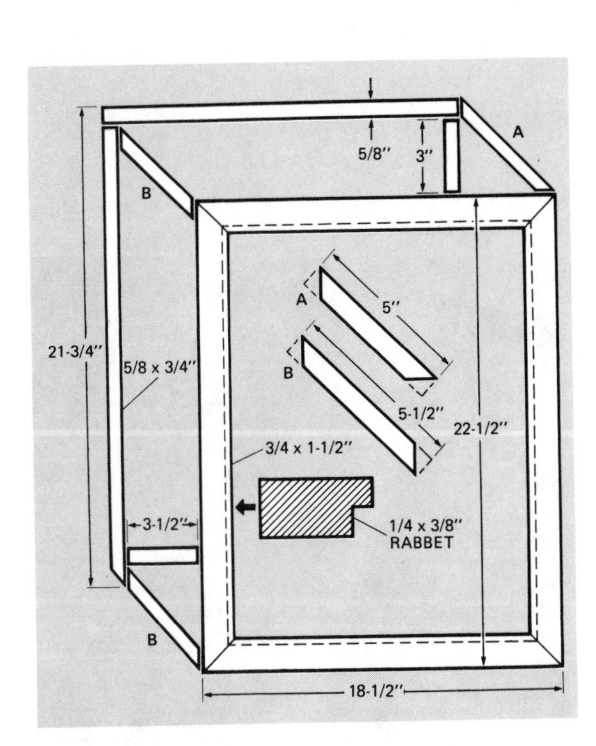

BECAUSE OF its apparent depth, this frame gives a picture a three-dimensional appearance—even though the frame lies flat against the wall. The frame is easy to make, and in all probability the small amount of materials needed can be ripped from scrap stock that you have lying about the shop.

All of the members are cut from ¾-in. stock. The main frame is 1½ in. wide while the "boxing" strips are ⅝ in. wide. The dimensions given in the drawing at left are for a frame that will accommodate a 16x20-in. picture. Size, of course, can be increased or decreased to suit the picture that you want to hang.

The small picture-frame clamp shown above makes assembling the mitered corners a snap. Most hardware stores stock such clamps.

To assemble, start by fastening the short slant strips to the main frame and then add the boxing strips. The two thin pieces go in last; these are simply glued in. Use a finish of your choice.

SEE ALSO

Clamps . . . Frames, art . . . Mountings, photo . . . Photo hints . . . Photography . . . Prints, photo

A pier set for your foyer

Here's a low-cost way to finish up your front hallway, using mitered filigree to enhance a mirror and a small table that fastens to the wall

By ROSARIO CAPOTOSTO

LAY A THIN BEAD of glue in mirror-frame grooves and insert mitered filigree.

WHEN WE FINISHED dressing up our foyer, I thought the project would end there. But my wife was so pleased with the results that she started dreaming up ways of utilizing what, at that time, was a stretch of wasted wall just inside the living room. We finally decided to add a wall-hung pier set for those last-minute appearance checks that always seem necessary before we leave the house.

The filigree of the frame is the same material I used in the entry divider. (It's made by Masonite Corp., 29 North Wacker Drive, Chicago, IL 60606.) And a piece of scrap Marlite wall paneling was used to back up the mirror. Total cost of the set was less than half the price of a ready-made unit. But I haven't seen any I like as well as the modern set I made.

On the prototype shown, the same hardwood framing that was used for the room divider served perfectly for the mirror frame. I simply

STURDY EYEBOLTS installed through the frame edge, joined with picture wire, hang the mirror.

SEE ALSO

Entryways . . . Fasteners . . . Remodeling ideas . . . Room dividers . . . Wall decorations

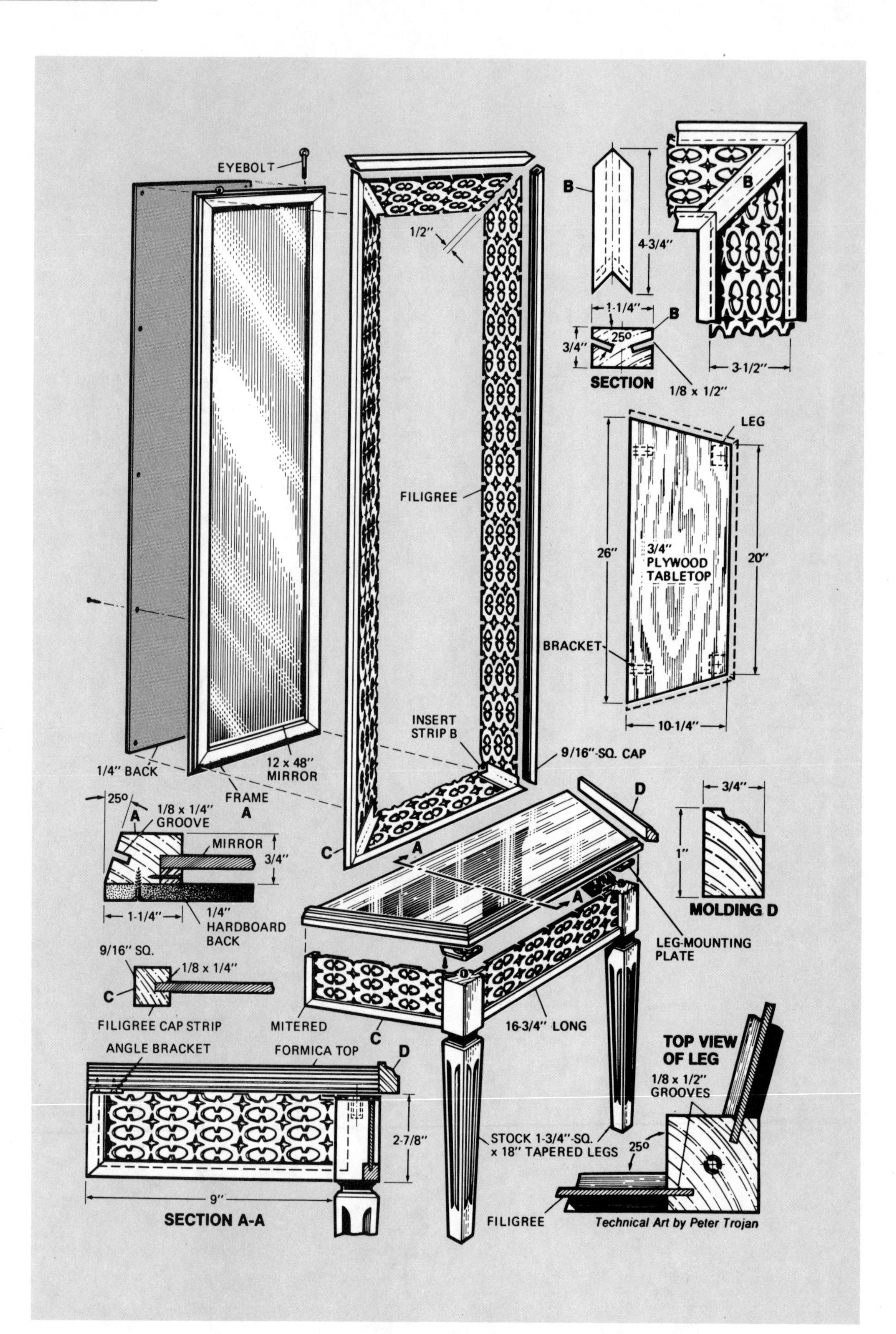

Technical Art by Peter Trojan

enlarged factory grooves in the wood frame to accept a 1x4-ft. mirror that I bought. (If you wish, you can run a rabbet in the framing strips and use a cleat to hold the mirror.) Next, make a 25° bevel cut to remove some of the excess width along the solid edge, leaving about 1 in. across the face. Then plow a ⅛-in. groove about ¼ in. deep perpendicular to the beveled edge. This groove receives the filigree.

Miter the corners of the strips to form a frame around the mirror, and for rigidity, back up the mirror with a piece of Marlite or hardboard as mentioned above.

Glue and screw three sides of the frame only to this backing. The bottom frame is joined with screws only so that the mirror can be inserted after most of the carpentry is completed. And, if your mirror should ever become cracked, this makes replacement a simple task.

To hang the frame, two eyebolts are installed on the back and fitted with an appropriate length of picture wire. Make certain that these bolts do not enter the groove that is intended to receive the mirror, and install them before inserting the mirror.

To attach the mitered filigree sections, squirt a bead of white glue into each outside groove. Notice in the photo at the right that the mitered filigree ends do not meet. This is to insure room for the reinforcing corners. Here you should allow about a ½-in. space which will be bridged by the insert.

figure the angles

Cutting these inserts is truly an exercise in angle cutting. The lead end is an inside miter while the tail end is the reverse. The tail end also slants back 25° toward the bottom to assure a good fit at the frame corner. Finally, two angled grooves along the sides permit it to slide over the mitered filigree. Since the face of the insert is left flat it won't fit flush with the 9/16-in.-sq. strip which surrounds the outer edge of the filigree and is not intended to. Glue the inserts in place first and add the square strips last.

The table is made using a pair of factory-made legs purchased at a lumberyard and a ¾-in. plywood top. Grooved slots cut into the leg tops secure the filigree. A piece of molding (D) was used to enclose the table top which I first covered with white paneling. You could use decorative laminate here.

The console can be stained or painted. I sprayed mine all white to contrast nicely with a green wall in back.

INSTALL MIRROR before the final section of the frame is placed. This last piece goes in without glue for easy replacement, should the mirror crack.

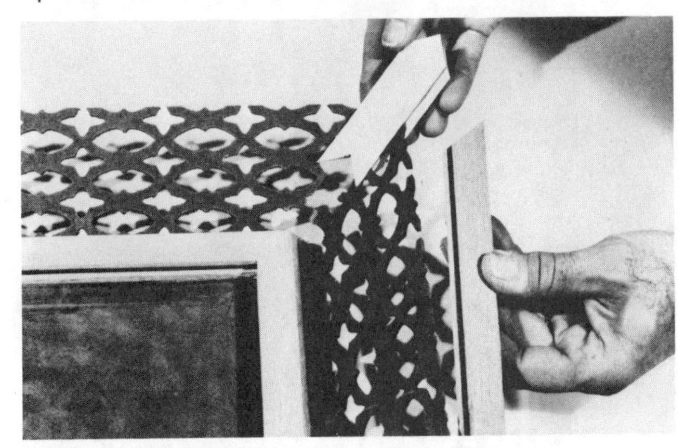

ARROW-SHAPED reinforcing corners provide an exercise in angle cutting (see text for details). Glue is used in groove here; edge cap goes on next.

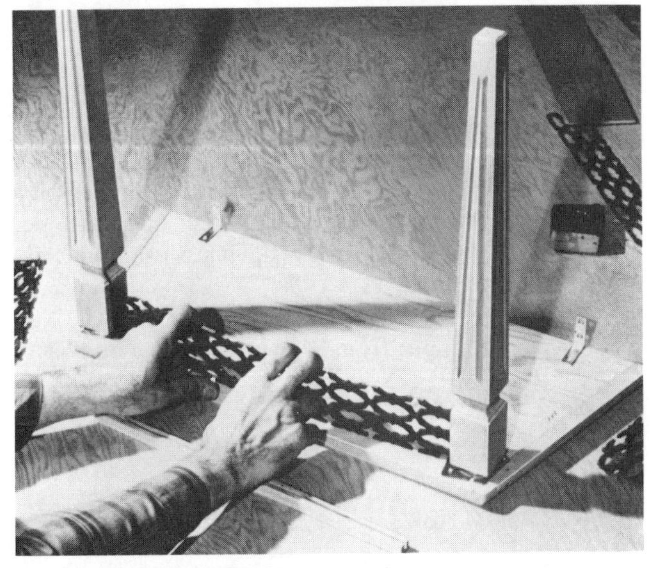

FACTORY-MADE TAPERED LEGS must have grooves cut in at top to receive filigree—which is cut a bit long, then bowed and sprung into place.

Two tub planters for the price of one

By WAYNE C. LECKEY

■ FOR HALF OR LESS the price you pay at a patio shop, you can make a pair of handsome, sturdy planter tubs by sawing a used whiskey barrel in half.

Where do you get a used whiskey barrel? You can order one from G. I. Frazier Co., Box 8275, Louisville, KY 40208.

SEE ALSO
Bars . . . Decks . . . Garden shelters . . . Gazebos . . . Patios . . . Strawberry barrels . . . Window boxes

When you get it, the chances are its metal hoops will be rusty, but a little elbow grease and a wire brush will soon get rid of the rust (an electric sander will speed the job). When you saw the barrel in half, you'll know it once held firewater because its charred interior will reek of bourbon. But this won't hurt your plants one bit; the smell will soon dissipate.

A homemade T-square with a thin bendable blade is used to mark the barrel around its circumference, and a sabre saw will cut the barrel in half quickly. Drain holes are required in the bottom of each tub, and you have a choice of painting the oak staves or sanding and varnishing them.

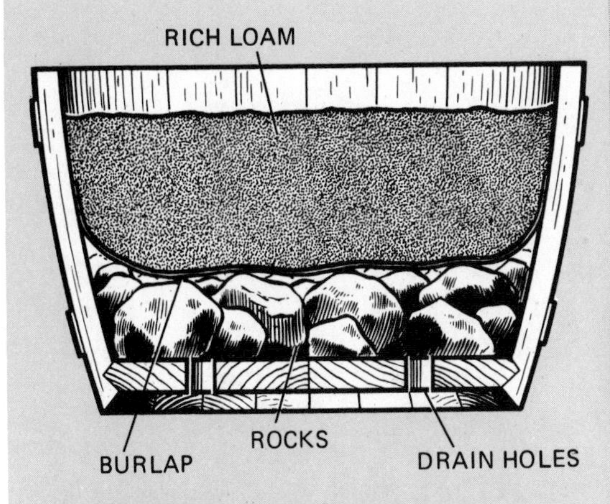

ELECTRIC SANDER and coarse abrasive paper will derust the hoops in a hurry; or do it by hand with a wire brush. For a varnish finish, sand the staves for a new-wood look.

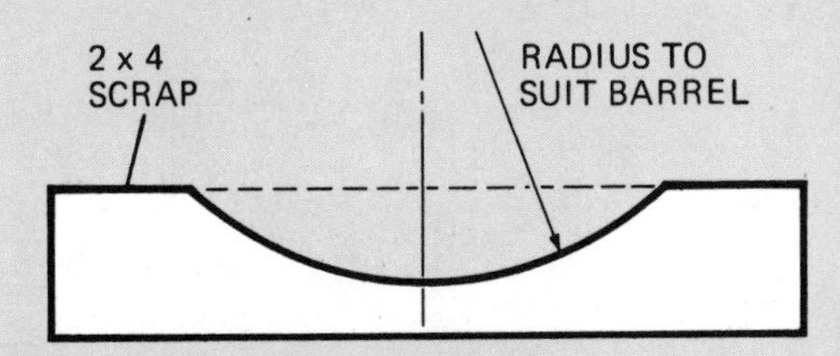

BARREL STAYS PUT for sawing when cradled with wood blocks at each end. Mark cutting line around circumference, plunge cut with a sabre saw, then rotate barrel.

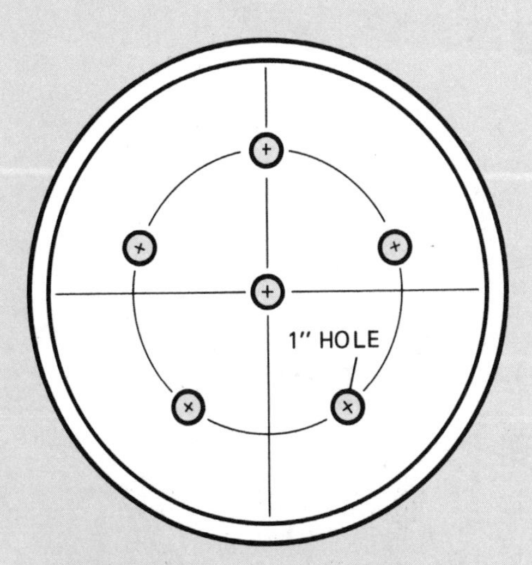

DRILL SIX DRAIN HOLES in the bottom of each tub; when you're ready to add plants, place rocks in the bottom, cover them with burlap and fill tub with potting soil.

Planters for your garden

■ SOMETHING DIFFERENT in the way of planters are these niches that are framed as part of the fence. Besides being a novel feature that serves to break up a long expanse of plain fence, the enclosures actually afford protection to a plant from strong winds and at the same time provide extra bracing to the fence itself.

A small bridge, such as the one below with its built-in planter boxes, will add charm to a fish pond and rock garden. When building both these projects from long-lasting California redwood, use noncorroding nails (hot-dipped galvanized, aluminum alloy or stainless steel) so the nails won't discolor the wood.

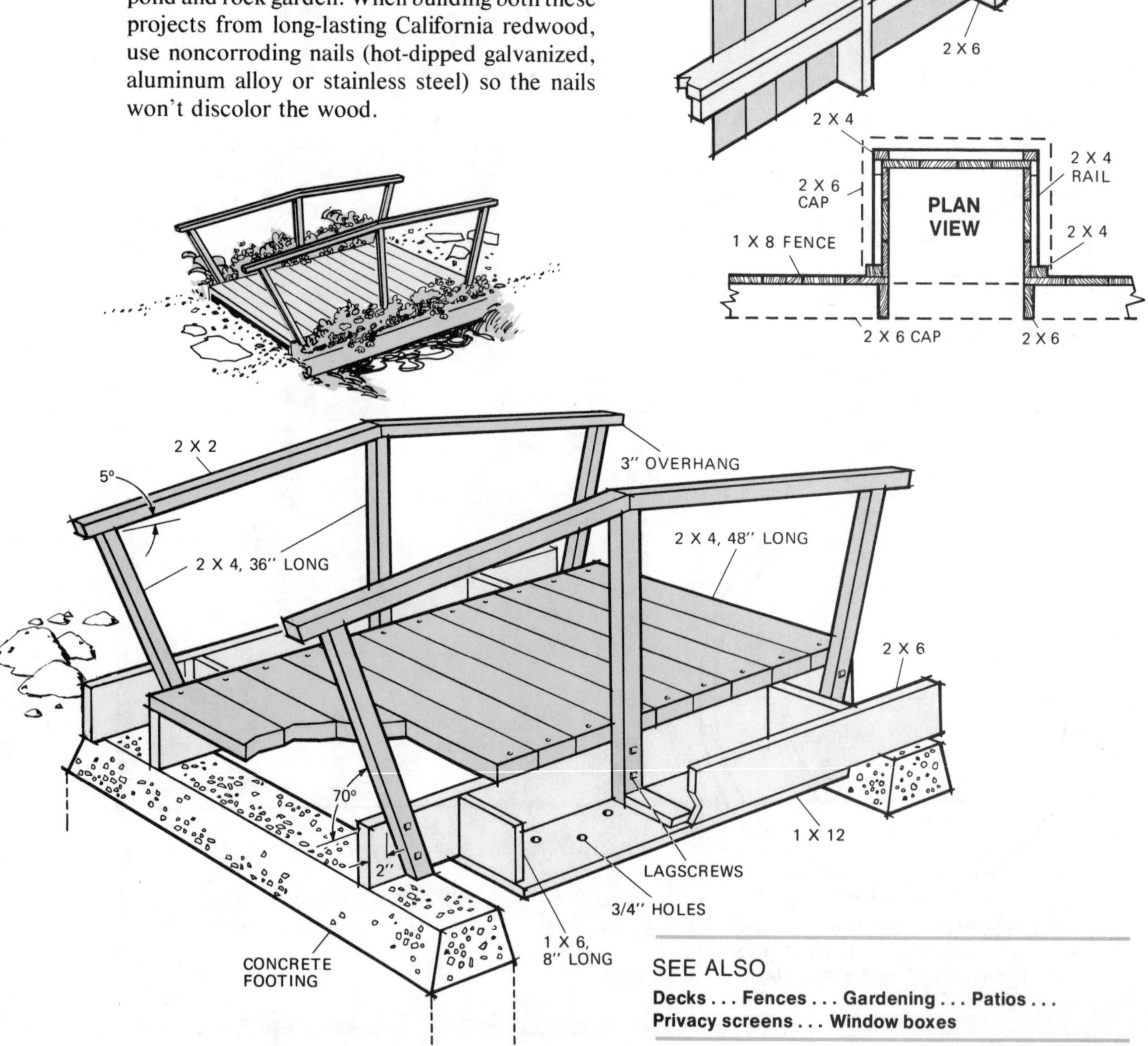

SEE ALSO
Decks . . . Fences . . . Gardening . . . Patios . . . Privacy screens . . . Window boxes

A wheelbarrow planter

By BOB CORLEY

THIS LITTLE patio planter is fun to build whether you are a dyed-in-the-wool woodworker or a guy taking his first whack at a project. Douglas fir was used here but other material can be used. To start, lay out and make all straight cuts for the bottom, side panels and the two end pieces that make up the wheelbarrow bucket. Next, set the saw blade at a 30° angle and make the bevel cuts in the two end pieces. To keep construction simple, use butt joints for all assembly. Make certain that edges to be joined are perfectly square. Finally, cut the handles and the wheels. The plans call for all parts to be cut from ¾-in. (actual) stock. The wheel axles are 3-in. lengths of ½-in. dowel.

SEE ALSO
Decks . . . House plants . . . Patios . . . Strawberry barrels . . . Window boxes

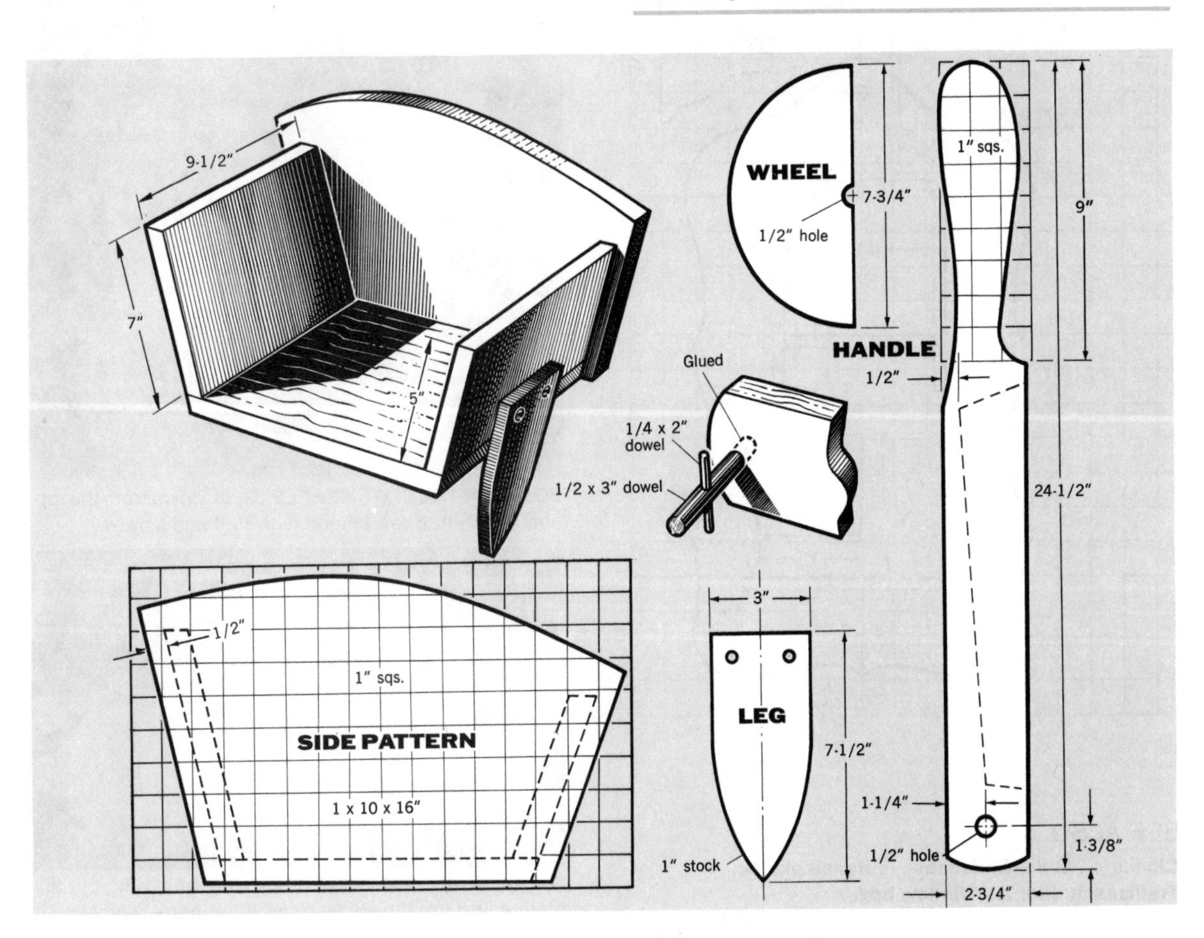

An early American clock-planter

By DON SHINER

IF YOU HAVE cast aside an old, yet serviceable, alarm clock, you can find new use for it as a wall clock in this handsome early American piece. A shelf holds the clock and a trough holds a plant.

Make paper patterns of all the parts and trace them on ½-in. material. Cherry, pine and walnut are appropriate woods. Chances are you'll have to glue up the 10¼-in. back from two or more pieces to build up the width. Simple butt joints are used throughout; screws from the back attach the clock shelf and the planter. You can add a finishing touch by shaping the edges of all parts with a router before assembling. A Styrofoam block in the planter will hold plastic plants.

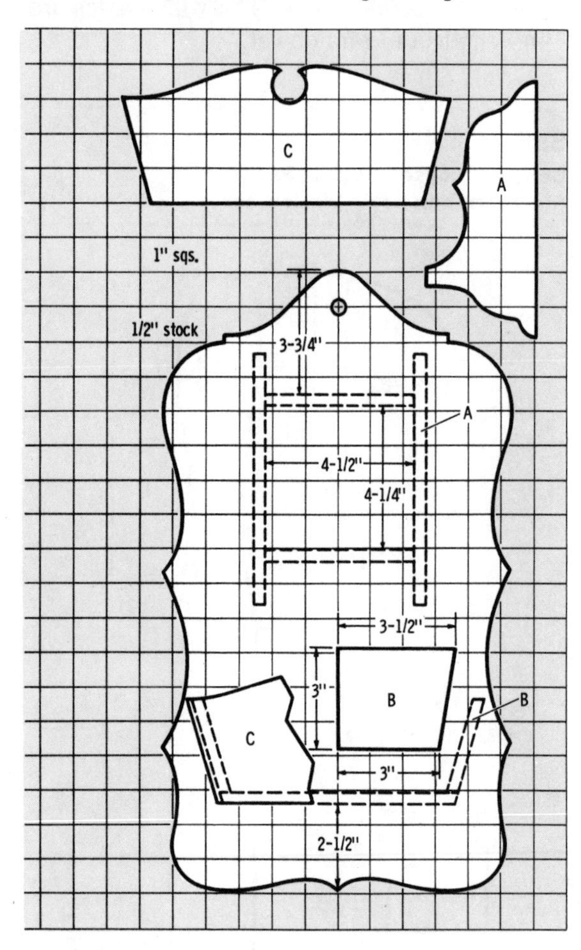

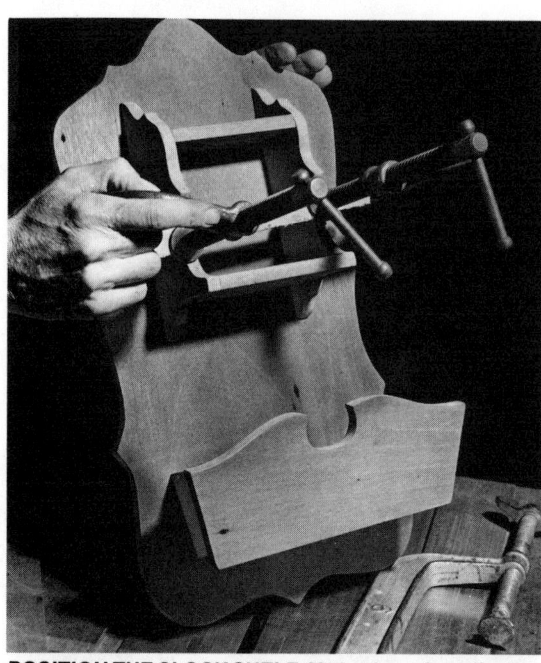

POSITION THE CLOCK SHELF 3¾ in. down from the top and attach it to the plaque with flathead screws.

BAND OR JIGSAW makes quick work of sawing out the plaque and the three other scroll-cut parts required.

SEE ALSO

Clocks . . . Gifts, Christmas . . . House plants . . . Trellises, indoor . . . Window boxes

With flexible vinyl molds, casting plaster figurines is easier than ever. If you follow directions, you'll reproduce objects without loss of fine detail

Easy-to-make plaster casts

IMPROVED CASTING PLASTERS take the quesswork out of the hobby of casting. Flexible vinyl molds (above) produce fine details. Procedure (below): 1. Cover your work table with multiple thicknesses of newspaper, then make a support for your mold by cutting a hole in a cardboard box. 2. Mix plaster and water and pour the mixture slowly and steadily into the supported mold. 3. After plaster has set, remove mold from support, lubricate exterior with hand lotion or liquid dishwashing soap, then grasp mold flange and peel off mold. 4. Remove rough edges and irregularities with a knife; smooth with an emery board.

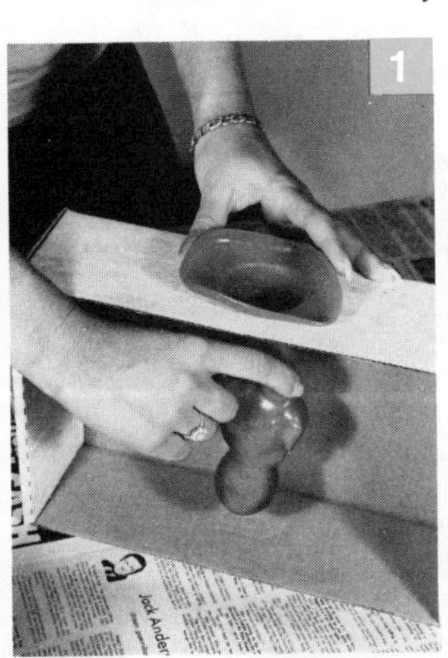

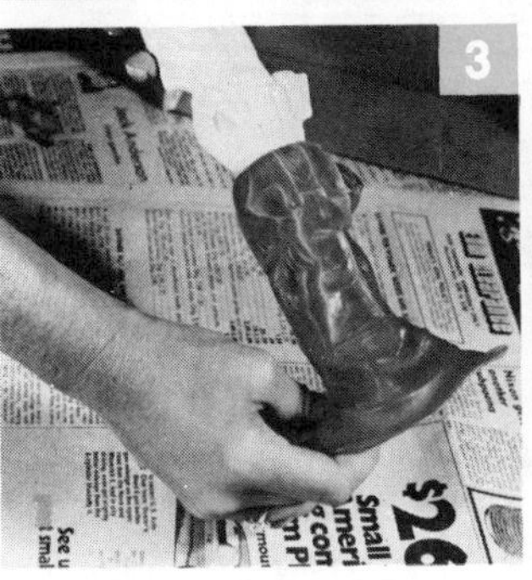

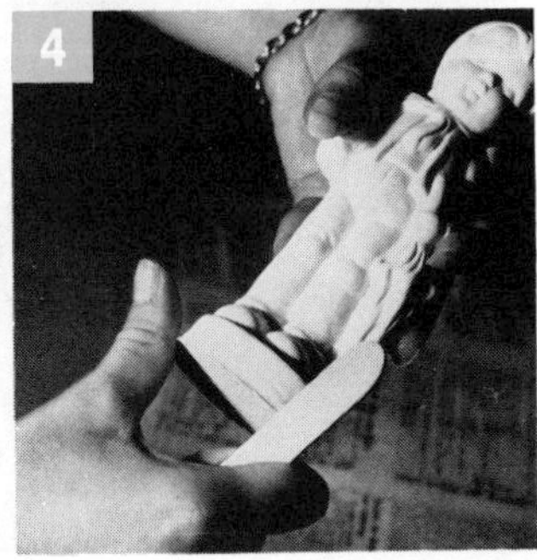

THOUGH PLASTER CASTING has been around a while, the latest casting plasters and molds make it easier than ever to turn out handsome figures. The reusable, flexible molds are called Flexo Mold by the manufacturer, Fibre Glass-Evercoat, Inc., 6600 Cornell Rd., Cincinnati, OH 45242. Like the casting plaster, they are available at hobby and department stores.

Figuring the plaster-to-water ratio is quick and easy. To do it, you simply fill the mold with water, then pour off approximately one-fourth of the water. The remaining three-quarters is then poured into the mixing bowl. Sift or sprinkle plaster onto this water until the plaster is barely covered with water. *Never dump the plaster into the water in a lump.*

After letting the plaster sit undisturbed for five minutes, stir the mixture gently. Pour the contents slowly—but steadily—into the supported mold. Important: As you pour, tap the mold side to release trapped air bubbles. After the plaster has hardened, the mold can be removed as shown. *Caution: Never dump unused plaster in a sink or toilet.*

SEE ALSO
Art glass . . . Bottle craft . . . Metal casting . . . Potter's wheels . . . Toys

How to work with plasterboard

GYPSUM-CORE plasterboard provides a low-cost interior-finish wall that is an ideal surface for both paint and wall coverings. When it is installed properly, your walls can have the smooth look of plaster. Plasterboard is available in fire-resistant grades that meet most building codes too. Most codes require this type on walls between house and attached garage.

Many of the techniques for repair of plasterboard surfaces are the same as for new installation, and professionals frequently use plasterboard to replace large areas of damaged plaster.

When joints, nailheads and corners in an installation are finished, allowed to dry thoroughly and sanded, the entire surface should receive a coat of vinyl or oil-base primer-sealer to assure uniform absorption of paint or wall-covering adhesive.

Estimating materials
NAILS

Wallboard thickness	Nail type	Per 1000 sq. ft. of wallboard
3/8″, 1/2″	1 1/4″ annular-threaded wallboard nail	6 lbs.
5/8″	1 3/8″ annular-threaded wallboard nail	6 lbs.

PREMIXED JOINT COMPOUND AND TAPE

Plasterboard (sq. ft.)	Ready-mix joint compound (gals.)	Wallboard tape (rolls)
100-200	1	2/60′
300-400	2	3/60′
500-600	3	1/250′
700-800	4	1/250′, 1/60′
900-1000	5	1/250′, 2/60′

Start by making a drawing of the surfaces to be covered with plasterboard and planning the arrangement of panels. Use the longest panels you can to reduce the number of end joints. Horizontal application to a wall is often preferred for this reason. Vertical application is desirable where the ceiling height of a wall is more than 8 ft. 2 in. or the wall space to be surfaced is 4 ft. wide or narrower. Where end joints cannot be avoided, they should be staggered.

The installation method that uses both an adhesive and nails is not only quicker, because there are fewer nails to drive and conceal, but also means a better-quality installation than nails alone. With this method, you will require about half as many nails as indicated in the chart at left above; for a professional-grade installation, you will need a quart tube of adhesive for every two 4x8 panels (64 sq. ft.).

Use the chart above to estimate the quantities of wallboard tape and ready-mix joint compound (spackling compound) you will need. Joint compound is also available in dry powder form; allow 60 lbs. per 1000 sq. ft. of surface.

Tools required

1. Wallboard cutting knife or utility knife
2. Wallboard hammer or crown-head claw hammer
3. 4-ft. T-square or steel straightedge
4. Steel tape measure
5. Keyhole saw or sabre saw
6. Joint-finishing knives, 4- and 10-in. blades
7. Pan for joint compound (mortarboard)
8. Medium-grade sandpaper and block
9. Cartridge-type caulking gun (for adhesive)
10. Corner-taping tool (optional)

SEE ALSO

Ceilings . . . Family rooms . . . Hardboard . . . House additions . . . Nails . . . Painting, interior . . . Paneling, hardboard . . . Paneling, plywood . . . Paneling, wood

Cutting plasterboard

Using a T-square to get an aligned straightedge, hold a wallboard or utility knife perpendicular to the surface and score completely through the face paper. The board can then be snapped with a firm, even pressure. Folding back the snapped-off section, cut through back paper with the knife. Use sandpaper to smooth any rough edges. Use a keyhole saw or sabre saw to cut any needed openings in panel; be sure to measure them carefully.

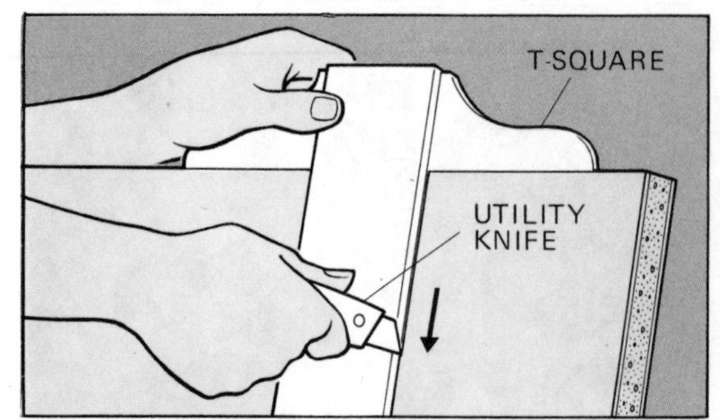

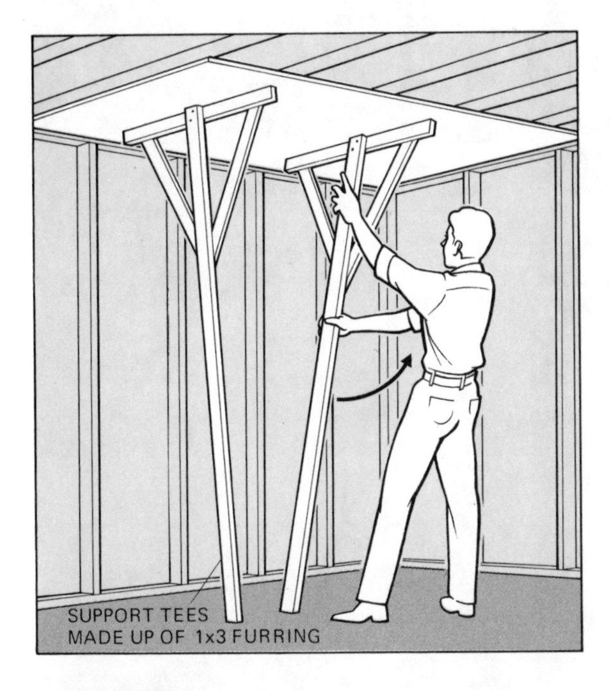

Ceiling installation

Ceilings should be covered before walls. Panels are held in place for nailing with support tees; make them about 1 in. longer than floor-to-ceiling height. Place nails 7 in. apart. If the adhesive-and-nails method is used, all edges should still be nailed, but only one nail per ceiling joist will be required in the "field" of the board. Drive nails to bring the panel tight to framing, then strike each nail one more time to "dimple" (set) the head, taking care not to break face paper.

Wall application and corners

In horizontal application, bottom panels are installed first; the second row can then be rested on the first. Nails are spaced 7 in. apart and dimpled. No nail in the top course should be less than 7 in. from the ceiling. If adhesive is used, no nails in the field are required unless a panel is bowed—then it may be nailed temporarily while adhesive sets. In a vertical corner, the panel edge that is lapped over need not be nailed.

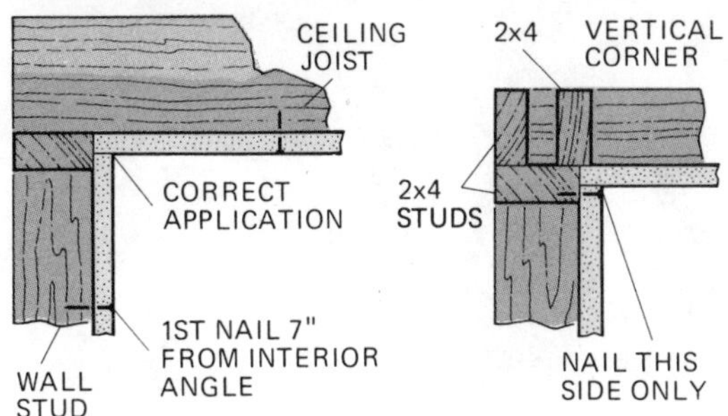

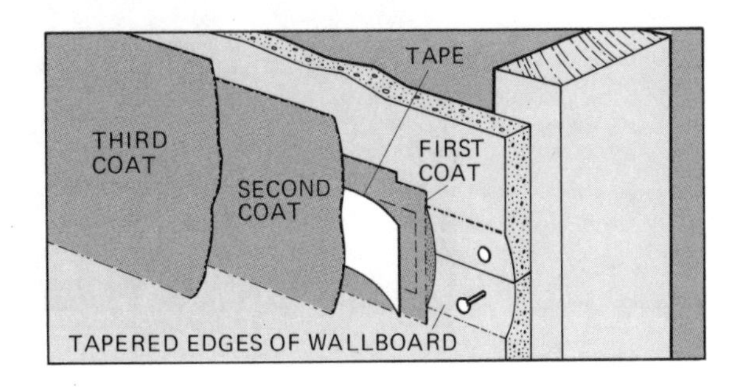

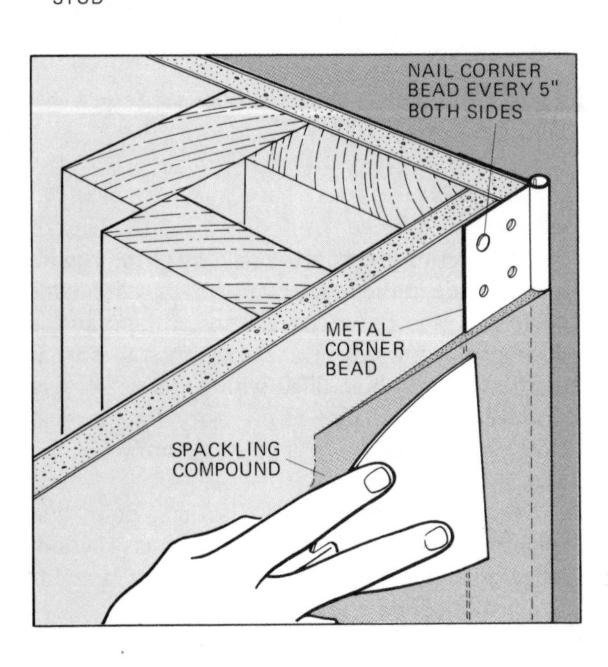

Finishing joints

Joints are filled, reinforced and finished as shown. First coat of joint compound is applied with 4-in. joint knife and tape pressed into it with knife held at 45° angle. Allow at least 24 hours for each coat to dry. Second and third coats are sanded and third feathered-out with 10-in. joint knife to a total width of 12 to 14 in. Treat end and butt joints the same way, with final coat 14 to 18 in. wide. Nailheads get three sanded coats of compound, no tape unless paper is broken.

Finishing corners

Two coats of compound may do for an outside corner. Final coat should extend 7 to 9 in. back from nose of corner. Tape creased lengthwise is embedded in inside corners, topped with one or two feathered coats of compound. To halt cracking, use the least possible compound in crease line.

A jungle-gym tree house

■ A COMBINATION JUNGLE GYM and tree house such as this can be constructed for about $65. The whole thing is designed to take advantage of standard lumber lengths and widths, which simplify construction. All you have to do is cut the various members to length.

The main platform is 6 ft. off the ground and supported by four 4 x 4 corner posts that are buried in 2 ft. of concrete. Each of the two levels measures 4 x 4 ft. square which means that both platforms can be cut from one 4 x 8-ft. sheet of ½-in. exterior-grade plywood. A 24-in. square hole is made in the lower platform for a fireman's pole. The pole is 1¼-in. galvanized pipe and is anchored at the top in a 2 x 4 crossrail and at the bottom in a hole filled with concrete. A seesaw uses the same pipe to pivot on. Two vertical ladders and a third one at approximately 60° are used here.

Designing different levels, ladders, poles and trapeze bars can be half the fun of construction. After all, your kids and their interests are different from all others!

SEE ALSO
Sandboxes . . . Swings

A stilt-house slide

■ YOUR KIDS will get your money's worth of fun and then some from this combined stilt house, playground slide and monkey bars. It's inexpensive to build, and remember, it's an item you'll be able to sell when your moppets outgrow it. With this in mind I made it in sections and bolted them together for easy dismantling. Other than the pipe bars, you'll find all materials at your lumberyard. The drawings give you all the construction data you need. Set it on bricks so the legs don't sink in the ground. Coat the slide with a clear sealer and then paint the rest of the structure in bright colors.

By R.S. HEDIN

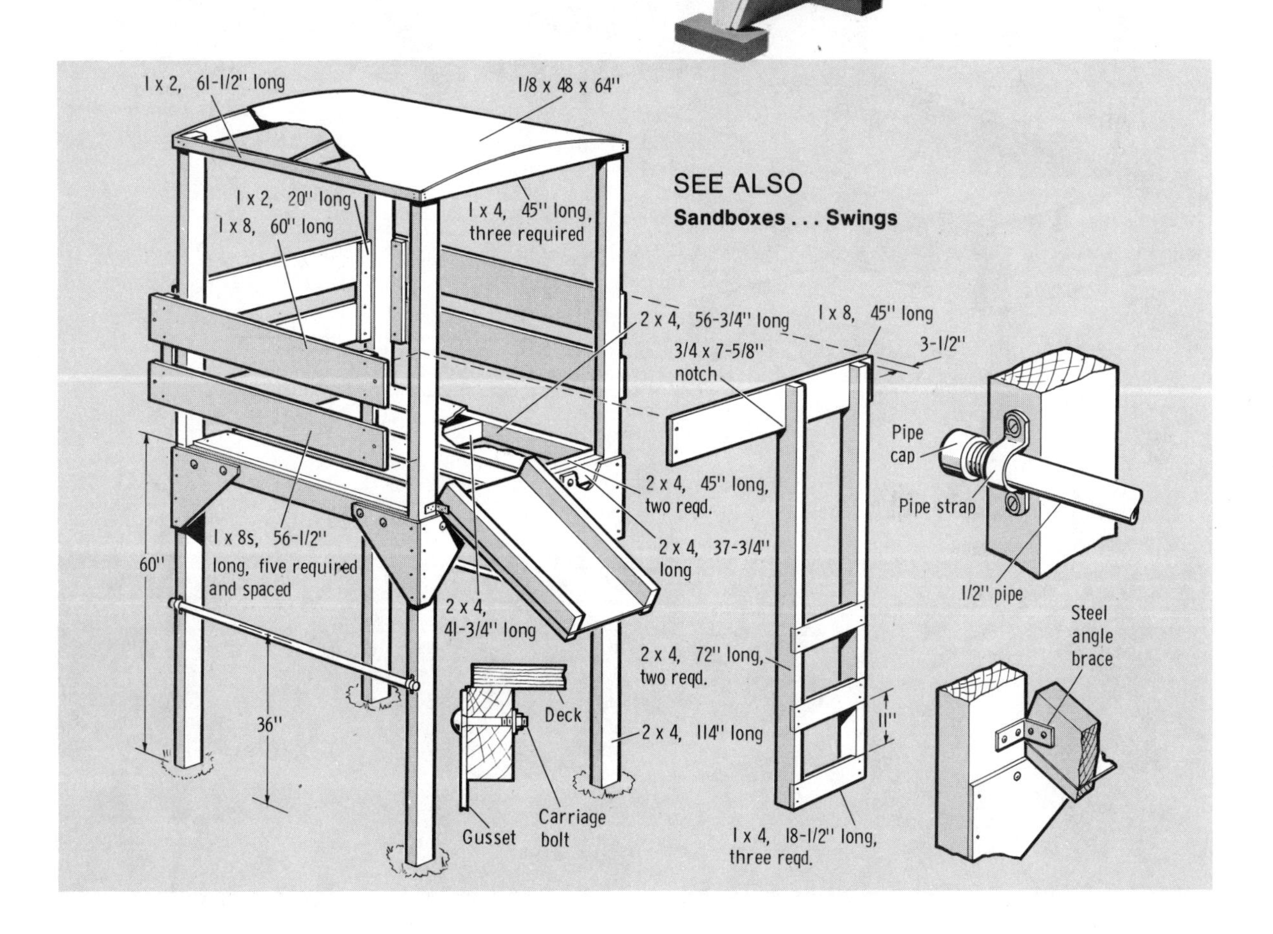

SEE ALSO
Sandboxes . . . Swings

YOU CAN BRING a touch of old Coney Island into your back yard by building this simple roller coaster. The wood rail sections can be propped up with boxes or, for a more permanent arrangement, secured to posts planted in the ground. Notice that sections are pivoted together with bolts so that the entire set-up can be quickly disassembled for relocation or storage. There's no limit as to how long the coaster track can be.

Wheels fit between the guides to keep the cart on the rails. Here is where accuracy is a must. Build the roller assembly first, and then measure for wheel placement so there can be no side wobble. An old rug around the last rail tie makes a good brake for stopping.

Back-yard roller coaster

By R. S. HEDIN

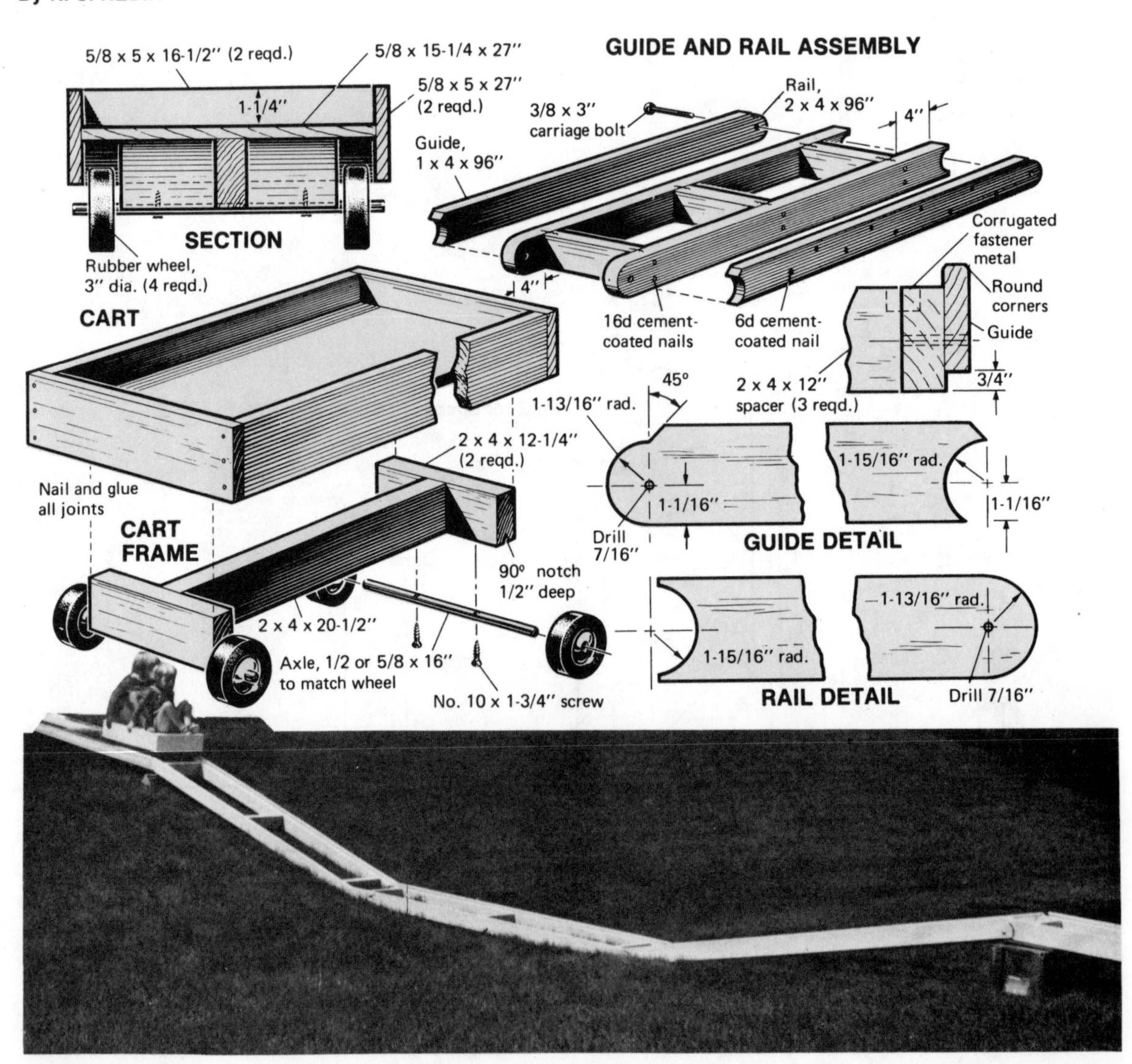

Playground fun

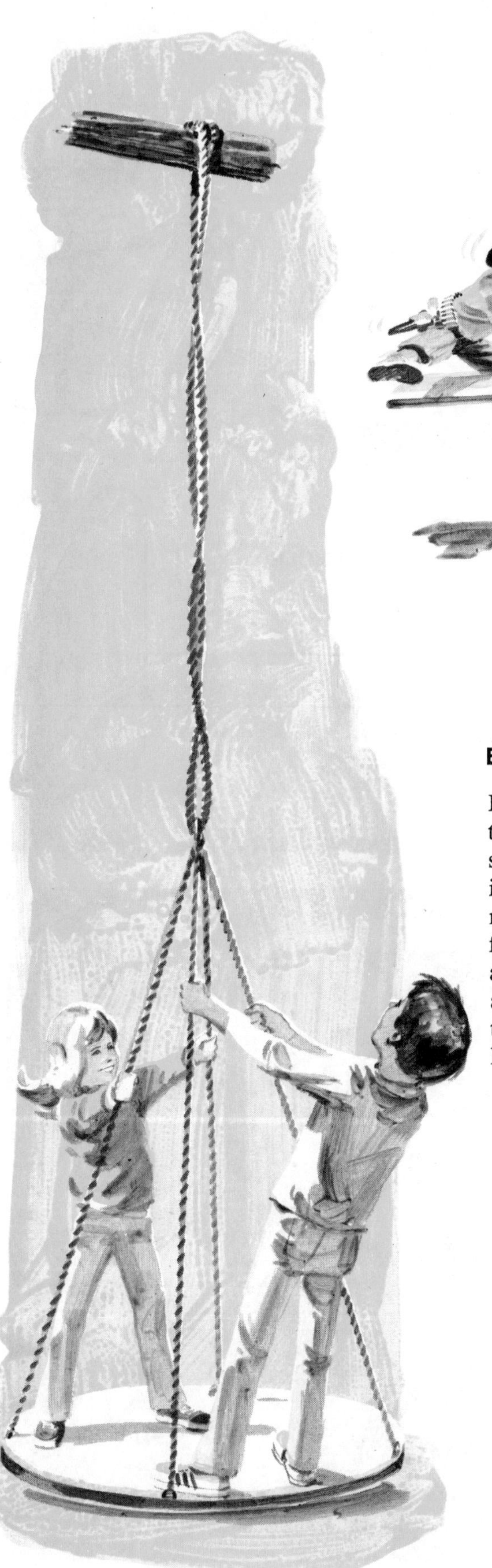

BOUNCING TEETER BOARD

IT'S POSSIBLE to add playground equipment to your back-yard "family-fun center" without spending a great deal of money. With a little imagination, you can convert everyday items that no longer serve their original purpose into games for your youngsters. The teeter board, for example, is simply four coil springs from a car attached to an old wheel hub. Use a heavy truck tire for a base and a 2x10 plank for the board. Paint in bright colors.

MERRY-GO-ROUND SWING

WHEN YOU LAY out the location for this toy, allow plenty of room so the kids can swing and twist on it in all directions. For a base, cut a 3-ft. disc from ¾-in. exterior plywood. Bore four holes equidistant around the circumference 2 in. from the edge. Secure with short hemp ropes knotted below and fasten to a length of rope attached to an overhead horizontal crosspiece between two trees.

SEE ALSO
Sandboxes . . . Swings

Seesaw with a new twist

By R. S. HEDIN

THIS SEESAW has a new twist and is sure to be irresistible to kids of all ages. In addition to the usual up-and-down movement, the seat board rotates on a vertical shaft that's fitted with a thrust bearing. The shaft in turn fits inside a pipe post that's anchored and braced solidly to a nontipping base of 2 x 4s. For safety, you would be wise to rope off the area in which the seesaw rotates and provide only one entrance to eliminate any possibility of a child who's among the spectators getting bowled over and injured.

Use a sound 2 x 8 plank for the seat board and round all edges to prevent splinters. To finish the seesaw, apply two coats of exterior house paint. You'll probably want to use a lubricant on the moving parts to assure a quiet, trouble-free action. Notice that conduit clamps are used to attach the seat board to the steel rod that pivots in pipe-nipple bearings. A ⅜ x 5-in. carriage bolt is used to secure the seat board support to the 1-in. pipe used for the pivot.

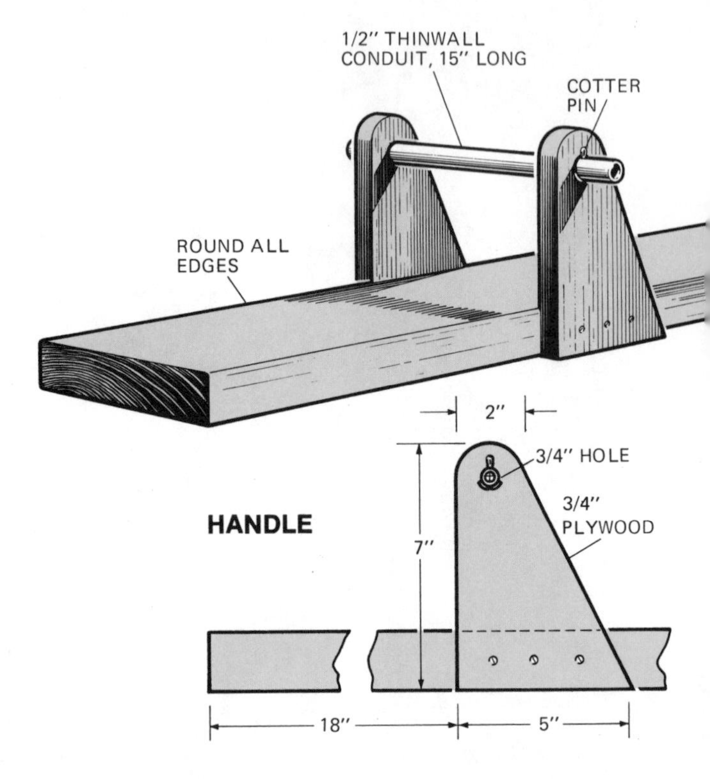

SEE ALSO
Sandboxes . . . Swings

YOUNGSTERS GET lots of exercise on this seesaw that takes them around as well as up and down.

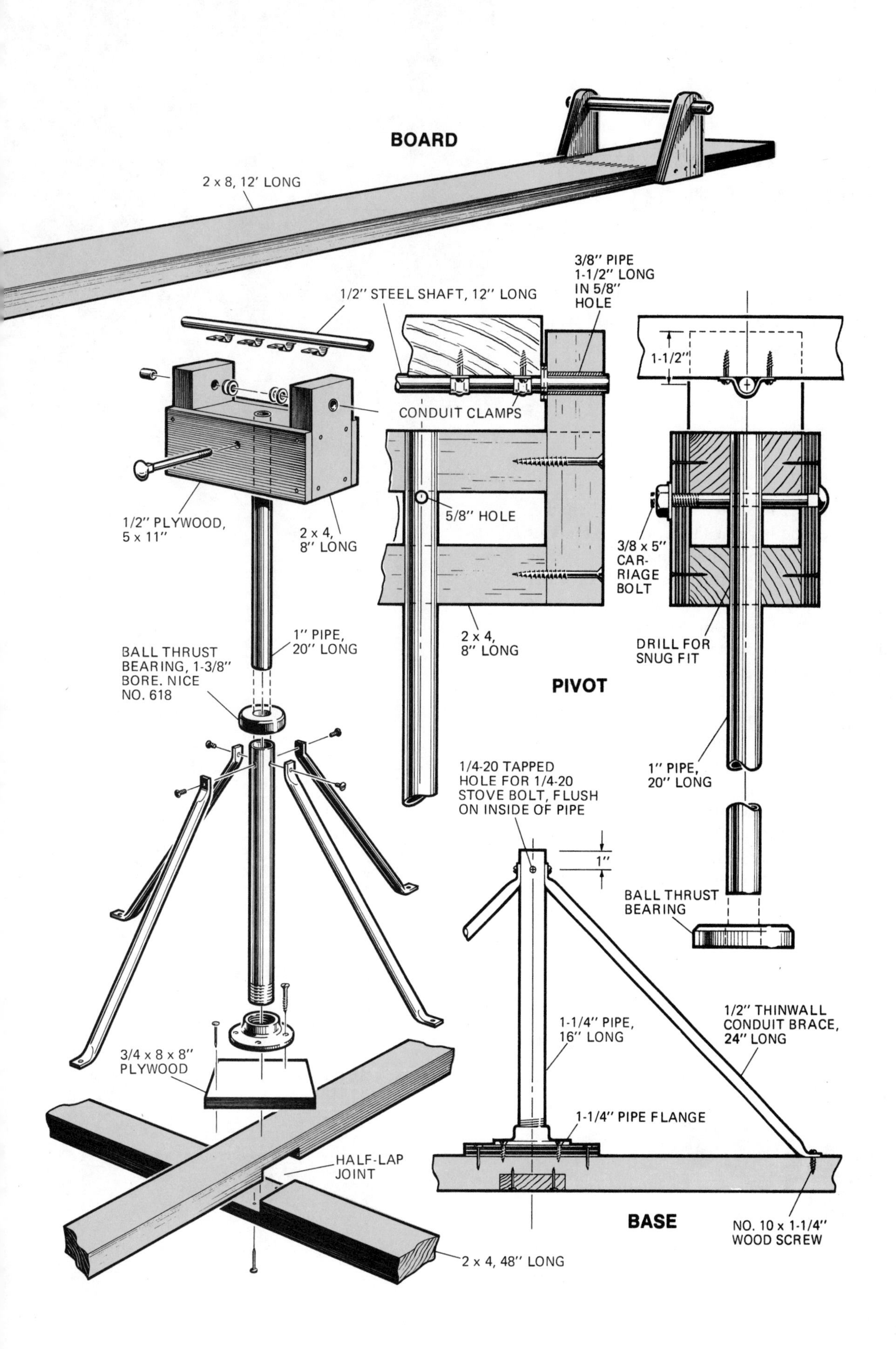
BOARD
2 x 8, 12' LONG
1/2" STEEL SHAFT, 12" LONG
3/8" PIPE 1-1/2" LONG IN 5/8" HOLE
1-1/2"
CONDUIT CLAMPS
5/8" HOLE
1/2" PLYWOOD, 5 x 11"
2 x 4, 8" LONG
3/8 x 5" CAR-RIAGE BOLT
1" PIPE, 20" LONG
2 x 4, 8" LONG
DRILL FOR SNUG FIT
BALL THRUST BEARING, 1-3/8" BORE. NICE NO. 618
PIVOT
1/4-20 TAPPED HOLE FOR 1/4-20 STOVE BOLT, FLUSH ON INSIDE OF PIPE
1" PIPE, 20" LONG
1"
BALL THRUST BEARING
1/2" THINWALL CONDUIT BRACE, 24" LONG
1-1/4" PIPE, 16" LONG
3/4 x 8 x 8" PLYWOOD
1-1/4" PIPE FLANGE
HALF-LAP JOINT
BASE
NO. 10 x 1-1/4" WOOD SCREW
2 x 4, 48" LONG

For summer fun— a water hoop

This project serves two purposes— the kids have a ball jumping "rope" while you sit back and watch as your lawn gets well watered

THIS ROLLICKING water hoop enables you to water the lawn at the same time the kids are having a ball jumping "rope" and getting drenched as the hoop turns. Strong jets of water escaping from pinholes drilled in opposite ends of the hoop cause the hoop to turn Ferris-wheel fashion when it's connected to a hose.

The toy was invented by Frank Reed and Marty Trent of Palos Verdes Peninsula, Calif., and you can make one like it from ½-in. PVC pipe and standard plumbing fittings. The hoop turns on two supporting posts anchored in the ground, and a double female hose coupling prevents the garden hose from twisting into a pretzel as the hoop turns. PVC pipe tees, plus short pipe nipples, provide axles at the center point of the hoop. The hoop is easily assembled with regular PVC cement.

HOSE HOOKUP is assembled from standard brass fittings. Adapter threads take PVC nipple.

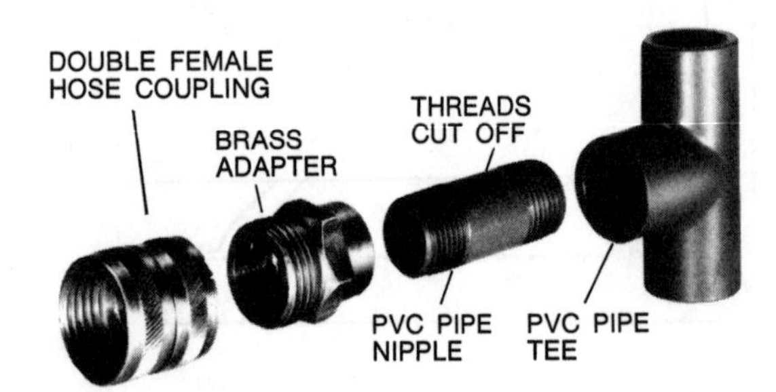

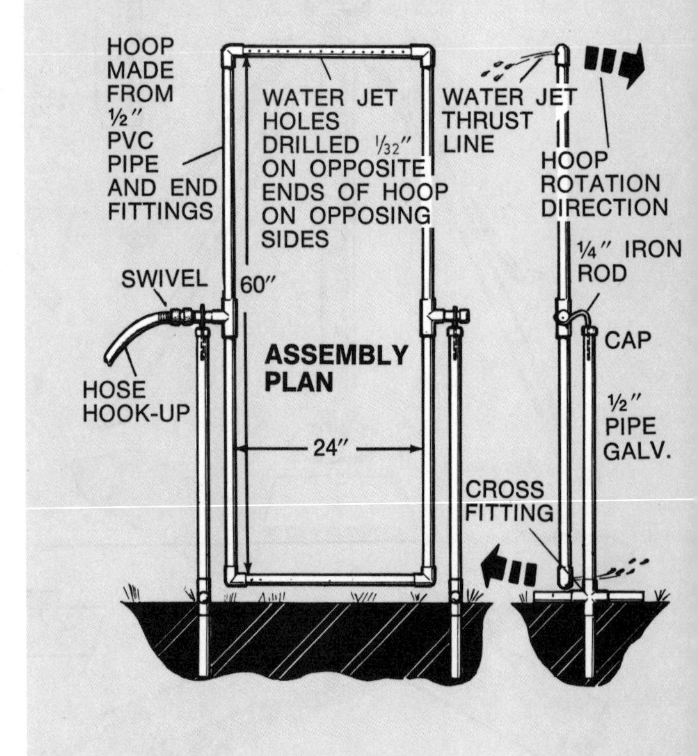

SEE ALSO
Sandboxes . . . Swings

By JOHN L. KUIK

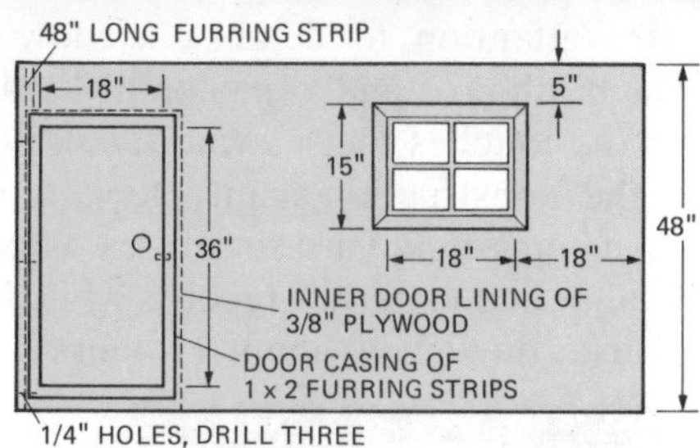

The fun of an outdoor playhouse moves indoors with this easy-to-build plywood version. Because it is easy to set up and knock down, it can be folded and stored conveniently out of the way for the night

Indoor playhouse

MATERIALS for the playhouse are ¼-in. plywood for the walls, a sheet of paneling for the roof, furring strips and 2x4 scraps, beveled and slotted for the roof supports. The corner is held together with three ¼-in. bolts through the furring strips on both plywood walls.

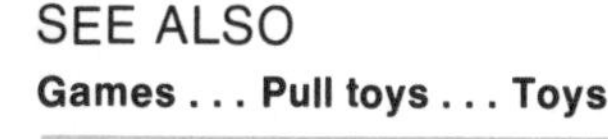

SEE ALSO

Games . . . Pull toys . . . Toys

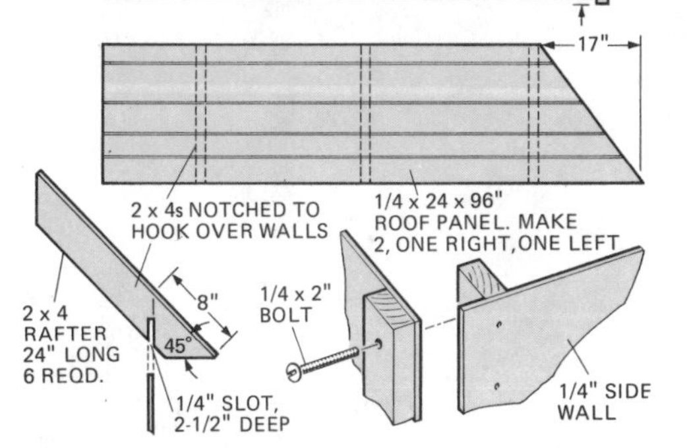

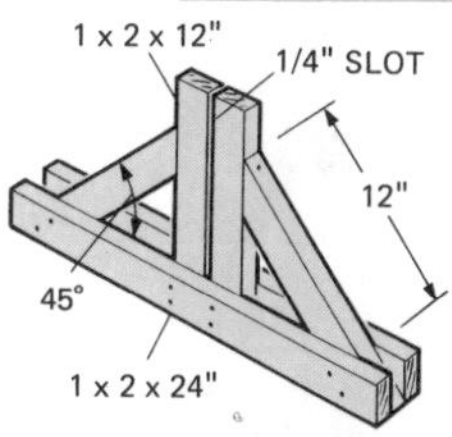

THIS QUICK-TO-SET-UP playhouse will delight your youngster. Walls can be ¼-in. plywood painted to suit or prefinished ¼-in. paneling. If the door opening is cut carefully, the cutout can become the door; window panes are also cut out, leaving muntins and bars. Furring strips for corner assembly and casing are glued and nailed; note that one longer corner strip serves to level walls held in end stands. Plywood strips lining door opening inside protrude ½ in. inward in order to keep the door from swinging in. Finishing touches are curtains and doorknobs, the latter made from thread spools.

Build a pretty little playhouse

By BRAD SNYDER

This charmer can serve other roles, too—giving you much greater storage space for lawn toys and games and yard tools

WHETHER YOU NEED a playhouse for the youngsters, a summer office, pool cabana or more storage space for yard equipment, a lawn building lets you make greater use of your property.

Once we decided to build one, the next step was to decide its architectural style. This was solved by selecting the Western-style model shown which matched our home exterior. Elevations for it (and the alternate Western Side Door) are shown on these pages.

slab or piers are ok

Though the house could have been built on a slab, I elected to construct it on four concrete-block piers (in my area, exempt from tax assessment). After evaluating exactly what would be stored in the shed, I actually built it slightly larger than shown on the plans.

Extra attention to details—window boxes, cupola birdhouse and ornamental hardware—yields the touches that elevate this little house from the construction-shanty look frequently found in home-built yard structures. I kept complete labor and materials records while building the house; they show about 35 hours of labor.

SHED FRAMING rests on four piers (upper left). Then flooring is nailed to joists and trimmed in place.

SPEED CONSTRUCTION by assembling each wall on the ground (left), then hoisting it into place as a unit.

PLACE END WALLS (above) and hold them temporarily with diagonal bracing. Ends equal the platform width.

SEE ALSO

Cabanas . . . Gazebos . . . Poolhouses . . . Storage buildings

a pretty playhouse, continued

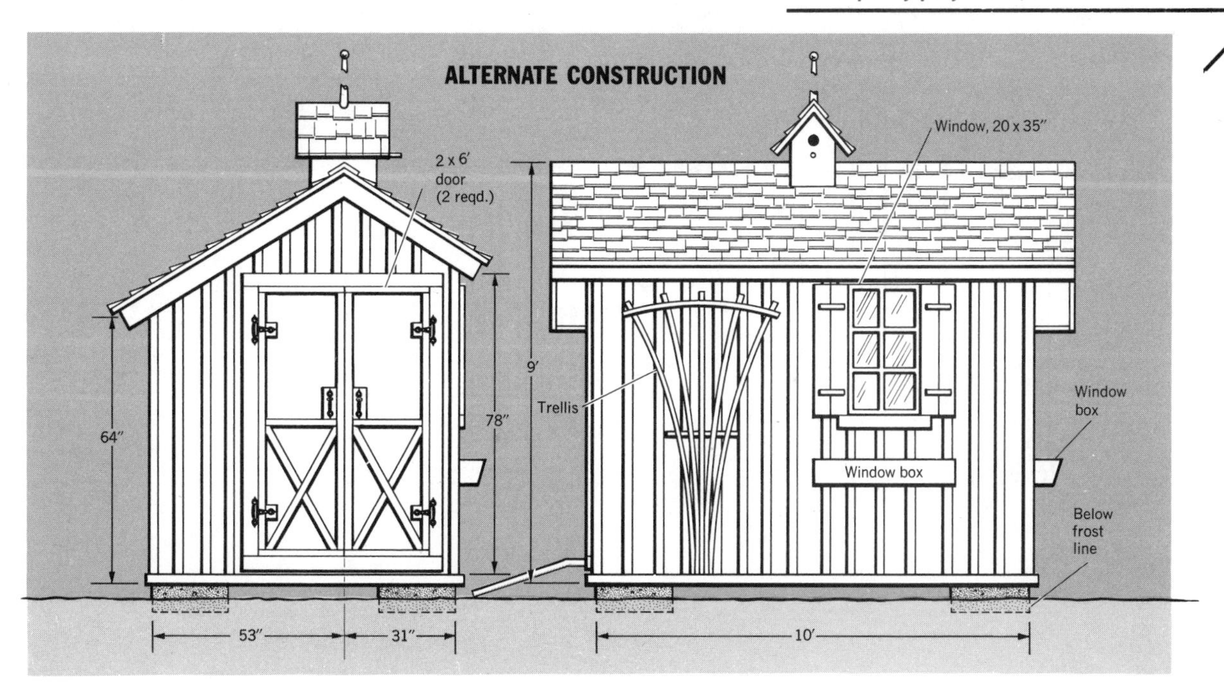

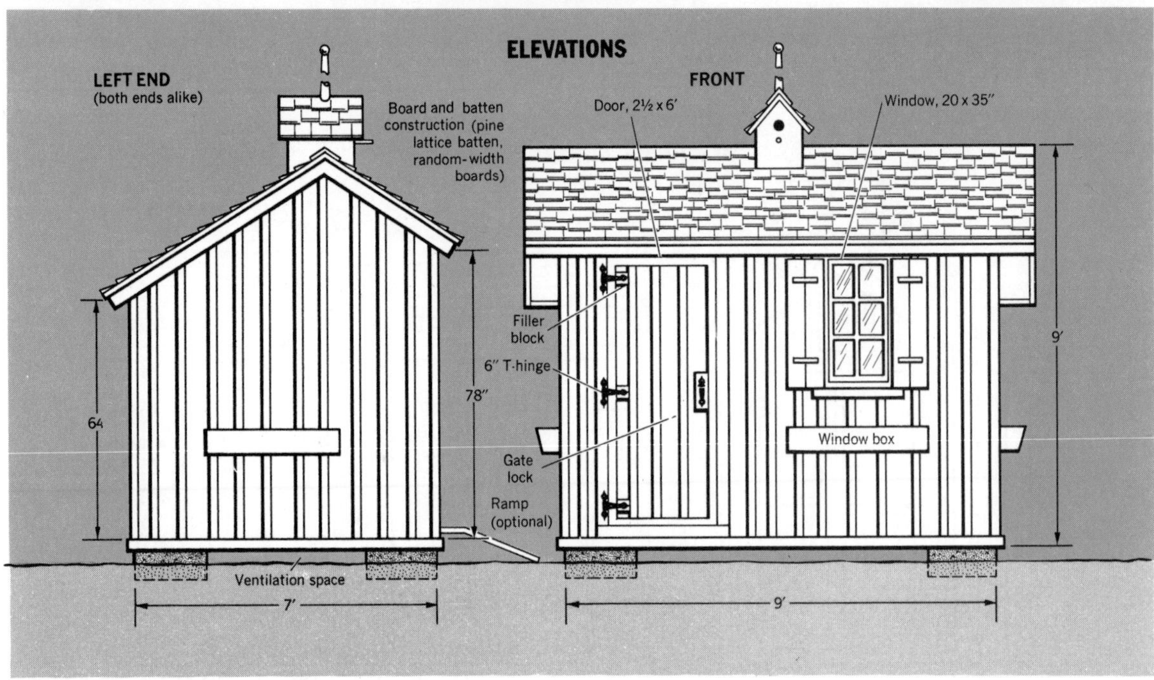
ELEVATIONS
LEFT END
(both ends alike)
Board and batten construction (pine lattice batten, random-width boards)
FRONT
Door, 2½ x 6′
Window, 20 x 35″
Filler block
6″ T-hinge
78″
64
9′
Window box
Gate lock
Ramp (optional)
Ventilation space
7′
9′

SHEETS of amber Plexiglas were used to make this handsome see-through coffee table, compatible with modern decors.

How to work with Plexiglas

■ ALTHOUGH MANY beginning do-it-yourselfers think otherwise, there's no ironclad rule that says an exciting, functional product must be hard to build. The well-designed, easy-to-make projects on these pages prove that's not so. Created from acrylic sheet plastic such as Plexiglas (TN), they are typical of the gleaming transparent, translucent, or opaque household items that are now so popular in the fashionable gift shops and better department stores.

SEE ALSO
Aquariums . . . Coffee tables . . . Gifts, Christmas . . . House plants . . . Internal carving . . . Ladder-chairs . . . Magazine holders . . . Occasional tables . . . Telephone centers . . . Wine racks

CLEAR PLASTIC has many applications. This fish tank is made of it. It can replace glass in doors, for safety, and can be used to make sliding cabinet doors.

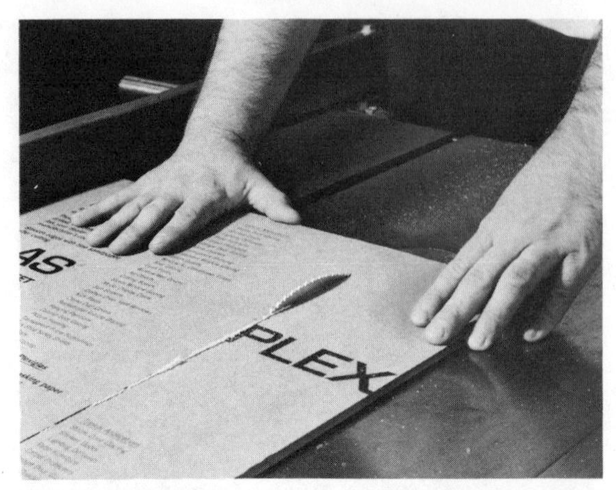

CIRCULAR SAWING: Use a fine-tooth "plywood" blade and set the blade a little higher than the thickness of plastic. Hold material firmly and work slowly.

SCRIBING: Plastic up to ⅛-in. thick can be cut by scoring with a pointed tool. Make the score along a straightedge, four or five times through the paper.

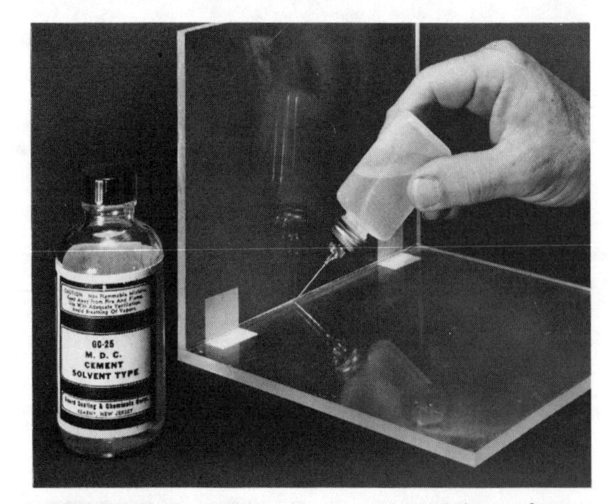

CEMENTING: Remove the paper and sand the surfaces to be cemented. Tape the work and apply solvent to joint with needle-spout unit.

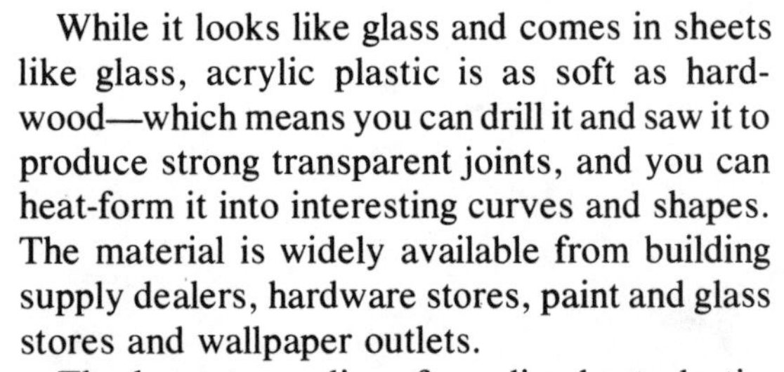

While it looks like glass and comes in sheets like glass, acrylic plastic is as soft as hardwood—which means you can drill it and saw it to produce strong transparent joints, and you can heat-form it into interesting curves and shapes. The material is widely available from building supply dealers, hardware stores, paint and glass stores and wallpaper outlets.

The largest supplier of acrylic sheet plastic, Rohm and Haas, makes it in two forms: Plexiglas K (safety glazing grade), with thicknesses ranging from .080 in. to 3/16-in.; and Plexiglas G (safety glazing and decorative grade), with just two thicknesses—⅛-in. and ¼-in. The only significant difference between the two, says the manufacturer, is that Plexiglas K, which is less costly, cannot be solvent cemented.

You can buy sheets in sizes ranging from 18x24 in. to 36x48 in. There are more than 40 standard colors of Plexiglas, in various tones and eight textured surface patterns.

The cost for ¼-in. Plexiglas G at presstime was about $3.00 per sq. ft. for clear and 10 percent more for colors. Plexiglas K was about 25 percent cheaper.

Although acrylic plastic will scratch more readily than glass, it comes with a protective

SABRE SAWING: The blade should have 14 teeth per inch. Use a strip to guide the saw in straight cuts and hold the work firmly on curves.

BANDSAWING: The blade should have a minimum of 10 teeth per inch. Pass the work slowly through the saw. Use protective paper to draw the cutting line.

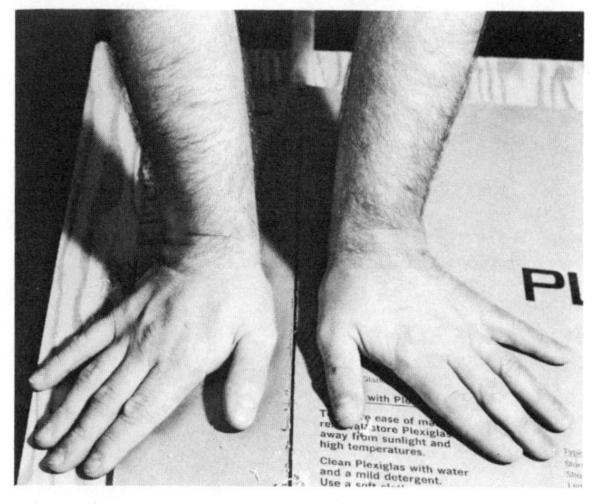

BREAKING: Position the score, face up, directly over a ¾-in. dowel. Hold sheet with one hand and press down with the other. Continue along the score.

DRILLING: Use a regular twist drill and press lightly. Back up the work with a wood block and a clamp. Drill slowly and don't remove the paper.

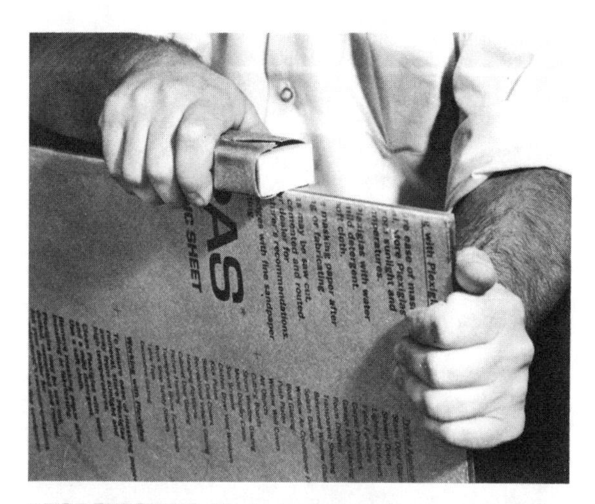

EDGE FINISHING: Marks are removed by scraping with a knife or by sanding with 60 to 80-grit paper, followed by 150-grit "wet or dry."

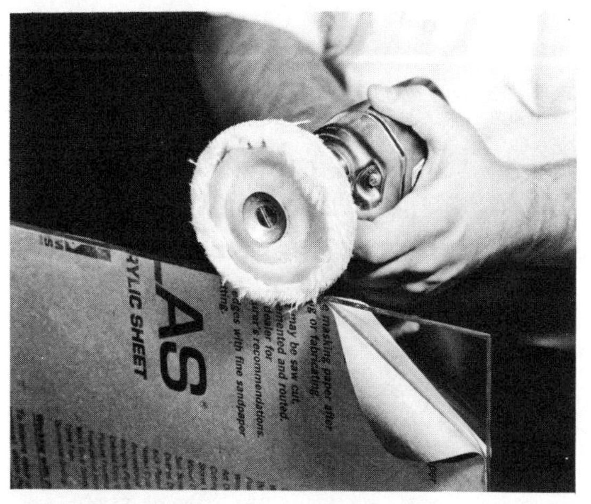

POLISHING: To produce a transparent edge, continue sanding with grits up to 400. Buff with a compound-coated muslin wheel and a cotton-flannel wheel.

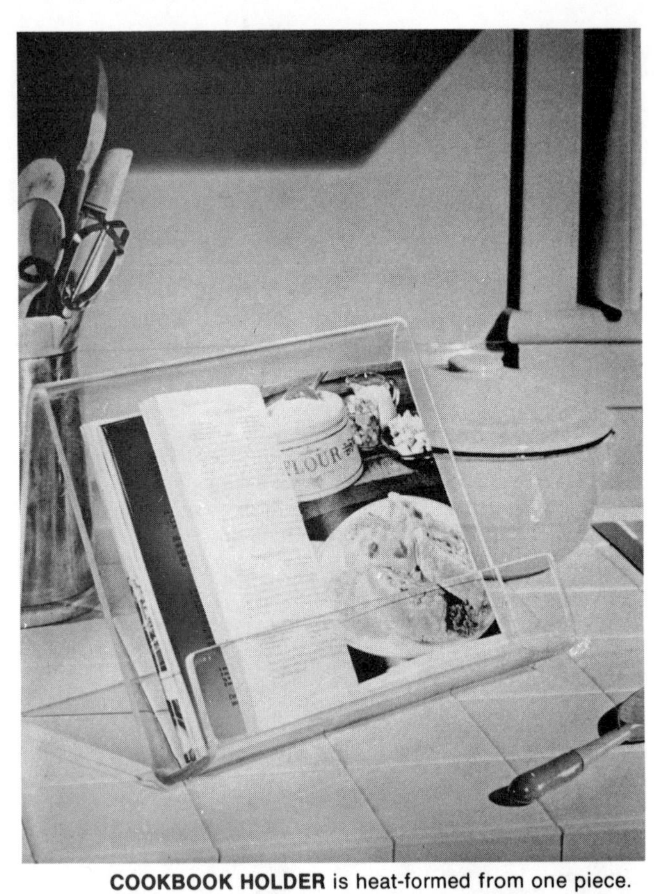

COOKBOOK HOLDER is heat-formed from one piece.

TERRARIUM is a good project for beginner.

TRISECTED TABLE: Top rests on bent sheets.

TELEPHONE STAND requires careful heat-forming.

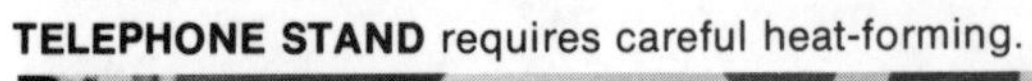

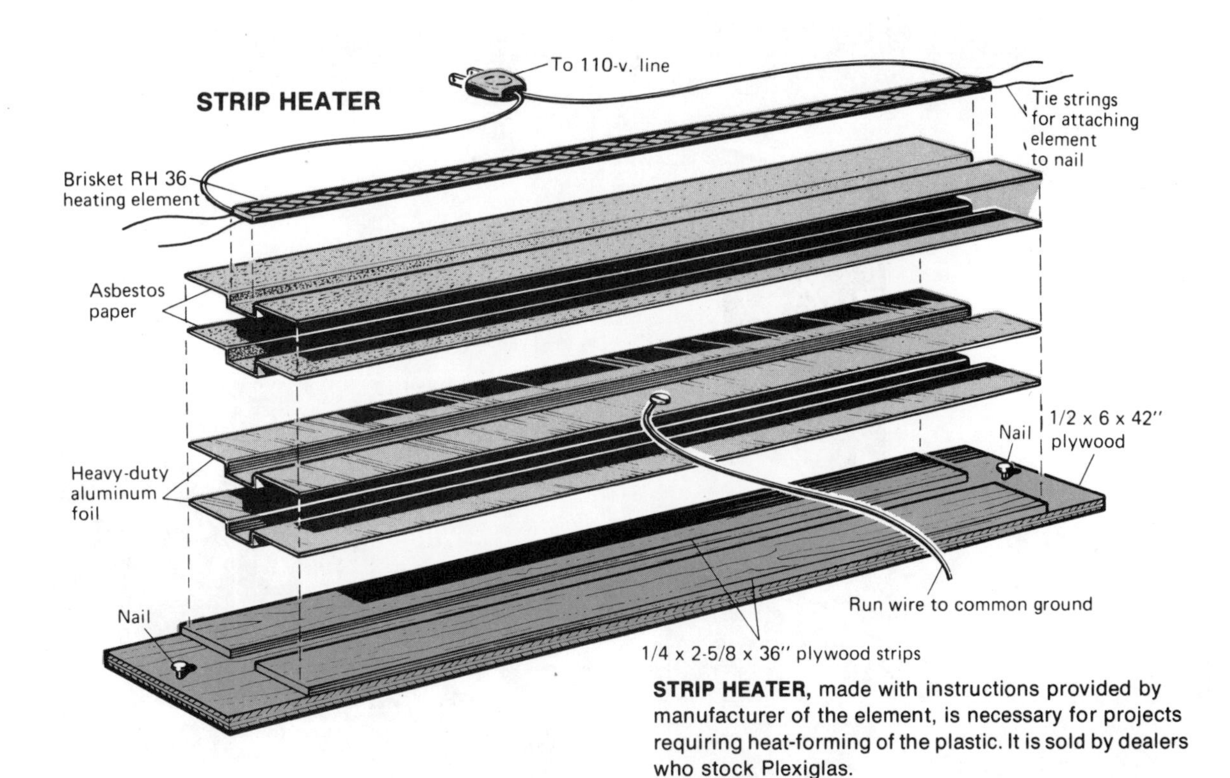

STRIP HEATER, made with instructions provided by manufacturer of the element, is necessary for projects requiring heat-forming of the plastic. It is sold by dealers who stock Plexiglas.

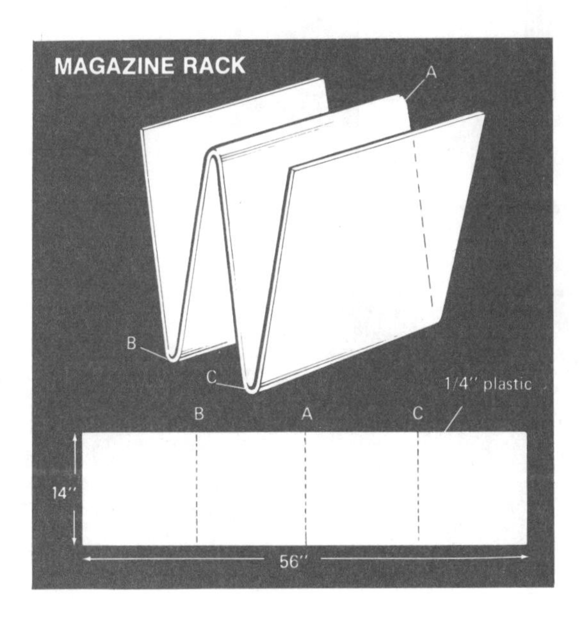

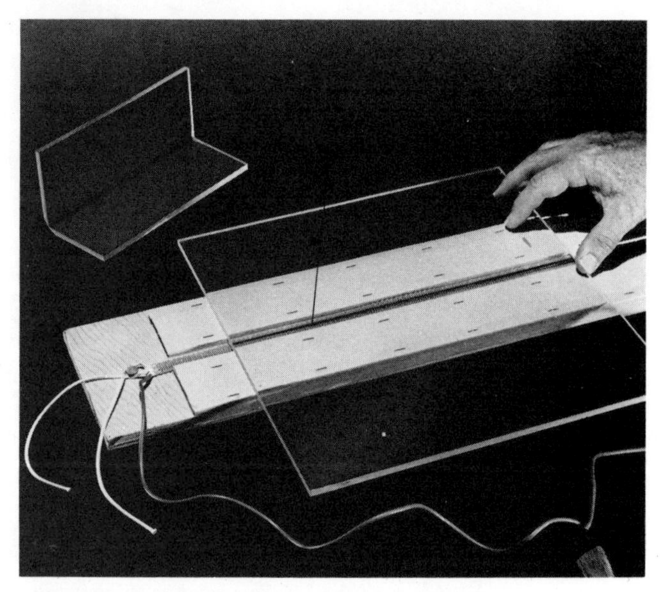

TO BEND PLASTIC, protective paper is removed and plastic is placed over heat tape in strip heater.

paper stuck to both sides which is usually left in place while the pieces are being handled and cut.

When working on the projects described on these pages, or one of your own designs, you will want to keep the following in mind:

• **Cutting.** Plastic up to ⅛-in. thick can be cut by scoring and snapping. After it is scored four or five times with a scratch awl, the scored line is centered face up over a ¾-in. dowel. Then the plastic is pressed down on each side to snap it. The minimum snap-off width is about 1½-in. Patterned plastic cannot be scored and broken; it must be sawed.

• **Sawing.** Use either a sabre saw equipped with a fine-tooth blade (32 teeth per inch) or table saw with a plywood-veneer blade. Hold the sheet down firmly and move it slowly through the saw; do not force. You can also make straight cuts

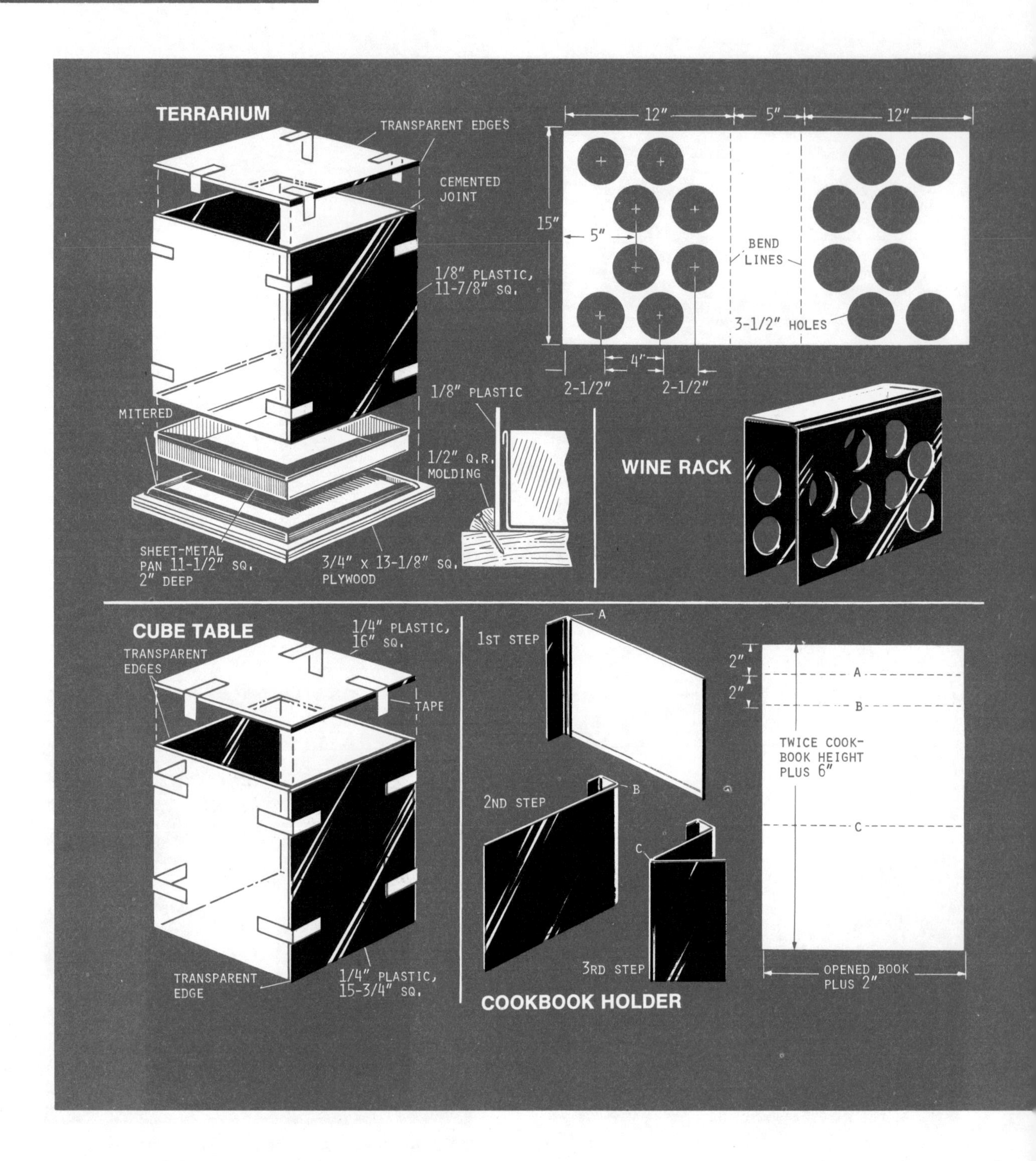

with a special hand tool obtained from the dealer who sold you the plastic.

• **Drilling.** You can use conventional twist drills to bore holes by hand. To do it, back the plastic with a clamped block of wood and be sure the drill is sharp.

To bore with power, use a specially ground high-speed twist drill (available from your sheet-plastic dealer). For best results, use a slow speed and minimum pressure: too fast and the plastic will spin with the bit, while too much pressure causes chipping on the back side of the hole.

• **Edge finishing.** Saw and other tool marks should be removed by scraping the edge smooth with a sharp knife or by sanding with a medium-grit (60-80) paper, followed by sanding with "wet or dry" (150) grit paper. For a satin finish, continue to sand with increasingly finer (220-320) wet-or-dry paper. For a transparent finish, sand with finer grit (400-500) wet-or-dry paper and

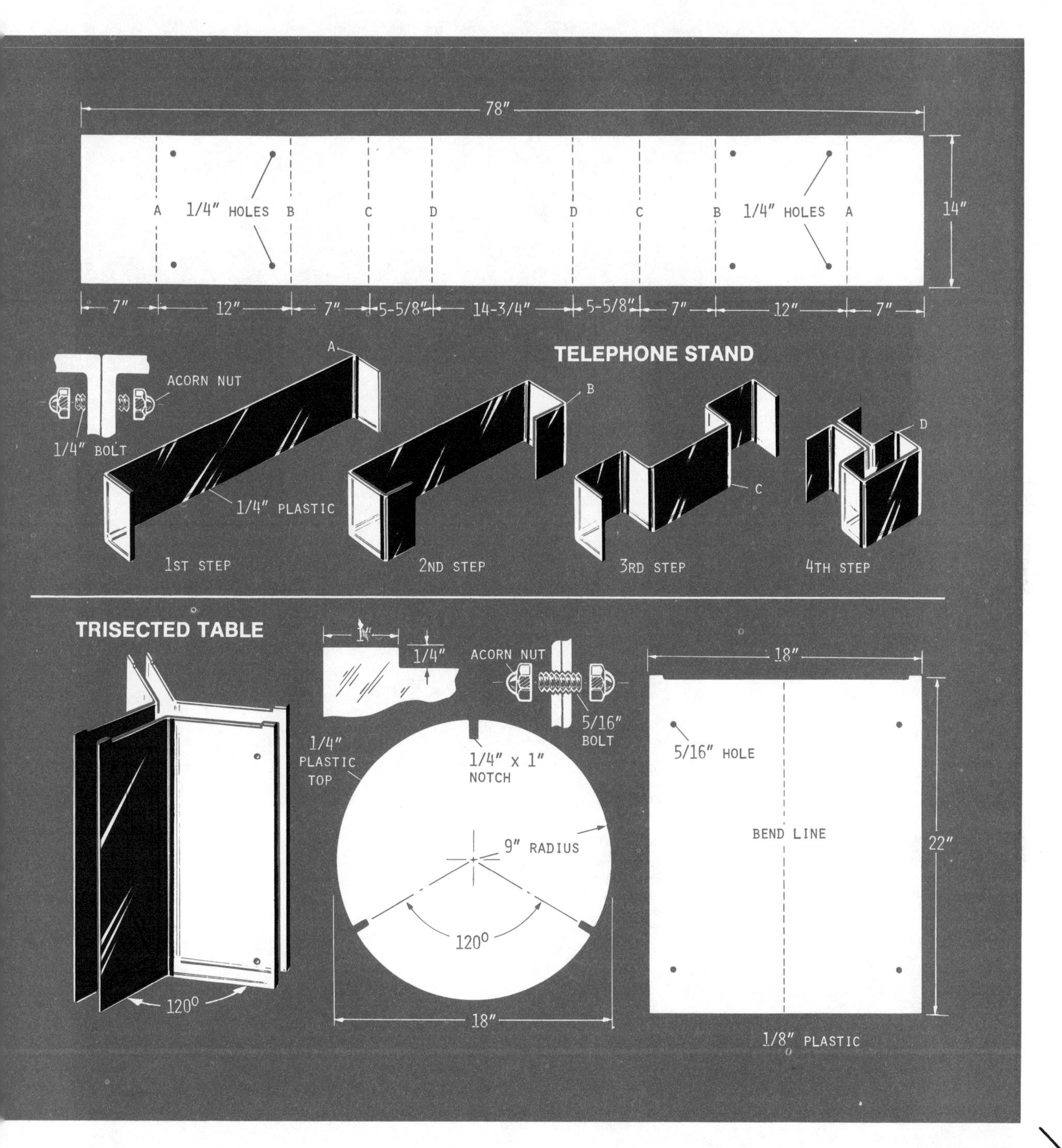

continued

then buff the edges with a clean muslin wheel dressed with a good grade of fine-grit buffing compound. (Note: Buffing kits, with compound, are sold at plastics dealers.)

• **Cementing.** Capillary cementing with a special solvent such as IPS #3 or methylene chloride is an easy and sure way of joining, literally fusing, two pieces of Plexiglas G and similar sheet acrylics. First, remove the protective paper from the plastic and sand the edges to a satin finish, as already described. (To save time, bind four panels together and sand the edges simultaneously.) Then place the workpieces together, hold the joint with tabs of masking tape and apply the liquid solvent with a needle-nose applicator made for this purpose (or use an eyedropper, syringe or small paintbrush—not as satisfactory). The liquid will quickly flow into the joint and create an immediate bond. Let it set 20 minutes before removing the tape.

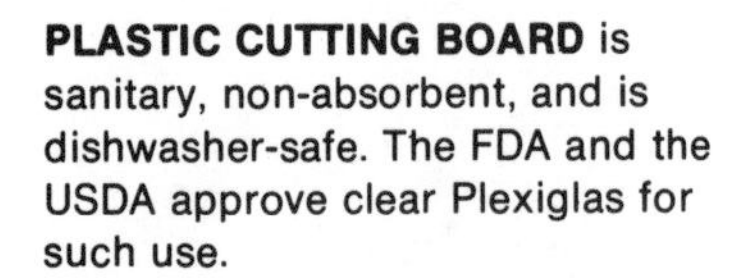

PLASTIC CUTTING BOARD is sanitary, non-absorbent, and is dishwasher-safe. The FDA and the USDA approve clear Plexiglas for such use.

DIAGRAM shows you how to make hat-coat rack shown on the opposite page.

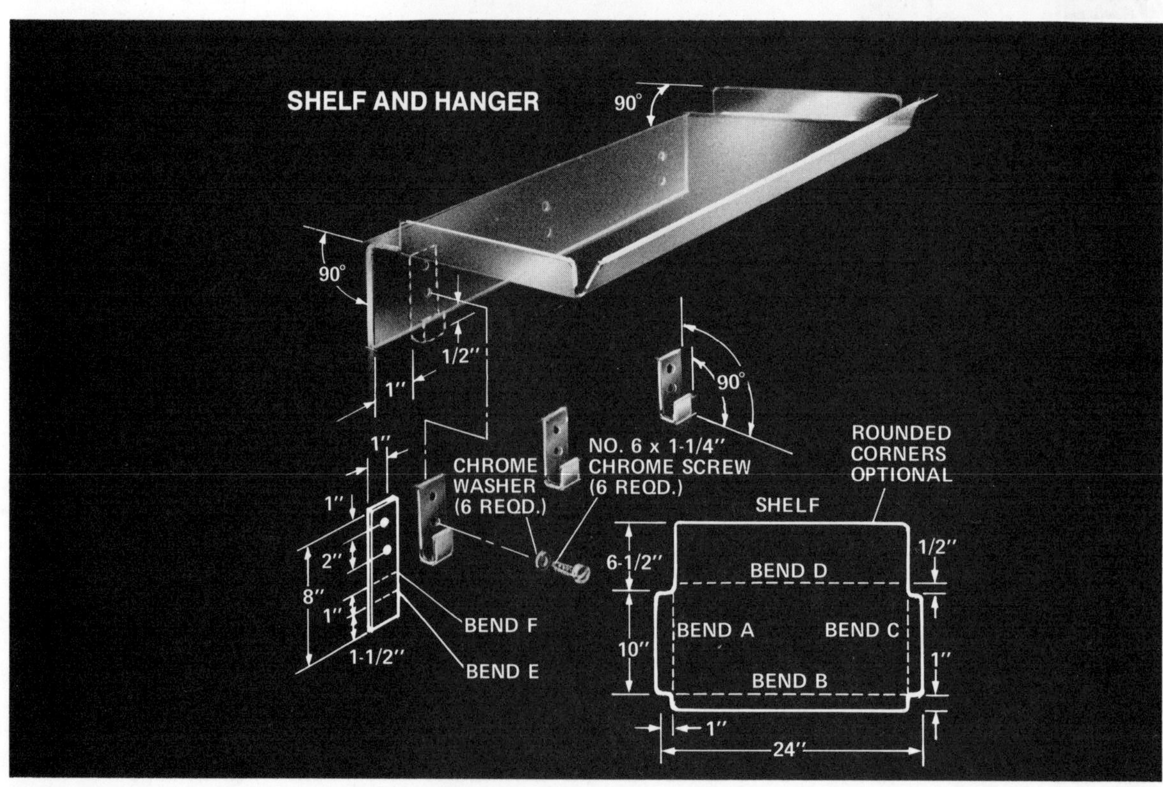

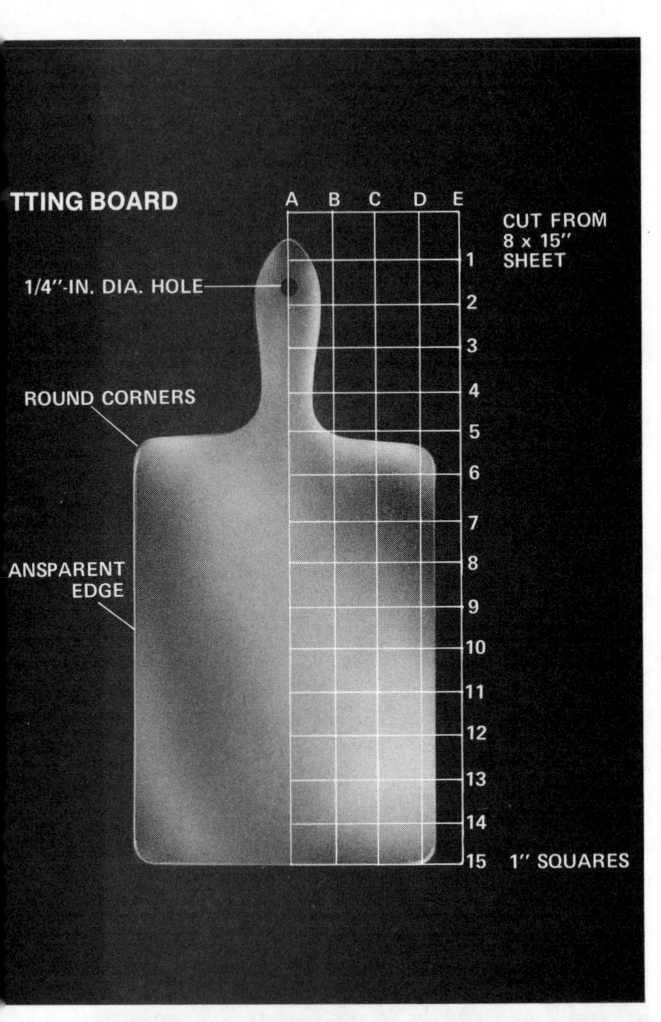

With type K Plexiglas, capillary solvent cannot be used. Follow the above directions, except use a thickened cement such as Daybond or IPS Weld-On #16 and clamp the joint for two hours.

Caution: Avoid dripping solvent on the surface of the polished plastic as it will deface it; also work in a well-ventilated room, as solvents may be toxic if inhaled for extended periods. Keep solvents away from flame and children.

• **Bending.** To make a bend, you will need a strip heater, such as the homemade unit shown on these pages that employs a heating element sold by plastics dealers. First, remove the protective paper from the plastic. Then use a grease pencil ("china marker") to mark the plastic where it is to be bent and center the pencil mark over the heater element. It will take from 8 to 10 min. at the desired temperature of about 290°F to heat ¼-in.-thick plastic to a bendable state. Make the bend slowly, on the line, while the plastic is still on the heater. You'll find that the plastic has a tendency to "spring" back as it cools, so you must compensate a bit when forming a right-angle bend. Hold the bent material until the softened plastic cools and hardens.

Be careful not to overheat the plastic; it will scorch and bubble if you do. Bending it before it

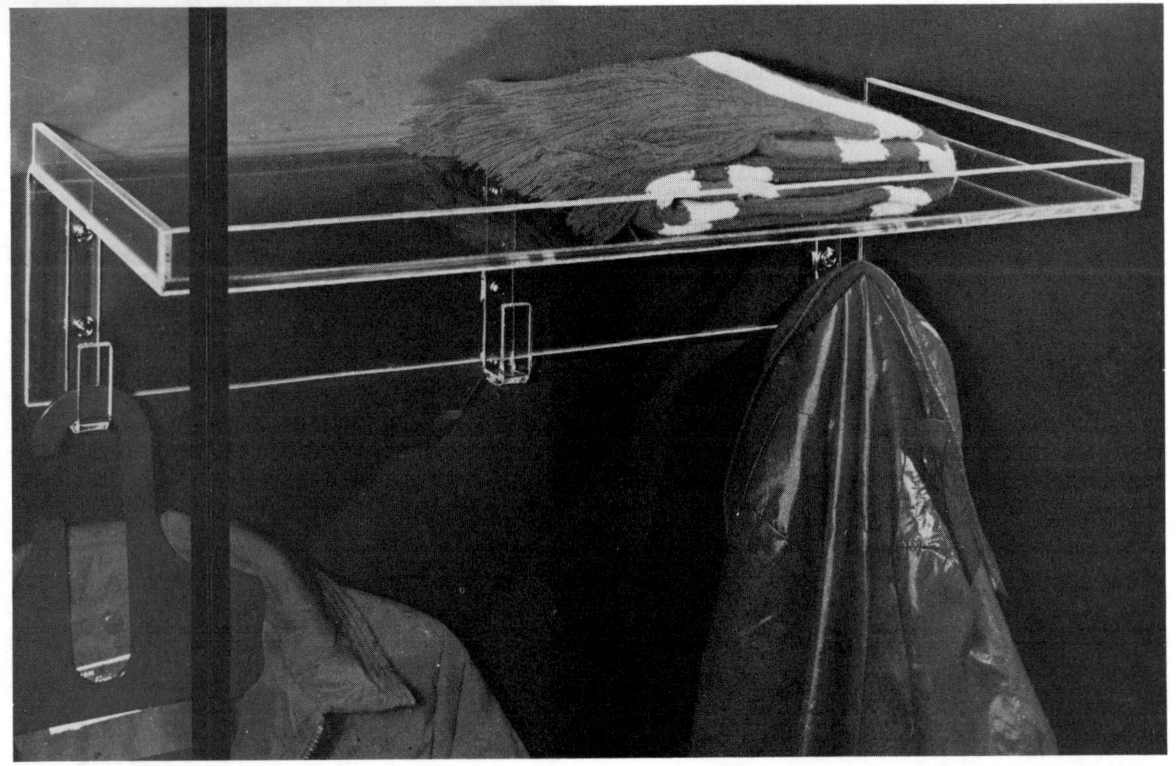

COFFEE TABLE, which stands 16 inches high, is made by combining a favorite wood with a pair of U-shaped legs fashioned of clear plastic. The result is an uncluttered, airy, floating effect.

is soft enough will cause stress crazing (small internal fractures) at the bend. Practice on a scrap first. The temperature of the plastic should not be greater than 340°F., and don't try to bend plastic more than ¼-in. thick with the heater. In any event, *do not* heat sheet acrylic in your oven; doing so could cause an explosion.

For more information about working with sheet acrylic, write to Rohm and Haas Co., Box 9730, Philadelphia, PA 19140. For a small sum they will send you a package containing a list of project plans, a do-it-yourself booklet of project designs and fabrication techniques, a booklet on the use of plastic as a safety measure in doors and windows, and a list of distributors. The firm also supplies a strip-heater kit and most of the special tools and cements mentioned here.

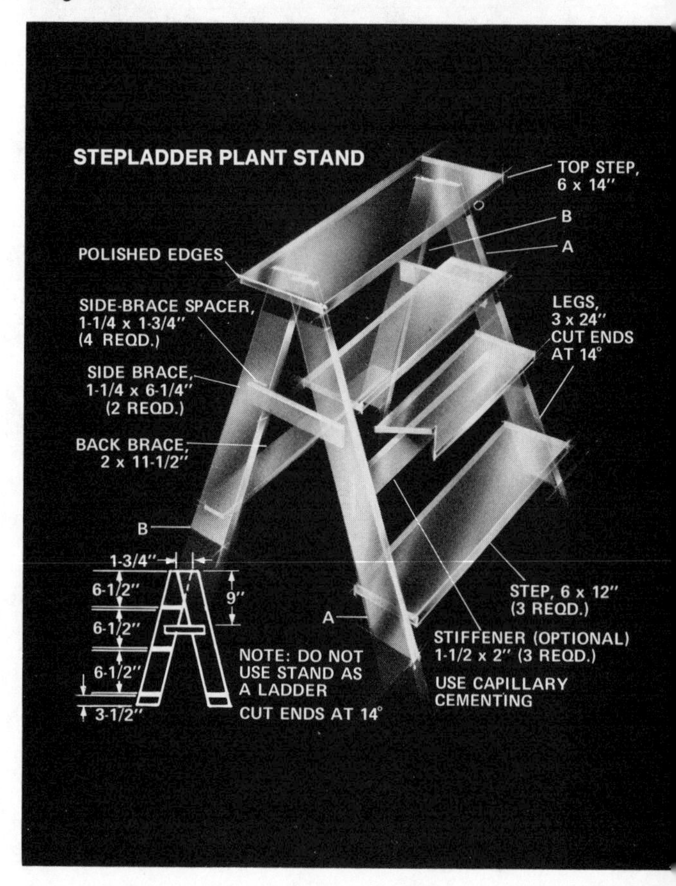

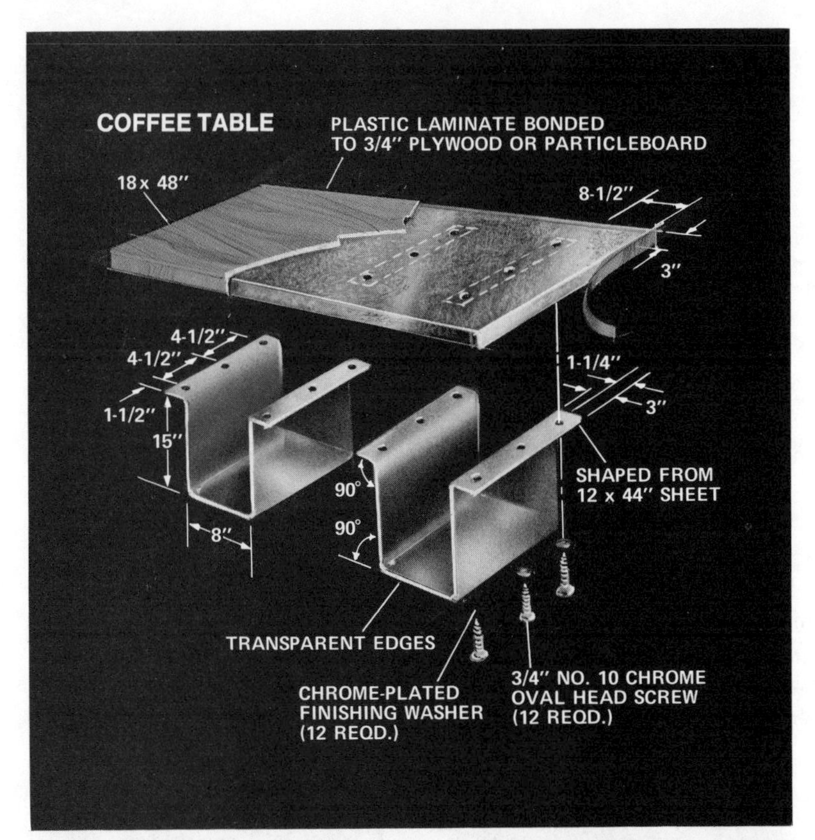

PLAN is for the coffee table shown on opposite page. The stepladder plant stand shown is excellent for displaying indoor plants; it can go anywhere.

Be your own home plumber

Experience, special tools, and local codes make big jobs a challenge, but a basic understanding helps when there's trouble.

IN CASE YOU DON'T already know it from end to end, it needn't take you long to become well acquainted with your home's plumbing system. And it's certainly worth your while. Understanding is vital to normal maintenance of the system, to say nothing of its importance to small repairs.

Start where the water supply first enters the house. The water meter's location will make that easy to find. A shut-off valve comes just before the line from the main, from out in the street, reaches the meter.

The water meter, if you have one, and most of the basic water system will be in the basement. In houses built on a concrete slab, it may be in a utility room. In such cases, as well as in houses set over a crawl space, builders try to locate plumbing centrally so they need to provide only short pipe runs—within the walls—to various fixtures.

Homes with basements are the more common, and understanding the system there will help to clarify layouts in houses of other kinds. A typical water-system layout is shown here. There will, of course, be variations on this arrangement, but the principles involved are constant.

As you trace that first (cold water) supply line, you'll see that it branches to serve a variety of functions and fixtures. Basement branches will go to sill cocks and laundry tubs. One will supply the boiler's water jacket if that's the sort of heating system you have.

SEE ALSO
**Bathrooms . . . Bathtubs . . . Drains . . .
Drinking fountains . . . Faucets . . .
Garbage disposers . . . Heaters, water . . .
Septic systems . . . Toilets . . . Well driving**

TYPICAL WATER SYSTEM

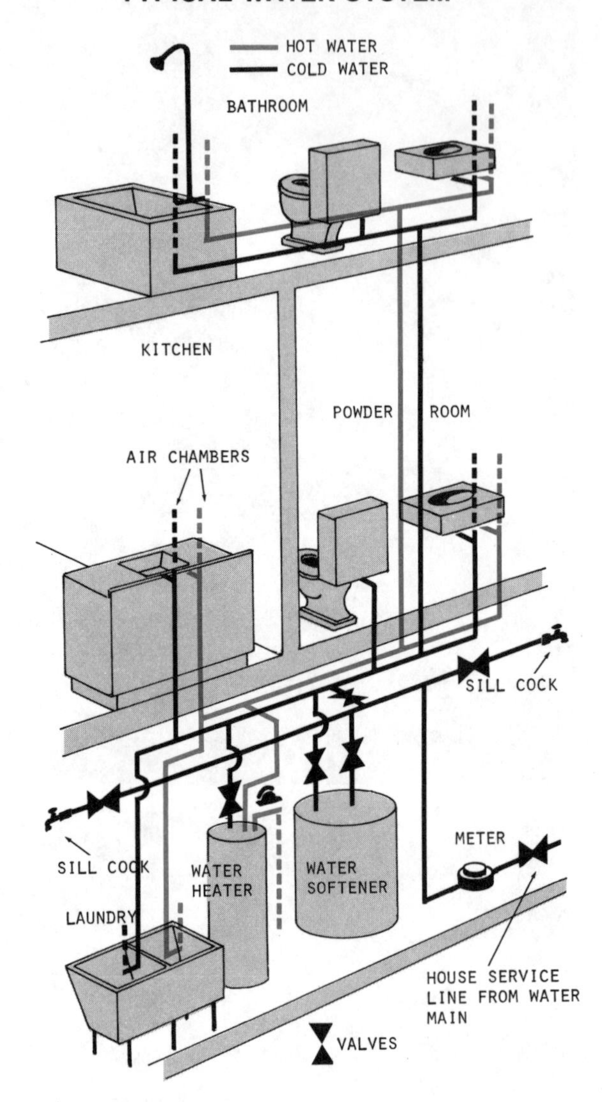

The sill cocks are the faucet-like fittings to which you hook your hose when watering the lawn or washing the car. Where freezing weather is a potential threat, provision is normally made to protect that section of pipe that reaches through the basement wall to the outdoors. Just inside the wall, sill-cock lines usually have shut-off valves. Thus you can close off that final leg and drain it by opening the sill cock. In better-built houses, you may be able to drain that leg as well as the body of the shut-off valve from inside the basement. The valve itself may have a small, knurled cylinder projecting from one side. That's the drain fitting; just turn it to open it.

Other branches from the main supply line will head upstairs to provide cold water to the kitchen, bathroom, and powder room if any. Normally they go up through interior walls.

TYPICAL DRAINAGE SYSTEM

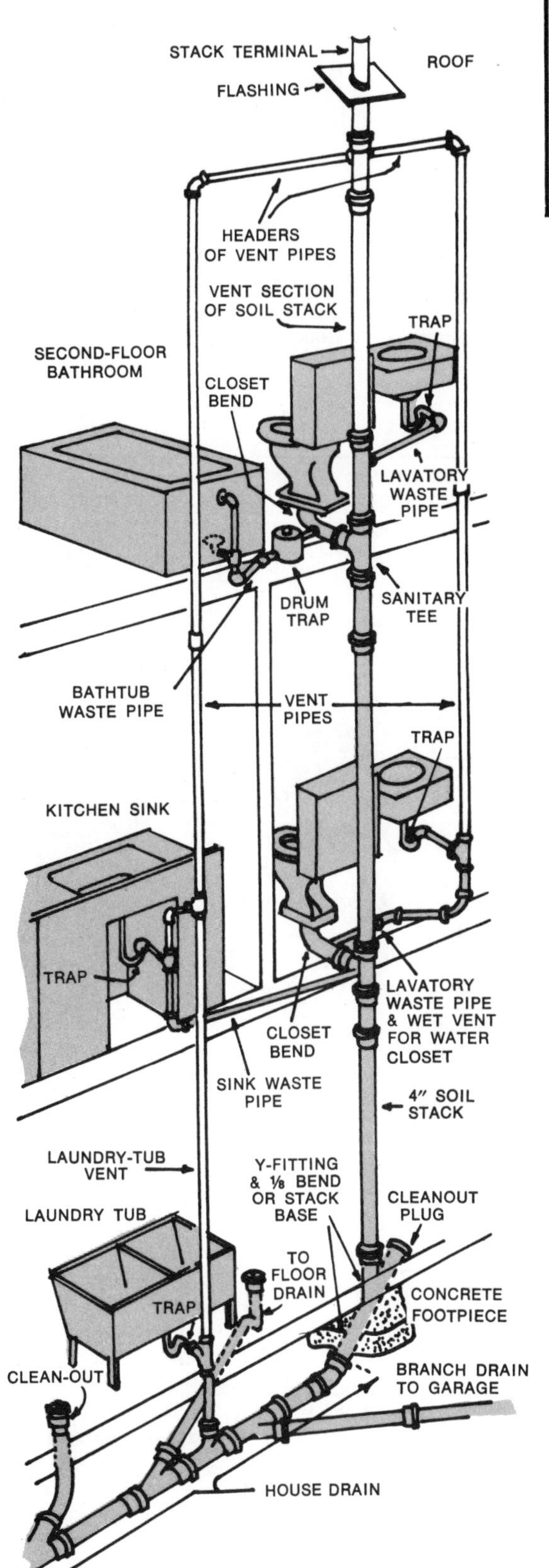

HOW MUCH PIPE FITS WITHIN A FITTING?			
Nominal Size	Normal Engagement For Tight Fit	Nominal Size	Normal Engagement For Tight Fit
1/8"	1/4"	1"	9/16"
1/4"	5/16"	1 1/4"	9/16"
3/8"	3/8"	1 1/2"	9/16"
1/2"	7/16"	2"	5/8"
3/4"	1/2"	2 1/2"	7/8"

MATERIAL DIFFERENCE

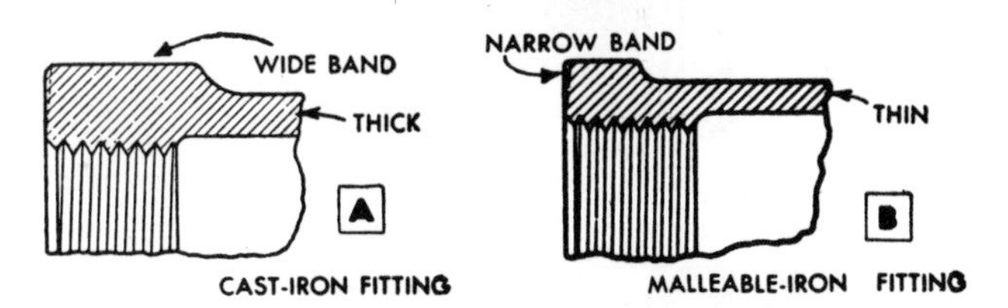

MALLEABLE FITTINGS

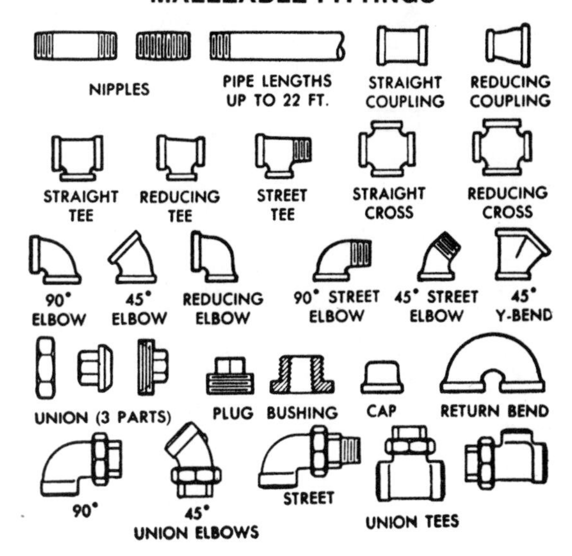

MALLEABLE PIPE fittings are somewhat more costly than cast iron drainage fittings. The fittings shown above are the most common. Ask for fittings by name if possible.

DIMENSIONS OF K, L AND M-TYPES COPPER TUBING FROM ⅜" TO 2"

Nominal Size	Outside Diameter	Inside Diameter			Wall Thickness		
	Types K-L-M	Type K	Type L	Type M	Type K	Type L	Type M
⅜	.500	.402	.430		.049	.035	
½	.625	.527	.545		.049	.040	
⅝	.750	.652	.666		.049	.042	
¾	.875	.745	.785		.065	.045	
1	1.125	.995	1.025		.065	.050	
1¼	1.375	1245	1265	1291	.065	.055	.042
1½	1.625	1481	1505	1527	.072	.060	.049
2	2.125	1959	1985	2009	.083	.070	.058

(All Dimensions in Inches)

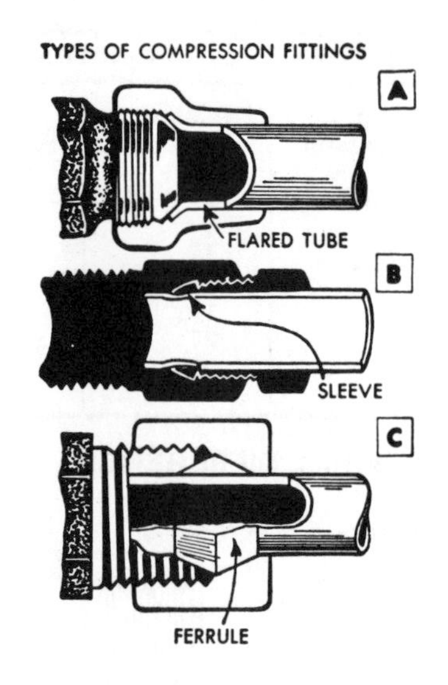

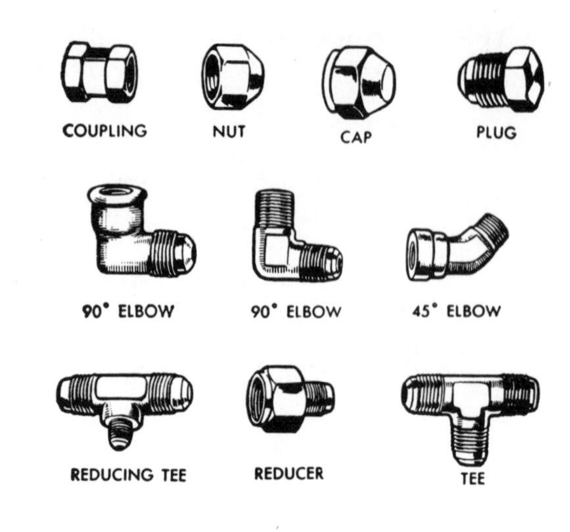

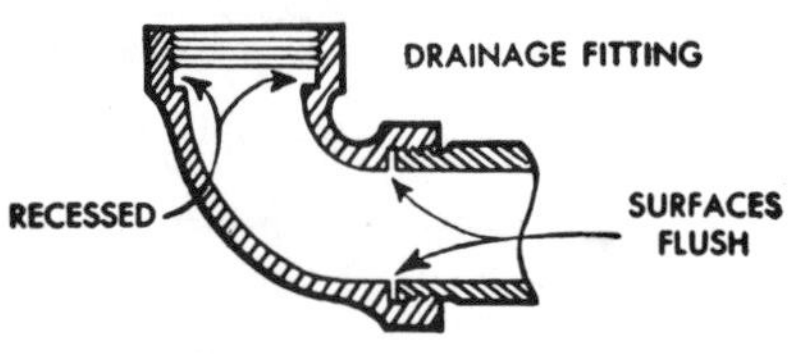

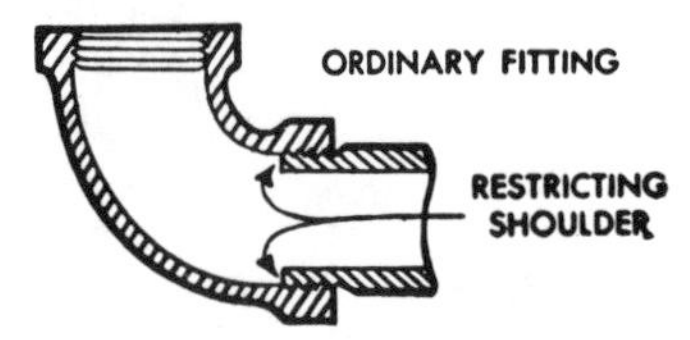

DESIGNED DIFFERENCE

LEAD PIPE FOR VENT AND DRAINAGE LINES			
I.D. (In.)	Wall Thickness (In.)		
1¼	.118	139	171
1½	.138	165	191
2	.142	177	205
2½, 3, 4, 5, 6	125		250

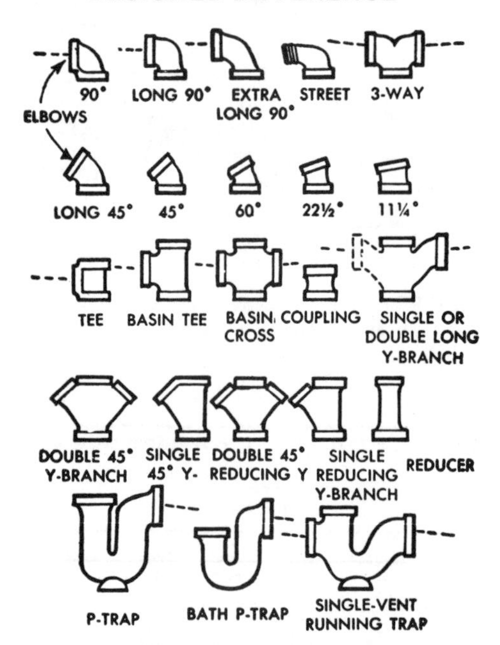

DRAINAGE FITTINGS

CAST IRON drainage fittings, in many cases, have a slight pitch built into one face. The pitch assures the proper flow through the drainage system.

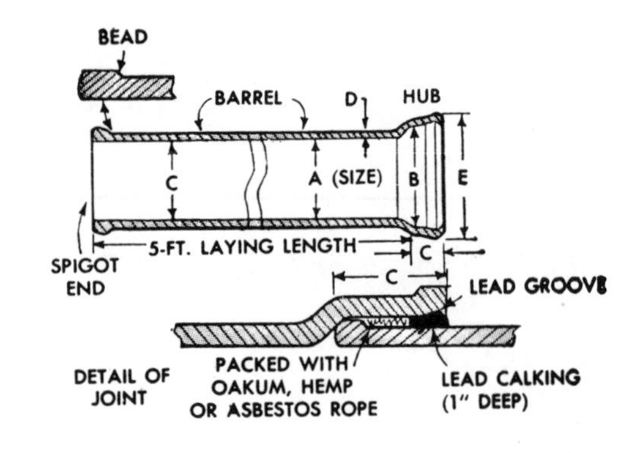

CAST-IRON HUB-AND-SPIGOT SOIL PIPE

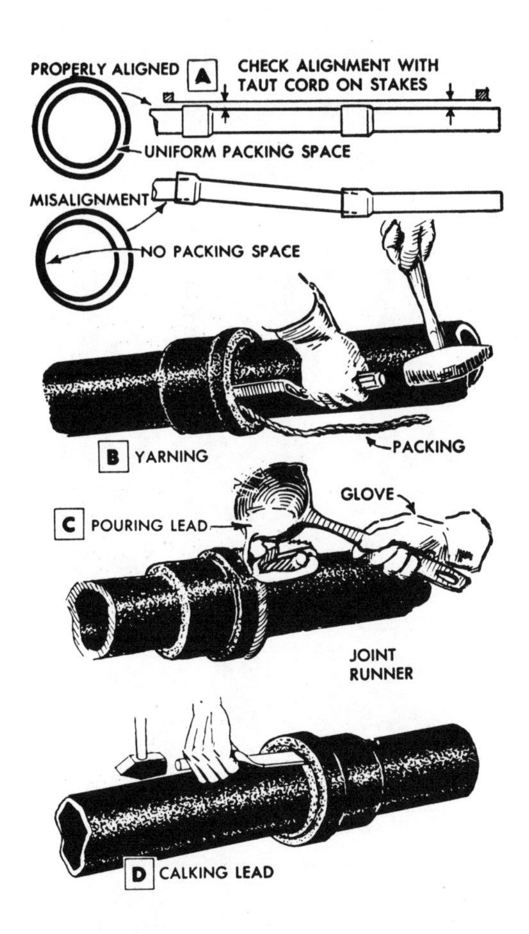

PROPER ALIGNMENT of soil pipe lengths can be difficult, but is essential if the joints are to be well calked. Hubs are always "upstream."

Builders like, as much as possible, to concentrate vertical plumbing lines in a single interior wall, often referred to as the plumbing wall.

Now let's tackle the most complex branch. That's the one that goes first to the water softener, then to the water heater. It becomes the entire hot-water circuit. (In the specimen layout, all water is softened.)

It's pretty simple to sort out the lines atop the water heater. One, with a relief valve in it, is a safety. If, for some reason, temperature or pressure gets too high, the valve lets go and this line leads it down to a foot or so above the floor. Excess water is taken past the flame or heating coil and toward a floor drain. Of the other two lines at the water heater top, the supply line will feel cold and the output line hot.

After leaving the water heater, the hot leg branches out further, supplying hot water to the laundry tubs, kitchen bath tub, and bathroom and powder-room lavatories. Many sections of hot line will parallel a cold, one pair heading toward the kitchen, one toward the bath.

Even a novice will quickly learn to distinguish between water lines and electrical conduit despite their similar sizes. If the difference in tubing surface doesn't do the trick, check fittings. Remember that conduit is often bent to make a 90° turn while plumbing relies on elbows.

It's a bit less obvious to distinguish water from gas lines, especially if some of the basement ceiling is finished off. Trace the lines carefully. Being sensitive to the function of each will help to ensure an accurate analysis.

On a gas-fired water heater, for example, the line that feeds the lower area of the appliance will be the gas supply.

drainage: a separate system

The drainage system is, of course, totally separate and quite different from the water system. Its fittings may seem to be counterparts of the water system's elbows and tees, but they're properly in a classification all their own. Instead of being galvanized steel, they're usually cast iron. Exceptions to that generalization come where local building or plumbing codes have been modernized to allow drain systems of newer materials—certain plastics or DWV (drain-waste-vent) copper.

Especially in older houses, the main drain lines are likely to be of rough cast-iron soil pipe. Straight runs, vertical or horizontal, are of 5-ft. lengths of hub-and-spigot pipe. The spigot end of one length fits, rather crudely, into the hub of the next at big, bulgy joints. The original plumber will have packed each joint—commonly with oakum—and poured it full of molten lead. The task is one that takes experience.

As you trace out these large lines, you'll find from time to time that they have openings stoppered with huge brass plugs carrying big, square bosses that take a man-sized wrench. These clean-outs provide a location where a plumber's "snake" can be fed into the drain system to open up any blocked areas.

The drain system is vented to the outside to help it flow well. You'll see at least one and maybe two vents sticking through your roof.

Traps are scattered throughout the drainage system, a trap of some kind at every fixture. Each holds some amount of water for an airtight seal that prevents sewer gas from backing up into the house. One vent function, incidentally, is associated with the traps: Vents ensure that a slug of waste water, plunging down the soil-pipe stack, won't create suction to pull water from the traps.

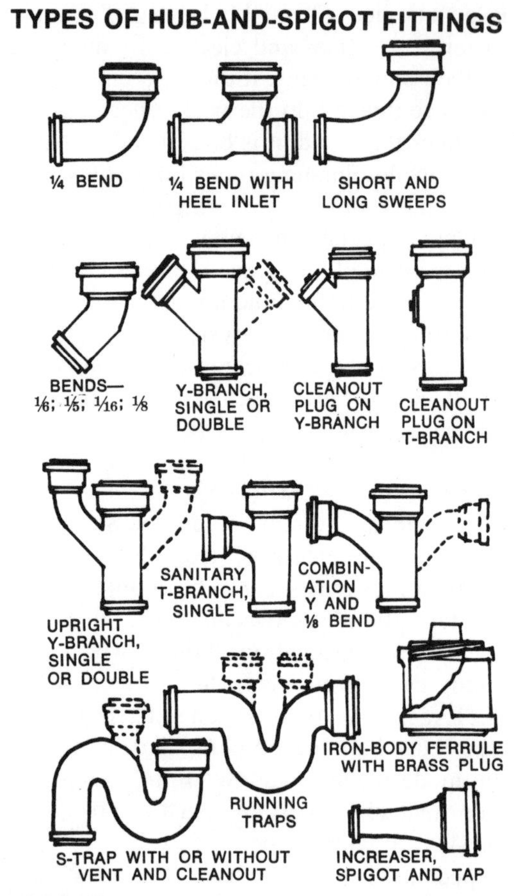

HERE ARE the more common types of drainage fittings found inside the house.

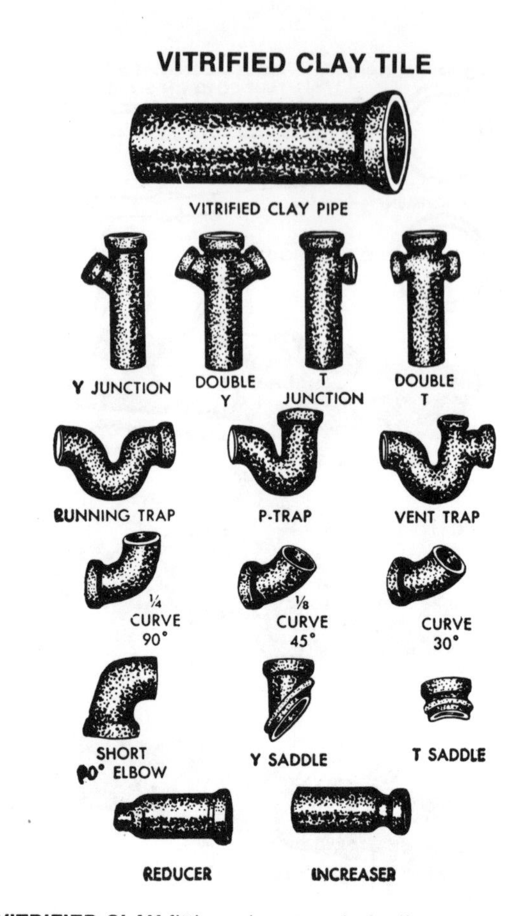

VITRIFIED CLAY fittings, in general, duplicate cast iron fittings. Clay tile usually is used for drainage beyond the foundation.

The trap in the water closet or toilet is molded into the stool itself. All the others, however, are specific plumbing fittings. Under the bathroom floor, there's a drum trap in the drain line from the tub or shower. Other fixtures—sinks, lavatories, or laundry tubs—all have hook-shaped P-traps just beneath them.

materials are changing

Pipe of other materials is gradually displacing the old reliable cast iron and wrought iron (malleable) pipe and fittings in new construction. Where local codes allow, copper pipe is used more and more widely in new residential and commercial construction, or even in major remodeling jobs. But they require special adapters when the new materials are joined to an old system—and these may not be available at the corner store.

But if you lean toward copper as more manageable material, be sure you get what you should have. It comes in types K, L, and M; the outside diameters are constant for each nominal size, but wall thicknesses vary. Plastic pipe, too, has a variety of characteristics. There are at least three general kinds: rigid, semi-rigid, and flexible. Only some are suitable for hot water use.

There's also concrete pipe, asbestos-cement pipe, and a bituminized-fibre pipe, all intended as kinds of soil pipe. Asbestos and bituminized are considered the most durable, but some codes specify they're for outdoor use only. Sections are joined with special fittings that use rubber rings and machined tapers. The joints are considered waterproof and root-proof.

Then there's vitrified-clay pipe, with its extremely hard, glazed surface, immune to acids, alkalies and solvents. Clay and concrete pipe joints are usually sealed with portland-cement mortar. Special fittings are available to connect vitrified clay to cast iron.

"So that's all," you say. "It's pretty simple. I can repair and maintain this whole system myself—and save a bundle."

Watch yourself! There are some jobs you'll have to reserve for the plumber. Plumbing and building codes often are complex. Some jobs take costly equipment that's rare in the ordinary household. And several take skills that can be accumulated only with experience.

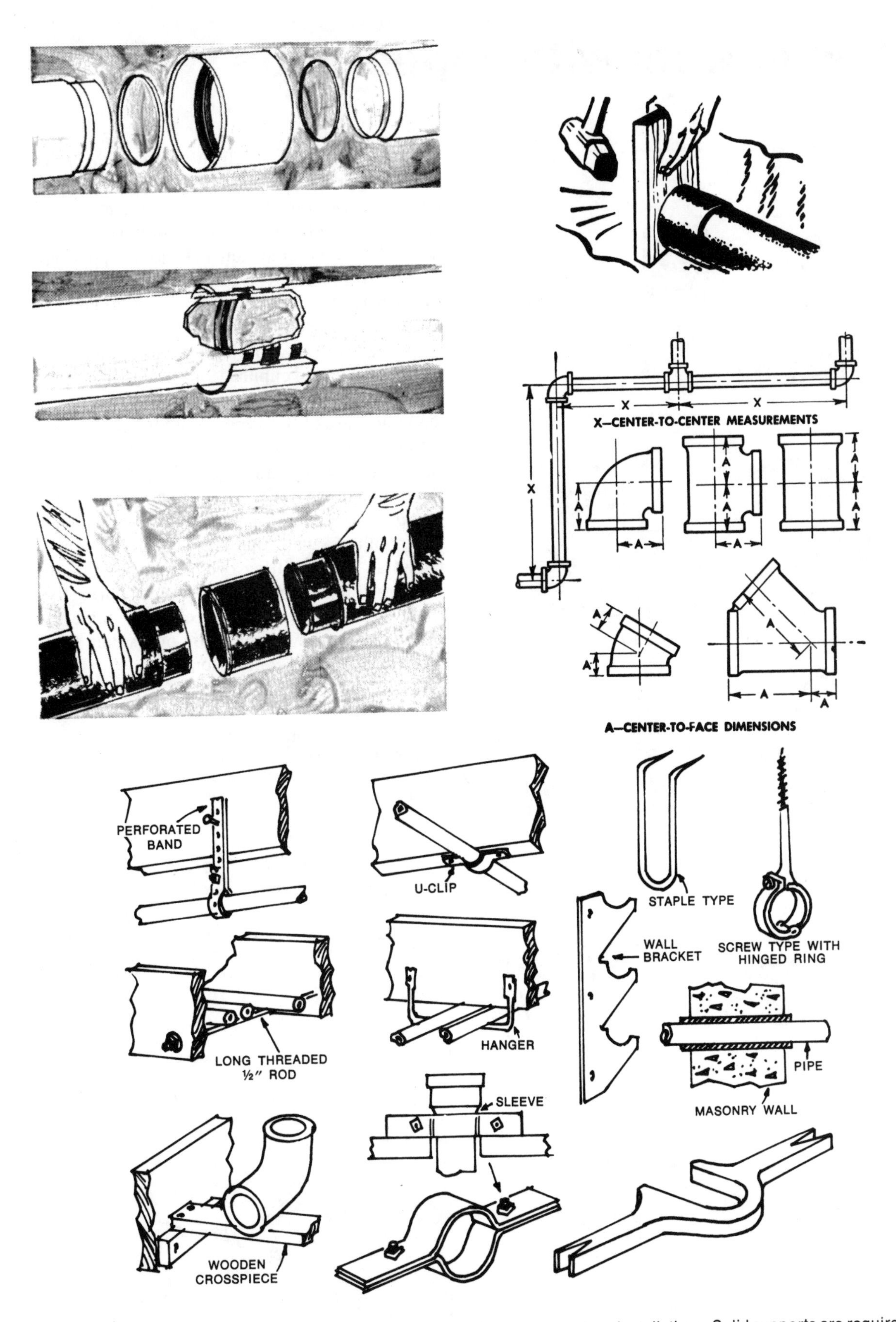

HERE ARE THE COMMON fixtures and hangers for supporting pipe in various installations. Solid supports are required to prevent joints from developing leaks. Drawing above right shows how to measure pipe runs.

How to work with copper pipe

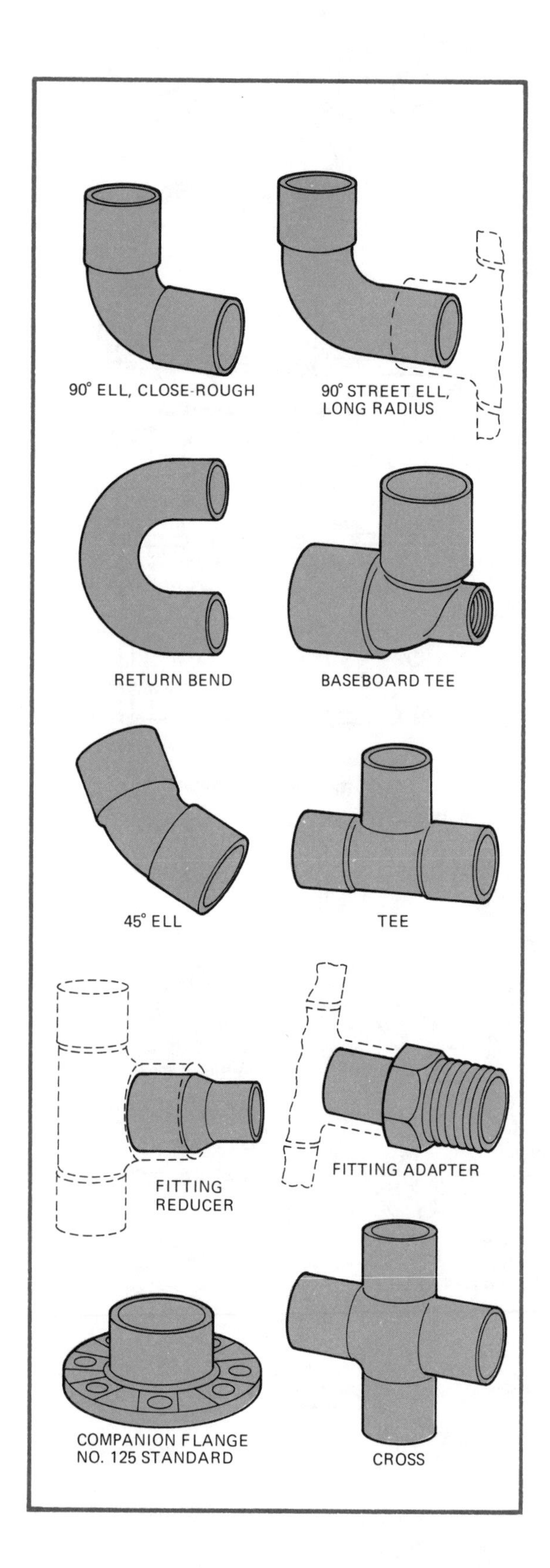

■ COPPER PIPING is light and extremely durable, requires no threading of the ends to join it, comes in varying diameters, wall thicknesses and degrees of hardness, and is suitable for both hot and cold-water systems. To join copper piping, there are many types of fittings to cover every part of the plumbing layout. A number of common fittings are shown at the left.

Copper pipe can be joined using either soldered (also called capillary or "sweat" joints) or screwed (compression fitting) joints. Compression joints are of two types. With the first, called a "bead" fitting, the tubing is pushed into the fitting, a bead of jointing paste is applied around the tubing in front of a compression nut, and the compression nut is tightened onto the fitting. The result is a watertight fit. The second type is called a "flare" fitting because the end of the tubing is funnel-shaped with a special flaring tool (below). This shaped end receives the male end of the fitting; the compression nut is then tightened to finish the connection.

SEE ALSO

Bathrooms . . . Bathtubs . . . Drains . . . Drinking fountains . . . Faucets . . . Garbage disposers . . . Septic systems . . . Soldering . . . Toilets . . . Torches . . . Well driving

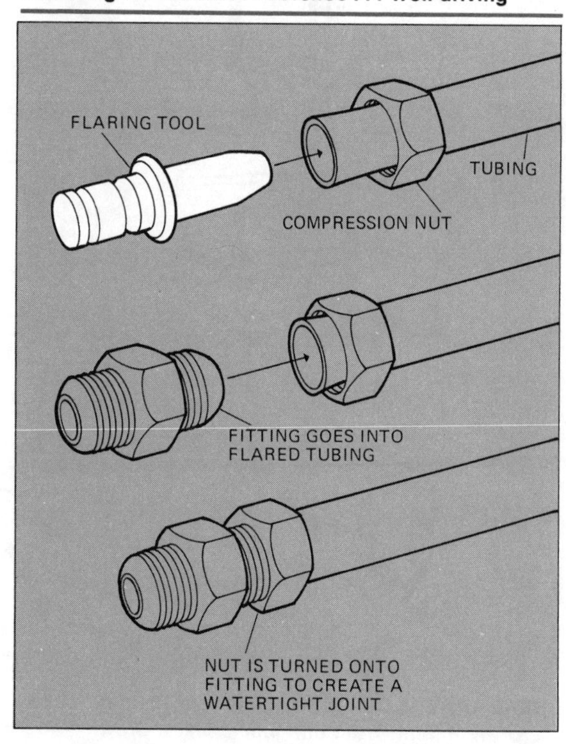

Types of copper piping

Type	Temper
K	Hard (rigid) or soft (flexible)
L	Hard or soft
M	Hard only

To be sure the type of copper piping that you use for a specific application complies with local plumbing code, always check with your local building department. In general, Type L can be used below ground, Type M above ground. For a superior installation, use Type K below ground and Type L above ground.

Equipment needed

Propane torch	Tubing cutter with reamer
Hacksaw	Sandpaper or fine steel wool
Smooth file	Solder
Tubing bender (also known as a "hickey")	Flux

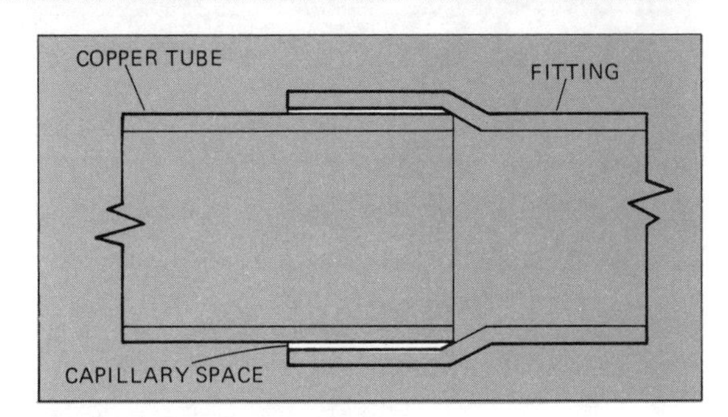

Capillary or 'sweat' joints

Properly prepared, a sweated joint will provide many years of troublefree (nonleaking) service. Although your joint may leak the first couple of times you attempt to sweat pipe, you'll soon be sweating copper pipe just like a pro by getting a little practice under your belt and by following the rules outlined on these pages.

To understand the principles of sweating pipe, you should understand how capillary action works. When the end of a copper pipe is inserted as far as possible into a fitting, a small amount of space will remain between the inside wall of the fitting and the outside wall of the pipe. When the fitting is heated with a propane torch and solder is applied around the pipe at the outer edges of the fitting, the solder will be drawn into this space by capillary action, bonding the pipe and fitting together securely. Such action will be the result regardless of whether the piping will be running horizontally or vertically.

If you're repairing or adding to an existing copper piping system, remember that all parts to be joined first must be completely dry. After the soldering is done and the joint cooled to room temperature, test the work for possible leaks.

Cutting and cleaning

Cut pipe to length using a tubing-cutter (1) or a fine hacksaw blade. Make sure the cut is square and the pipe remains round and true. Cutting with a hacksaw blade leaves rough edges on the inside and outside of the pipe, while a tubing cutter leaves rough edges on the inside of the pipe. Remove burrs on the outside of the pipe with a smooth file or sandpaper and on inside with a reamer (2) or rattail file. Clean the end of pipe with steel wool or a strip of sandpaper (3).

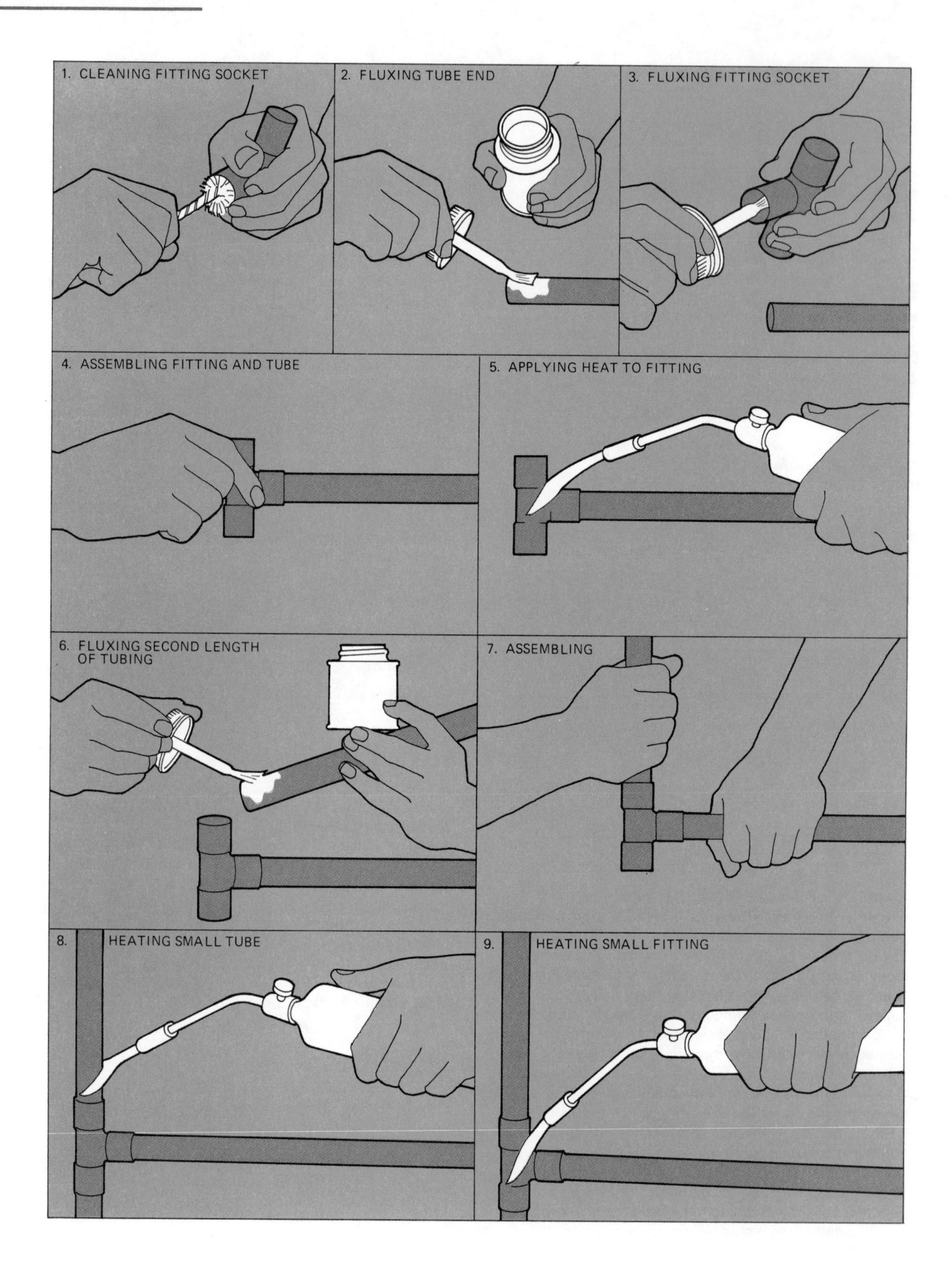
1. CLEANING FITTING SOCKET
2. FLUXING TUBE END
3. FLUXING FITTING SOCKET
4. ASSEMBLING FITTING AND TUBE
5. APPLYING HEAT TO FITTING
6. FLUXING SECOND LENGTH OF TUBING
7. ASSEMBLING
8. HEATING SMALL TUBE
9. HEATING SMALL FITTING

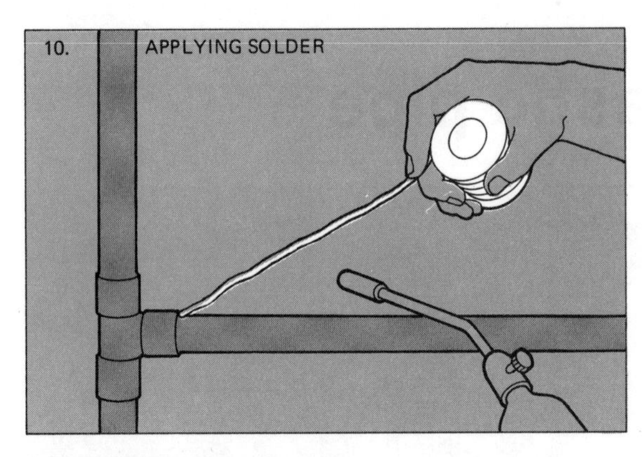

Assembling copper system

After you have thoroughly cleaned the inside of the fitting socket (Step 1, left), apply a thin coat of flux to the end of the pipe (Step 2) and the inside of the fitting (Step 3) with a small, clean brush. Then push the tubing tightly into the fitting (Step 4) and twist the pieces slightly in order to distribute the flux evenly. Wipe off any excess flux that remains and apply heat with a propane torch to the fitting (Step 5).

In the same manner, apply flux to the second length of tubing (Step 6), insert in the fitting (Step 7) and apply a flame to both the tubing (Step 8) and fitting (Step 9). Melt the solder from a spool of soldering wire around the tubing-fitting joint (Step 10, above).

Flux for soldering is mildly corrosive. It contains zinc and ammonium chlorides in a petroleum base, and is used as a protective coating on the metal and as an agent to help the solder flow. Always stir flux before you use it.

The cardinal rule in choosing a solder is to buy a quality solder. Most solders for household plumbing jobs are composed of 50 percent tin and 50 percent lead. If the joint requires a solder of greater strength, use one comprising 95 percent tin and 5 percent antimony.

Do not clean, flux and assemble more copper piping than you can solder in about two hours.

Soldering tips

Remember to align joints with adequate support before soldering, and to place no strain on them. When soldering, use torch with sweeping motion—tubing and fitting should be at same temperature for best flow of solder into joint. If solder forms lumps, joint is not hot enough. If there is no question that the joint is hot enough but solder still does not flow freely, overheating resulting in burned flux is likely, and the joint must be started again from Step 1. As soon as solder has set, use a wet brush or rag to crack and remove flux (remove it from inside of pipes by flushing with water); remove all flux before pressure-testing the joint—if necessary use a wire brush. If you have to redo a joint, reflux the entire joint area before applying heat to unsolder.

Ten steps for assembling copper piping

Clean the inside of the fitting with a wire brush. A thorough cleaning is absolutely necessary because a "sweat" joint relies on capillary action and *any* dirt, grease, or surface oxidation on the pipe or the fitting will hinder the joining action. Because the pipe should fit tightly into the fitting, do not remove too much metal when sanding or the capillary space will be enlarged and the joint weakened.

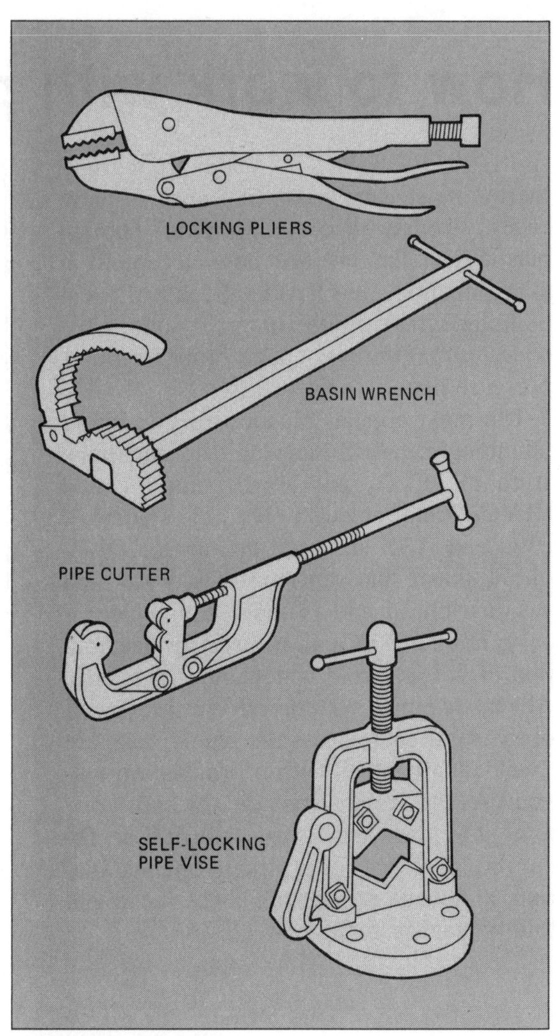

Toolbox additions

If you plan on doing most of your own plumbing jobs, the four tools shown above can be valuable additions to your toolbox. The two pictured at the top are available at most hardware stores, while you may have to visit a plumbers' supply house to find the lower two.

Vise-grip pliers, with serrated jaws and locking nut, are especially useful when working with small-diameter pipes. A basin wrench, whose gripping head is adjustable, will save you many bumps and knocks on head and hands when you are installing a basin where there is little room for swinging ordinary wrenches.

A pipe cutter, which is faster and more accurate than a hacksaw when cutting iron or galvanized pipe, is operated simply by starting the cutter over the pipe, and, as it is revolved, tightening the handle gradually to deepen the cut. Thread-cutting oil should be applied to both the cutter and the pipe.

A self-locking pipe vise has V-shaped jaws that grip the pipe from both top and bottom. It eliminates the need for a helper to hold the pipe while you do the cutting.

How to work with plastic pipe

■ PLASTIC PIPE is made from rigid thermo-plastic materials that are, in many cases, stronger than metal piping. Though plastic installations are now accepted in many localities, it is best to check with local building authorities in advance. Some local codes *forbid* the use of plastic pipe for water pressure lines.

The most popular plastics for household plumbing are ABS (acrylonitrile butadiene styrene), PVC (polyvinyl chloride) and CPVC (chlorinated polyvinyl chloride). PVC and ABS are used mainly for DWV (drain, waste and vent) systems, water and gas distribution and as underground electrical conduit. CPVC can be used for distribution of hot and cold water under pressure. All plastic piping systems have fittings made of the same material as the pipe. These are "welded" together with a brushed-on solvent. As the cement dries rapidly, work one joint at a time—and always test-fit first. *Do not mix* two types of plastic in one installation, and when cementing, always read and follow manufacturers' directions.

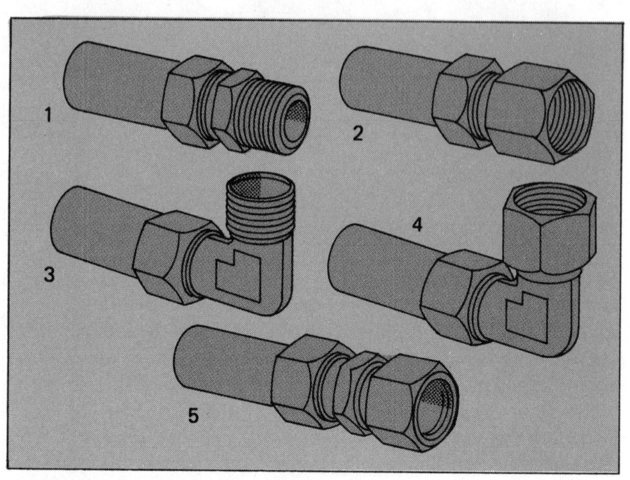

Typical pipe adapters
Adapters permit transition from metal pipe and tubing systems to plastic pipe. Nos. 1 through 4 are for use with threaded iron pipe—1 and 3 for connection to female fittings, 2 and 4 for connection to male fittings. Elbow adapters, 3 and 4, are designed for close angle connections and help where space is tight, as is the case with in-the-wall plumbing. The copper tubing adapter, No. 5, is nonthreaded.

SEE ALSO
Bathrooms . . . Bathtubs . . . Drains . . .
Drinking fountains . . . Faucets . . .
Garbage disposers . . . Septic systems . . . Toilets . . .
Well driving

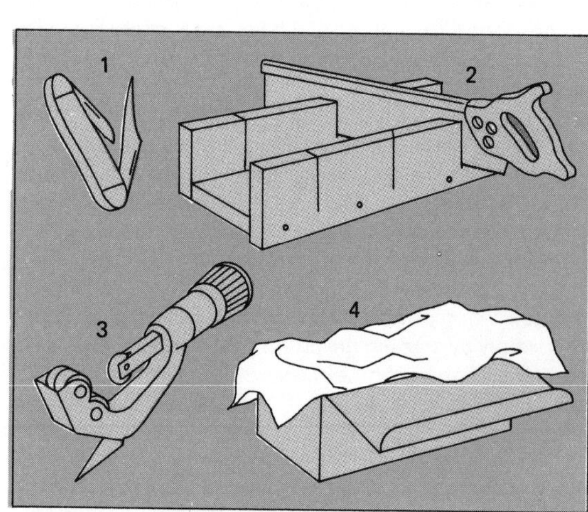

Tools for working plastic pipe
You probably have most of the equipment you need to work with plastic pipe. Basic tools include: 1) pocketknife, 2) miterbox and backsaw, 3) tubing cutter with cutting wheel recommended for plastic pipe and 4) clean rags. *Do not* use paper products to wipe solvents.

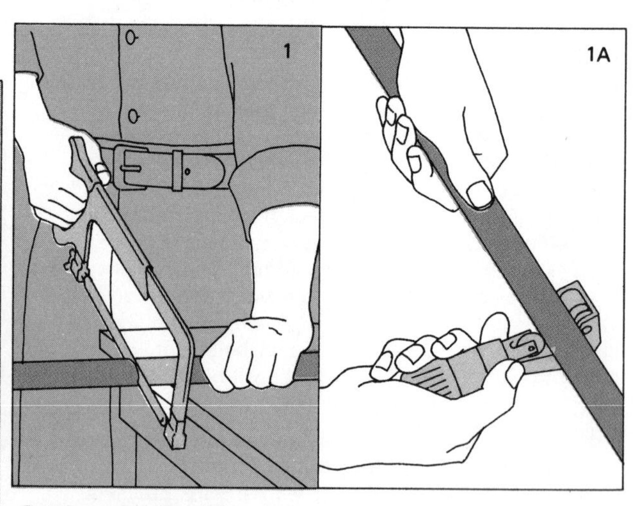

Cutting plastic pipe
After measuring the length (or run) of pipe needed, cut pipe to proper length, *allowing for the distance it goes into fittings.* Though miterbox and backsaw or tubing cutting are neatest, pipe can also be cut freehand with hacksaw (Fig. 1) if your eye and hand are steady. Tubing cutter, Fig. 1A, is rotated around the pipe and tightened after every few revolutions until the cut has been completed.

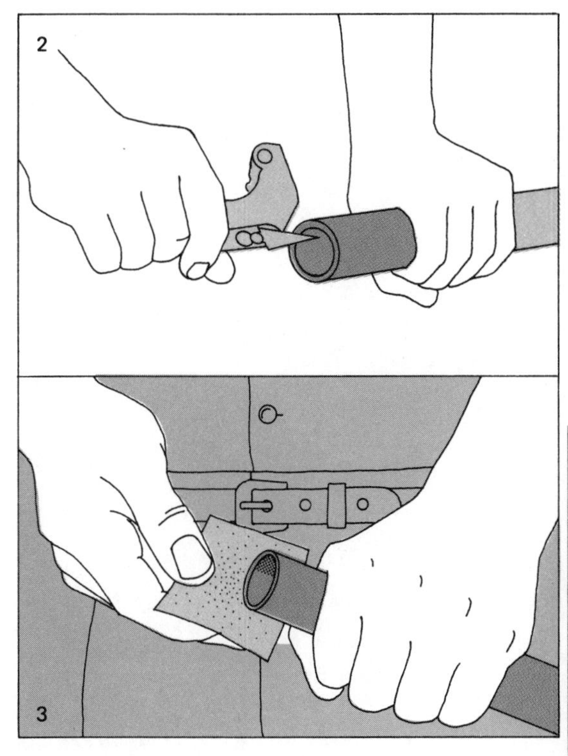

Deburring the pipe

Burrs and ridges from cutting must be removed with knife or tubing reamer (on cutter) so that ends are smooth inside and out. Check fit next. Pipe should enter fitting socket, but fitting should not fall off when pipe is pointed downward. Next, remove surface gloss from both pipe end and inside of socket with either fine sandpaper or a cleaning solvent made specifically for the type of plastic pipe used.

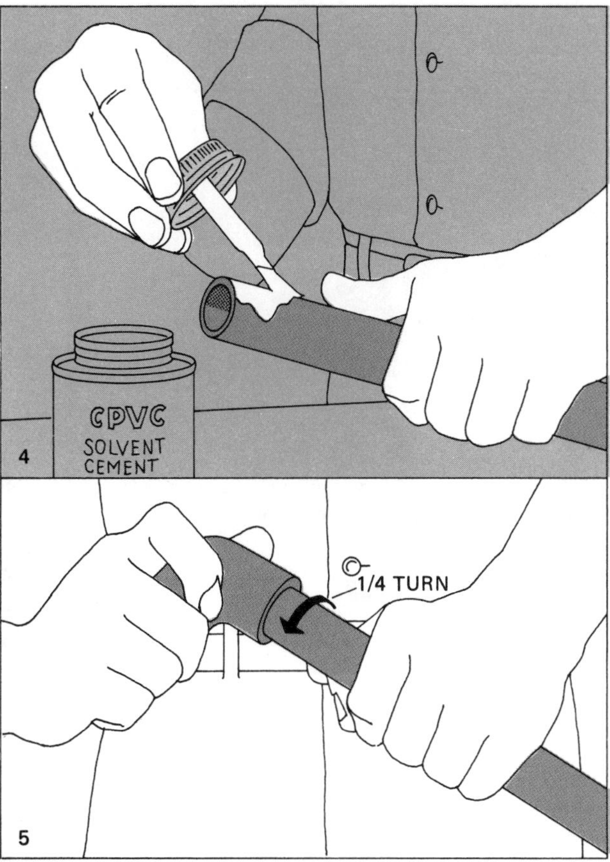

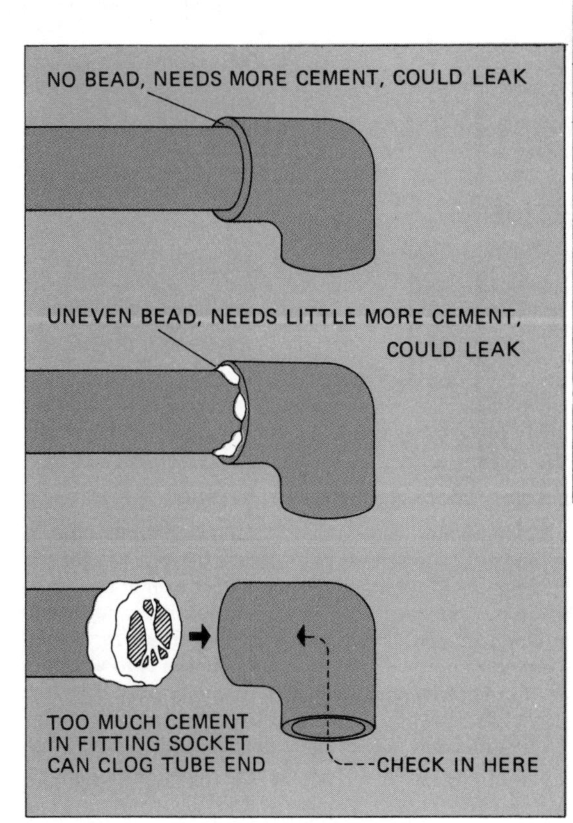

Applying solvent cement

Using a narrow brush—width equal to ½ pipe diameter—apply thin coat of cement on pipe end. Dip the brush again and apply a thin coat to the socket. Dip once more and recoat the pipe end. Push pipe and fitting together and give joint a quarter turn to spread cement evenly; adjust for proper angle immediately. Hold together for at least 15 seconds, then wipe off excess cement.

Three cementing faults are depicted at the left. Wait an hour—overnight is better—before filling system with water. Check new work for leaks immediately.

How to silence plumbing noises

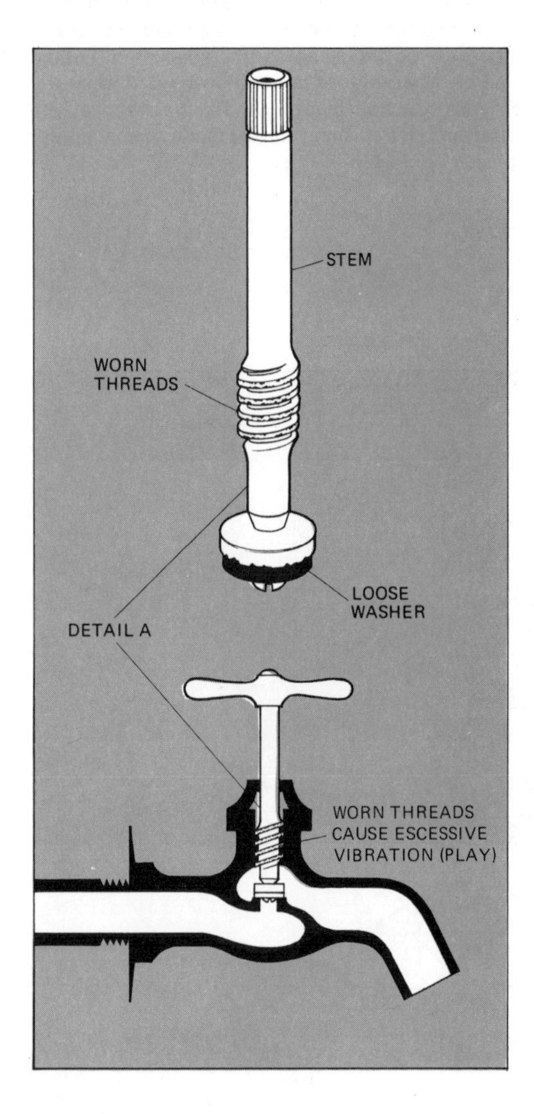

Noisy faucet

Chattering and whistling are the most common faucet noises. When this happens in a compression-type faucet (above), the usual cause is either a loose or worn (corroded) internal assembly. To remove faucet stem, turn off water supply, loosen cap nut and unscrew spindle (stem) assembly. First check small screw at end of stem; if loose, tighten to seat washer firmly. If washer is worn, replace it. When screwing stem assembly back in place, check whether it has any "play" (movement up and down) caused by worn threads. If assembly is loose, replace it with a new one. Occasionally, faucet noises are caused by a defective faucet design. In this case, replace the entire faucet.

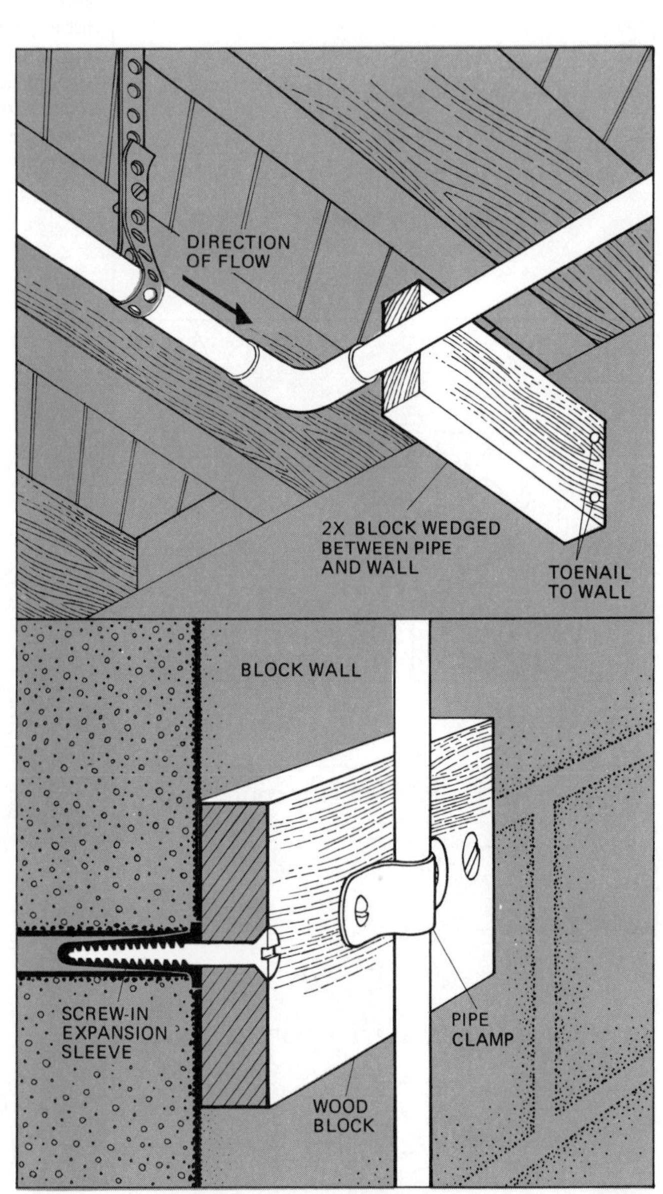

Water hammer (knocking, banging) in pipes

When fast-moving water, especially in a long horizontal pipe, is suddenly turned off, a shock wave often occurs between faucet and where the pipe changes direction. The result is hammering due to severe vibrations. To lessen such noise and rattling, anchor the pipe firmly along its run. One method of further securing long horizontal piping hung by strap-type pipe hangers is to wedge a scrap piece of 2x4 between pipe and wall, toe-nailing block to wall with masonry nails. (*Caution:* Avoid oversized wedge that creates pressure on the pipe and may cause a nearby joint to leak.) Pipe clamp and wood block, fastened to concrete wall as shown above, will secure the riser and also reduce vibration.

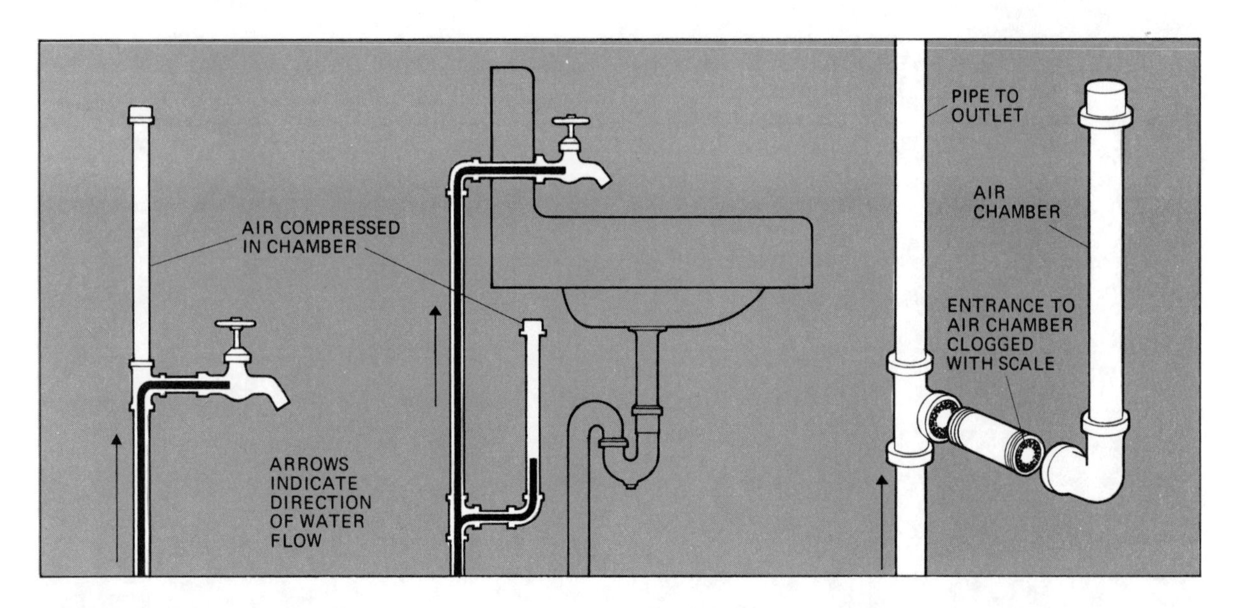

Noise-reducing air chambers

Air chambers also help minimize water hammer. When a faucet is closed quickly, water rushes into the chamber and the compressed air cushions thrust of the water (above, left and center). Since the air cushion is gradually absorbed by water under pressure, water must occasionally be drained from the chamber and air replaced. To drain, turn off water, open drain valve below the level of the air chamber and remove cap at upper end of chamber. Short, horizontal pipe leading to chamber (above, right) which often becomes clogged with scale, should be periodically checked and cleaned.

SEE ALSO

Bathrooms . . . Bathtubs . . . Drains . . .
Drinking fountains . . . Faucets . . .
Garbage disposers . . . Septic systems . . . Toilets . . .
Well driving

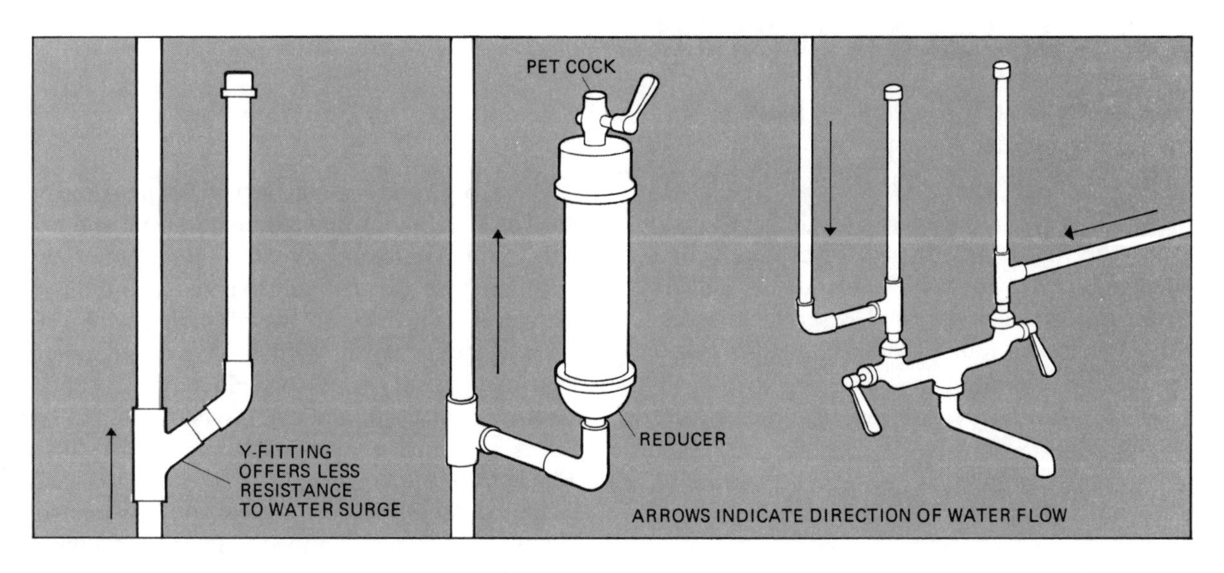

Air chamber positions

An air chamber that is a direct continuation of a pipe (positioned as shown at top, left of page) is best because it then receives the full thrust of rapid-moving water. A "Y" (45°) fitting (above, left) offers less resistance to water surge than a 90° fitting. An air chamber that needs draining frequently can be made more convenient by addition of a pet cock on cap of chamber (above, center). Effectiveness of a chamber is increased if inlet opening at bottom is about half size of connecting pipe (note reducer shown). Faucet, below level of chambers (above, right), acts as a drain valve.

HIGHLY DECORATIVE plywood paneling for study or office is called "Brushed reverse board and battin."

All about plywood

By W. CLYDE LAMMEY and RICHARD NUNN

■ IF YOU'RE NEW to doing it yourself you should think of plywood as a single board measuring up to 4 feet wide and 8 feet long with a thickness from ¼ to ¾ in. Some lumber dealers furnish it in smaller sizes and lesser thicknesses, in panels from 1 foot in width up, and in thicknesses down to ⅛ in.

This range of dimensions opens new fields to the do-it-yourselfer.

SEE ALSO
Finishes, wood . . . Lumber . . . Nails . . . Paneling, plywood . . . Plywood jigs . . . Sanding . . . Table saws . . . Wood finishes . . . Woods

Also, plywood is available faced with some of the finest cabinet woods, both domestic and exotic, from ash to zebrawood. Some of the finer wood facings are relatively expensive, but those plywoods with the softwood facings are relatively inexpensive. With such a broad range you can use plywood to build houses, boats, cabinets, furniture and even toys.

two basic types

In general, plywood comes to you in two basic types, the one with *hardwood* facings of a wide variety, the other in a variety of *softwood* facings. The latter are most widely used in common applications, largely because of versatility and lower cost per square foot. Plywood is sold almost anywhere lumber and other building materials are sold.

MANY TEXTURED, as well as plain, panels are offered by plywood manufacturers.

hardwood-faced plywoods

Hardwood-faced plywoods are graded somewhat differently than softwood-faced panels. The best grade is *custom* grade (No. 1), free of the patches, knots and plugs that are permissible in the lower grades. It's suitable for the finest work where the wood must be exposed.

Next comes *good* grade (No. 2) with clean, smoothly cut facing and the joints precisely matched so the grain runs true.

The *sound* grade, commonly No. 3, has no open, visible defects but the grain may not be as closely matched and minor mineral streaks and stains are permissible.

In the *utility* grade (No. 4) somewhat greater defects and discolorations are more or less general and in the final, or *reject* grade (No. 5) knot holes and splits are permissible in manufacture. The latter two or three grades are suitable only for rough work where sectional strength and not appearance is the desirable feature.

Hardwood-faced plywoods also come to you in three types of bonds (adhesives) classified as *waterproof, water resistant* and *dry*. You would specify *waterproof* bond where the plywood is to be exposed to weathering and dampness, as in exterior applications. Specify the *water-resistant* bond for interior applications where the panels will not be exposed to extremely high humidity or directly to the elements. Lastly you can use the dry bond in locations where panels will not be exposed to water, excessive dampness or a condition of high humidity.

softwood plywoods

Most plywoods used for medium and light construction and do-it-yourself projects are commonly termed "softwood plywoods" and these are generally classified by wood species, type and grade. As an example, Group No. 1 in the classification of species includes facings of Douglas fir, western larch, and the southern, loblolly and longleaf pines. Group No. 2 includes Douglas fir, western hemlock and Sitka spruce. In all, there are some 30 species of woods classified into four groups.

IN PANELING A WALL, furring strips are applied to fit panels, then adhesive is applied to strips.

PANELING IS APPLIED over the furring strips. Be sure the edge of first panel is vertical.

cores for softwood plywoods

Panels are available with three different types of cores—*veneer, lumber* and *particleboard. Veneer* cores consist of a series of laminated veneers, the laminations alternating at right angles. In *lumber* core the center consists of solid wood strips, edge-glued; the core thus built up is faced with a series of laminated veneers. This plywood is widely used in furniture construction and built-ins. *Particle-board* core is actually a board made up of resin-coated wood particles to a given width and then faced on both sides with laminated veneers in the same manner as lumber core.

All these panels are lightweight, easily workable with hand or power tools and are exceptionally stable, free of the tendency of solid-stock construction to warp or "wind."

exterior and interior types

The softwood panels are manufactured in two types. *Exterior* type has a 100-percent waterproof glue while *interior* type has a highly moisture-resistant glue. The veneers in the backs and inner plys of the exterior type are a higher grade than those of the interior type. *Exterior* grade panels may be used for boats, farm structures, siding and other applications where the material will be exposed to constant wetting, drying, soaking or other moisture conditions, including those involving constant high humidity. *Interior* grade plywood is recommended for use where the material will not be exposed to moisture or continuing high humidity, such as paneling, indoor furniture, wall sheathing, roof decks and other structural applications.

Plywood produced by mills belonging to the American Plywood Association is in strict accordance with government standards. APA has registered certain grade-trademarks which are used by the member-manufacturers. Within each type there is a variety of appearance, generally determined by the grade of veneer used on the face and back of the panel. The grades are N, A, B, C, C-plugged and D.

softwood grades

N-grade is a special order "natural finish" veneer. It is select all heartwood or all sapwood. It is free of open defects, but allows some repairs.

A-grade is smooth and paintable. Neatly made repairs in the veneer are permissible. The panels may be used for a natural finish in less demanding applications.

B-grade has a solid surface veneer. Circular repair plugs and tight knots are permitted.

C-grade has knotholes up to 1-in. Occasional knotholes ½ in. larger are permitted providing the total width of all knots and knotholes within a

Guide to Appearance Grades of Plywood

	Common uses and descriptions	Use these terms when you specify plywood	Typical grade-trademarks	Grade inner ply	Common thicknesses (inch)					
					1/4	5/16	3/8	1/2	5/8	3/4
Interior Type	Natural finish cabinets • Furniture (Special order item)	N-N, N-A, N-B INT-APA	N-N G-1 INT-APA PS 1-74 N-A G-2 INT-APA PS 1-74	C						•
Interior Type	Paneling • Cabinets (Special order item)	N-D INT-APA	N-D GROUP 3 INTERIOR PS 1-74 000 APA	D	•					
Interior Type	Built-ins • Cabinets • Furniture • Partitions (Paintable, 2 smooth solid faces)	A-A INT-APA	A-A G-4 INT-APA PS 1-74	D	•		•	•	•	•
Interior Type	Same as A-A except appearance of 1 side less important. (Paintable, 1 smooth face.)	A-B INT-APA	A-B G-4 INT-APA PS 1-74	D	•		•	•	•	•
Interior Type	Paneling • Shelving • 1-good-side partitions (Paintable, 1 smooth solid face)	A-D INT-APA	A-D GROUP 2 INTERIOR PS 1-74 000 APA	D	•		•	•	•	•
Interior Type	Shelving • Walls • Workshop furniture (Utility panel, 2 solid sides)	B-B INT-APA	B-B G-3 INT-APA PS 1-74	D	•		•	•	•	•
Interior Type	Sides of built-ins • Shelving • Bins (Utility panel, 1 solid side)	B-D INT-APA	B-D GROUP 3 INTERIOR PS 1-74 000 APA	D	•		•	•	•	•
Interior Type	Paneling • Interior accent walls Built-ins • Counter facing (Usually textured)	DECORATIVE PANELS-APA	DECORATIVE B-D G-1 INT-APA PS 1-74	D			•	•	•	
Exterior Type	Fences • Outdoor built-ins • Signs • Boats (Paintable, 2 smooth solid faces)	A-A EXT-APA	A-A G-3 EXT-APA PS 1-74	C	•		•	•	•	•
Exterior Type	Same as A-A except appearance of 1 side less important. (Paintable, 1 smooth face.)	A-B EXT-APA	A-B G-1 EXT-APA PS 1-74	C	•		•	•	•	•
Exterior Type	Siding • Soffits • Fences • Tanks (Paintable, 1 smooth solid face)	A-C EXT-APA	A-C GROUP 2 EXTERIOR PS 1-74 000 APA	C	•		•	•	•	•
Exterior Type	Service buildings • Shelving outdoors, e.g., in carports, garages (Utility panel, 2 solid sides)	B-B EXT-APA	B-B G-1 EXT-APA PS 1-74	C	•		•	•	•	•
Exterior Type	Farm buildings • Bins • Ag equipment Tile backing (Utility panel, 1 solid side)	B-C EXT-APA	B-C GROUP 2 EXTERIOR PS 1-74 000 APA	C	•		•	•	•	•
Exterior Type	Cabinets • Counter tops • Tanks Concrete forms (Hard, smooth resin-fiber overlay 2 sides)	HDO EXT-APA	HDO A-A G-1 EXT-APA PS 1-74	C or C-Plugged			•	•	•	•
Exterior Type	Siding • Built-ins • Furniture (Smooth, paintable, resin-fiber overlay 1 or 2 sides)	MDO EXT-APA	MDO B-B G-4 EXT-APA PS 1-74	C			•	•	•	•
Exterior Type	Siding • Paneling • Accent walls Counter facing • Fences • Ceilings Storage buildings • Open soffits (Usually textured)	303 SIDING EXT-APA T 1-11 EXT-APA	303 SIDING 16 oc GROUP 1 EXTERIOR PS 1-74 000 APA 303 SIDING 16 oc T1-11 GROUP 3 EXTERIOR PS 1-74 000 APA	C			•	•	• •	•
Exterior Type	Boat hulls (A or B face and back. Available also HDO and MDO.)	MARINE EXT-APA	MARINE A-A EXT-APA PS 1-74	B	•		•	•	•	•

Guide to Engineered Grades of Plywood

	Common Uses	Use these terms when you specify plywood	Typical grade-trademarks	Grade inner ply	Common thicknesses (inch)					
					1/4	5/16	3/8	1/2	5/8	3/4
Interior Type	Wall sheathing • Roof sheathing • Subflooring	C-D INT-APA WITH EXTERIOR GLUE	C-D 32/16 APA INTERIOR PS 1-74 000 EXTERIOR GLUE	D		•	•	•	•	•
	Roof decks • Structural diaphragms Box beams • Gusset plates Stressed skin panels • Pallet bins	STRUCTURAL I C-D INT-APA STRUCTURAL II C-D INT-APA	STRUCTURAL I C-D 24/0 APA INTERIOR PS 1-74 000 EXTERIOR GLUE	Improved D		•	•	•	•	•
	Underlayment Subfloor-underlayment	UNDERLAYMENT INT-APA	UNDERLAYMENT GROUP 1 APA INTERIOR PS 1-74 000	C & D	•		•	•	•	•
	Cabinet and built-in backs Wall and ceiling tile backing (Not a substitute for UNDERLAYMENT)	C-D PLUGGED INT-APA	C-D PLUGGED GROUP 2 APA INTERIOR PS 1-74 000	D		•	•	•	•	•
	Subfloor-underlayment under structural or nonstructural floor covering	2•4•1 INT-APA	2·4·1 GROUP 1 APA INTERIOR PS 1-74 000	C & D	1-1/8					
Exterior Type	Subflooring • Roof decking Siding on service and farm buildings Pallet bins	C-C EXT-APA	C-C 32/16 APA EXTERIOR PS 1-74 000	C		•	•	•	•	•
	All engineered uses that demand full Exterior type plywood, as outdoor exposure of uses listed in Interior STRUCTURAL grades	STRUCTURAL I C-C EXT-APA STRUCTURAL II C-C EXT-APA	STRUCTURAL I C-C 48/24 APA EXTERIOR PS 1-74 000	C		•	•	•	•	•
	Underlayment • Subfloor-underlayment in moist conditions, as balcony decks Shower tile backing • Fruit pallet bins • Tanks	UNDERLAYMENT C-C PLUGGED EXT-APA	UNDERLAYMENT C-C PLUGGED GROUP 2 APA EXTERIOR PS 1-74 000	C	•		•	•	•	•
	Same as UNDERLAYMENT C-C Plugged EXT-APA	C-C PLUGGED EXT-APA	C-C PLUGGED GROUP 3 APA EXTERIOR PS 1-74 000	C	•		•	•	•	•
	Concrete forms	B-B PLYFORM CLASS I OR II EXT-APA	B-B PLYFORM CLASS I APA EXTERIOR PS 1-74 000	C					•	•

specified section doesn't exceed certain limits. Limited splits are permitted; minimum veneer.

C-plugged has improved C-veneer with splits limited to ⅛ in. in width and knotholes and borer holes limited to ¼ x ½ in.

D-grade permits knots and knotholes to 2½ in. in width and ½ in. larger under certain specified limits. Limited splits are permitted.

interior grade use-guide

What grade and type of plywood you buy depends, of course, on the project at hand. Below is a guide to interior appearance grades:

A-A INT-DFPA: Both faces are the highest standard veneer grade for use where both sides will show: built-ins, cabinets, furniture, partitions, etc. The most common thicknesses are: ¼ in., ⅜ in., ½ in., ⅝ in., ¾ in. and 1 in. The veneer grade is A face, A back and D-grade inner.

A-B INT-DFPA: This panel is similar to A-A, but it is used where the appearance of one side is less important, and two smooth solid surfaces are desirable. Thicknesses are the same.

A-D INT-DFPA: Used for built-ins, paneling, shelving, partitions, etc., where only one side will show. Thicknesses are standard, with D inner plys.

B-B INT-DFPA: An interior utility panel for use as partitions, utility built-ins, mounting boards, etc. Both sides are smooth and may be painted. Thicknesses are standard, with D inner plys.

B-D INT-DFPA: For use where one smooth side is needed. Shelving, sides and backs for built-ins, economy cabinet work, slip sheets, separator boards and bins. Standard thickness; inner plys, D.

DECORATIVE PANELS: This material is rough sawn, brushed, grooved, striated or embossed on one side. Use it for accent walls, paneling, counter fronts and where wood with various surface textures is desired. The most common thicknesses are 5/16 in., 3/8 in., and 1/2 in. Veneer grade is C or better face, plys, D back and D inner.

PLYRON: These panels have a hardboard face and back and are used for built-ins, cabinet doors, countertops, worktables and furniture. The faces may be tempered, untempered, smooth or screened hardboard. The most common thicknesses are 1/2 in., 5/8 in. and 3/4 in., with C and D inner plys.

N-N INT-DFPA: A natural finish cabinet-quality panel, designed to be used where both sides will show. Both sides are select all heartwood or all sapwood veneer. Typical uses are for cabinet doors, built-ins and furniture having a natural finish. The panels are usually a special order item. In thicknesses of 3/4 in. only with C inner plys.

N-A and N-B INT-DFPA: This is similar to the grade listed above, but it permits an A or B-grade veneer on the backside. The panel is designed for economy when building cabinet doors, built-ins, furniture. It is a special-order item in 3/4-in. thickness only with C inner plys.

N-D INT-DFPA: One side is select all heartwood or all sapwood veneer. Use it for interior paneling that will have a natural finish. Usually a special order item in 1/4-in. thickness only with D inner plys.

UNDERLAYMENT INT-DFPA: For underlayment or combination subfloor-underlayment under resilient floor coverings. Ply beneath the face is C or better veneer; it is sanded or touch sanded as specified. Most common thicknesses: 1/4, 3/8, 1/2, 5/8 and 3/4 in.

2-4-1 INT-DFPA: A combination subfloorunderlayment panel for use with supports on 4-ft. centers. The panels provide a good base for direct application of resilient flooring. Available square-edged or tongue-and-grooved two or four sides as specified. Thickness: 1 1/8 in. only; D back and other inner plys.

A-A EXT-DFPA: Designed for exposed applications where both sides will show: fences, windscreens, exterior cabinets and built-ins, boats, etc. The most common thicknesses are: 1/4, 3/8, 1/2, 5/8, 3/4 and 1 in. Panels have an A face and back with C inner plys.

A-B EXT-DFPA: Similar uses to A-A EXT, but where the appearance of one side is less important. The thicknesses are the same with C inner plys.

MDO EXT-DFPA: A medium-density overlaid plywood panel with opaque resin-impregnated fiber overlay, heat-fused to one or both panel faces. It provides an ideal base for paint. Uses including siding, soffits, windscreens, exterior painted cabinet work, etc. Thicknesses: 5/16, 3/8, 1/2, 5/8, 3/4 and 1 in. Veneer grade is B face, B or C back, C or C-plugged inner plys.

TEXTURE 1–11: The unsanded panels have parallel grooves 1/4 in. deep, 3/8 in. wide on 2-in. or 4-in. centers. The edges are shiplapped for a continuous visual pattern. Uses include siding, accent paneling, fences, etc. It is available in 8 and 10-ft. lengths and sanded or with MD overlay. Thicknesses: 5/8 in. only; C or better face, C back and inner plys.

303 SPECIALTY SIDING EXT-DFPA: The grade covers proprietary plywood products for siding, fencing, soffits, windscreens and other exterior applications or interior panels. The

PLYWOOD VENEERS AND THICKNESSES[a]

	Thickness (in.)								Striated	
Product	1/8	1/4	5/16	3/8	1/2	5/8	3/4	13/16	7/16	3/8
Softwoods:										
Douglas fir		I-E	I	I-E	I-E	I-E	I-E		I	E
California pine		I		I	I	I	I	I		
Idaho knotty pine		I				I				
Sitka spruce		I	I	I	I	I	I			
Cedar		I								
Hardwoods:										
Maple		I		I			I-E			
Oak	I	I		I	I		I-E			
Walnut	I	I		I	I		I-E			
Birch	I	I		I	I		I-E			
Southern gum	I	I		I	I		I		I	
American elm		I								
Philippine mahogany		I		I			I		I	
African mahogany	I	I		I	I		I-E			
Korina	I	I		I			I-E			
Primavera	I	I					I-E			

[a] I = Interior grade.
E = Exterior grade.

HERE'S A TEXTURED exterior paneling, easy to apply, called "Rough sawn reverse board and battin."

panels have special surface treatments which include rough-sawn, striated and brushed, and may be V-grooved, channel-grooved, etc. It is available in redwood, cedar, hemlock, Douglas fir, lauan and other woods. The most common thicknesses are ⅜, ½ and ⅝ in. The veneer grade is B or better face, C back and plys.

PLYRPN EXT-DFPA: The panels are surfaced on both sides with tempered hardboard with smooth or screened surfaces. Thicknesses are ½, ⅝ and ¾ in. The panels have C inner plys.

MARINE EXT-DFPA and SPECIAL EXTERIOR DFPA: Marine-grade panels are made only with Douglas fir or western larch, and a special solid joined core construction. The panels are subject to special limitations on core gaps and the number of face repairs. Use them for boat hulls. The panels are also available with overlaid faces. Exterior is a premium panel similar to the marine grade but permits any species covered under PS 1–66. The most common thicknesses are ¼, ⅜, ½, ⅝, ¾ and 1 in. The veneer grade has an A or B face and back with B inner plys.

C-C PLUGGED EXT-DFPA: For exterior underlayment, these panels are also ideal for tile backing where a permanently waterproof material is needed. The panels are sanded or touch sanded as specified. The most common thicknesses are ¼, ⅜, ½, ⅝, ¾ and ⅞ in. The veneer grade is C (plugged) face, C back and inner plys.

The types and grades mentioned above are available in 4 x 8-ft. panel. However, other lengths and widths are manufactured. Generally, larger sizes can be ordered by your lumber dealer.

shopping tips

Many lumber dealers have "plywood bins" in which random-size pieces and trimmings are available. Many dealers also will cut a panel for you in multiples of 2 ft. When buying plywood, it is often to your advantage to preplan the project at hand so the amount of material needed can be purchased at one time. Costs can be cut with quantity, and any irregular sizes can be picked out of the plywood bins—another saving.

working with plywood

Plywood panels are easy to work with, although there are several tips that will make the job even easier:

1. To prevent waste, lay out the panel for cutting. If there will be many pieces cut from a single panel, sketch the arrangement on a piece of paper before you transfer it to the panel as a cutting pattern. Allow for the saw kerf between the pieces. Have the grain of the panel running the long way of the piece, if possible.

2. If you use a handsaw, cut the panel with the best face up. Use a saw with 10 to 15 points to the inch and support the panel on sawhorses so it won't sag. Always use a sharp saw.

3. For power sawing on a table saw, cut with the good face of the panel up. Use a sharp combination blade or fine-tooth blade without too much set. The blade should be set so it protrudes above the panel about the height of the teeth.

4. With a portable power saw, place the good face of the panel down.

5. When planing edges, work from both ends of the edge toward the center of the panel. This will prevent splitting out the plys at the end of the cut. Always use a plane with a sharp blade and set it to take a fine shaving. Work slowly.

6. Since plywood is sanded smooth at the time it is made, sanding it before a sealer or prime coat of finish should be confined to the edges. After the surface is sealed, however, you may sand in the direction of the grain only.

7. It is difficult to nail or screw into the edges of veneer-core plywood. Plan your work so you can avoid these problems.

Plywood panels can be bent to certain minimum radii depending, of course, on the thickness of the panel. In some applications you may have to bend two thin panels to build up a particular thickness. For example, ¾-in. panels can be bent only in a circle with a 10-ft. radius, while ⅜-in. panels can be bent to a radius of 36 in. Two layers of the ⅜-in. material will produce a much sharper bend and yet will give you the same effect as a ¾-in. panel.

finishing plywood

Fir plywood has a "wild grain" that must be "tamed" in finishing it. This reduces the contrast between the hard and soft growth in the tree. The American Plywood Association recommends the following steps (simplified) in obtaining a light-stain glaze. Here are the procedures:

1. If you want to whiten the panel, apply a coat of interior white undercoat thinned with an equal amount of turpentine. This may be wiped with a rag for more grain "show through."

2. Seal the wood. Apply one coat of thinned white shellac or clear resin sealer.

3. If you want to color the panel, apply a color coat of thinned undercoat or enamel, or color-in-oil. Light stains may also be used. The color coat is wiped to the proper tone.

4. To make a wearing surface, apply a coat of flat varnish.

5. When using conventional stain, first apply a clear resin sealer or thinned white shellac to subdue the contrast.

6. To prepare plywood panels for wallpapering, fill all the joints and prime the panels with thinned, flat-white paint. Next, coat the surface with wheat-flour paste combined with a glue size. Then apply a smooth wall liner or felt. Apply the wallpaper over this liner.

7. To paper an enameled wall made of plywood, first apply a painter's canvas or unbleached muslin, following the steps outlined above. Then apply a coat of glue size, and finish with the paper of your choice.

8. Conventional paint finishes are possible if high-grade paints are used. To be on the safe side, first apply a clear resin sealer, shellac or flat-white paint, followed by a prime coat and finished coat.

9. In exterior finishing, the prime coat is most important. It should be a high-grade primer thinned with a pint of raw linseed oil per gallon of paint. Over this apply the second and third coats. All edges should be well sealed.

MANY PLYWOOD PANELS are available prefinished. Prices range from very low to ultra-high.

ONE OF THE MOST POPULAR exterior panelings of all time is the attractive "Texture 1-11."

16 ways to hide plywood edges

PLYWOOD HAS long presented the home workman with the problem of hiding the material's laminated edges from view. The simplest do-it-yourself technique has been to cover them with paper-thin wood tape. It's sold in rolls in a choice of woods and merely glued on. This is okay for book shelves and perhaps the square edges of a tabletop, but it's not too durable a solution if the project will get lots of handling and wear. And wood tape, limited to plain square edges, is no help when you want shaped edges on a piece of furniture. But here are many ways to hide the laminations and add eye appeal at the same time. They range from comparatively simple to more involved approaches.

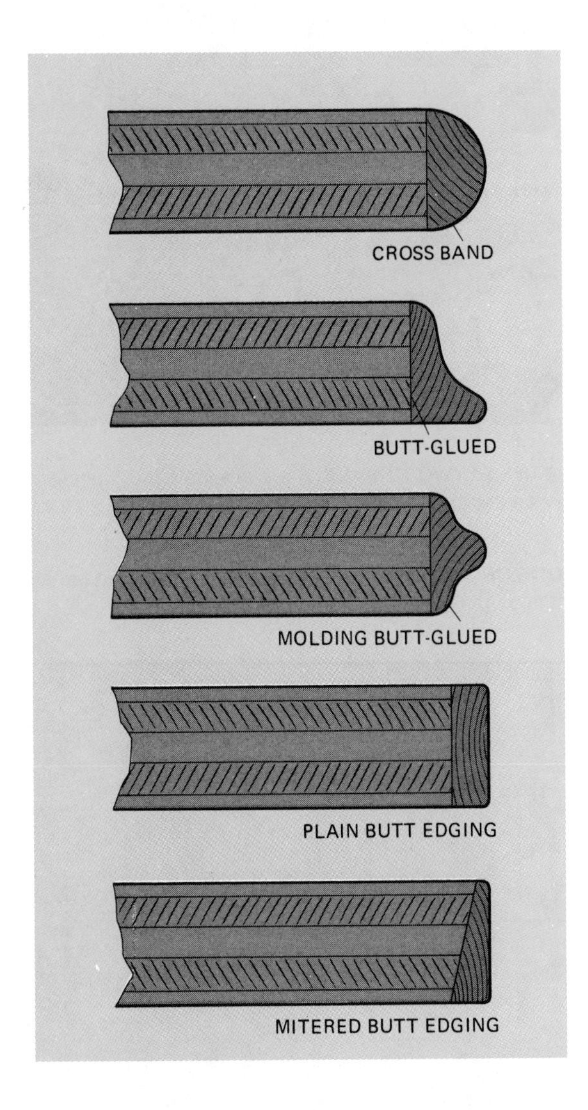

SIMPLE BUTT-GLUING moldings to straight plywood edges can dress them up. Five approaches are shown at left. Small finishing nails or brads are added, their heads set and puttied over. For the ultimate in hiding nails, a small gouge is often used to lift a chip of wood first. The nail or brad is then driven and the chip is glued back in place over the head. On fairly small projects, rubber bands cut from a large inner tube are handy for clamping molding to the plywood edge.

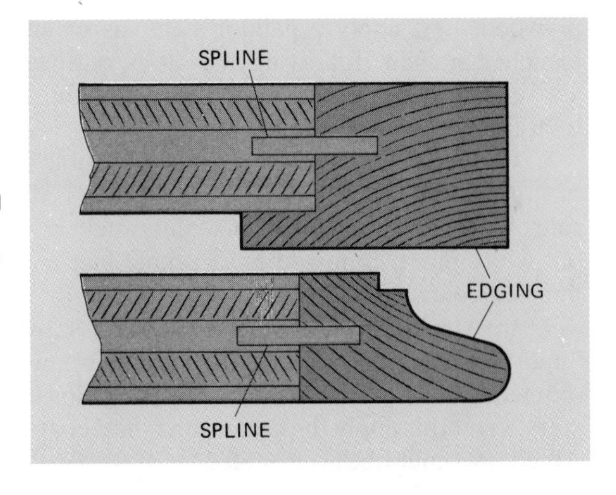

SPLINES FORM exceptionally strong joints. They're popular where there is room for them, as with wider moldings such as those at the right. With a table saw, run kerfs in both the molding and plywood and rip thin wood splines to fit the kerfs. A rabbet in the molding (top right), plus the spline and glue, makes a joint so strong that the edge stiffens the plywood.

SEE ALSO

Joinery . . . Moldings . . . Paneling, plywood . . . Plywood jigs

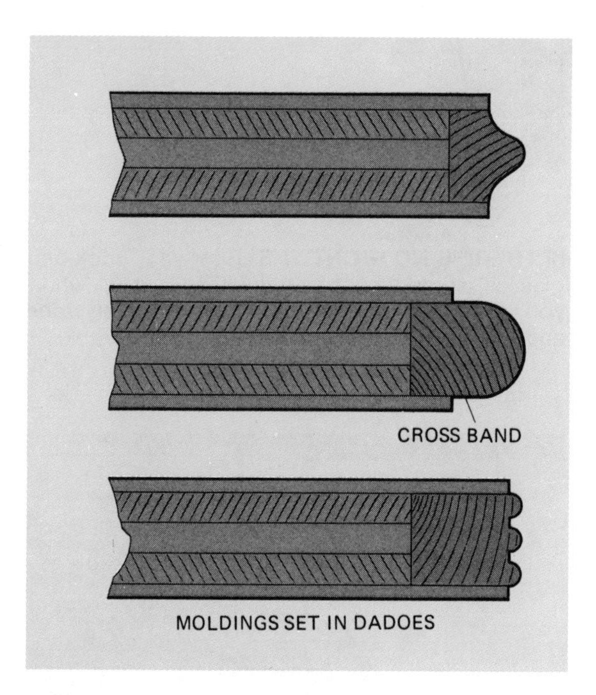

INSETTING MOLDINGS in dadoes turns the plywood veneer plies into a part of the decorative edge. A dado in the core laminations gets a depth to suit the molding. At the top, that depth brings the veneer ply flush with the molding, but the outer veneers can also make decorative shoulders. Pinch clamps will hold surface veneers against the molding while glue sets.

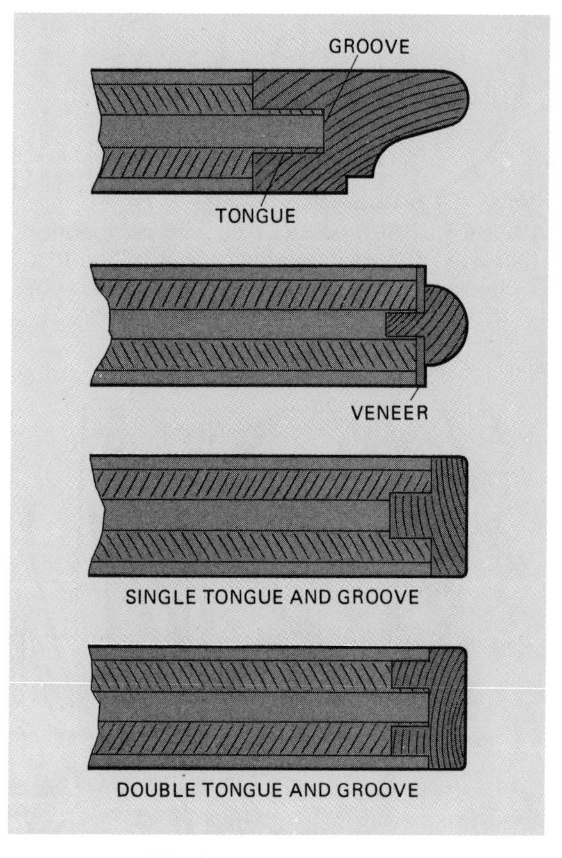

TONGUE-AND-GROOVE joints are far less likely to pull loose. Grooves can be cut in the plywood, as in the center examples above, or in the molding. The second drawing shows how an edge treatment can be built up, with narrow molding added to a veneer strip.

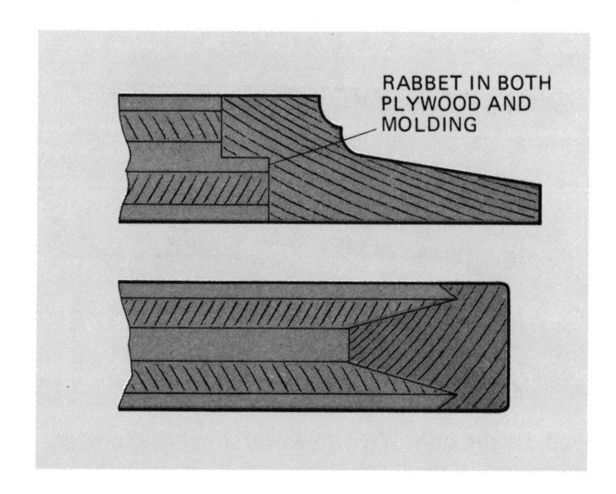

IN SPECIAL approaches at the left, you see how fancy, wide picture-frame molding can be the edging (top). Below it is perhaps the strongest joint of all—but one that takes special cutters to form both the plywood groove and the molding. After such a start, you might end up by shaping the exposed face of the molding itself.

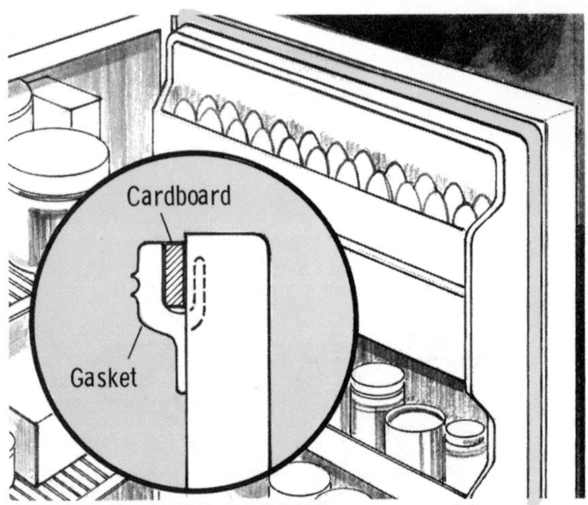

AS THE RUBBER GASKET on your refrigerator door ages it loses its sealing power. When this happens, you can add new life to the gasket by inserting cardboard behind it.—*Jean Dunn.*

IF THERE'S NO NIGHT TABLE for your book and glasses, a holder such as this will do the trick when you're ready to drop off. It's made of a thin plywood and hooks over the bedrail.—*Roy Alkenbrack.*

A STRIP OF PLASTIC BLEACH BOTTLE, 1x6 in., will make a better putt-putt "motor" for your kid's bike than a card and clothespin. Just wrap it around a seat support and fasten with a bolt.—*Joe Reinhardt*

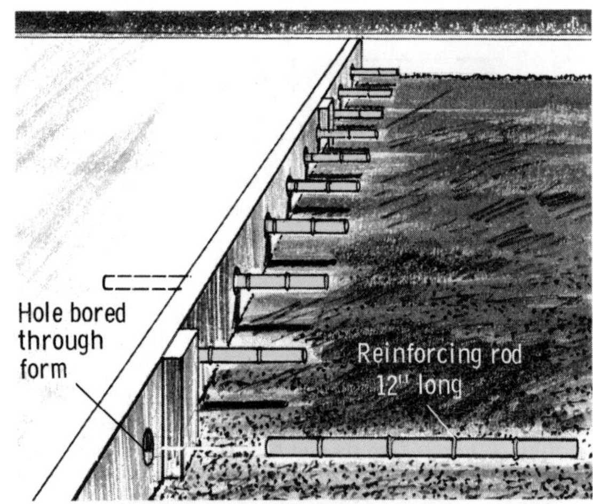

WHEN YOU POUR A SLAB in sections, avoid future cracking at the joint by reinforcing it with short rods. Bore oversize holes in the dividing form board and insert rods into the wet concrete.—*Victor H. Lamoy.*

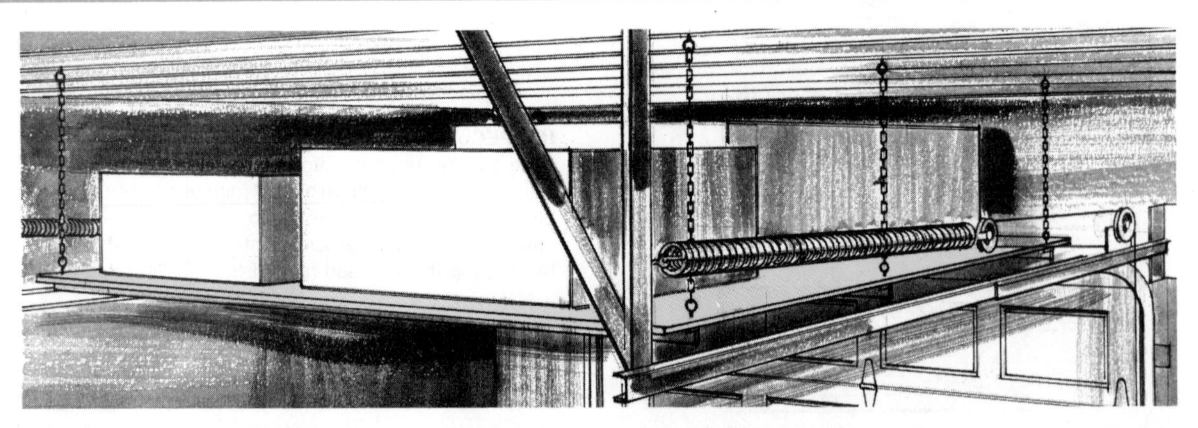

SPACE IS GOING TO WASTE between tracks of your overhead garage door. Two plywood sheets supported by lengths of 1-in. angle iron and hung with chain will add 64 more sq. ft. of storage.—*W. F. Wilson.*

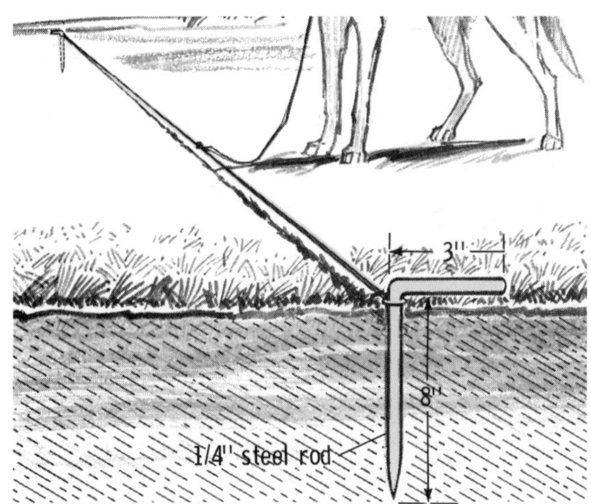

TWO L-SHAPED IRON STAKES passed through eyes in the ends of a galvanized wire and then driven into the ground, make a non-trip-over tether for your dog. The dog's leash is snapped to the wire.—*John Krill.*

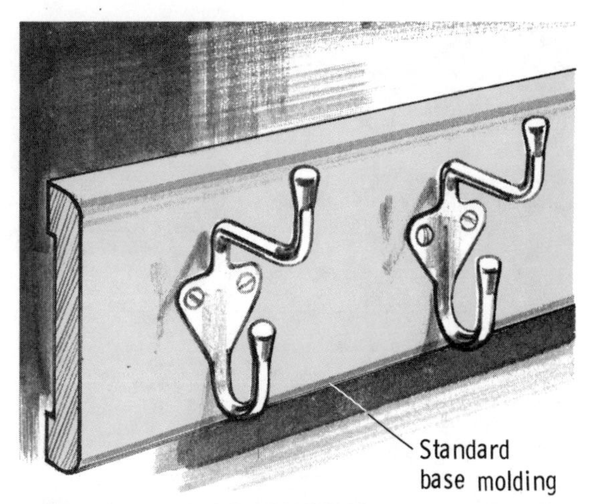

WHEN ADDING COAT HOOKS to a closet wall, a strip of door casing makes a neat rail on which to screw them. Besides being nicely shaped, the casing provides a solid surface for screws.—*Daniel Bousha.*

WHEN WATER MUST BE CARRIED in an open container in the car, it will be sloshproof if you first line the pail with a plastic bag. After filling, bag is tied at the top with a bit of string.—*Andrew Vena.*

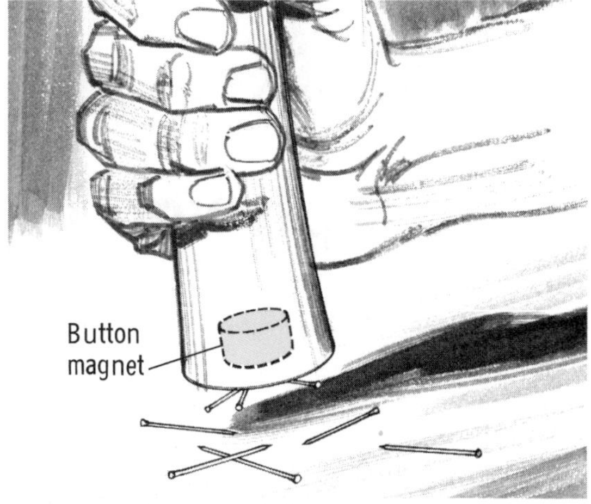

PICKING UP TINY NAILS is no problem if you embed a small button magnet in your hammer handle. Drill a hole slightly smaller than the magnet and tap the latter in place.—*Joseph Braunstein.*

YOU CAN SAVE YOURSELF STEPS when you make use of a grass catcher to increase the capacity of your wheelbarrow. Use pieces of wire to hang it between the handles of the barrow.—*Victor H. Lamoy.*

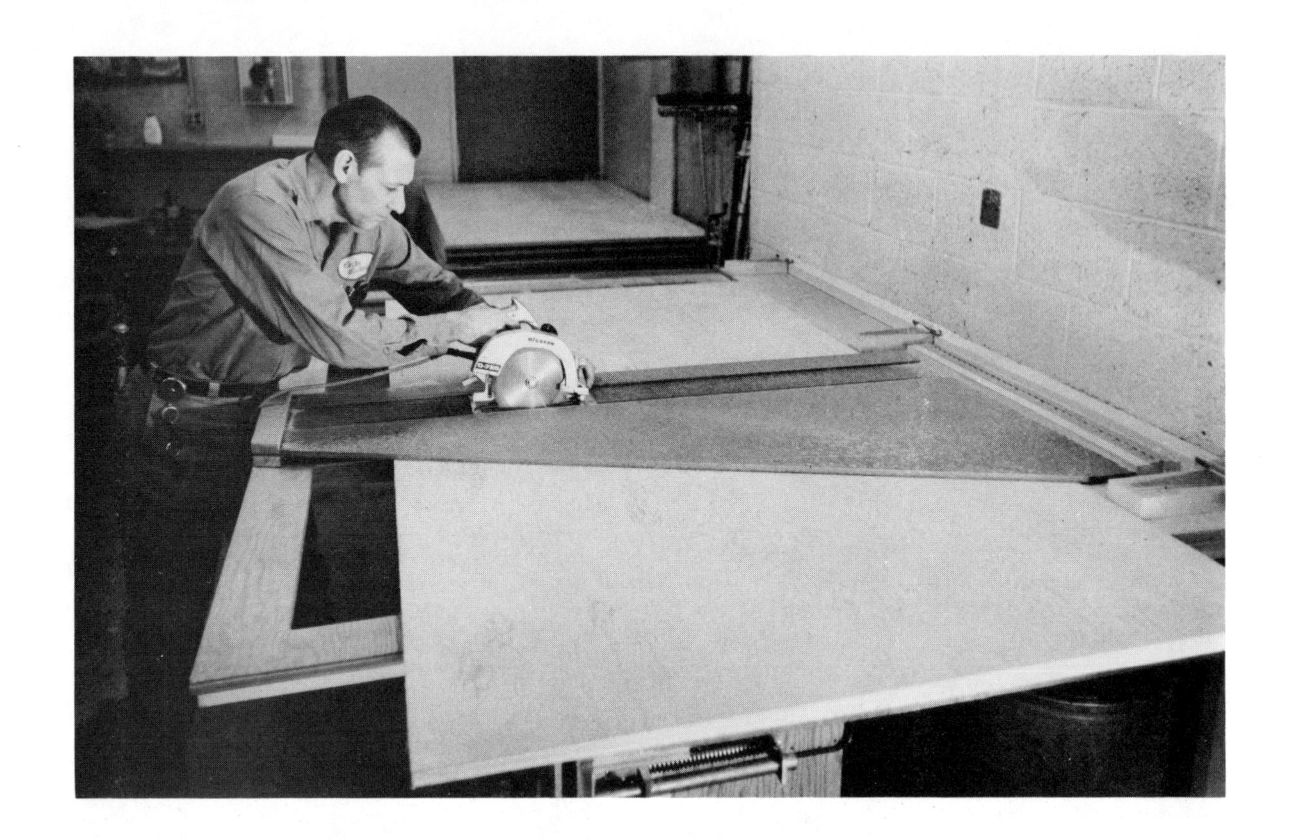

Build a plywood cutoff jig

By EBEN H. GUSTAFSON

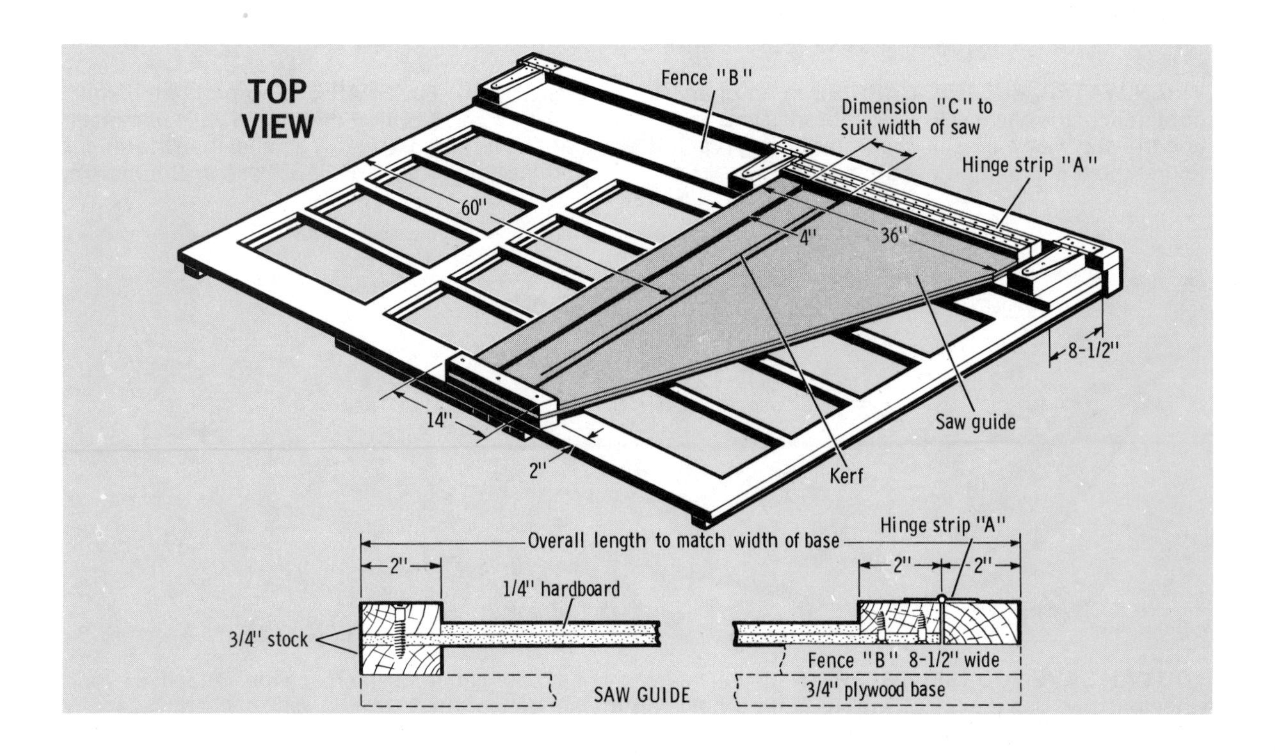

IF YOU NEED to cut up a full sheet of plywood only once in a while, you aren't going to bother making this cutoff jig. You'll first saw it roughly to a size that's fairly easy to handle and take it from there, not caring particularly if you waste some material in doing so.

However, if you run a small cabinet shop where you are working daily with these big, awkward sheets, it will pay you to make this handy labor-saver.

It consists of a 60x96-in. base on which the plywood sheet is placed, and a saw guide which is hinged to swing down on top of the work. A built-in track and kerf in the guide, which is made to fit your particular portable electric saw, lets you zip across the sheet in nothing flat, resulting in a perfect 90° cut.

When not in use, the jig is swung up against the wall, clearing the benchtop for other use. You can either attach the jig directly to the wall or bolt it to the rear edge of the bench on which it's used. A 1x2 handle hinged under the front of the jig is fitted with a spring-loaded bolt latch and chain to make it handy to swing the jig up against the wall and lock it securely in place. As an extra precaution, a king-size turnbutton will give added assurance that it won't come crashing down accidentally.

The details clearly show how it's made. The base is a 4x8-ft. sheet with a 20-in. piece splined to it to make it 68 in. wide, then cut as shown to make it lighter and self-clearing of sawdust. It's important in hinging the hardboard saw guide to be sure that it is exactly 90° to fence "B."

The jig will accommodate both plywood and lumber up to ¾ in. thick. Thinner stock is cut by shimming it up with scrap pieces. The track for the saw is made just wide enough to let it slide smoothly, yet without any side play.

JIG STORES AGAINST WALL when not in use. Note latch-fitted handle to raise and lower jig.

SEE ALSO

Circular saw blades . . . Circular saws, portable . . . Paneling, plywood . . . Plywood . . . Power-tool stands

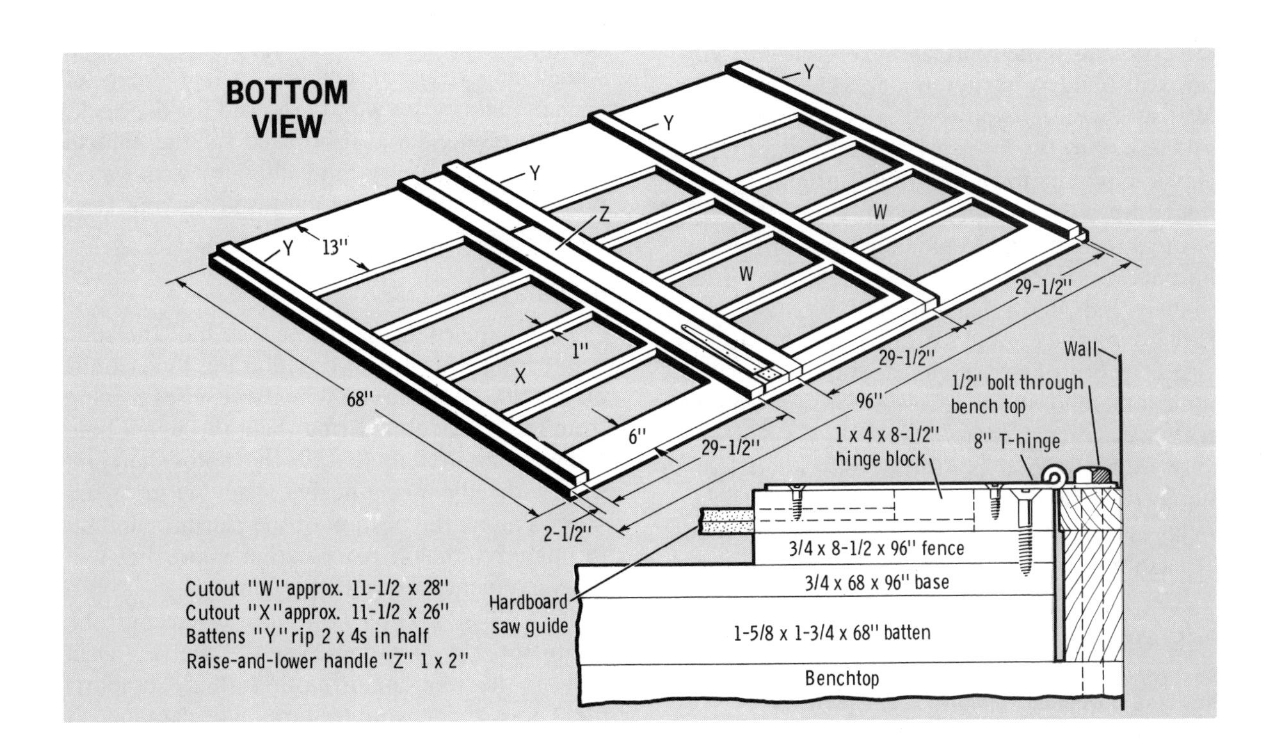

It took only a week of evenings and $385.65 to build this simple and handsome pontoon deck boat. That price includes two electric outboard motors

Build this raft boat for $450 —with power

By MICHAEL MCDOUGALL

IN SEVERAL EVENINGS' WORK you'll be ready to launch, once you start building this attractive pontoon boat. It is simple to construct, performs well, and the price is right. My cost was $385.65, and though prices have gone up, you can still build yours for under $450, including twin-screw electric power.

One key to the low cost is the availability of plastic-covered foam pontoons originally designed for a catamaran sailboat. I ordered each of them for $65 plus $5 handling f.o.b. from the Formex Corp., Box 812, 505 Belvedere Rd., Elkhart, Ind. 46514. They are now about $85 plus $5 handling apiece, and worth it. The ABS covering of the Styrofoam gives the pontoons a handsome look, and fittings recessed fore and aft into each make them easy to attach. With a simple 6 by 8-foot plywood platform, reinforced by a supporting frame of 2x4s, the strong but lightweight pontoons will support a whole family or two couples.

SEE ALSO

Boat repair . . . Boating safety . . . Boats . . . Canoes . . . Kayaks . . . Outboard motors . . . Sailboats

use two electric motors

I chose two trolling electric outboard motors to provide a comfortable 2 to 3-knot speed and a method of steering without a rudder. Mounted on the platform as far apart as possible, the motors will turn the boat in one direction or the other; you simply switch off the motor on the inside of the turn. To turn in one boat length, you reverse one motor.

Construction is simplified by the aluminum castings molded into the top of the Formex pontoons. They contain four ⅜-inch tapped holes to which the platform can be bolted. The 6 by 8-foot platform, reinforced by the 2x4s on 16-inch centers, provides a good compromise between weight and strength. One and a half sheets of ½-inch exterior plywood are used for the deck, and the remainder can be used for the control console. Coat everything liberally with wood preservative and marine paint so that your boat will last against the elements.

mounting the motors

To mount each motor, saw in half the tube connecting the control box and the lower unit. Splice No. 14 or heavier wire to the wires coming from the lower unit. Bring them through a hole drilled in a crutch tip that fits the motor shaft and seal with silicone adhesive. Run wiring from motors along the bottom of the platform and up through the console to a location where they will be convenient for your operation.

The console contains the battery and controls. Drop-front doors can enclose the shelves. Drill holes in the door enclosing the battery compartment to provide ventilation while charging. A lock on one compartment and a cutoff switch inside can prevent unauthorized operation. I included a waterproof plug on the outside of the console to make hooking up a battery charger easy.

finishing off

Cover the platform with indoor-outdoor carpeting and trim the edges with aluminum carpeting threshold. The safety stanchions are 1½-inch pipe screwed into pipe flanges. I covered them with plastic posts from a garden supply store and added plastic chain. Swimming steps are mounted forward and fold back under the deck. Install more rugged railings for fishing, or gas outboards for added speed. And get ready for questions and compliments as you float--with power—into the distance.

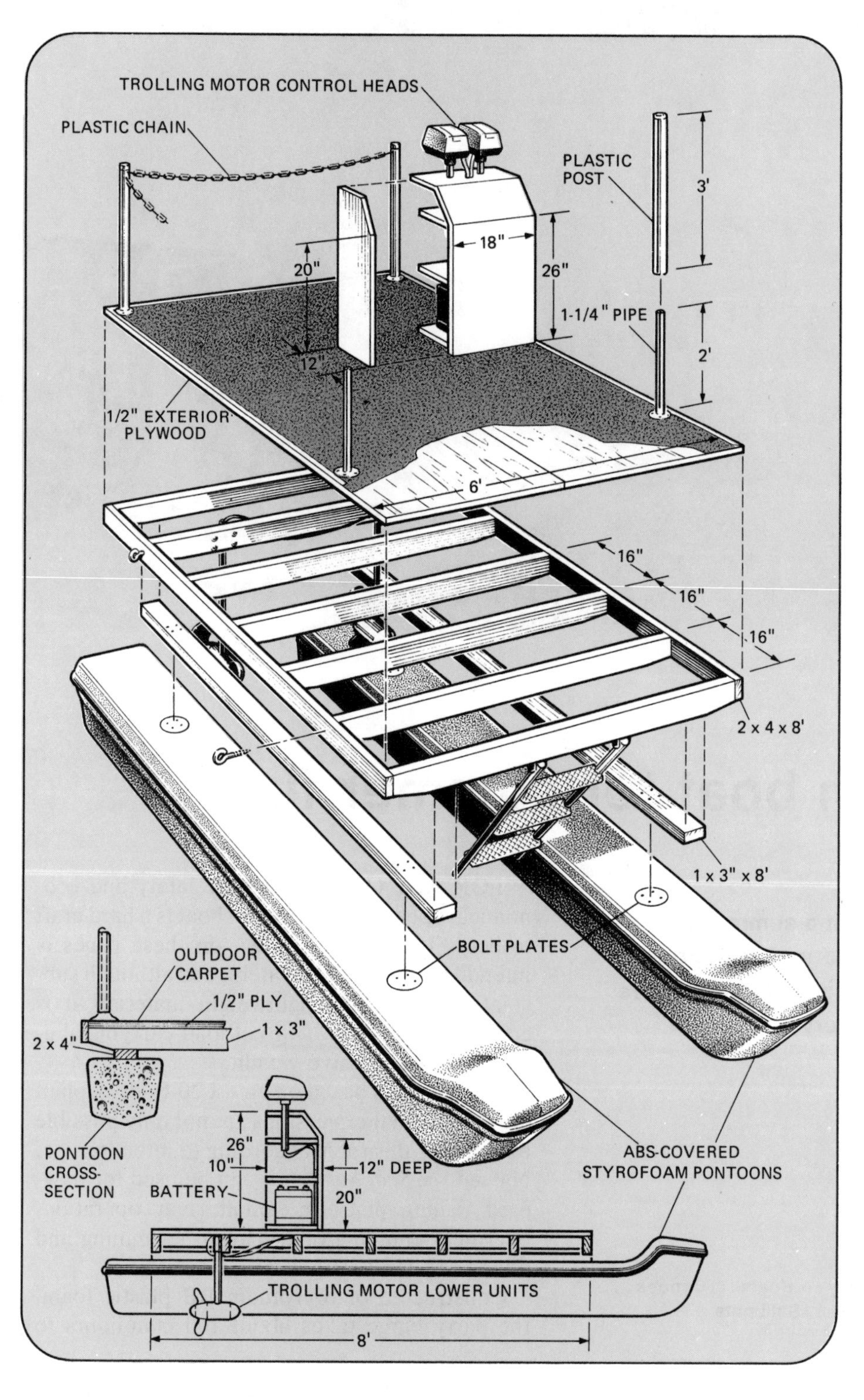

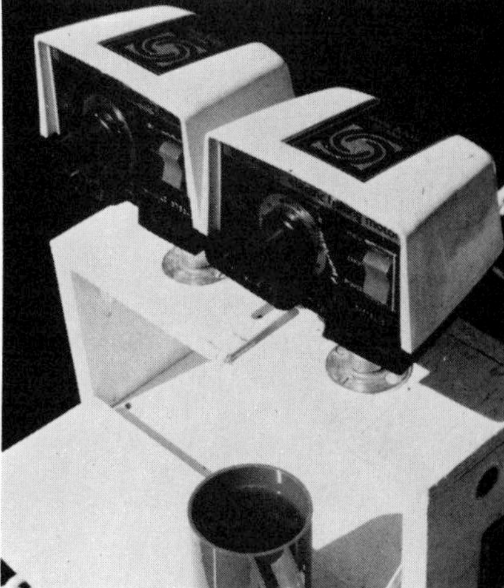

TO STEER you turn power knobs. Drop-down door becomes shelf.

RAFT BOAT PARTS LIST

Item	Cost
Lumber	
7 pcs. 2x4—6′	$ 6.16
2 pcs. 2x4—8′	2.00
2 pcs. 1x3—8′	3.68
2 4x8′ pcs. ½″ exterior-grade plywood	11.00
Accessories	
Carpeting (felt polypropylene)	34.00
Double-stick tape (attach carpet)	2.50
4 8′ sections aluminum threshold	12.00
4 pcs. 1¼″ x 2′ threaded pipe	8.16
4 1¼″ pipe flanges	4.76
22′ plastic chain	4.14
Miscellaneous	
2 electric trolling motors	80.00
2 ABS-covered Styrofoam Formex pontoons, $65 each plus $5 handling (f.o.b); now $85 plus $5	140.00
Heavy-duty 12-volt battery	41.25
Wood preservation and paint	20.00
Hardware	16.00
Total cost	$385.65

A pontoon boat for summer fun

You'll have nothing but a summer of fun on your own floating platform. It is supported by billets of buoyant plastic foam that are almost unsinkable and very lightweight

By HARRY WICKS

SEE ALSO

Boat repair . . . Boating safety . . . Boats . . . Canoes . . . Kayaks . . . Outboard motors . . . Sailboats

FOR ALL-OUT water fun, safety and economical operation, a pontoon boat is a hard craft to beat. The version shown on these pages is intended for protected waters, and although substantially built, the lightweight materials it is constructed of provide great load-carrying ability without excessive weight.

The design is based on an 8 x 20-ft. deck plan. However, smaller versions are not only possible but may be desirable according to intended use. Named the *Sea Surrey* it can be used for powered fishing platform, small river operation, overnight camping or just plain swimming and diving-raft fun.

Constructed of Styrofoam BB plastic foam, the party barge takes about 100 man-hours to

FOUR BUOYANCY billets are used for the two flotation pontoons. Bow ends (left) are notched to receive the wood framing members. Plastic foam doesn't lose buoyancy even if it's punctured. One cubic foot of the foam will hold up 55 lbs. The frames are joined using bolts, Anchorfast nails and waterproof resorcinol glue. The wood is preservative-treated to reduce the chance of decay from moisture. This also helps reduce attack by insects. All nonglued surfaces are covered with Cuprinol. The bow is skinned with ¼-in. exterior plywood (above). The edges should be carefully sealed to keep the water out. To protect the pontoons from gas and oil, which will dissolve them, apply two coats of water-mix exterior paint to the foam plastic. The styrofoam may also have to be covered with hardboard or wire netting to keep muskrats from burrowing in it.

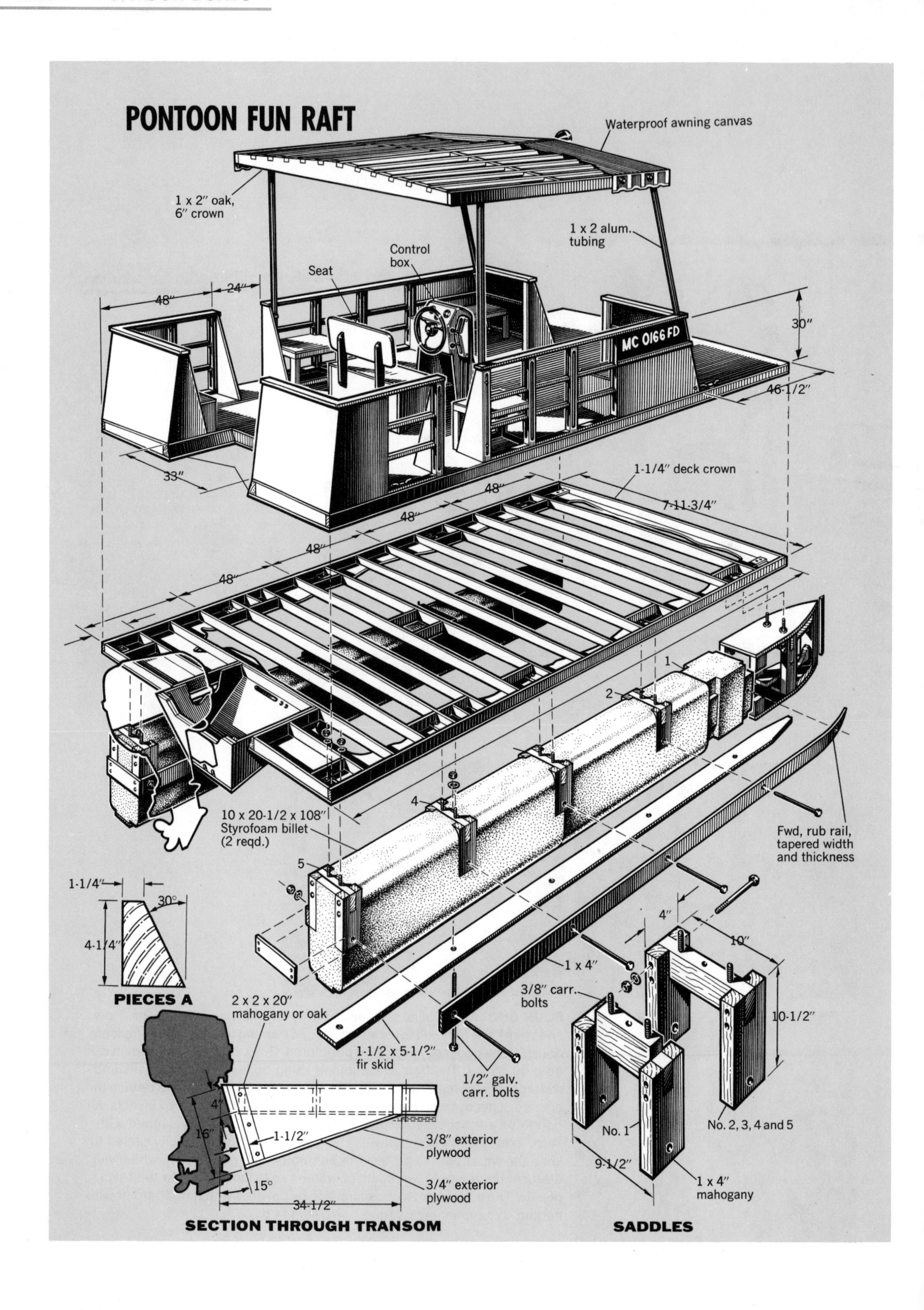
PONTOON FUN RAFT
Waterproof awning canvas
1 x 2" oak,
6" crown
1 x 2 alum.
tubing
Control
box
Seat
48"
24"
30"
MC 0166 FD
46-1/2"
33"
1-1/4" deck crown
48"
48"
7-11-3/4"
48"
48"
1
2
4
10 x 20-1/2 x 108"
Styrofoam billet
(2 reqd.)
5
Fwd, rub rail,
tapered width
and thickness
1-1/4"
30°
4-1/4"
PIECES A
1 x 4"
4"
10"
3/8" carr.
bolts
10-1/2"
2 x 2 x 20"
mahogany or oak
1-1/2 x 5-1/2"
fir skid
1/2" galv.
carr. bolts
4"
16"
1-1/2"
3/8" exterior
plywood
No. 1
No. 2, 3, 4 and 5
9-1/2"
15°
3/4" exterior
plywood
1 x 4"
mahogany
34-1/2"
SECTION THROUGH TRANSOM
SADDLES

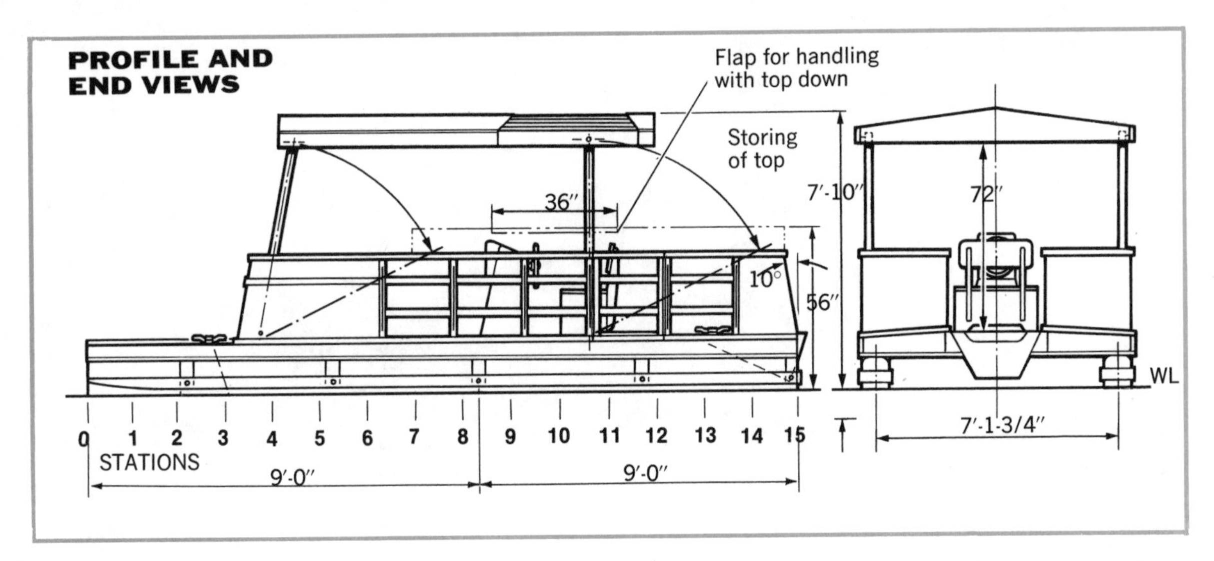

build. Though we've shown construction drawings on these pages, a brochure on the craft, which includes complete construction details, is available free at your Styrofoam dealer or directly from Styrofoam Buoyancy Plans, Functional Products & Systems, The Dow Chemical Co., Midland, MI 48640.

The plans call for a railing, a control box for steering and controlling the craft, a captain's seat and a "surrey" top. In constructing any of the topside area, you can turn your imagination loose, and vary or customize to suit your needs and imagination. If you plan to add power, the *Sea Surrey* is designed to accommodate outboard motors from 5½ to 40 hp.

treat the wood

You would be wise to use only treated wood, or wood naturally resistant to decay or insect attack, for the wooden parts of the boat to make them last longer. If you choose the first, make certain it is clean, dry and free of oily residue. (Clean wood treated with pentachlorophenol is suitable for fresh-water structures.) If you treat the wood yourself, avoid spilling the liquid preservatives on the Styrofoam BB (buoyancy billet) plastic since they will dissolve the foam. If the craft is to be used in saltwater, protect all submerged parts the way you would a wooden hull boat. In some locations muskrats like to burrow in styrofoam. To solve the problem, cover it with hardboard or wire netting.

For surfaces above the waterline, a spokesman for Dow recommends an undercoat and finishing coat of a good quality marine topside paint. If desired, the deck can be fiberglassed. But if you plan to, don't apply preservatives to any surface to be fiberglassed.

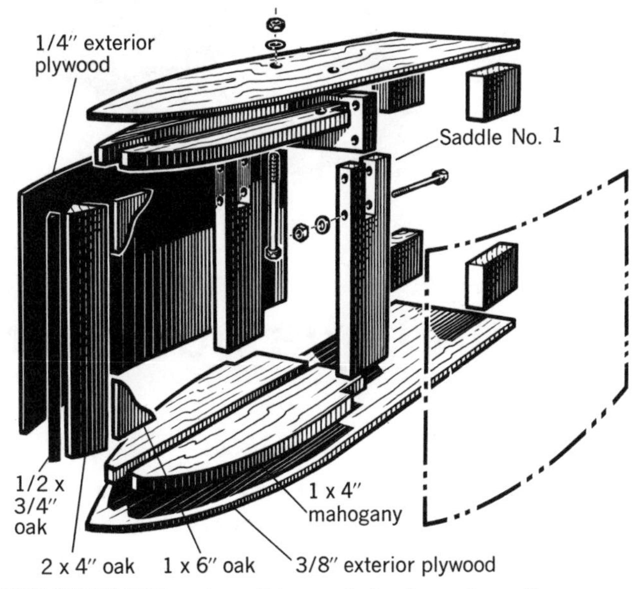

FOR OVERLAND portage, it is easy to haul your fun raft from lake to lake using an ordinary boat trailer.

Build this beautiful pool table

By JOHN CAPOTOSTO

With billiards growing rapidly as a favorite indoor sport, everyone wants a pool table. You can build this sturdy, full-size model yourself and save nearly $200

IF YOU HAVE DONE any shopping lately you know that a pool table is an expensive item to buy. However, if you are good at working with tools you can save almost $200 by building this beauty. Believe it or not, I only spent about $107 to build it, and that includes everything—even the balls and cues. Such hard-to-get items as billiard cloth, cushion rubber and foam padding come in a kit (a source of these necessities for any pool table is given at the end of the article).

This table is well-designed and if constructed

SEE ALSO

Air games . . . Chess sets . . . Cribbage boards . . . Family rooms . . . Game tables . . . Games . . . Party tables . . . Shuffleboard tables

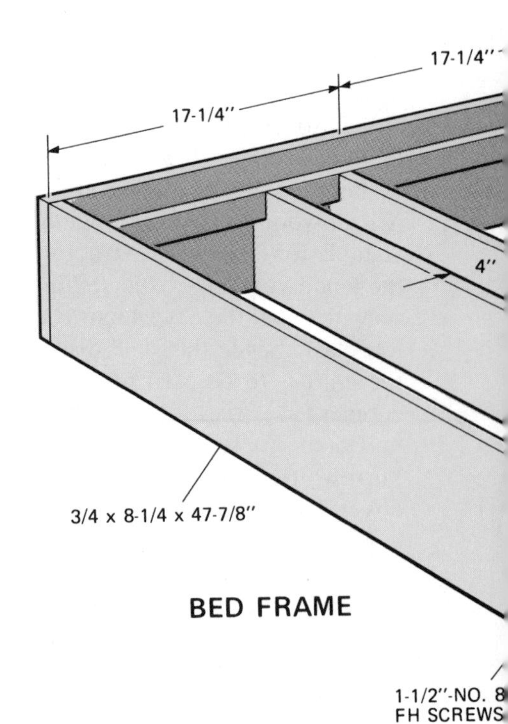

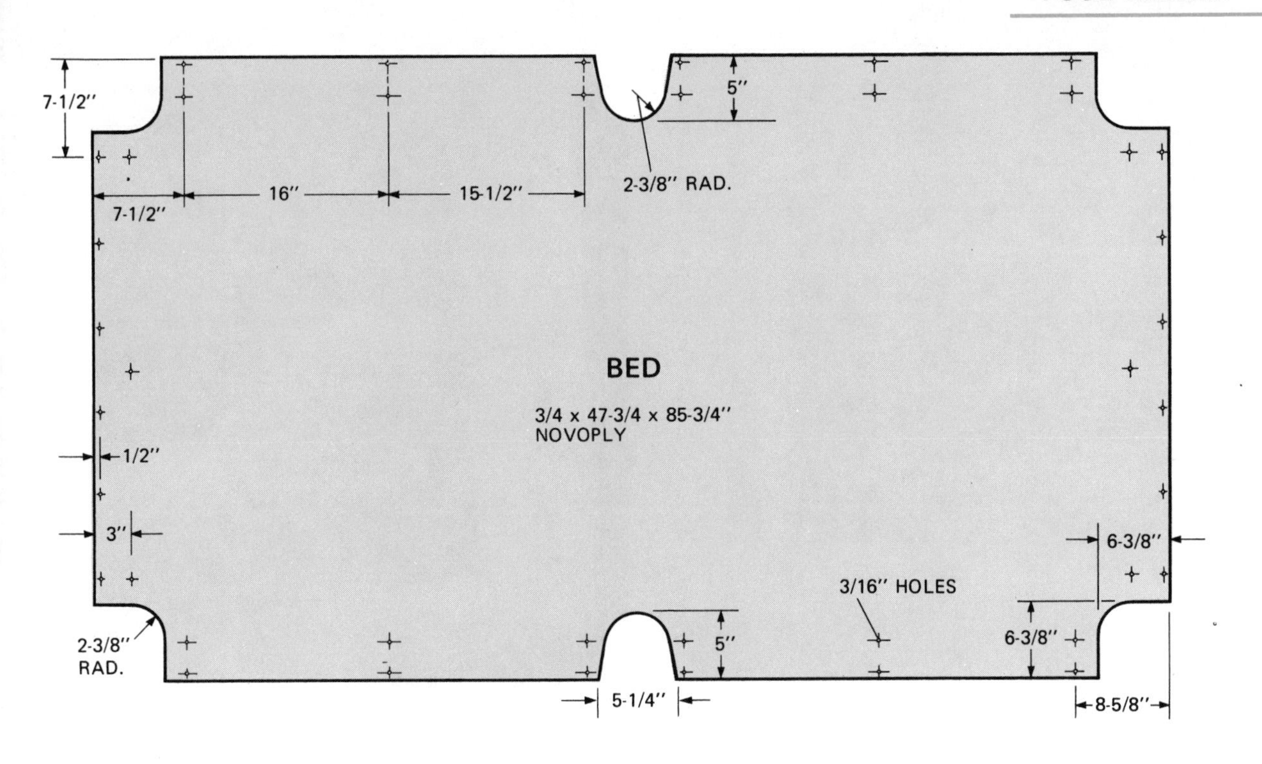
BED
3/4 x 47-3/4 x 85-3/4"
NOVOPLY
7-1/2"
16"
15-1/2"
2-3/8" RAD.
5"
7-1/2"
1/2"
3"
6-3/8"
3/16" HOLES
6-3/8"
2-3/8"
RAD.
5"
5-1/4"
8-5/8"

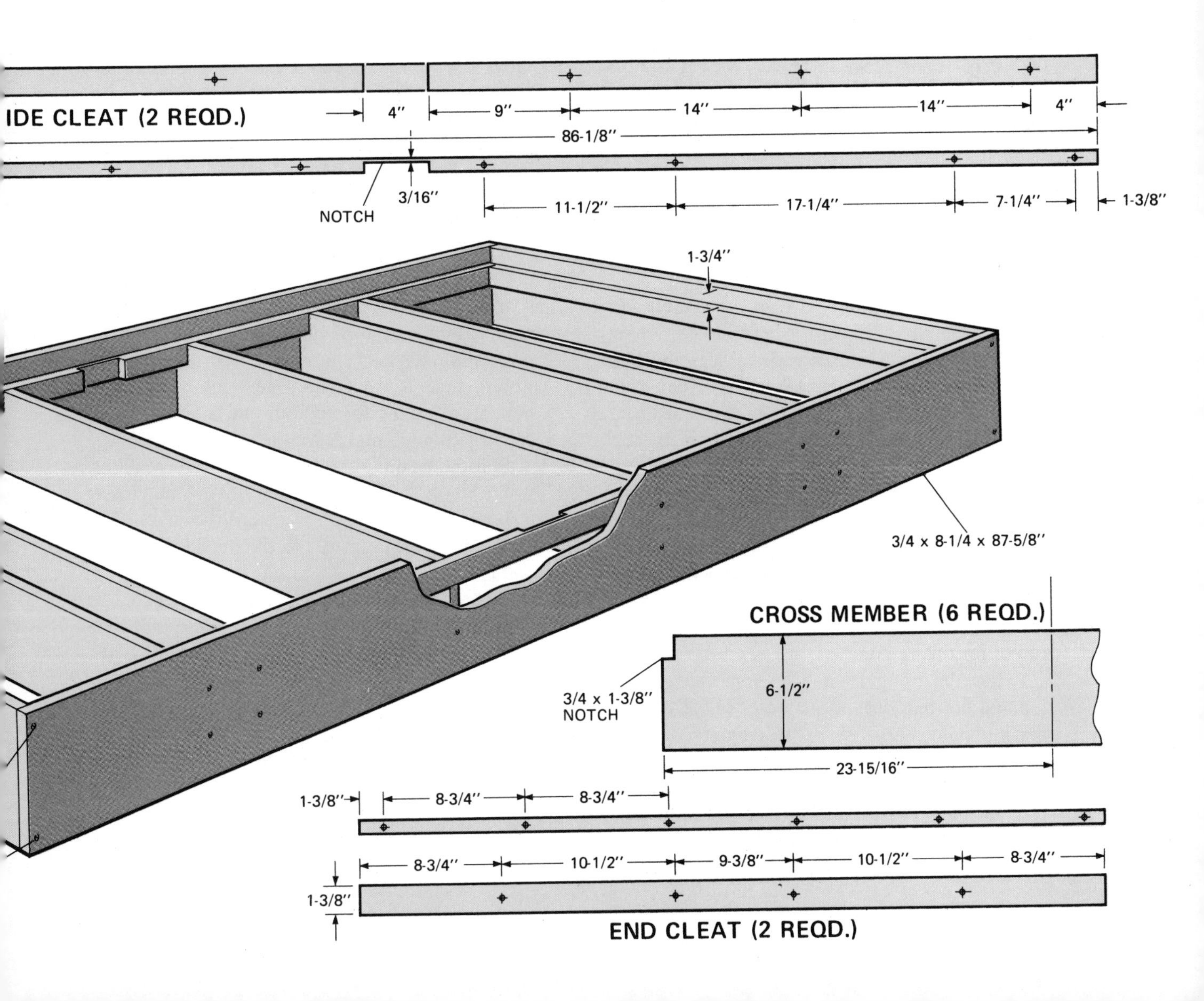
IDE CLEAT (2 REQD.)
4"
9"
14"
14"
4"
86-1/8"
NOTCH
3/16"
11-1/2"
17-1/4"
7-1/4"
1-3/8"
1-3/4"
3/4 x 8-1/4 x 87-5/8"
CROSS MEMBER (6 REQD.)
3/4 x 1-3/8"
NOTCH
6-1/2"
23-15/16"
1-3/8"
8-3/4"
8-3/4"
8-3/4"
10-1/2"
9-3/8"
10-1/2"
8-3/4"
1-3/8"
END CLEAT (2 REQD.)

APRON ASSEMBLY is squared up with temporary diagonal braces of scrap across two corners.

SCREWDRIVER BIT in a variable-speed drill makes quick work of driving home the many screws needed.

with care, it can prove to be very strong and durable. It features a sturdy pedestal base, plastic-laminated aprons, drop pockets which simplify the construction, and padded rails—an extra usually found only on more expensive tables.

The table is standard size (3½ x 7 ft.) and uses 2¼-in. balls.

materials readily available

• **Base.** All materials used in the table are readily available. Except where noted, ¾-in. plywood is used. Even the pedestal legs and base are made of plywood, using box-type construction which adds much to rigidity and sturdiness. Leg uprights are rabbeted to minimize edge grain, and base sections are butt-joined.

To insure accuracy and to simplify assembly, the uprights should be temporarily mounted to the pedestal *before* the scallop at the bottom of the pedestal is cut. Mount the uprights individually before they are "boxed." You will note in the material list that extra length has been allowed for this reason.

Miter the uprights at 14° from the vertical, top and bottom, then at the center of the pedestal mark two lines 8 15/16 in. apart. Align the uprights on these marks, keeping the bottom even with the bottom edge of the pedestal. Tack the pieces in place with 1¼-in. brads, then drill pilot holes for the screws. Use four screws in each upright for added strength. Once located, you can remove the uprights and cut the scallop in the pedestal and recut the bottoms of the uprights to match the scallop. Uprights now may be permanently glued. The leg filler pieces are rabbeted, leaving ⅛ in. of stock as indicated. These are glued just short of the top and extend slightly into the base.

Note: When gluing edge-grain stock, glue-size the edges. Apply thinned glue (thin with water if white glue) to edges and allow to dry before regular application of glue. This seals the edge, preventing excessive absorption of glue which would cause a weak joint. Remember, this is to be a sturdy table throughout and a good careful construction job makes that possible.

Before installing the base pads to the scallops, drill a ½-in. hole at the center of each and insert a T-nut. These are for the leveling jacks. The flange of the nut must be to the outside when the pad is mounted.

When the pedestals are completed, add two furring strips to the upper ends; these will help support the table and simplify mounting the pedestal later.

now make stretcher

The stretcher can be made now and the two pedestals connected to it. Lagscrews are driven from the inside to join the pedestals. Do not use glue as you may need to disassemble the table to move it to its final destination. Lagscrews can

LAGSCREWS attach table to base. Do not use glue so the table can be dismantled easily for moving.

TEMPORARY JIG nailed between uprights of base assures accuracy during assembly.

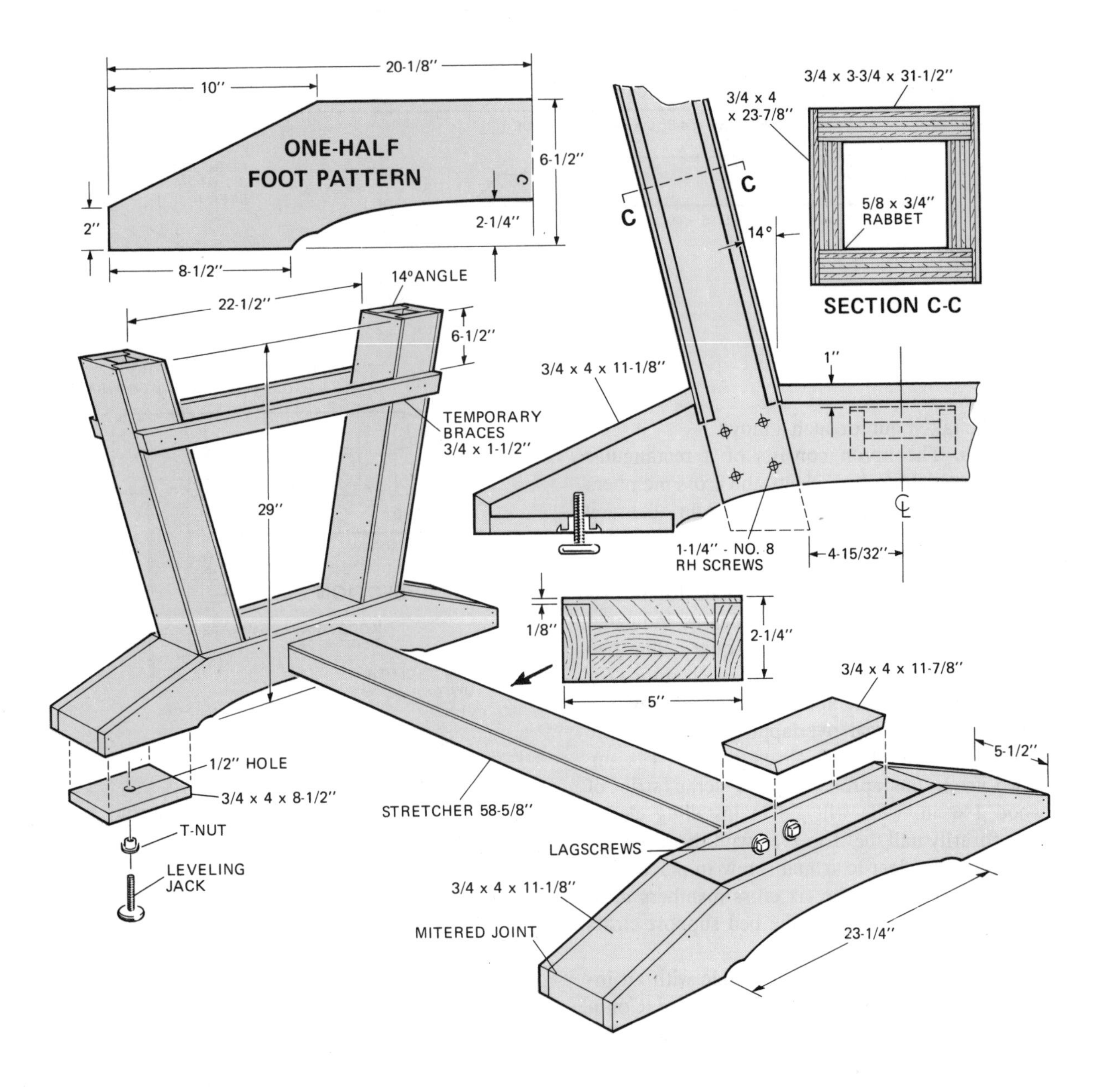

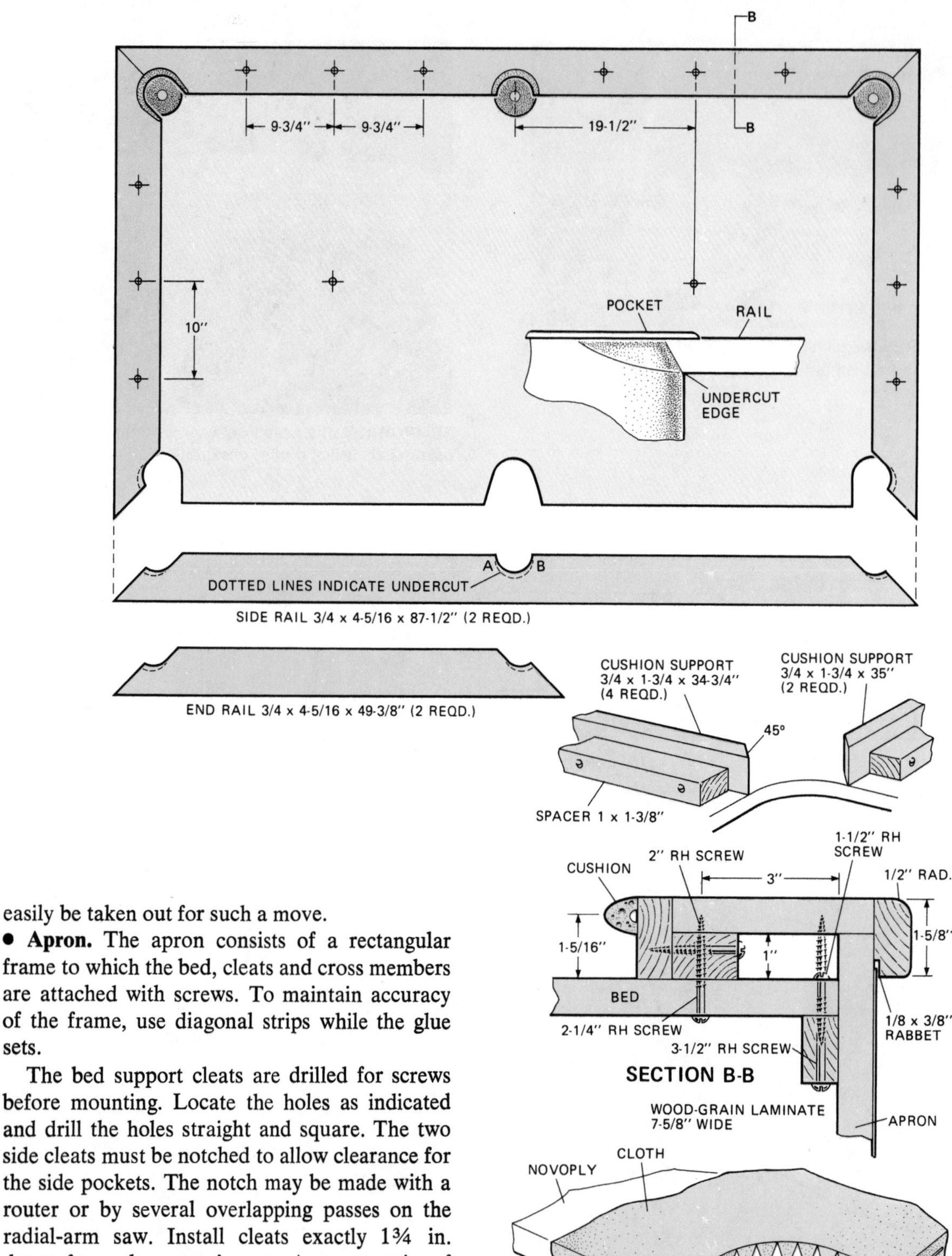

easily be taken out for such a move.

• **Apron.** The apron consists of a rectangular frame to which the bed, cleats and cross members are attached with screws. To maintain accuracy of the frame, use diagonal strips while the glue sets.

The bed support cleats are drilled for screws before mounting. Locate the holes as indicated and drill the holes straight and square. The two side cleats must be notched to allow clearance for the side pockets. The notch may be made with a router or by several overlapping passes on the radial-arm saw. Install cleats exactly 1¾ in. down from the apron's top. A scrap strip of wood 1¾ in. wide will aid in installing cleats. Temporarily nail the strip even with the top edge, then butt the cleat to it and screw in place after gluing. Top edge of the six cross members must be flush with top edge of the bed support cleats as shown.

I covered the aprons on my table with an inexpensive, wood-grained laminate called Conolite, which is applied with contact cement. It's

SLIT FABRIC at drop-pocket cutouts and staple it to the underside of the rail, then along rail edges.

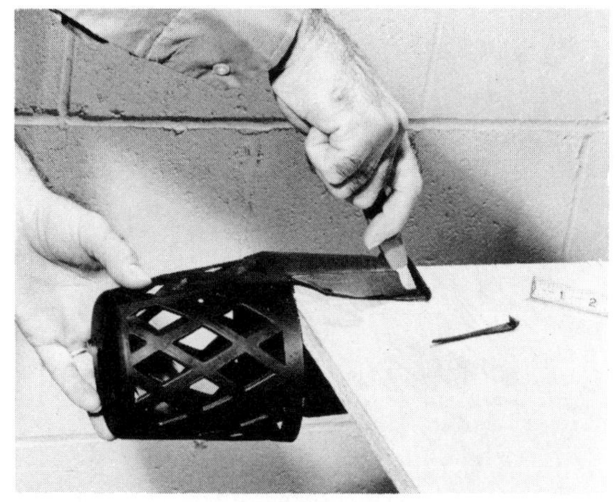

TRIM POCKETS to fit—differently at the sides than at the corners. See the drawing, above right.

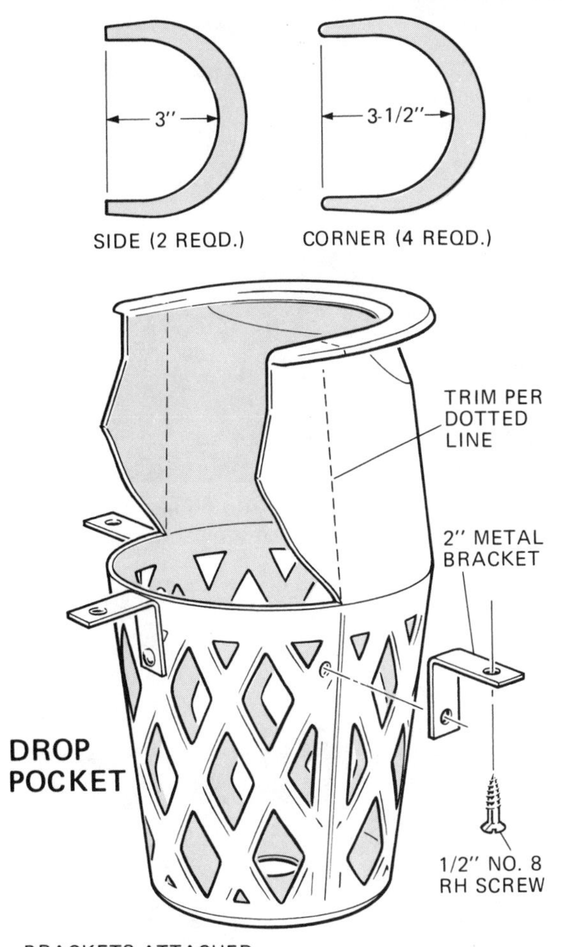

METAL ANGLE brackets are used to attach drop pockets in cutouts after trimming the pockets.

offered in rolls 36 in., wide and sold by the foot. It is easy to install and gives the table a nicely finished look. Various colors, patterns and grains are available. It can be cut with scissors, but you may find it easier to score the surface with an awl and snap it along the scored line.

Cut the laminate slightly oversize and apply contact cement to it and to the wood surface. Allow the cement to dry until it loses its tackiness, then apply carefully. Once in place, it cannot be moved. The top edge of the laminate is set 11/16 in. below the top edge of the apron. The sides and bottom should overhang slightly. Trim excess with a router fitted with a laminate trimmer or by hand with a plane. Cover the end aprons first, then the longer sides.

• **Bed.** The bed is cut from a sheet of ¾-in. particleboard. Notice that ¼ in. is trimmed from the 48-in. dimension. The length of the bed is 85¾ in. The material is dense and tough, but it is easily cut with ordinary tools such as a portable saw, sabre saw, or even a handsaw. Lay out the corner and side-pocket cutouts according to the diagram. After cutting, break all sharp edges with sandpaper. Drill the mounting holes, then cover with billiard cloth. The cloth is stapled to the underside of the bed. Do the long sides first, then the ends. Slit the cloth at the pockets, stopping the slits just short of the cutouts. Pull the cloth evenly around the pockets and staple to the underside of the bed. (Before installing the cloth remove wrinkles with a steam iron.) The bed and the felt on it are two of the most critical parts of any pool table.

• **Rails.** The rails require some tricky sabre-saw cutting. Cut the sections to size and miter the ends 45°. Place the four pieces on a flat surface and lay out the 4⅛-in.-dia. cutouts.

Make cutouts in the usual manner using a sabre saw. After all corner and sidepocket cutouts have been made, tilt your saw's base to 30° and recut the section of the cutout from points A and B. Undercutting is needed to clear the drop pockets.

The outer edging for the rails is cut and rabbeted as in the drawing. Two passes on the table

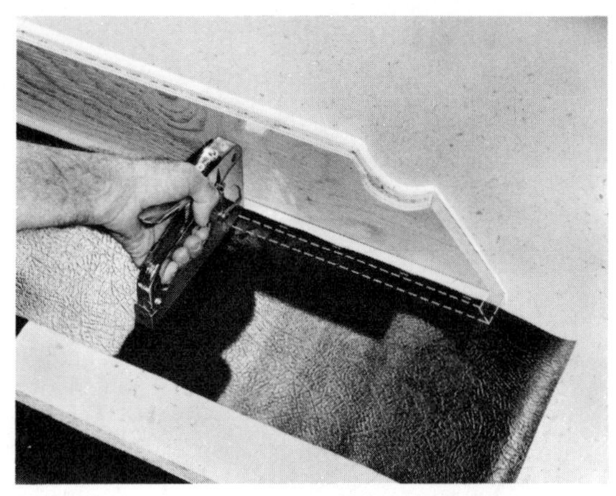

FABRIC-BACKED vinyl is stapled to the underside of rails with 5/16-in. staples spaced about 1 in. apart.

COVER CUSHIONS with 5-in. wide strips of billiard cloth, pulled taut and stapled to the rear side.

CUSHION ENDS are glued as shown, then cloth is pinched and trimmed neatly with a razor blade.

HERE'S HOW a drop pocket fits the corner hole. Front padded rail has been removed for clarity.

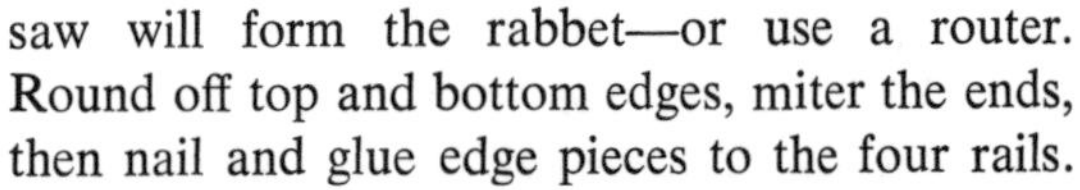

saw will form the rabbet—or use a router. Round off top and bottom edges, miter the ends, then nail and glue edge pieces to the four rails.

Padding the rails is not too difficult. Glue a 5-in.-wide strip of foam to the rear edge of the rail just before the round starts. Use rubber cement or Pliobond *only*. Contact cement, white glue and animal glues destroy the foam. If you use rubber cement (sold at stationery and art stores), apply it to both surfaces and let it air-dry about five minutes before joining the parts. Apply a narrow strip of cement about ½ in. wide.

Cover the rails with a strip of fabric-backed vinyl. This is upholstery material; two well-known trade names are Naugahyde and Boltaflex. Cut it in 9-in.-wide strips and let the ends overhang the rails slightly. Staple one edge of the vinyl to the rabbeted part of the rail back. Pull this taut toward the front of the rail and staple it again on the front edge, with staples about 1 in. apart. At the cutouts, slit material and staple it to the underside as shown on page 181. At the ends of the rails, trim the excess and where impractical to staple, use cement.

When all rails are covered and mounted to the table, there will be a slight gap at the miters. This is rectified by inserting corner fillers made by folding a piece of vinyl over a foam strip. Insert in corners before permanently mounting the rails.

• **Cushions.** The rubber cushions are cemented to the wood cushion supports with rubber or contact cement. The cushion rubber is not symmetrical, but has a top and bottom. It's mounted right when the nose of the rubber is 1 15/16 in. from bottom edge of the support. Miter the supports as indicated, then mount the rubber. Let rubber extend past the miter, then trim it flush with a sharp knife. It's much easier to cut if the blade is dipped in water first.

Covering the cushions is next. Cushion cloth in the kit is 10 in. wide, with a small slit at the

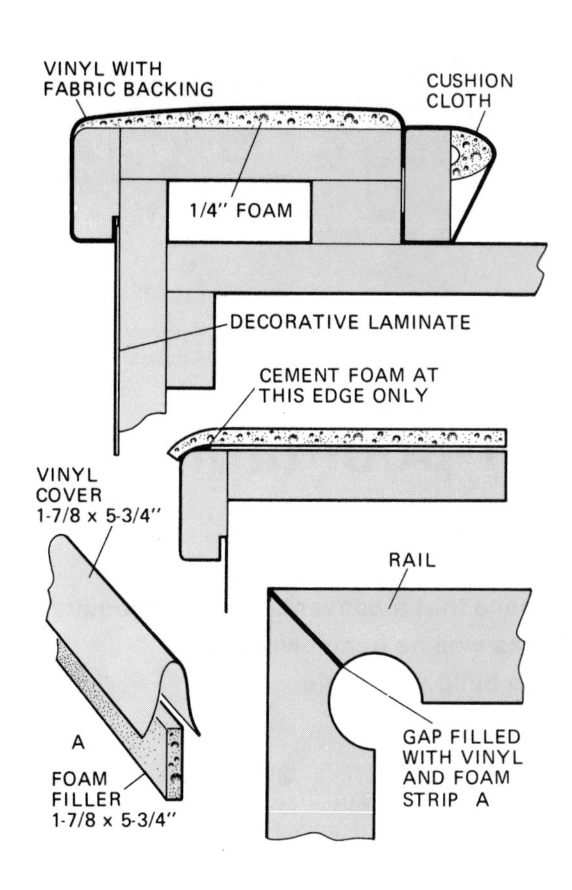

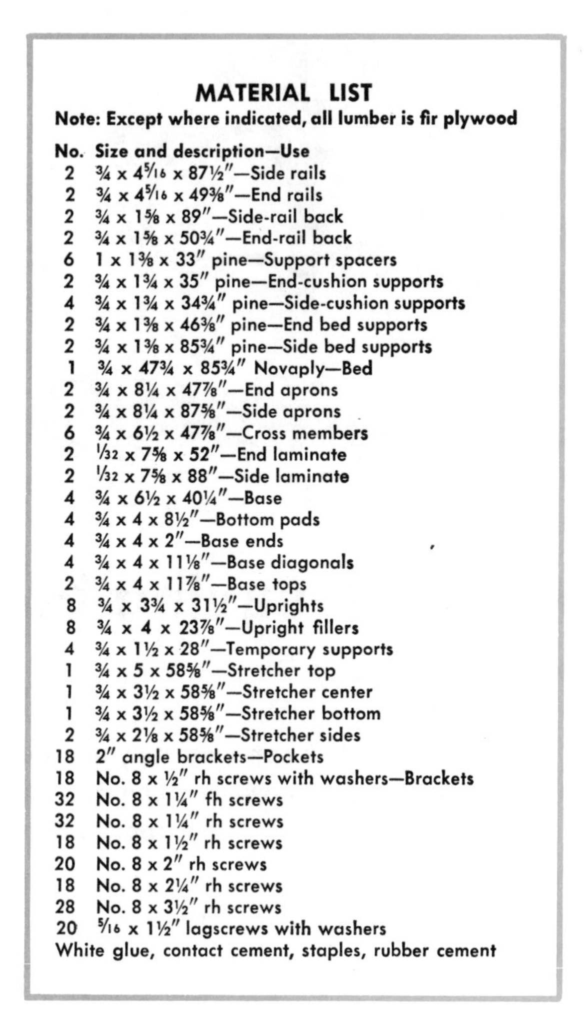

MATERIAL LIST

Note: Except where indicated, all lumber is fir plywood

No.	Size and description—Use
2	¾ x 4⁵⁄₁₆ x 87½"—Side rails
2	¾ x 4⁵⁄₁₆ x 49⅜"—End rails
2	¾ x 1⅝ x 89"—Side-rail back
2	¾ x 1⅝ x 50¾"—End-rail back
6	1 x 1⅜ x 33" pine—Support spacers
2	¾ x 1¾ x 35" pine—End-cushion supports
4	¾ x 1¾ x 34¾" pine—Side-cushion supports
2	¾ x 1⅜ x 46⅜" pine—End bed supports
2	¾ x 1⅜ x 85¾" pine—Side bed supports
1	¾ x 47¾ x 85¾" Novaply—Bed
2	¾ x 8¼ x 47⅞"—End aprons
2	¾ x 8¼ x 87⅝"—Side aprons
6	¾ x 6½ x 47⅞"—Cross members
2	¹⁄₃₂ x 7⅝ x 52"—End laminate
2	¹⁄₃₂ x 7⅝ x 88"—Side laminate
4	¾ x 6½ x 40¼"—Base
4	¾ x 4 x 8½"—Bottom pads
4	¾ x 4 x 2"—Base ends
4	¾ x 4 x 11⅛"—Base diagonals
2	¾ x 4 x 11⅞"—Base tops
8	¾ x 3¾ x 31½"—Uprights
8	¾ x 4 x 23⅞"—Upright fillers
4	¾ x 1½ x 28"—Temporary supports
1	¾ x 5 x 58⅝"—Stretcher top
1	¾ x 3½ x 58⅝"—Stretcher center
1	¾ x 3½ x 58⅝"—Stretcher bottom
2	¾ x 2⅛ x 58⅝"—Stretcher sides
18	2" angle brackets—Pockets
18	No. 8 x ½" rh screws with washers—Brackets
32	No. 8 x 1¼" fh screws
32	No. 8 x 1¼" rh screws
18	No. 8 x 1½" rh screws
20	No. 8 x 2" rh screws
18	No. 8 x 2¼" rh screws
28	No. 8 x 3½" rh screws
20	⁵⁄₁₆ x 1½" lagscrews with washers

White glue, contact cement, staples, rubber cement

5-in. mark. Grasp the cloth at one end and pull apart at the slit into two 5-in-wide strips. Cover the cushions by stapling the cloth to the rear side, a trifle above center. Pull the opposite end taut and again staple at rear of the support. Work from the center out. Be sure the staples set flush. If not, hammer them all the way home. Do likewise with the rail. Ends of the cushion cloth are cemented. Pull the cloth toward the center, then carefully cut the excess with a razor blade. Pull loose ends to the back and cement.

The support spacer is attached to the cushion support with five 2-in. rh screws in each piece. Drive the screws tightly.

• **Final assembly.** Place the support spacer under the rail and screw rail into place with 3½-in. rh screws. Force the cushion as tight as possible against the rail and attach with the 2¼-in. screws. Have an assistant help you. If you can't get 2¼-in. screws, use 2½-in. ones with several washers under the heads to keep points from penetrating.

• **Drop pockets.** The molded-rubber pockets are made slightly oversize so they may be trimmed to fit various tables. Pockets in the kit are cut with a sharp knife or scissors. Three metal brackets hold each pocket in place, using Pop-rivets. The other end of each bracket is attached to the table with a ½-in. screw. Since bracket holes vary, no dimensions are given. If too large or too far in from edge, drill new holes as necessary. Press top of the pocket down firmly against the padded rail when positioning brackets.

Rail markers are ⅜ in. pressure-sensitive paper discs available at art and stationery shops. Peel off protective backing and press them in place. Paint the base as desired.

The kit, with four leveling jacks, 22 ft. of cushion rubber, billiard cloth, six drop pockets and a ¼ x 5 x 280-in. urethanefoam strip can be ordered from The Armor Co., Box 290, Deer Park, N.Y. 11729.

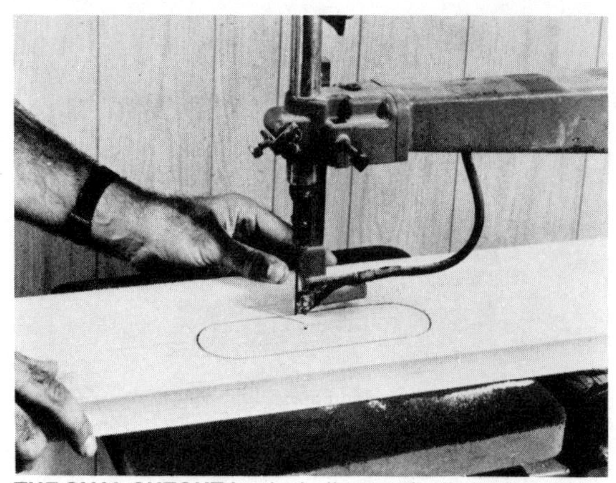

THE OVAL CUTOUT for the ball return in the end panel is made before assembly. Use a jig or sabre saw.

THE BALL-RETURN BOX is simply constructed with butt joints. The box bottom slopes slightly toward opening.

A space-saving bumper-pool table

By JOHN CAPOTOSTO

It takes approximately one-third the space that a conventional table requires. That means apartment dwellers can now enjoy pool as well as homeowners with spacious family rooms. Here's how to build your table

■ POOL HAS LONG been favored as an American family pastime, but two obstacles—cost and space—have kept pool tables out of most homes. Now, by building a regulation-size bumper-pool table yourself, you too can get in on the fun of skillful pool playing.

The most important feature of a good pool table is rigidity. Our version, with its ¾-in. particleboard bed, stacks up against good commercial tables. Also, the one shown boasts aprons and legs of 5/4 (1⅛-in.) stock. Though designed so that construction is simple, quality has not been sacrificed. And, to make shopping for materials an easy task, all the specialty pool items are available by mail order from one source.

The pool table measures 32x48 in. Some lumberyards will (and some won't) sell you the particleboard cut to size. When buying, it's important to make sure that the board is free of any warp.

Lay out the hole locations for the bumpers and drill them with a 1⅜-in. bit. Cup holes will have to be cut with a sabre saw, but before sawing them in the particleboard, check for size on a piece of scrap. When testing the cup liners for fit, drape several pieces of cloth over the holes; the fit should be fairly snug.

Apron members are cut to size next. Choice of lumber is optional but, if you plan to paint your table, a less expensive wood (such as fir) will do. If you prefer stain, consider a hardwood with an attractive grain (walnut or birch, for example). Lay out the oval ball return openings on the end panels and cut them with a sabre saw or jigsaw.

Add the cleats to the apron members, using flathead screws and glue. Position the cleats accurately as they will indirectly determine the cushion height, which is very important. Notice the counter-bored holes drilled in the cushion liner for the bed-to-liner screws.

Next, cut and assemble the legs. These are attached to the 2x3-in. frame as shown. Drill the clearance holes for the leg levelers and then drive home the special Teenuts. Use lagscrews to join the leg assembly to the bed. *Caution:* Take care when working with particleboard—overtightening a screw can strip the hole.

Cut the wood cushion liner to size, mitering the corners, then undercut the ends (see inset in

SEE ALSO

Air games . . . Chess sets . . . Cribbage boards . . . Family rooms . . . Game tables . . . Games . . . Party tables . . . Shuffleboard tables

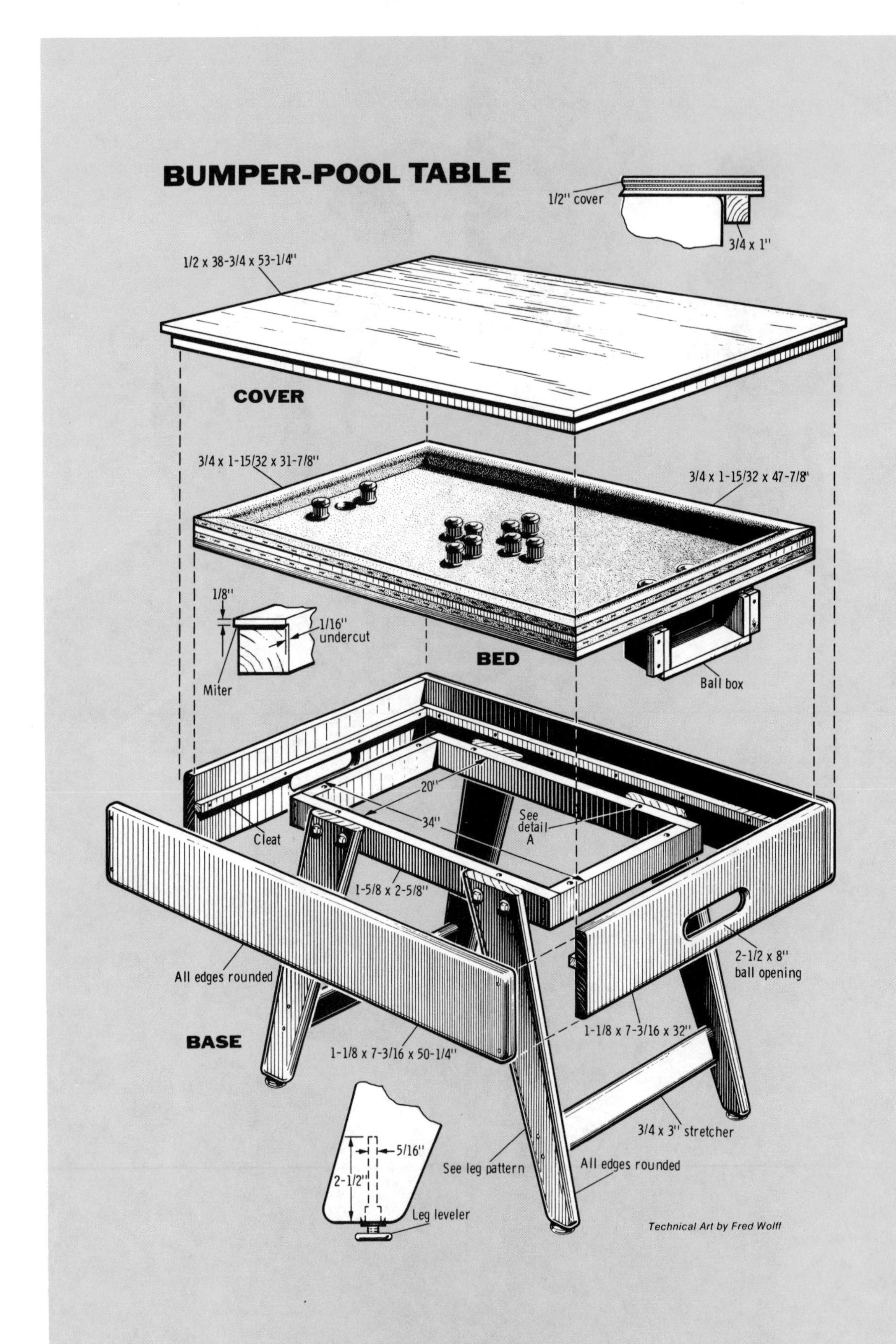

Technical Art by Fred Wolff

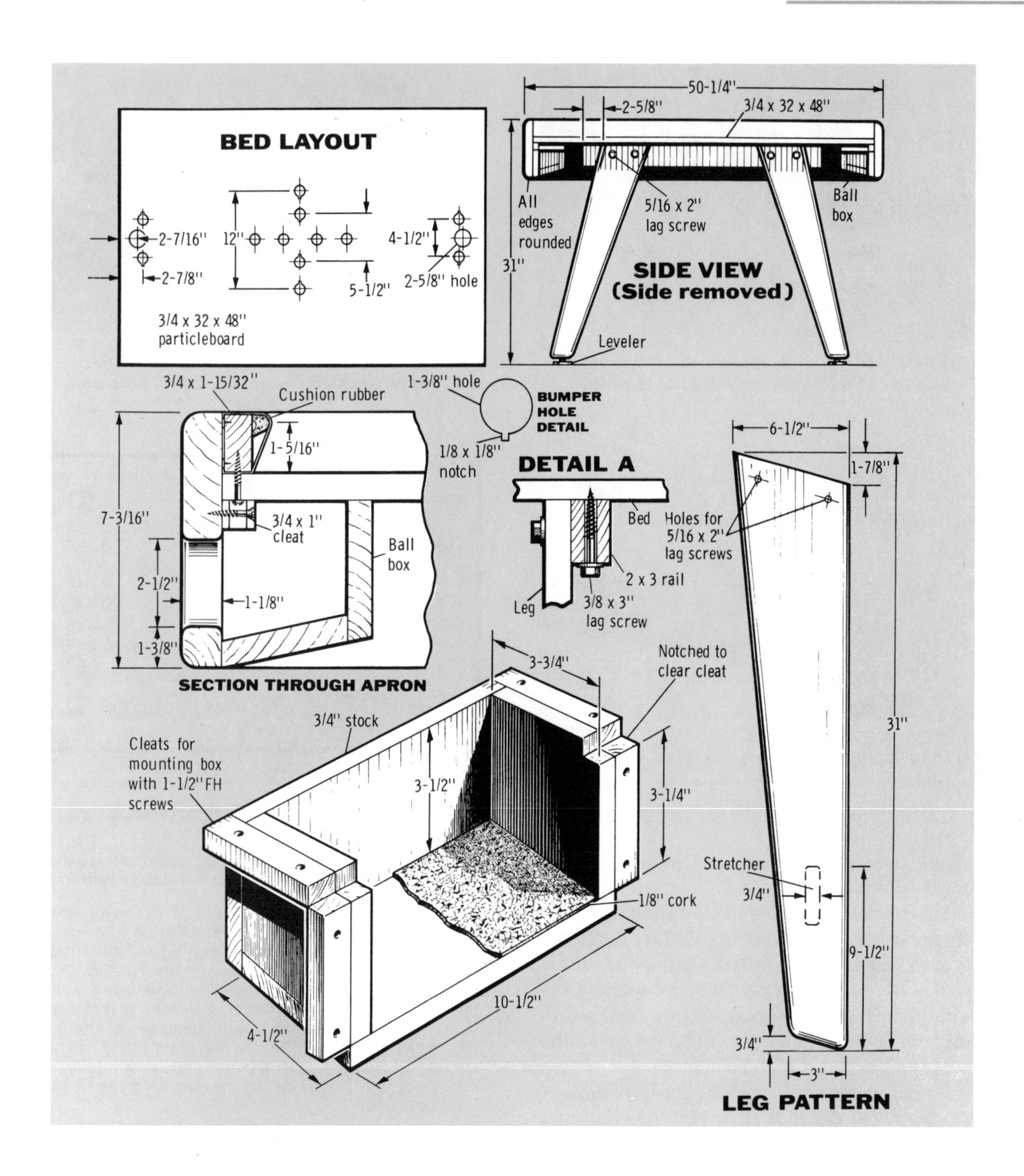

photo at top right of page 2396). The undercut is necessary to allow clearance for the gathered felt at the ends of the cushions. After mitering the lines, lower the blade ⅛ in. and recut the ends.

The cushions are now added. Cut the strips a trifle longer than the liner and apply a coat of contact cement to both surfaces. Allow this to set, then join the pieces carefully. If you examine the rubber in cross section, you'll notice it has a shallow and a deep curve. The shallow part is the top, therefore mount it accordingly to the liner. Trim ends to match the mitered liner. Use a sharp knife, after dipping it in water, to lubricate the blade or you'll have trouble cutting the rubber.

Cover the cushions and bed next. If the cloth is wrinkled, press it carefully on the *wrong* side with a steam iron set on low. Drape the cloth over the bed and tack with staples spaced 1 in. apart: first at the four corners, pulling the cloth taut before stapling; next along the ends, and finally along the long sides. After stapling com-

THE BED CLOTH is stapled around the perimeter every inch or so. Knife for trimming should be razor sharp.

THE CUSHION RUBBER is cut a bit oversize and attached with contact cement (see inset). Next, trim.

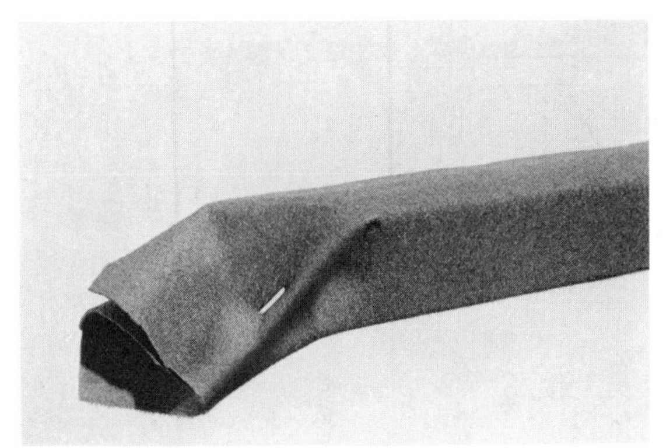

FELT IS FOLDED over the ends, and tucked beneath the undercut in the liner. Finally, staple and trim.

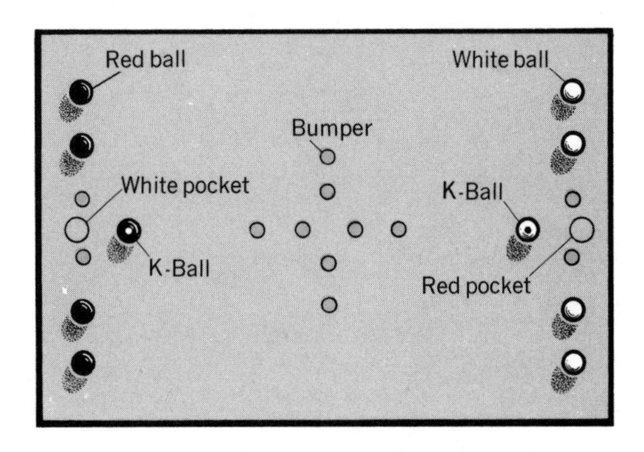

pletely around the perimeter of the bed, trim the excess cloth with a knife.

Slit the cloth over the holes with a sharp blade, stopping just short of the edges. Make eight slits in each hole area. Tap the pocket liner into place so that the edge is just a trifle below the surface. The bumpers are inserted into the holes with their projections aligned with notches of the holes and fastened with nuts.

Staple cushion covers along the back edge of the liner. Do the ends first; pull material taut, then staple at 1-in. intervals all along. Pull cloth around cushion and repeat the procedure on other edge of the cloth. Fold ends over as shown and staple gathered felt in the undercut section. Cut off excess cloth, and attach cushions to the table with roundhead screws driven from below.

Make and attach the ball boxes as shown. A plywood cover with attractive decals protects your table and completes the job.

Specialty items are available from Armor Co., Box 290, Deer Park, NY 11729. Write for free price list, with parcel-post rates and state taxes where applicable.

HOW TO PLAY BUMPER POOL

Number of players: two to four. Each side has five balls: one side red, one white. In each set ball marked with spot is called the king (K) ball.

STRATEGY OF PLAY

Balls are spotted as shown above; white balls shoot toward white pocket and red toward red. To start play, both players shoot their K balls simultaneously toward their respective pockets. The player whose ball is closest to his pocket has the right to continue to shoot. After he "makes" (pockets) his K ball, he may shoot at *any* ball on the table. *Important:* Until a player makes his K ball, he may shoot only for his pocket; he may not try to hit his opponent's ball.

SKILLFUL PLAY

The strategy is to keep your opponent from having an open shot at his pocket while you leave yourself open to shoot at your pocket. This is usually done either by knocking your opponent's ball out of position, or by positioning your own ball in such a manner as to block his shot. The player who pockets his five balls first wins.

PENALTIES

If a player sinks one of his balls before the K ball, opponent pockets any two balls and shoots.

If a player causes a ball to jump the table, his opponent places the jumped ball wherever he chooses (including in the center of the eight-bumper cluster), pockets any two balls and shoots.

If a player pockets an opponent's ball, it is a scratch and he loses his turn. The pocketed ball stays in the pocket.

Quiet that floor

Every time we move, the floors squeak underfoot. I have a full basement, can reach the floor from underneath, but what can I do to stop the squeaks?—Paul Hanlan, Detroit

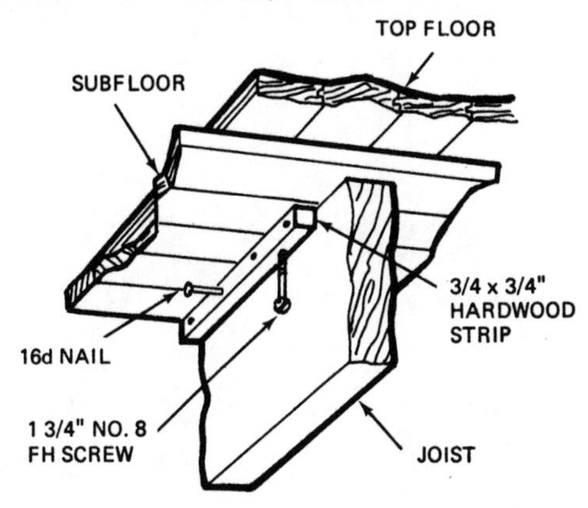

One way that seems to be effective in nearly all instances is shown in the illustration above. First, locate the squeaks from the basement by having someone walk about on the floor. Then nail strips to the joists, spanning the areas of the squeaks, and making sure that the strips are pressed tightly against the floor as you nail them in place. Then have someone stand on the spot while you drive screws through the strips, through the subfloor and into, but not through, the top floor.

Loose register vanes

Two wall registers in my warm-air heating system won't remain open. The vanes drop to their closed position as soon as the control level is released. Can these be repaired?—R. Hanscom, Joplin, Mo.

Chances are the pivots at the ends of the vanes have become worn through usage. Turn out the two screws holding the unit in place, lift it out and you'll see the vanes are pivoted on rivets that normally are set with just enough friction to hold them in place at the desired setting. Stand unit on end with heads of several rivets resting on a sturdy metal surface and tap each lightly. Test for free movement as you go to make sure you don't overtighten them, which would make the vanes difficult or impossible to adjust.

60°F. basement

The temperature in my basement stays at 60°F. all winter, so my workshop is always cold and damp. How can I eliminate this condition? My furnace is in a separate room on a different floor.—F.L., N.Y.

If it is not possible to tap into ducts or pipes to conduct heat into the basement, then the only practical solution remaining is to go to a vented gas heater (which can be suspended from the ceiling or installed between studs in a conventional framed wall). Such heaters are quite efficient and come with a circulating fan for more uniform heat distribution.

For summer months, you might consider the installation of an automatic dehumidifier to keep the moisture content of the air at a given level.

Quick drawer fix

I have an older chest in which the drawers have been heavily loaded at times. As a result, the bottom edges of the drawer sides are somewhat worn, making them difficult to slide in and out. There are no center guides. What can I do to make them slide more easily?—Mrs. J. Tenney, Fort Worth, Tex.

First, pull the drawers all the way out and check to see that the sides have not spread—that is, that the corner joints have not opened; if they have, add glue and tap the sides until the joints are tight. Then drive a large-headed thumbtack in the position shown in the illustration, the head centered under the lower edge of the drawer sides. Spray the lower edges of the sides with a silicone lubricant, which you can buy from your paint or hardware dealer.

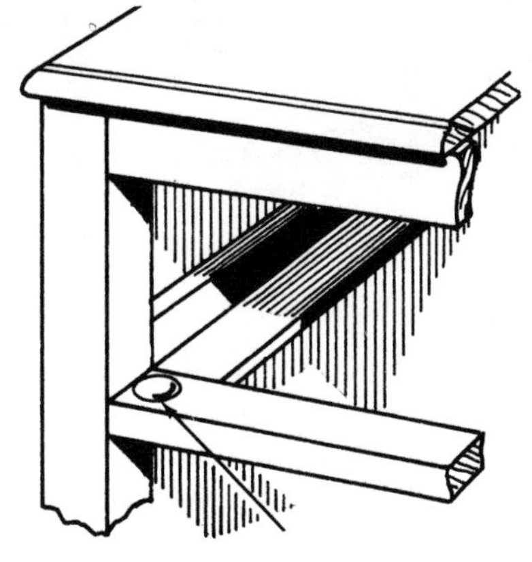

Orienting your new house

We plan to build a new house on our lot next spring. Can you outline briefly how to place a house to gain best advantage of sunlight, air circulation and privacy?—A.L., Tex.

Consider first your local building restrictions, then plan window sizes and exposure to sunlight the year round, direction of prevailing winds, location of plantings and use of fencing or shrubbery or both to attain the desired privacy. A simple penciled plotting of these various features will help you plan your home.

by W. Clyde Lammey

Build a cabana for your pool

You can use this standard-built structure all year long. In the summer it makes a great changing area and in the winter it can be used for storage of yard equipment

By DON SHINER

SEE ALSO
**Cabanas . . . Carpeting, outdoor . . .
Garden shelters . . . Gazebos . . . Playhouses . . .
Storage buildings . . . Swimming pools**

■ THERE ARE two distinct advantages to be gained from erecting a small structure adjacent to your pool. For one thing, you'll keep wet bathers from dripping water throughout the house because they'll have a convenient place to dry off and change. And when the pool is closed down at the end of the season, the little house can be put to good use for winter storage of seasonal items such as tractors, lawn furniture and the like.

The handsome cabana shown to the left gives 84 sq. ft. (it measures approximately 7 x 12 ft.) for year-round use to suit your family's needs. Construction is conventional as can be seen in the drawings that follow. Our experience has proven that it is far more convenient if it is located close to the pool. If the apron around your pool is too narrow to accommodate the house, it is well worth the slight extra effort and investment to increase the apron on one end, or, if you would rather have the house located elsewhere, simply add a connecting flagstone walk between the new slab and the existing apron next to the pool.

The house is built following standard building procedures. First, stake out the desired location and remove all topsoil. Dig and pour footings around the perimeter to meet local area requirements and then pour a 4 to 5-in.-thick slab. *(Editor's note:* Before starting actual construction, check with your local building department; you may be required to obtain a building permit.) In my case, the existing pool slab was wide enough to accommodate the little house so I simply laid a double bead of caulking on the concrete over which the sole plates were laid. Use screws and lead anchors to secure them.

The 2x3s used for the studding provide more than adequate strength because there is a rather steep roof pitch to eliminate snow (load) ac-

CABANA PROVIDES SPACE for bathers changing to swim togs and, as a bonus, there is extra storage for all of your lawn equipment and a tractor rider-mower.

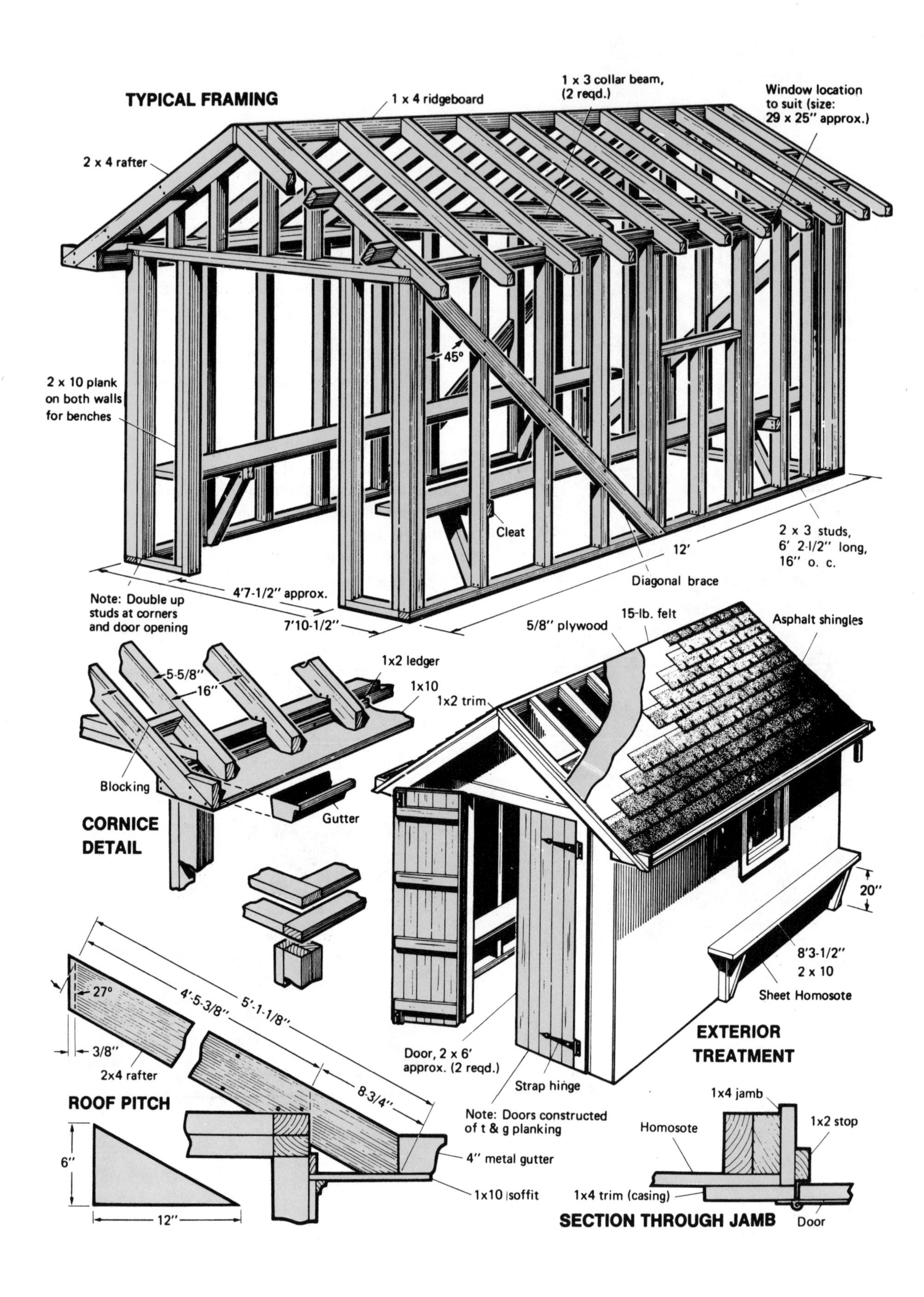
TYPICAL FRAMING
1 x 4 ridgeboard
1 x 3 collar beam, (2 reqd.)
Window location to suit (size: 29 x 25" approx.)
2 x 4 rafter
45°
2 x 10 plank on both walls for benches
Cleat
2 x 3 studs, 6' 2-1/2" long, 16" o. c.
12'
Diagonal brace
4'7-1/2" approx.
Note: Double up studs at corners and door opening
7'10-1/2"
5/8" plywood
15-lb. felt
Asphalt shingles
1x2 ledger
5-5/8"
16"
1x10
1x2 trim
Blocking
Gutter
CORNICE DETAIL
20"
8'3-1/2"
2 x 10
Sheet Homosote
27°
4'-5-3/8"
5'-1-1/8"
3/8"
2x4 rafter
8-3/4"
Door, 2 x 6' approx. (2 reqd.)
Strap hinge
EXTERIOR TREATMENT
ROOF PITCH
6"
12"
4" metal gutter
1x10 soffit
Note: Doors constructed of t & g planking
1x4 jamb
Homosote
1x2 stop
1x4 trim (casing)
SECTION THROUGH JAMB
Door

2-FT.-WIDE DOORS open up to make way for a riding tractor. If you don't have a tractor, a single door will do.

cumulation during the winter months. The rafters are nominal 2x4s nailed 16 in. o.c., each directly over a stud. For ventilation, I installed a window on each side of the house. Window size can be determined by personal choice or by what windows might be on sale at the local lumberyard. The rafters are covered with ⅝-in. plywood, followed by 15-lb. felt and asphalt shingles. Wall construction was kept simple (and economical) by using 4x8-ft. sheets of Homosote, which stands up well against the weather. It can be painted at first, and, as funds are available, covered with siding or shingles to match your home.

If desired, the cabana can be partitioned inside to provide individual dressing rooms. We chose to leave it as one big room so that the winter storage would not be cut down or made impractical.

The doors are constructed of boards held together with horizontal strips nailed on the inside. Barrel-type door bolts are fastened to one door at top and bottom to enter holes drilled in the slab and header. Add a standard doorknob and strap hinges to complete the door hardware.

We chose to install two 2-ft.-wide doors because of a riding tractor. If you don't own one, or will never have the need for one, you might prefer to install a standard 2½ to 3-ft.-wide single door in the conventional manner.

Since there was no reason to do any fancy finishing, I chose to leave the interior unfinished. For convenience, however, I installed two 2x10-in. benches the full length of both walls. The diagonal bracing (as shown on the facing page) provides more than adequate strength and there has been no noticeable sagging. Because the house is next to the pool, a short bench was fastened along an outside wall. Thus, whenever our youngsters have a gang in, there is more than enough seating for everybody.

DOORS ARE held closed by a pair of sliding bolts on one, and a latch and pull combination on the other.

The basics of portrait photography

IF YOU THINK that portrait photography is for professionals only, take a few minutes to study the pictures and diagrams on these pages. They show that portrait lighting is not only basically simple—it's also a lot of fun to try because there are so many unusual effects.

Shooting a portrait does require some know-how, but it doesn't take a studio full of fancy equipment. You can create just about any lighting setup you want with four ordinary mushroom-type photo-floods available at photo shops.

There are four basic light positions. Your lights don't always have to be in exactly these positions, but they give you a starting point from which to try other variations. The main or "key" light is usually placed to one side of the camera so it lights the subject from an angle. This cross light casts shadows that give depth and shape to the subject's facial features.

A "fill" light at or near the camera illuminates the side of the face that's away from the key light and softens the shadows so they don't become too harsh. A third flood is used to light up the background so the subject stands out clearly. A fourth flood, called a "hair" light, is placed so it

HOW YOU BUILD UP BASIC FOUR-POINT LIGHTING

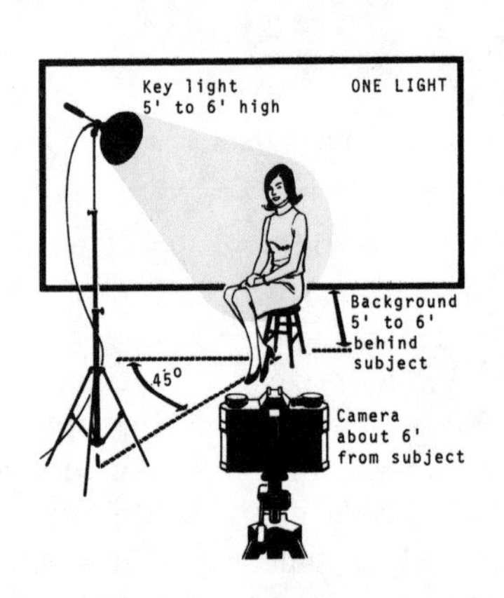

THE SEQUENCE of photos above and on opposite page shows what happens as you add one light at a time. Using a rubber ball helps to illustrate the dramatic effect that each light produces. Key light (1) provides main illumination. Placed off to the side, it creates strong shadows. Adding fill light (2) softens shadows and evens lighting.

shines down on the subject's head from the rear. Using various combinations of the four lights, you can actually make 15 different setups. Not all will produce pleasing or useful results, but they'll let you see the wide variety of effects that are possible.

Proper location of the key light is important. The familiar "45/45" rule—angled 45° from the

SEE ALSO
Backdrops, photo . . . Cameras, care . . . Close-up photos . . . Enlarging, photo . . . Exposure meters . . . Floodlights . . . Lenses, photo . . . Photo hints . . . Photography . . . Prints, photo

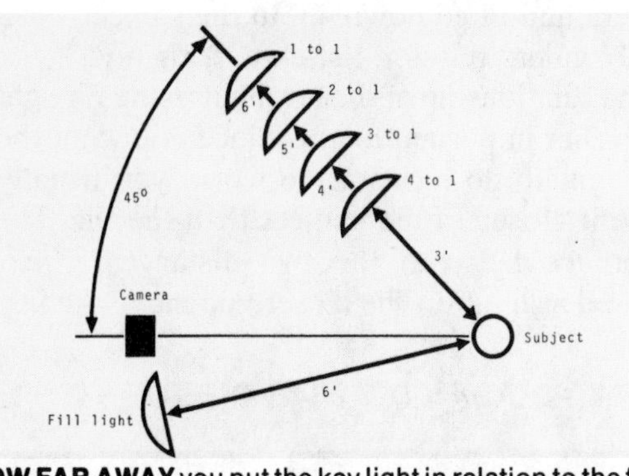

HOW FAR AWAY you put the key light in relation to the fill light determines your "lighting ratio." When both are at the same distance, their ratio is 1 to 1, and they illuminate the subject more or less equally. As the key light is moved closer, its ratio increases. It becomes stronger and the fill light gets weaker. The higher the "lighting ratio" is, the deeper the shadows and the more contrast to your photo.

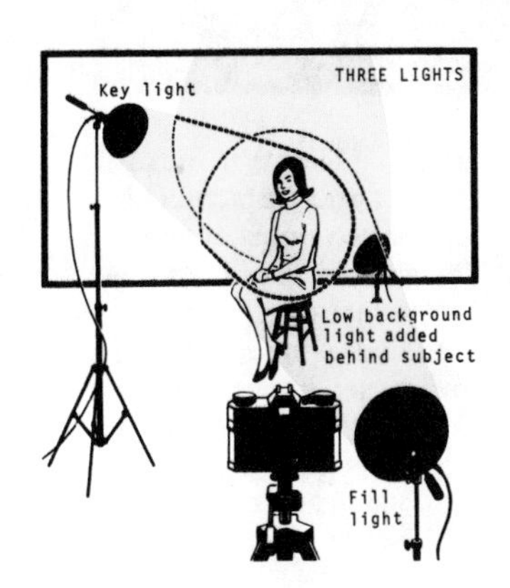

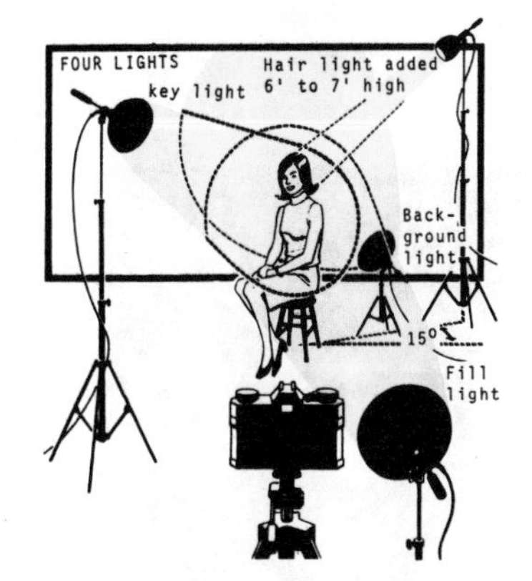

BACKGROUND LIGHT (3) outlines the subject's head by lighting up the background. This is used to separate the background from the subject so it will stand out clearly. The final light (4), sometimes called a "hair" light is placed so that it shines down on the subject's head from the rear and gives an attractive sheen to her hair.

camera and tilted down 45° to the subject—is a handy guide, but don't stick to it rigidly.

The relationship of the key light to the fill light is another important factor. Since you want the key light to do most of the work, you usually place it closer to the subject than the fill. The difference between the two distances is expressed as a ratio. The closer you move the key light to the subject, the stronger it becomes in relation to the fill light and the higher the ratio. Its shadows become deeper and more pronounced as the effect of the fill light gets weaker.

Watch your background, too. One of the most common mistakes in portrait photography is to place the subject too close to the background. This causes the subject to cast ugly multiple

WHAT YOU CAN DO WITH ONE OR TWO LIGHTS

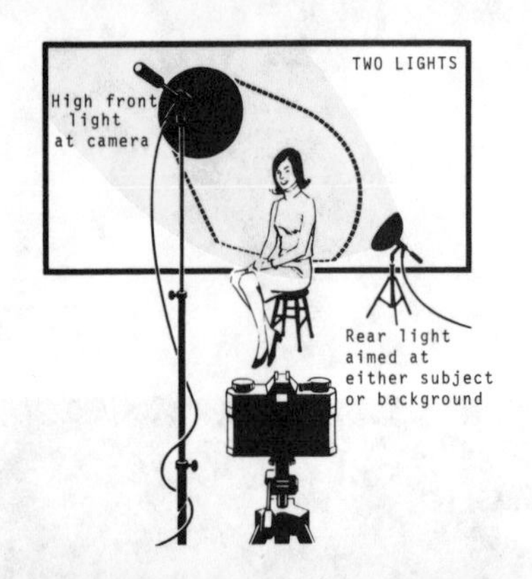

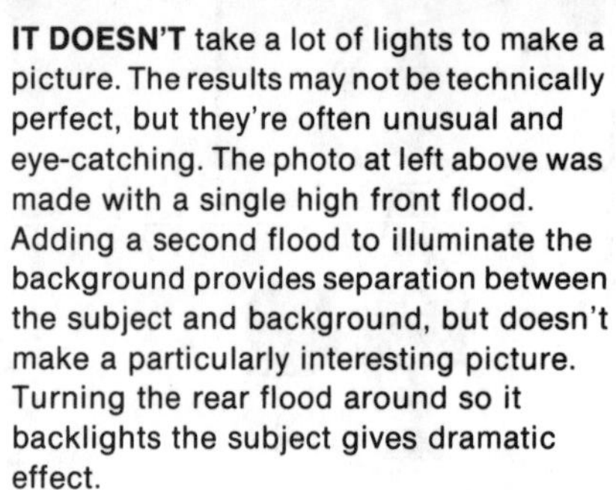

IT DOESN'T take a lot of lights to make a picture. The results may not be technically perfect, but they're often unusual and eye-catching. The photo at left above was made with a single high front flood. Adding a second flood to illuminate the background provides separation between the subject and background, but doesn't make a particularly interesting picture. Turning the rear flood around so it backlights the subject gives dramatic effect.

NEED AN extra light? The two photos below show how a white cardboard reflector can serve the same purpose as a light. Here, it acts as a front fill, and the key light is swung around almost broadside to the subject to provide a dramatic cross light. The photos show the effect without the cardboard on the left and with it added on the right. It casts just enough light to open up the dark side of the face.

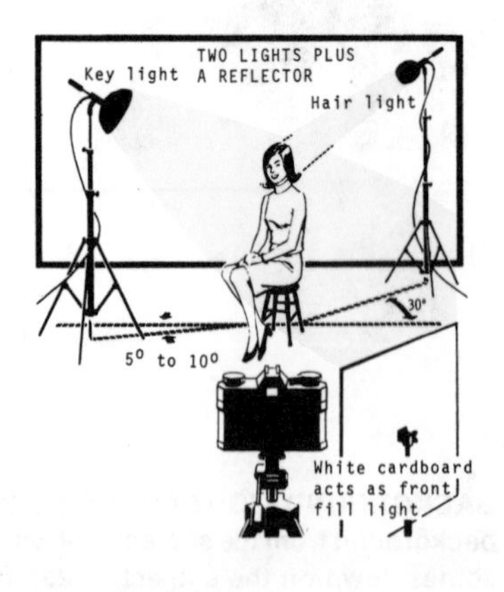

shadows all over the background. Also, your lights will wash out the background, especially if you're deliberately trying to keep it dark. Light falling on a black background will actually make it look light gray or almost white in the picture.

Keep your subject well in front of the background—as much as five to six feet. If you want the background to go dark, don't put a light on it.

Keep the background plain and uncluttered. For a convertible backdrop, paint a sheet of thin plywood or hardboard white on one side and black on the other.

It's best to establish your exposure with a light meter, although you'll be surprised to find that it will change very little no matter how many lights you use or how you move them around.

THREE WAYS TO CREATE SPECIAL EFFECTS

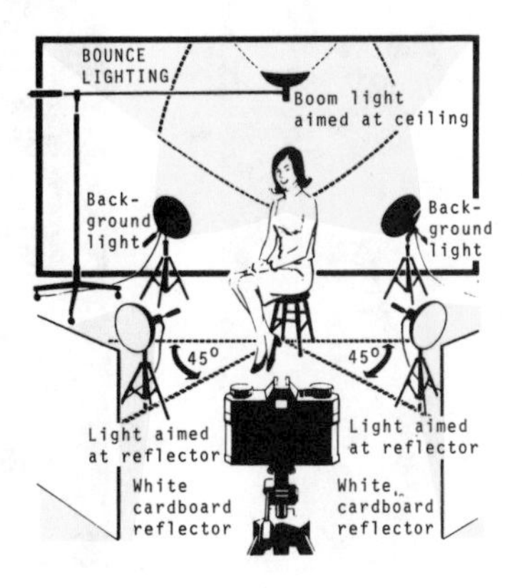

BOUNCE LIGHTING creates a soft, pleasing effect without shadows. While not as dramatic as direct lighting, it's often more flattering, especially on subjects with prominent features that cast deep shadow lines. Here, the illumination is entirely by reflected light. Front lighting is provided by two photofloods aimed away from the subject at white cardboard reflectors. Two more floods light up the background. A fifth light is aimed straight up so it reflects downward, casting a highlight (if ceiling isn't white, tack up a white bedsheet to give good reflection).

A FEW simple photo props can completely change a subject's appearance and personality, as shown at left. The background is an old piece of black paper deliberately crinkled. A peaked cap and high-necked sweater give the subject a tough, sexy look. Note there is no fill light to soften shadows cast by the key light. This heightens the dramatic effect. Hair and background lights complete the setup.

RANDOM SHADOW patterns often add an interesting, unusual touch to an otherwise routine picture. You'll find many objects around the home that can be used to create interesting shadow effects. You'd never quess that the mottled background at left was produced by an ordinary kitchen stool turned upside down. One light is placed so it shines through the stool, casting shadows of its legs on white background paper. Locating the light low and off to the side, as shown at right, lets you throw shadows behind the subject without tne stool itself getting in the way. Try moving the light around. It was discovered that moving the light closer or farther away from the stool varies the shape and intensity of the pattern. This picture also shows an entire setup. Notice that there is a key light (behind camera), a hair light overhead and a fill light at the left. Study what the light does in different positions. Don't be afraid to experiment with "strange" or unusual props. It is through this experimentation that you will get the most pleasing effects.

Shoot portraits with a single bounce light

PORTRAIT PHOTOGRAPHY doesn't necessarily require a lot of fancy equipment. You can shoot excellent informal portraits with a single light—even a flash. The trick is to bounce the light off a curved reflector. This floods your subject with light without any hot spots or harsh shadows. And your subject doesn't squint and squirm under a glaring battery of lights.

Furthermore, you don't have to change the setup every time your subject moves. It remains basically the same.

The method shown here works best with electronic flash, but you can try it with flashbulbs and photofloods. An old umbrella, sprayed white inside, makes a fine reflector. The bracket, as shown, is an easy way to support the umbrella after you've cut off the handle. The flash unit, aimed at the center of the umbrella, slips into an accessory flash shoe clip.

Positioning the rig is easy. It's the classic old 45/45 arrangement—45° from the camera horizontally and 45° above your subject vertically.

Use a dark wall or blanket as a backdrop and keep your subject two to three feet in front. This will give you a crisp black background with your subject lighted dramatically in front.

Exposures are calculated on the basis of flash-to-subject distance in the same way as for regular flash shooting except that you must compensate a bit for light lost in the bounce process. Total flash-to-subject distance is the distance from flash to umbrella, plus that from umbrella to subject. Divide this into the guide number for your flash to find the f/stop, then open up one stop wider to give the necessary added exposure. Experiment with different distances and exposures until you find the best combination. Once you have established this, you can shoot just about any type of portrait with the same setup, and the results will always be identical.

SEE ALSO

**Backdrops, photo . . . Cameras, care . . .
Close-up photos . . . Enlarging, photo . . .
Exposure meters . . . Floodlights . . . Lenses, photo . . .
Photo hints . . . Photography . . . Prints, photo**

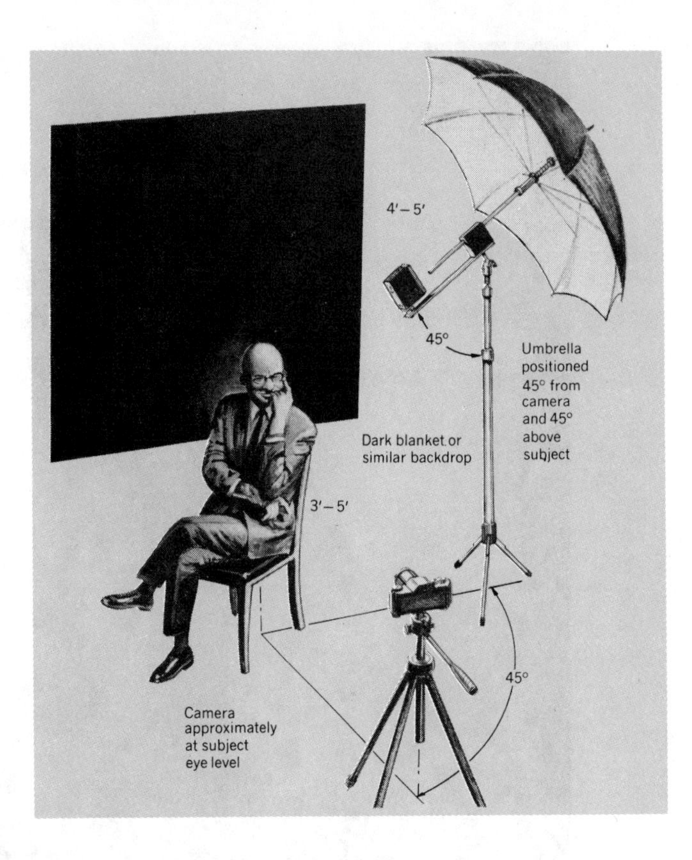

THE HOMEMADE BRACKET, shown at bottom and in the drawing, holds the umbrella shaft in a wood block with the flashgun in an accessory flash shoe clip. The block allows the umbrella to slide back and forth to adjust distance to flash. The rig mounts on a light stand with a ball-and-socket swivel and adapter fitting. Swivel, adapter and flash clip are stock photo accessories. At lower left is an alternate mounting arrangement using a photographic clamp. Spray the umbrella with several coats of white enamel.

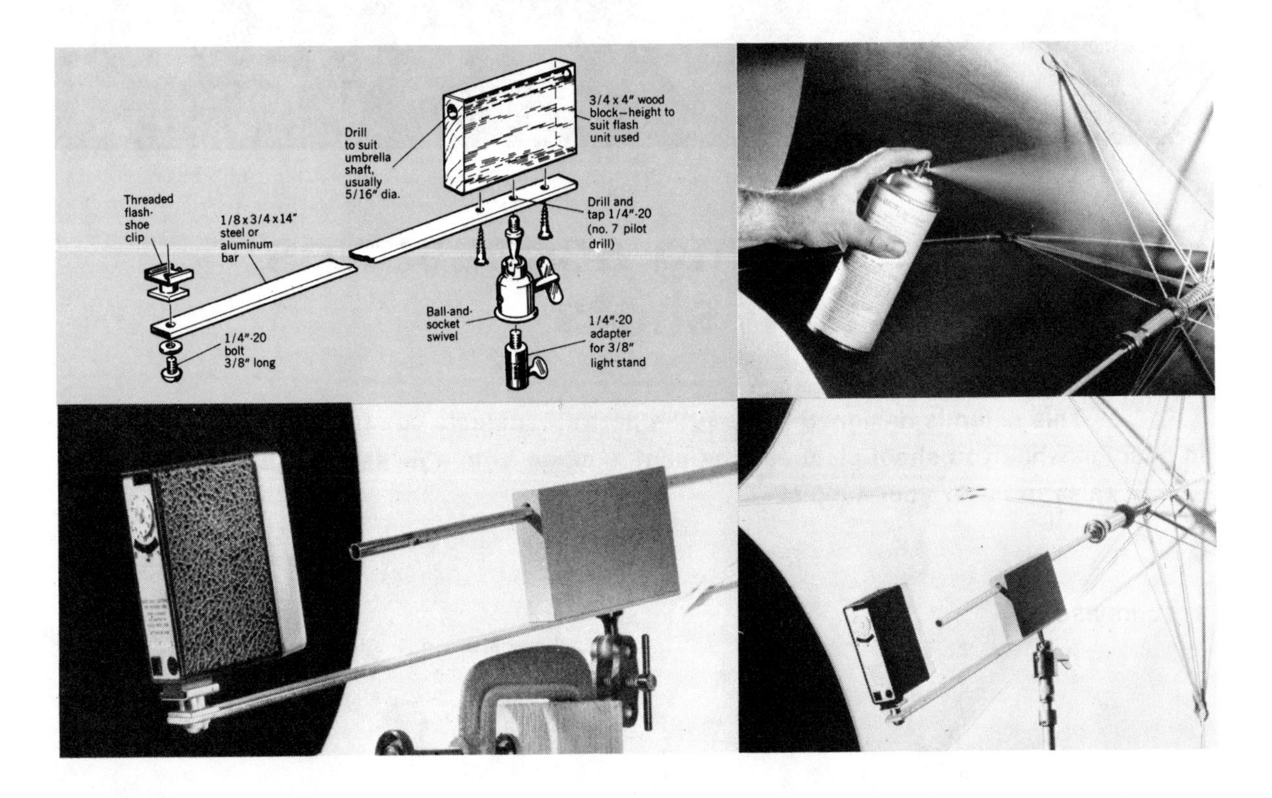

Build these posing accessories for your portrait shots

This setup is designed to keep the portrait subjects comfortable and in position while you shoot pictures. The seat is made from a jackscrew that can raise or lower your subject

By ED JOHNSEY

SEE ALSO

Backdrops, photo . . . Close-up photos . . . Enlarging, photo . . . Exposure meters . . . Floodlights . . . Photo hints . . . Photography . . . Prints, photo

■ THREE ACCESSORIES that every portrait photographer can use are a posing stool that swivels and adjusts for height; a narrow table for a hand and armrest; and a small platform to raise your subjects for low-angle shots. They're hard to buy, but easy to build. And since they'll be either out of the picture or covered with a rug, cloth, or paper when photographed, no great furniture-finishing or cabinet making skills are needed.

The stool is basically a five-ton jackscrew (Wards or Sears) topped by a seat made from two 8x12-in. pieces and two smaller (say 5x5-in.) pieces of ¾-in. plywood. These are joined with the two smaller pieces under the center of the seat. Drill a hole through the four layers of plywood to accept the jackscrew head, and permanently secure with epoxy cement. The stool's base is another sandwich consisting of two ¾ x 8-in.-dia. plywood discs with a 4½-in. hole cut in one disc to accept the base of the jack. A thin bed of epoxy adhesive holds the jack in place. The finished stool adjusts from 10 to 15 in. in height; the platform can add another 8 in. when needed.

The table consists of two 20-in. lengths of ½-in. galvanized pipe, fastened by flanges between 1½-in. "planks" made by laminating two pieces of ¾-in. plywood measuring 8 x 21½ in. Placing carpet or towels on the table can add interesting texture to your photos.

The platform is a ¾ x 24 x 24-in. piece of plywood glued and nailed to two ¾ x ¼ x 24-in. uprights. Notice the additional brace on one end made from a 22½-in. piece of 1x4 lumber. (Dimensions needn't be exact, but these allow the table and stool to be stored inside the platform.) Two 1x2s under the platform serve as centering tracks so you can mount the platform on the armrest table to make a 24-in. square tabletop for small-object photography. Heavy bolts through the platform let you secure it to the table with wingnuts. Attaching four 1 x 2 x 23¼-in. legs with carriage bolts converts the platform to a sturdy table for photographing children. The whole combination of posing aids nests and stores in less than two square feet of storage space.

POSING STOOL and armrest table nest inside platform (above), take less than two square feet of space. For tabletop photography (right), platform is supported by table; loop for background paper is stiff wire.

How to install a yard light

A YARD LIGHT does many things for a home. It bids welcome. It discourages prowlers. It adds nighttime beauty to the yard, and lights the way to your front door.

The biggest job in installing a yard light is digging the hole for the post and the trench for the cable. The required minimum depth is 18 in., and you'll find a narrow spade best for digging the trench.

Yard lights come with metal or wood posts, plain or fancy. The important thing when setting the post in concrete is to see that it's plumb before filling the hole. Here, in the case of a wooden post, a couple of C-clamps can be used to attach braces to it temporarily; with a metal post, notches in the braces will let you hook them over the top.

Use heavy-duty, flat, plastic-covered cable made for underground burial and run it up inside the yard-light post, leaving ample wire at the top for connecting it later to the socket. Buy three bags of dry-mix concrete to set the post, mix according to directions and fill the hole.

To connect the cable to an existing junction box in the basement, you have to pass it through a hole in the foundation wall or a hole in the joist header. The latter is an easier job if you have a poured foundation, but it means the cable must be partially exposed. In this case, the exposed part must pass through conduit before entering the house wall.

While they cost more, you can buy yard lights that turn themselves on and off at dusk and dawn by a built-in photoelectric control. This feature eliminates the need for a separate switch. However, the drawing on the opposite page shows how to install a separate switch at some convenient location in the house, and the wiring diagram below shows how you connect the wires of the cables to the black and white wires you'll find in the junction box when you remove its cover. Turn off the electricity when making the connections, and remember to connect black wires to black and white wires to white.

SEE ALSO
Electrical wiring . . . Extension-cord reels . . . Fluorescent lighting . . . House numbers . . . Patios . . . Testers, continuity . . . Wiring, electrical . . . Yard lighting

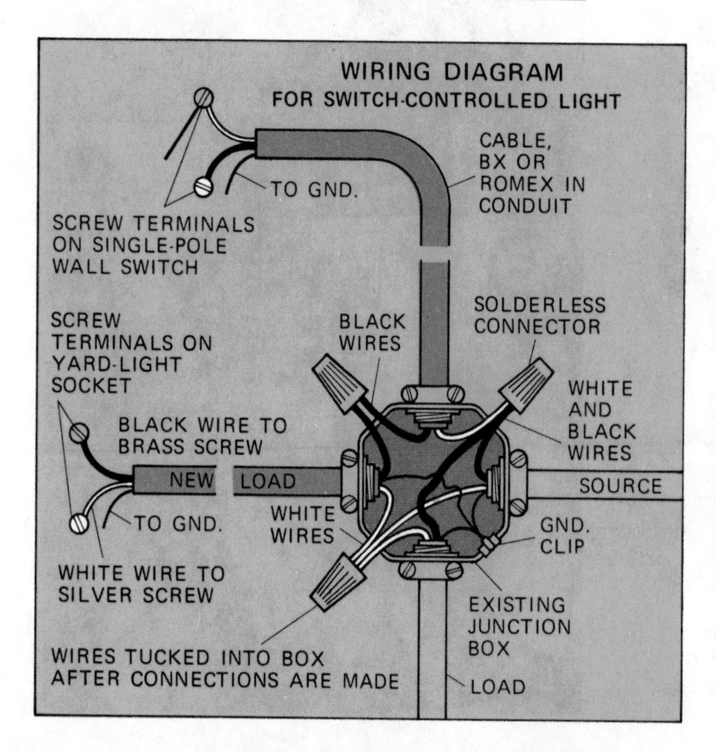

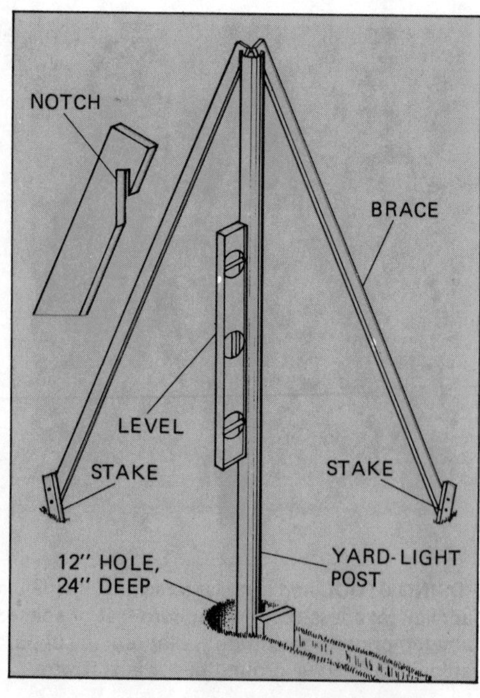

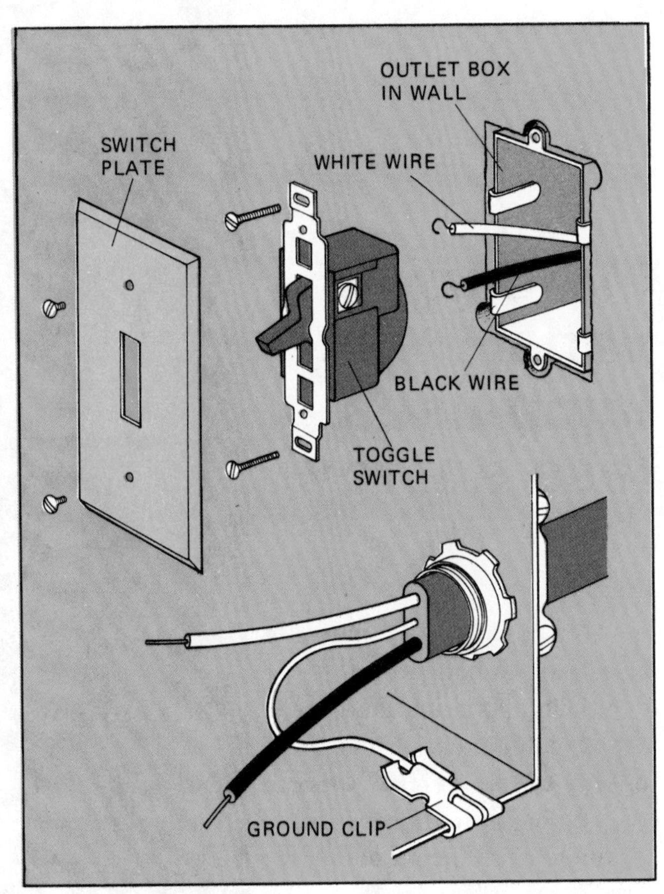
OUTLET BOX
IN WALL
SWITCH
PLATE
WHITE WIRE
BLACK WIRE
TOGGLE
SWITCH
GROUND CLIP

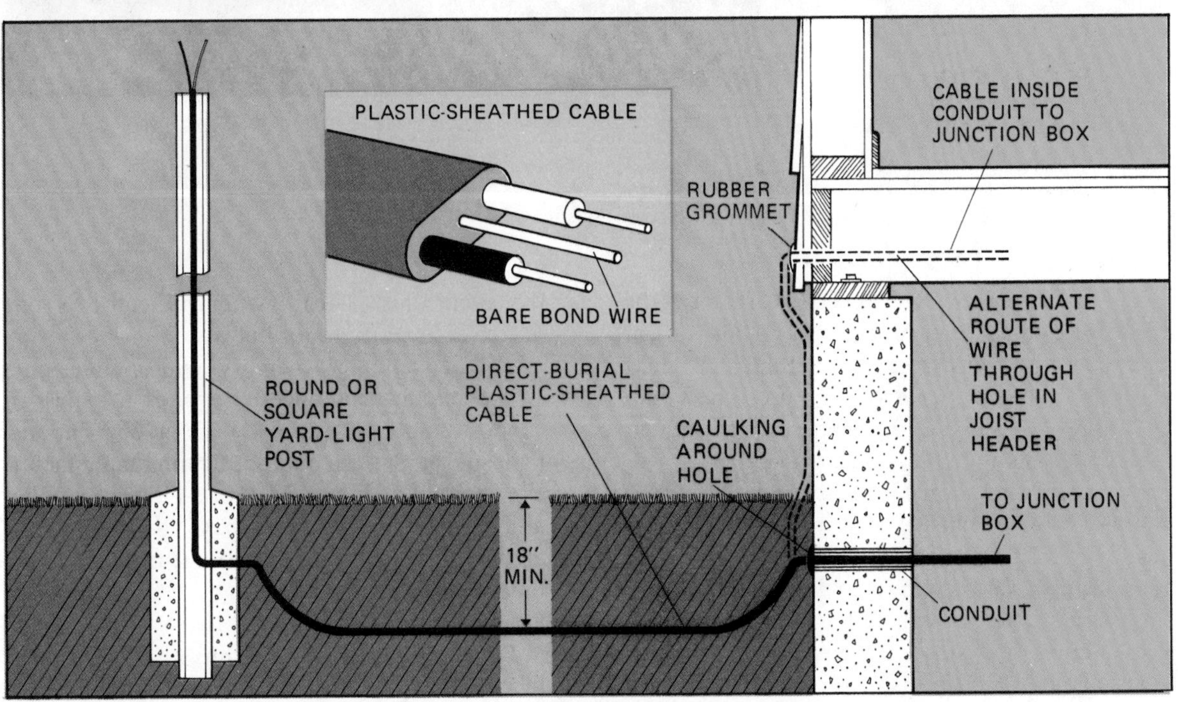
PLASTIC-SHEATHED CABLE
BARE BOND WIRE
CABLE INSIDE
CONDUIT TO
JUNCTION BOX
RUBBER
GROMMET
ALTERNATE
ROUTE OF
WIRE
THROUGH
HOLE IN
JOIST
HEADER
ROUND OR
SQUARE
YARD-LIGHT
POST
DIRECT-BURIAL
PLASTIC-SHEATHED
CABLE
CAULKING
AROUND
HOLE
TO JUNCTION
BOX
18"
MIN.
CONDUIT

Mercury vapor lamp uses less energy

You can install a new post lamp or convert an existing light and take advantage of this energy-saver. Mercury vapor bulbs burn brighter and longer than incandescent

By ROBERT W. TUREK

■ TODAY, ELECTRIC POST LAMPS offer the most economical and protective illumination for your driveway, walk, steps and entrances. Thanks to a new mercury vapor bulb, you can now illuminate the outside of your home with a brighter, longer-lasting light that uses less energy.

Compared to a typical 100-w. household-type bulb, a 50-w. mercury vapor bulb lasts 21 times as long and gives off almost twice as much light per watt. A 100-w. household bulb lasts about 750 hours (three months if lighted an average of eight hours a day), but the mercury bulb will burn about 16,000 hours (more than five years at the same daily rate). General Electric is one maker of mercury vapor bulbs.

The new elliptical mercury bulb operates on a 120-v. circuit. But since it requires a ballast, it cannot simply be screwed into a conventional light socket. Several outdoor lighting manufacturers, including Hacco, McGraw-Edison, Artolier and Montgomery Ward, have designed cast-aluminum postlight fixtures for the mercury vapor bulb. They offer excellent light distribution from an unbreakable lens.

Before installing a new lamp, check with your local building department to assure electrical code

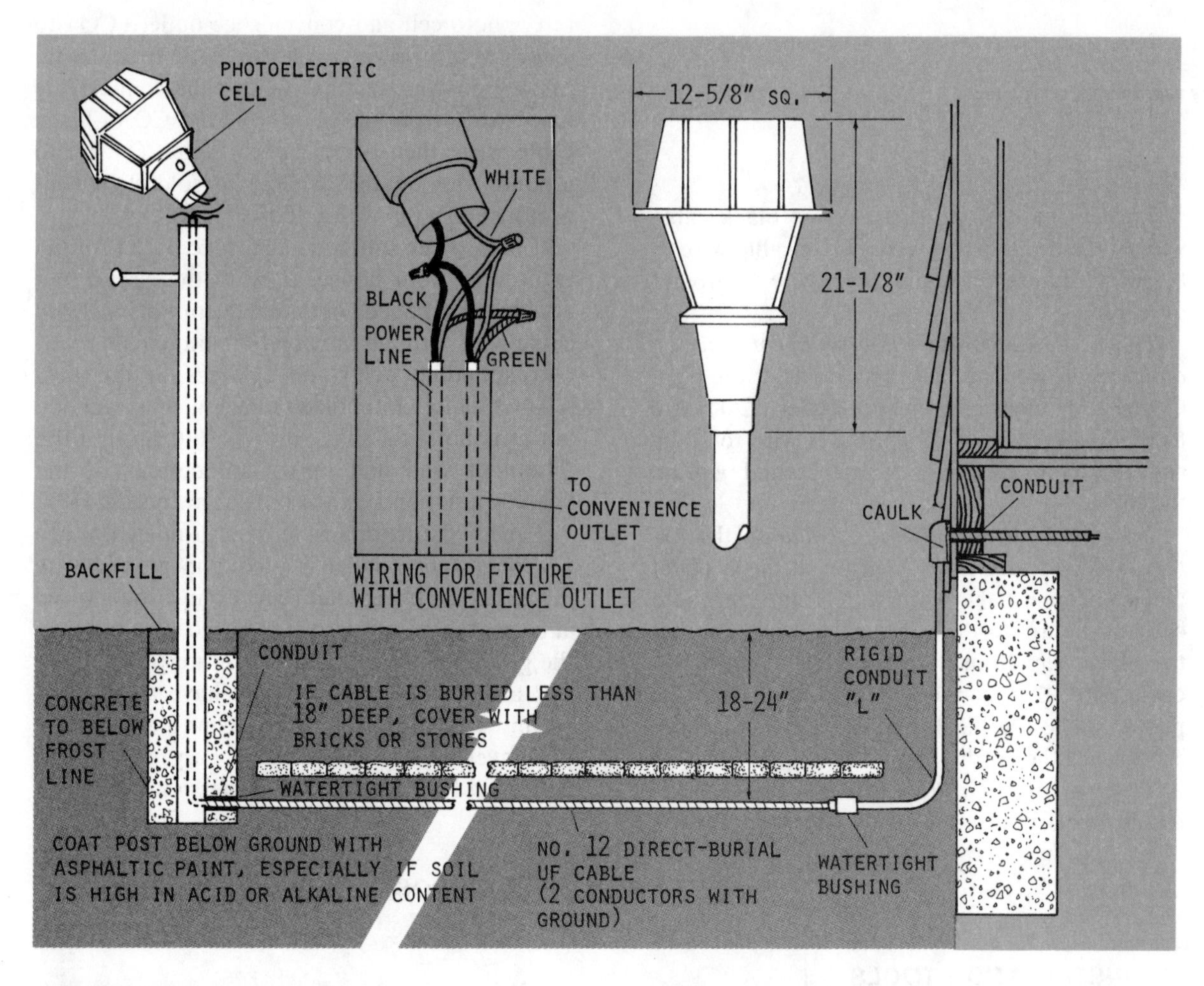

CONVERTING A standard electric post light can be as simple as removing the existing fixture head, and connecting the mercury vapor unit.

compliance. Then dig a post hole—lower than the area frost line—and a trench to the power source, following details in the diagram above. Once the cable is laid in the trench and wired through the post, place the post in the hole, plumb and secure it in both planes with rope and stakes (see page 2414). Usually a 45-lb. bag of concrete mix will fill the hole to about 6 in. below ground level. Backfill the hole and trench, and replace sod. Pull a plastic bag over the post top and seal it with tape to guard against moisture. Let concrete set 24 to 48 hours, then remove the bag and mount the fixture head by wiring as follows:

SEE ALSO

Electrical wiring . . . Extension-cord reels . . . Fluorescent lighting . . . House numbers . . . Patios . . . Testers, continuity . . . Wiring, electrical . . . Yard lighting

mercury vapor lamp, continued

To wire fixture only. Attach the black cable wire to the black fixture wire, white cable wire to the white fixture wire, and green wire to ground on cable.

To wire the outdoor, weatherproof convenience outlet to provide a plug-in receptacle at the post. Connect the black convenience-outlet (CO) wire to the black cable wire, white CO wire to white cable wire and green CO wire to ground wire on the cable.

To wire a photoelectric-cell collar to the fixture. (This device turns light on at dusk, off at dawn.) Connect the white wire from the photo cell and fixture to the white cable wire; connect the black wire from the photo cell to the black cable wire; then connect the red wire from the photo cell to the black fixture wire. Aim photo cell toward the north.

To wire a photoelectric cell, convenience outlet and fixture. Connect the white wires from the fixture, photo cell and convenience outlet (CO) to white cable wire; connect the black fixture wire to the red wire on the photo cell; connect the black wires from the photo cell and CO to black cable wire; then connect the green CO wire to ground wire on the cable. Use solderless connectors and wrap with electrical tape.

If the power source is a surface outlet on the exterior of your house, turn off the circuit and attach an L-shaped conduit to the outlet box. Pull cable wire through the conduit and connect it to corresponding color-coded wires in the outlet—white to white, black to black. If an outside outlet is not available, run conduit through the basement wall and make connections at the nearest junction box (see diagram, page 2413).

A metal fixture or post must be grounded. When no convenience outlet is used, run ground wire to fixture. With an outlet (which can also be wired at base of the post), ground the receptacle box to the ground post and fixture. A waterproof outlet box at the house entry should have an internal ground screw for ground-wire connection.

Converting a gas post light is easy, but the gas line should be capped by a professional gas-pipe installer.

INSTALLATION OF LAMP POST

KEEP POST PLUMB WITH ROPE AND STAKES WHILE CONCRETE SETS
PLUMB POST IN BOTH PLANES
POSTHOLE, 18-24" DEEP, 8" DIA.
TRENCH 18-24" DEEP FOR DIRECT BURIAL CABLE

INSTALLATION TOOLS AND MATERIALS

MATERIALS

1. No. 12 direct-burial type UF cable wire (2 conductors with ground)
2. Solderless connectors (6)
3. Plastic electrical tape
4. 45-lb. bag of dry concrete mix
5. Heavy-plastic bag (minimum 4-in. dia.)
6. Rope
7. Stakes (4)
8. L-shaped conduit
9. Conduit sleeves (2)
10. Watertight bushings (2)

TOOLS

1. Spade
2. Long-nose pliers
3. Wire stripper
4. Screwdriver

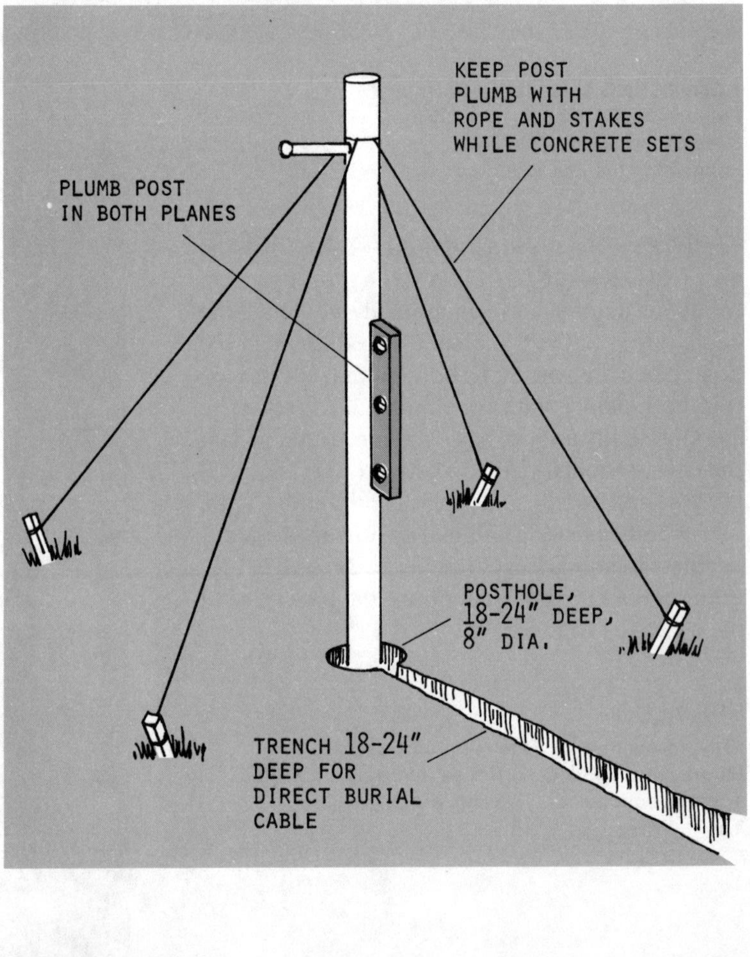

A shrubbery light for $3

By ARNOLD H. HUEHN

Add a little light to your yard with this clever inexpensive fixture made from a pie pan, a sign socket and a glass mayonnaise jar

■ AN ALUMINUM pie pan and a quart mayonnaise jar make an attractive shrubbery light.

The pie pan top is held in place by four wire braces and a metal collar. Cut the collar from 16-ga. sheet aluminum with a circle cutter on a drill press. Make holes 90° apart in both the collar and pie pan for ⅛-in. aluminum wire.

Replace the vacuum-seal jar cover with a metal disc made from a round outlet-box cover with a knockout hole in the center. Enlarge the knockout to accept a standard porcelain sign socket and solder the disc to a short piece of galvanized pipe. The disc and jar cover provide a watertight seal. Three setscrews hold the light to its 1¾-in. o.d. post. Friction tape around the top of the 30-in.-long post builds up its o.d. so it fits snugly inside the larger pipe. Use a 40-w. bulb.

For a yard light, attach the light to a 5-ft. post. In all cases, set the post in concrete and bring up ample wire inside the pipe to connect the socket. Run heavy-duty, direct-burial cable underground and wire the light to an inside switch.

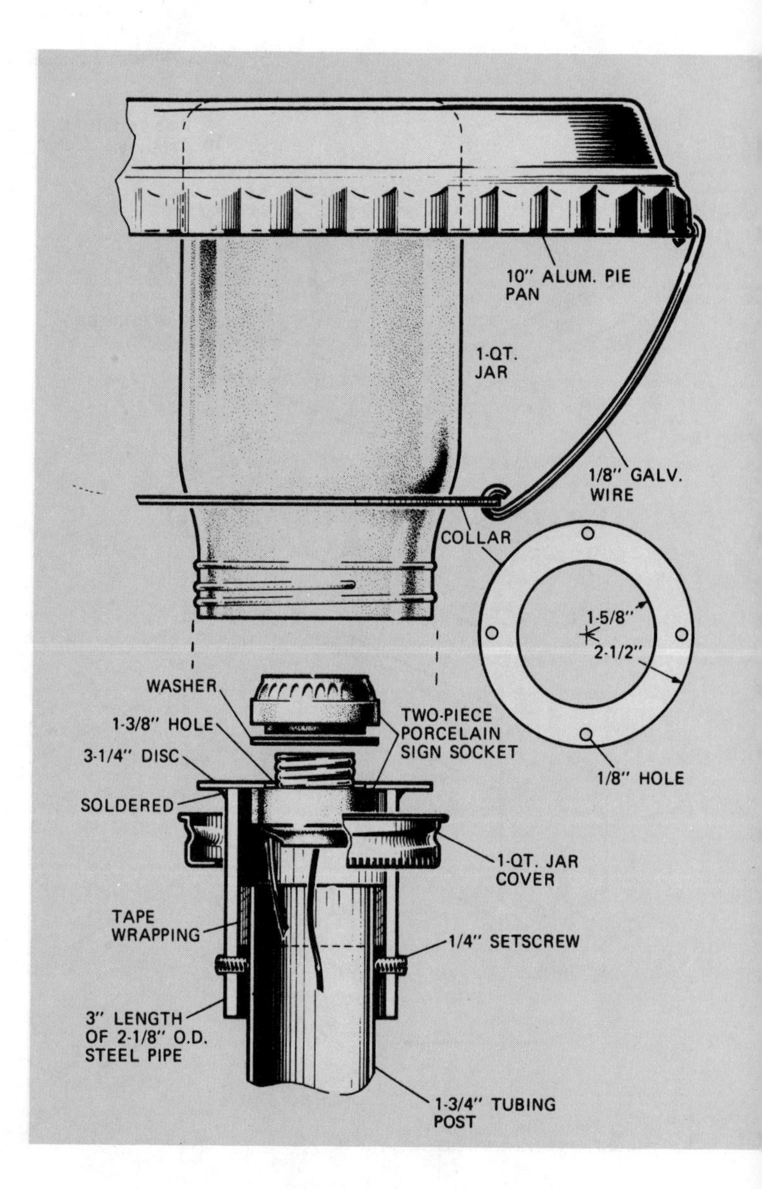

SEE ALSO

Electrical wiring . . . House numbers . . . Landscaping . . . Patios . . . Wiring, electrical . . . Yard lighting

Make your own potter's wheel

LIKE A FOREIGN LANGUAGE, such terms as "kicking," "wedging," "necking" and "throwing" are Greek to one who has yet to experience the fun of forming a hunk of clay into an attractive vase on a potter's wheel. But they soon become common parlance, and you'll know that necking in pottery means shaping the neck of a pot. I found that the best way to get started in pottery is to take lessons. The beginner can read how it's done and learn the fundamentals, but there's nothing like watching a skilled potter pull up a pot from a mass of spin-

BY SUSAN LANCASTER

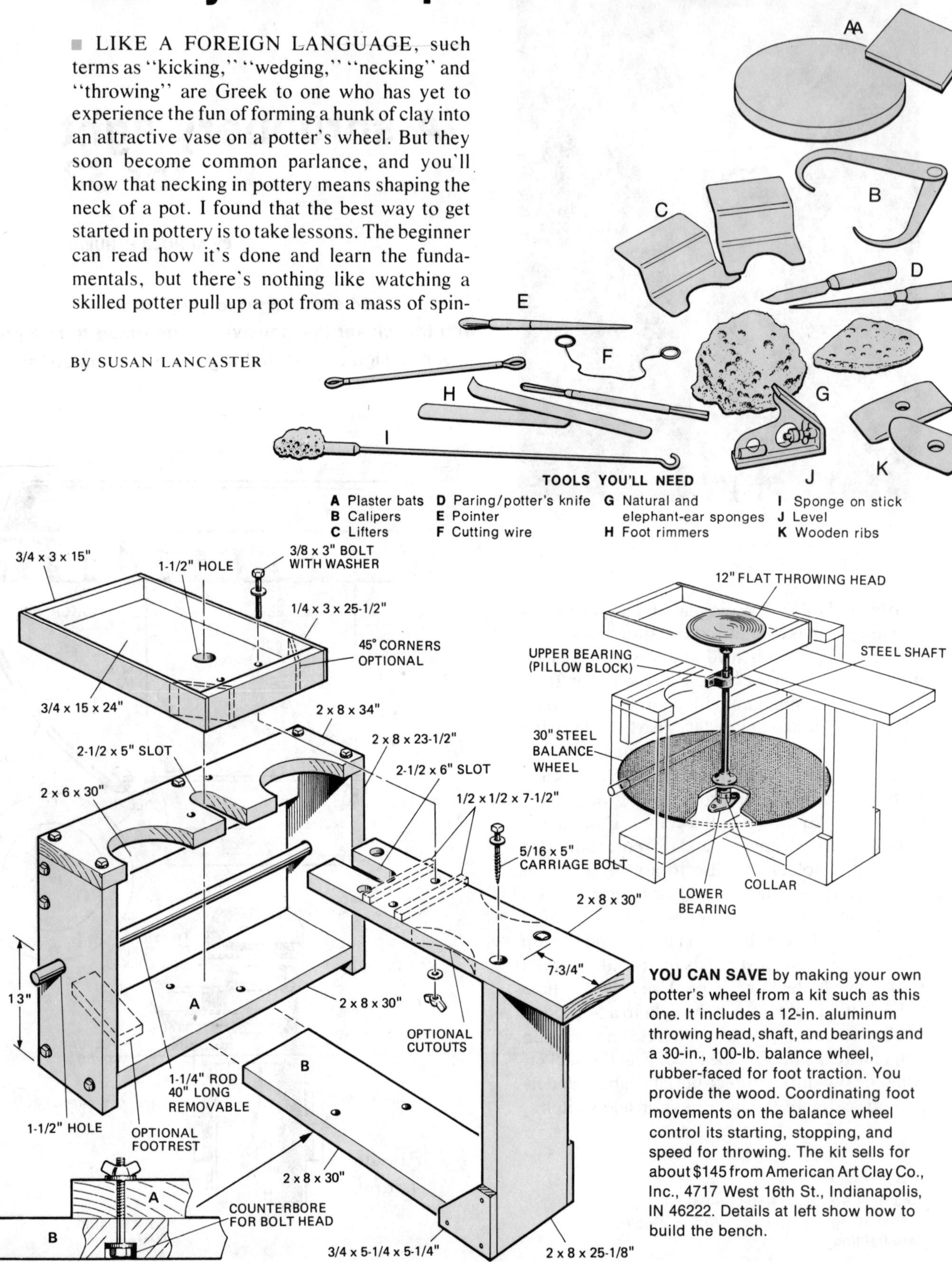

YOU CAN SAVE by making your own potter's wheel from a kit such as this one. It includes a 12-in. aluminum throwing head, shaft, and bearings and a 30-in., 100-lb. balance wheel, rubber-faced for foot traction. You provide the wood. Coordinating foot movements on the balance wheel control its starting, stopping, and speed for throwing. The kit sells for about $145 from American Art Clay Co., Inc., 4717 West 16th St., Indianapolis, IN 46222. Details at left show how to build the bench.

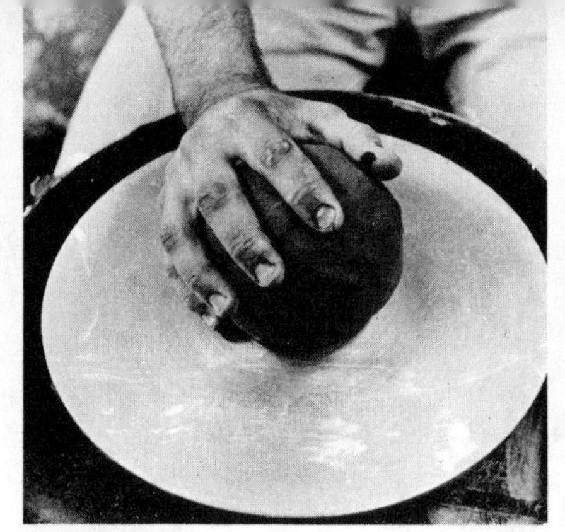

1. WEDGE clay to remove air bubbles and form two or three softball-size lumps. Then slam one lump on the center of the wheel head or on a moistened bat to make it stick firmly in place.

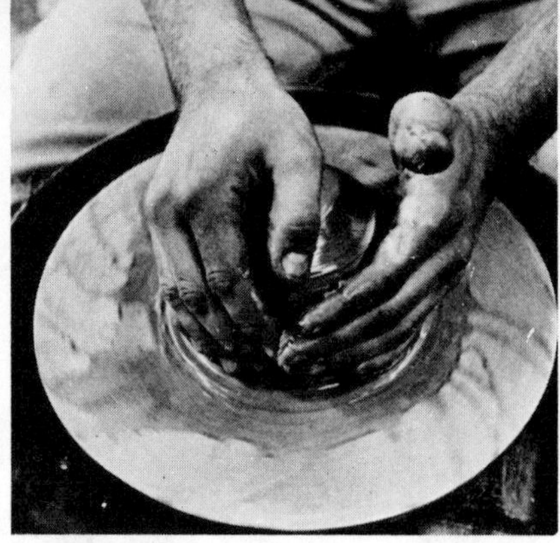

2. SET wheel in motion by kicking it forward with the right foot. When it spins remove the foot and begin working the clay ball with hands to the center of the wheel. Don't kick and shape at the same time.

3. WHEN clay is centered, open it with the thumbs, working them down slowly to about ¼ in. from the base. Steady hand control is important; brace your right elbow against your side to help.

HOW TO WEDGE CLAY

Your clay is made workable by a process called wedging. Similar to kneading dough, wedging is done before the clay is placed on the potter's wheel, a necessary step to remove air bubbles and pockets from the clay.

First your clay lump is cut in half. Then one half of it is slammed down on top of the other, with cut side out. This step is repeated many times until the pockets of air are forced from the clay, and finally the well-wedged lump is shaped into a four-sided loaf by patting the ends with the hands.

Wedging the clay is a most important step, not only in removing air bubbles but in producing uniformity of texture in the clay.

7. AS NEEDED, trim the uneven top with a pin tool to keep the clay balanced so the cylinder stays centered. Trim enough from the top so no segment is carrying an extra mass that could disturb balance.

8. CONTINUING upward pulls produce a larger cylinder with a thinner wall. As the wall thins, slow the kick-wheel speed. If the work collapses, you'll have to remove the clay and start over.

ning clay on a potter's wheel to really see how it's done. Even then, the beginner is not going to "throw" a perfect pot the very first try. Like all hobbies, it takes practice.

After the pot has been shaped, trimmed and dried, finishing it requires materials and equipment difficult for the beginning potter to assemble on his own. This is another good reason for the novice to link up with a studio. The place where you take lessons will usually let you glaze and fire your pieces for a fee even after the course is over. First the dried piece, known as green ware, is fired in a kiln, either gas or electric, until the clay takes on the characteristics of an ordinary flowerpot. It is now known as bisque and is ready for glazing. Some studios use ready-mixed glazes and some mix their own and store them in big crocks in which the pots can be dipped. After the piece is glazed, it is fired again at a very high temperature. At the studio where I work, stoneware pottery is fired to 2350°F. in a gas kiln. This final firing produces a glasslike surface and makes the pot extremely durable.

The main costs of starting in pottery are the purchase of a wheel or a kit to build one and the initial lessons. Typically, lessons cost $5 to $7 for a three-hour session and are given once a week for 10 to 14 weeks. A separate charge for clay, glazes and firing is made on top of this. However, clay is cheap—about 12 cents a pound for stoneware clay—and the tools needed by a beginner are simple and often can be found in your own home.

I started with a knife and fork from my kitchen, and a sponge (used to wet the clay while throwing) from the cosmetics section of a drugstore. I cut off the corner of an old chamois to smooth the rim of the pot after throwing it, and I found a thin but strong piece of wire in the toolbox to cut the pot off the wheel head. You do have to buy trimming tools to finish the bottoms of your pieces after they become partially dry—"leather-hard" is the term potters use. These tools are available at most art supply stores.

4. START FORMING your cylinder by pulling the clay upward with your thumbs. Use little pressure with the hands. Each upward pull will gradually thin the clay wall and make the cylinder taller.

5. FOR BETTER control, join your hands whenever possible, locking the thumbs together or resting the left thumb on the right hand. Place and remove your hands slowly so you don't move the clay.

6. CYLINDERS tend to flare out at the top; they must be closed in by necking. Cup your hands around the cylinder center—a maneuver that makes the wall thicken and, gradually, rise straight.

9. USE A taut wire to cut work free of the wheel head after trimming excess clay from the base with a wooden tool. Put the wire under the base and pull. If the work is on a bat, just lift it from the wheel.

10. IF NO BAT was used and the work thrown on the wheel head itself, slide the work gently, after cutting it free, onto a board or plaster bat and let it dry until it's ready for glazing and firing.

RECOMMENDED BOOKS

There are many books that are helpful to the beginning potter. Here are two suggestions:

The Complete Book of Pottery Making by John B. Kenny, Chilton Book Co., Philadelphia, publisher; $4.95

Throwing on the Potter's Wheel by Thomas Sellers. Professional Publications, Columbus, Ohio, publisher; $4

For the more advanced potter:

Pottery, the Technique of Throwing by John Colbeck. Watson-Guptill, Inc., New York, N.Y., publisher; $10.

Clay and Glazes for the Potter by Daniel Rhodes. Chilton Book Co., Philadelphia, Pa., publisher; $12.50.

Step by Step Ceramics by Jolyon Hofsted. Golden Press, Inc., New York, N.Y.; $2.95.

Later on I made some plaster bats—solid, dish-shaped slabs that you attach to the wheel head when throwing a pot and remove to let the pot dry. The plaster for making bats can be purchased from a hardware store, and pieplates make good molds.

Firing charges can be rather high, especially if you make big pieces. The rate might be $1 a pound at a commercial art center, somewhat less at an adult education center. This fee covers the cost of both firings and the use of the glazes. When you are more experienced, you can cut these costs by purchasing your own kiln and mixing or buying your own glazes. Although some people feel the gas kiln produces a more beautiful and subtle glaze, many find the electric kiln, with its more evenly distributed heat, provides more predictable results. Electric kilns range in price from $250 to $500 and portable gas kilns from $200 to $600.

For the beginner, however, developing skill on the wheel will be the primary concern. The accompanying pictures demonstrate the steps in forming the basic cylinder from which most shapes are made. It is useful to have such pictures to refer back to again and again as you work. But pictures and books can only go so far and a complete beginner will find it hard to learn without some instruction from a teacher.

For instance, the very first step in making a pot—kneading, cutting and pounding the clay to eliminate air bubbles and produce a uniform texture—is hard to pick up on your own. "Wedging," as the process is called, is most easily understood by watching a demonstration. Later, when your pot disintegrates in a soggy pile on the wheel head for the fifth time in a row, perhaps the teacher can tell you the one small thing you were doing wrong so that it won't happen again. It will be a while before the pot you see in your mind will be the one you end up with. But in time it will come and you will get great satisfaction from turning out handsome and useful things on your potter's wheel.

Build a power hacksaw from washing-machine parts

By BRADFORD DITTMER

In this ingenious adaptation, the back-and-forth mechanism of a discarded impeller-type washing machine pushes a saw instead of an agitator

SEE ALSO

**Arbor presses . . . Cutoff machines . . .
Hydraulic presses . . . Lead ladles . . . Machining . . .
Metal casting . . . Motors, shop . . .
Power-tool stands . . . Sheet metal . . . Torches**

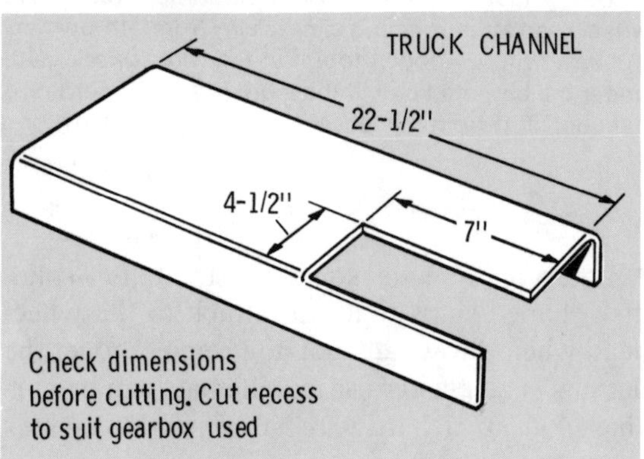

FOR ACCURACY, make a test stand using wood before cutting recess in the truck channel.

GEARBOX IS MOUNTED using ½-in. stock, washers and pins. First, test dimensions on wood base.

MOTOR IS MOUNTED on existing bolts on gearbox. Plate fastens to an angle to receive motor.

60-TOOTH GEAR is mounted on driveshaft against collar. Key parts line up on this gear's center line.

BRASS PLATE extended down one leg provides way to attach rack, takes springiness out of leg.

READY TO GO, saw includes counterweight added to outboard end of saw guide.

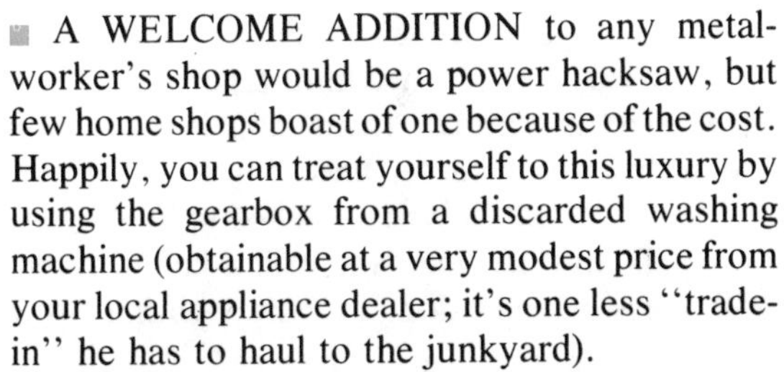

A WELCOME ADDITION to any metal-worker's shop would be a power hacksaw, but few home shops boast of one because of the cost. Happily, you can treat yourself to this luxury by using the gearbox from a discarded washing machine (obtainable at a very modest price from your local appliance dealer; it's one less "trade-in" he has to haul to the junkyard).

Though any make of washer having a back-and-forth impeller movement can be used with the rack-and-gear method to drive the saw, I used a Sears Kenmore. The gearbox has built-in gear reduction, existing lugs for attaching a motor mount and saw guides, plus a 7-in. driving pulley. Half of the housing is gray iron casting, the remainder die-cast of a light-weight alloy.

Two changes were necessary: A hole had to be reamed in the large lug on the underside of the iron casting to accommodate the ½-in. rod on which the motor rides in the base, and the impeller shaft had to be shortened about 8 in.

perfect cutting speed

If you slip a 16-pitch, 60-tooth gear over this ¾-in. shaft and drive the 7-in. pulley with a ¼-hp, 1725-rpm motor rigged with a 2-in. pulley, you get just about perfect cutting speed—72 strokes per minute. Stroke length is about 6¼ in.

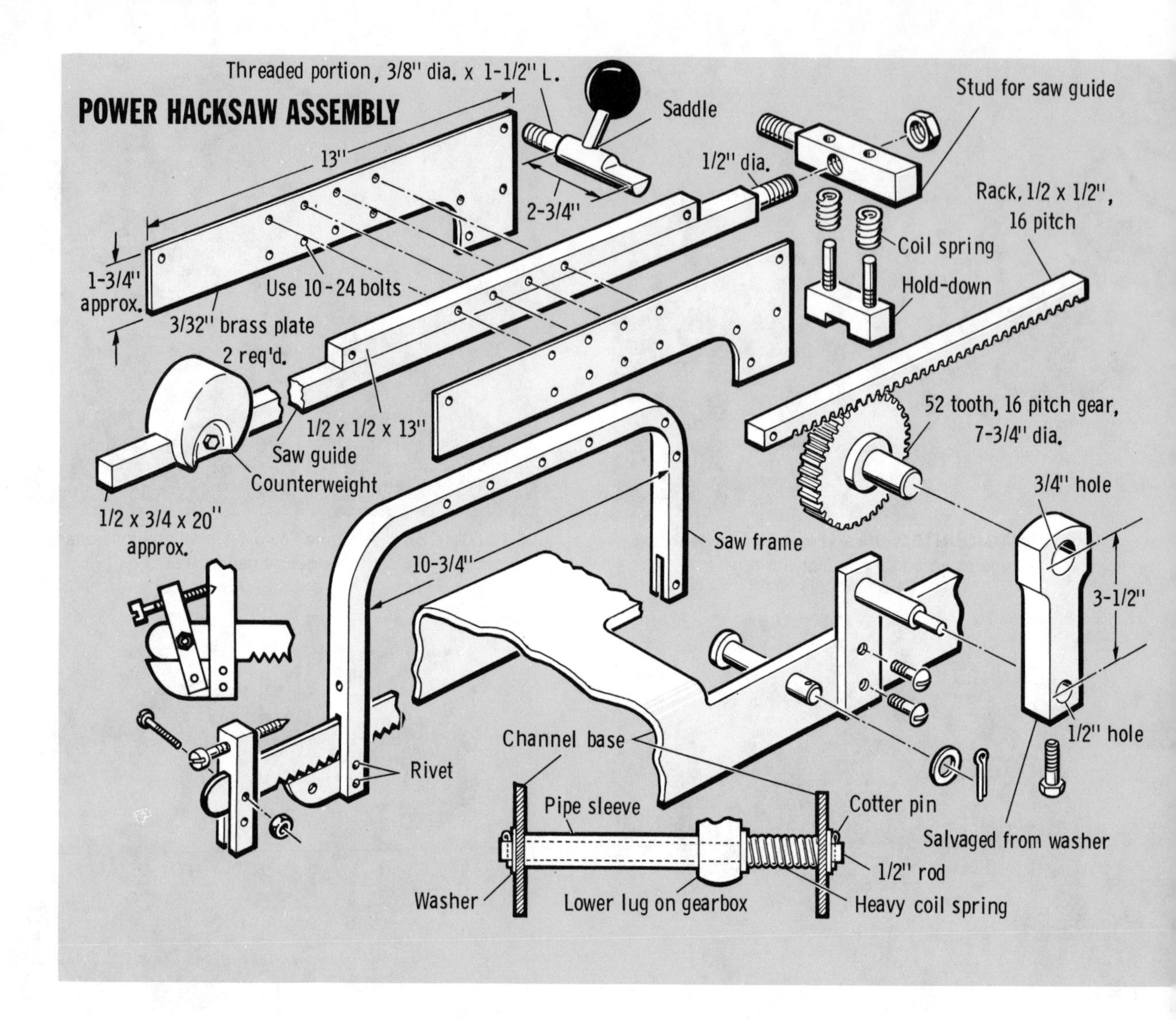

Of cold-rolled stock, the saw frame is made simply by heating and bending it, using a wood template. Slots to cradle the blade are hand-sawed with a hacksaw. They're cut to accommodate the 12-in. power-hacksaw blades that are sold by Sears.

Since the saw operates smoother if the flat surface contacting the saw guides is long, use a straightedge along the top of the frame after bending. Place the blade so it will operate as a drag saw.

trial-and-error base

Make a trial-and-error wood base for setting up the machine. Use about 30 in. of 2x8 stock and saw out the recess as shown. About 2½ in. back from the forward end of the recess and 1 in. down from the top surface, drill a ½-in. hole across the recess.

Next, mount the gearbox on a rod inserted across this recess. Block up the back of the box, set it in position, fit and assemble the rest of the fixtures. This done, you can then determine the measurements that you will need to build the permanent stand.

Place the gear on the driveshaft tight against the collar and fasten it with a taper pin. When assembled, all parts on the mechanism are lined up on this gear's center line.

The brass hold-down is notched to fit over the rack. Clamp it in place and drill a hole through both parts on each side of the rack with a No. 7 drill.

sliding fit

Next, tap ¼-20 threads and insert ¼-in. bolts in the holes and saw off the heads about 1¼ in. above the stock. If necessary, enlarge the holes in the stud to assure an easy sliding fit. The

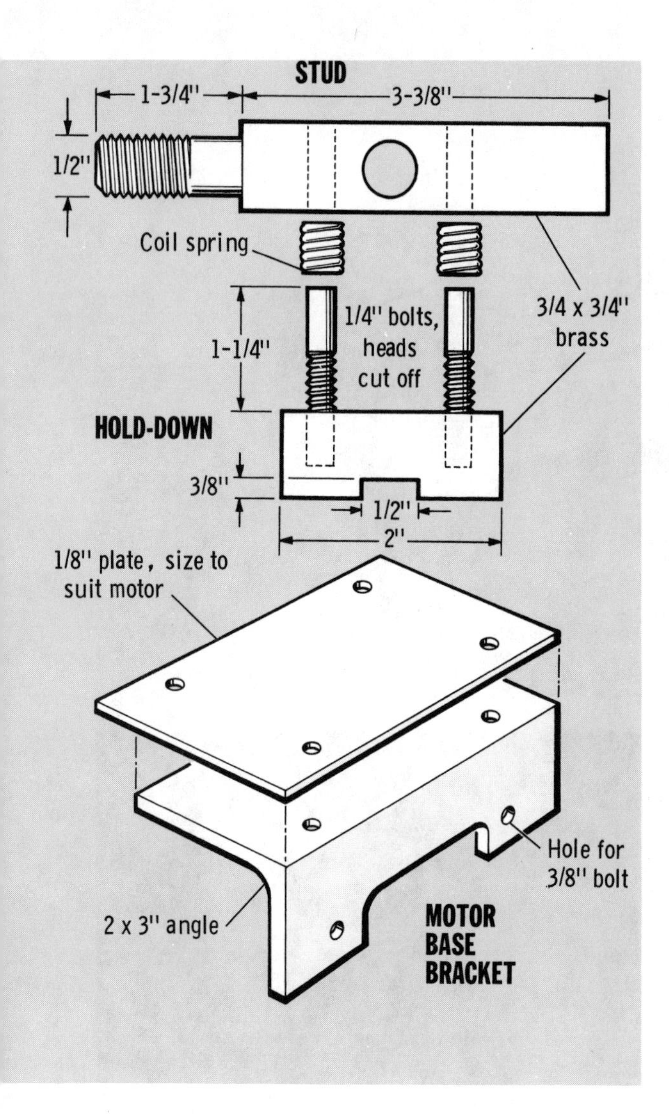

springs slipped over the studs should be of a suitable length to maintain a moderate down pressure on the rack.

To make the saddle, saw out a half-round section under the saw guide. This allows the saw to swing down far enough to finish the cut. Fit this part with a suitable handle for turning to up and down positions. Since the saw operates when the saddle is in any position, there is no need for an extra switch to stop the saw automatically after the cut.

The part salvaged from the washing machine (see drawing) is slipped over the small end over the ½-in. stud. The bronze, brushed end goes over the gear shaft to act as an outside bearing. Finally, add a ⅜-in. setscrew to hold it securely on the ½-in. stud.

Run the saw out to the end of the forward stroke. The face of the rear vise jaw should be set ½ in. ahead of the rear leg of the saw. The saw guide should be level when the blade is about ¾ in. above the floor of the vise. And, when the saw guide is level, the rack should be parallel.

When you have the rig checked out, use the measurements from your temporary setup to make the permanent one.

The base shown was made from 8-in. truck channel. (That explains those unused holes.) The legs are of light channel with the lower ends heated and bent to serve as feet.

setting the gearbox

To set the gearbox, drill holes for the ½-in. rod square with the sides of the channel and parallel to the top surface. Set the gearbox on the rod, block it in its final position and cut a pipe sleeve to fit over the rod between the lug and the far side of the channel. On the near side of the rod, place a stiff spring and use washers if necessary to hold the box in position.

Drill a ½-in. hole in a short piece of ¼ x 1¼-in. stock, and slip the hole over the ½-in. stud. Tip the gearbox to its vertical position, clamp the piece to the channel flange and drill for two ¼-in. bolts. If the spring on the rod is tight, your gearbox is set.

The motor-base bracket is cut from 1½ x 2½-in. angle to fit over two existing lugs on the back of the gearbox. Drill the bracket so it can be bolted onto the lugs with ⅜-in. bolts. Since the 2½-in. face is not wide enough to accommodate the motor base, use a plate—the size of the motor base—between the motor and the bracket. *Caution:* Be sure you set the motor so that the pulley is clear of the rack path on the back stroke.

construction tips

It's easier to assemble the saw sliding mechanism if you clamp the saw, saw guide and top slide together. The brass plates can then be clamped in place and holes bored for 10-24 bolts to hold the unit together. After removing the clamps, bore the remaining holes.

When using shims to insure a free-sliding fit, my experience has been that there is too much play when the shims are removed. Thus, I simply tightened the bolts to allow a free slide. It's not a must to use a 60-tooth, 16-pitch gear; a smaller gear—down to 50-tooth—can be used, but it will shorten the saw stroke.

Lengths of cold-rolled stock can be picked up at a local machine shop. If you have difficulty getting the gear and rack, write to Chicago Gear Works, 440 N. Oakley Blvd., Chicago, IL 60612.

Get more from your power hacksaw

By PARRY C. YOB

It's unquestionably a handy machine. Here are tips that will solve tough problems and make it even handier, plus safety and maintenance suggestions

■ YOUR DECISION to tackle a metal-working project—or *not* to tackle it—may often be based on the amount of time it takes to cut stock to length even before you begin machining or welding. Torch cutting is fast, but can cause poor fits. And a torch can't be used for such metals as brass, bronze or stainless steel.

SEE ALSO

**Arbor presses . . . Cutoff machines . . .
Hydraulic presses . . . Lead ladles . . . Machining . . .
Metal casting . . . Motors, shop . . .
Power-tool stands . . . Sheet metal . . . Torches**

WORK SUPPORT STAND is made of ¾-in. pine and built to a comfortable working height. Slots in the sides make it adjustable to particular tasks.

T-SHAPED SUPPORT speeds work by insuring prompt termination of cut. Support is bolted to permit its removal when you need to cut odd-shaped workpieces.

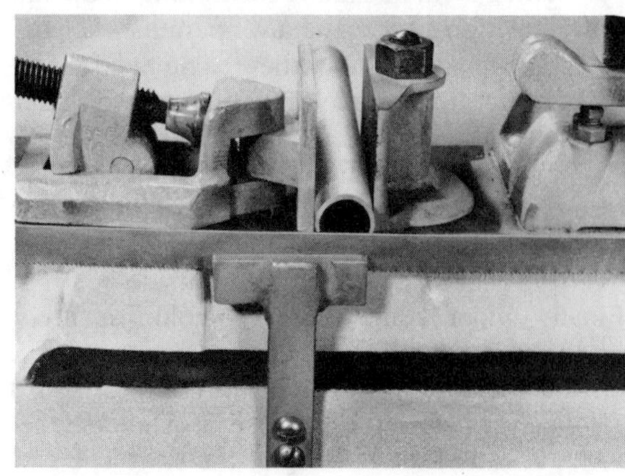

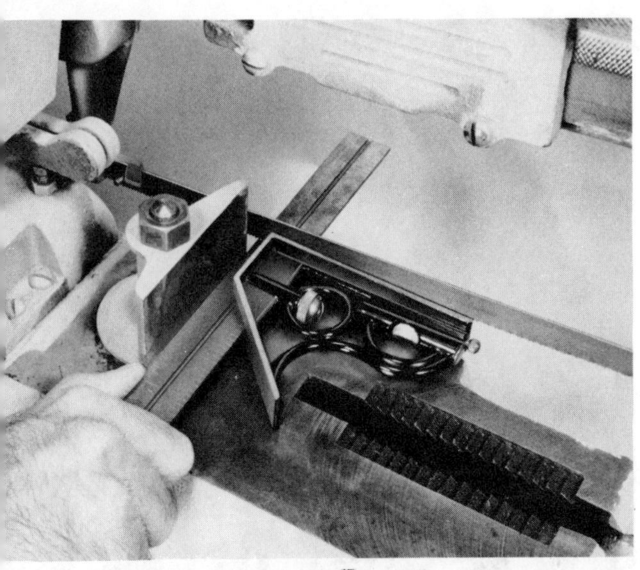

USE A SQUARE to check fixed-jaw adjustment on the saw vise. Remove the clamping jaw to make job easy.

METAL SHIM, properly placed, will keep blade from wandering. Without it, saw can drift ½ in. or more.

TO CUT SEVERAL PIECES from same-width stock, use block between jaw and work to distribute wear.

SHORT PIECES are held more securely in vise if you make a jack to spread, and keep jaws parallel.

The obvious alternative is a power hacksaw; I feel that the most satisfactory type is a small drag-cut machine. Although slower than the band type, its lower initial cost and cheaper blade cost make it attractive for home shop. Also, its automatic shutoff feature allows you to do something else while the machine is making a time-consuming cut.

To get the maximum from your power hacksaw, proper setup and maintenance are essential. For best performance, the saw and motor should be mounted on a suitable low base. Don't make the mistake of using a high, unstable stand and do allow at least two feet of space from the wall, or you will be moving the saw every time you need to cut a long piece.

The automatic shutoff works well when properly adjusted, but toward the end of the cut, the unsupported piece will bend downward, allowing the blade to cut into the face of the work. When the saw is unattended, the cut may run lengthwise of the bar for as much as a quarter of an inch before the piece falls free or the blade breaks. A simple T-shaped support, attached outboard of the saw blade, will prevent the sagging piece from working its way beneath the blade.

When cutting long pieces, it is convenient to have at least one work support stand of the type shown. The height of the uprights should be about an inch less than the distance from the floor to the bottom of the saw vise. The Vs in the

SMALL WOODEN FORM lets you mount an irregular piece in plaster cement. Coat part with grease first.

HELD SECURELY in cement casting, a difficult piece is easily cut. Cement cracks away with hammer taps.

adjustable pieces are cut at 60° to hold round or hexagonal stock. The ends can be reversed to provide support for flat or rectangular bar stock. A roller dolly may be used, but it can be a hazard unless clamps are provided to avoid movement and damage to the saw. The support shown here should always be placed near the point of balance.

Dos and don'ts. Except for making sure that the gibs and bearings are snug, adjustments for slanting cuts should never be attempted on the saw mechanism. Such adjustments would be futile, and could damage the machine.

Several factors control blade life. The first is the use of proper tooth spacing. It pays to follow the manufacturer's recommendations on this point. Never start a new blade in an old cut. Start a new cut to avoid losing the "set" of the teeth.

Workholding forms. Place equal volumes of plaster of Paris and common Portland cement on a piece of newspaper. Roll from corner to corner to mix, and break up any lumps. Place the dry mixture in a tin can, and mix with water to about the thickness of mayonnaise. Using a spatula or putty knife, pack the wet cement around the metal set in the form to fill the box. Allow the material to set for about 45 minutes. Then, remove the form-holding strings (see photo) and clamp the whole box in the saw vise as shown. The cement will have sufficient strength to hold the piece during the cut. When the cut is completed, spread the sides of the box near the top, and remove the plaster block. The box (form) may be retained for future work, and the plaster block will crack under light hammer taps.

Finally, if you plan to leave the area while the saw is in operation, additional precautions should be taken with the belt and motor pulley. If the belt is loose, a slight sticking of the blade may stop the saw, and the friction of the small motor pulley will frequently set fire to the belt. If you leave the room, you will have no chance to stop the motor before this happens. If the motor pulley becomes worn and polished to the point where slipping occurs, it should be replaced. Belts should be kept in good condition and tight.

With attention to the procedures outlined above, your experience with your power hacksaw should be safe and satisfying. The more you use this handy tool, the more uses you are likely to find for it and the more adept you will become.

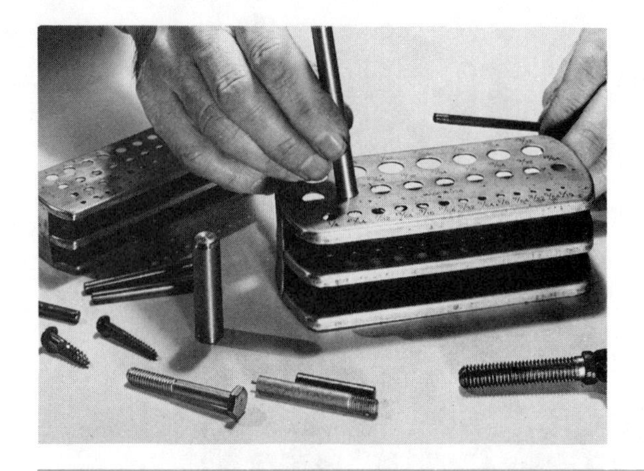

TO MEASURE the diameter of a rod, wire, bolt or screw shank when you don't have a regular caliper, try using your drill-bit stand. The holes are conveniently marked in fractions or decimals from about 1/16 to 1/2 in. Letter-type drill stands can also be used, but an equivalent table (in most shop handbooks) is needed to convert the letter to a decimal.—*Andrew Vena.*

TO REMOVE a number of fine scratches from a clear plastic box, a bit of liquid brass polish can't be beat. Simply charge a clean cloth pad with the polish and rub the scratched area with gentle strokes for a minute or two. Then use another clean cloth to remove excess polish and bring out the shine. Various other materials of a mildly abrasive nature can be used. However, try them on a piece of scrap, or on an area that will be hidden, before coating the entire object.—*Walter E. Burton.*

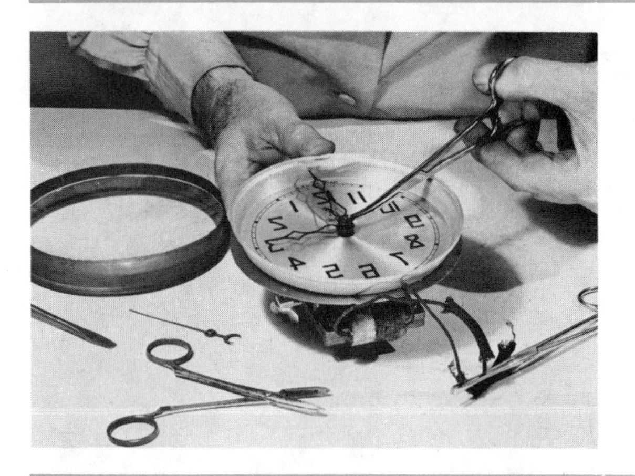

HEMOSTATS ARE INSTRUMENTS normally used in surgery to clamp blood vessels, but their quick-release, quick-clamping action can be extremely handy in a shop as well. They look like a combination between pliers and scissors, and usually have two or three locking notches as part of the handle. Thus, they are particularly useful as heat sinks, soldering clamps, or third hands, especially when working with tiny screws and nuts.—*Walter E. Burton*

A PARTIALLY EMPTY oil can may become contaminated if left uncovered around the home or shop. Most homeowners are faced with this potential problem if they use mowers, chain saws and other gasoline-powered tools. One solution is to cover the oil can with the plastic lid from a one-pound coffee can. The lid fits a quart-sized oil can snugly, keeps the oil clean and is easy to snap on and off as needed.—*William H. Kauffman.*

Stands for your power tools

By JACKSON HAND

There's valuable space going to waste under your power tools. Put it to work with these easy-to-build cabinets

SEE ALSO
Bandsaws . . . Bench saws . . . Drawers . . . Drill presses . . . Drill-press accessories . . . Drill-press techniques . . . Jigsaws . . . Motors, shop . . . Plywood . . . Table saws . . . Workbenches

■ The four cabinet-style bases shown here have an expensive look, but actually were made at an average cost of about $30 each for plywood, nails, glue, paint and a set of husky casters.

Each of these tool stands was made of sheathing-grade plywood, which is a couple dollars cheaper per sheet than A-D plywood. The rough surface of the sheathing makes little difference, but if you like things a little smoother, use A-D plywood.

To capitalize on the 4 x 8-ft. sheet, dimensions are kept at 12, 16, 24 and 32 in. when possible. Actually these dimensions are minus half the width of a saw kerf so that a sheet will cut up, for instance, into three pieces a shy 16 in. wide.

Nails and glue are used throughout, except for fastening the drawer dividers and glides to the sidewalls of the drill-press unit. These are screwed and glued. Since there is a back (or a divider as in the case of the bandsaw base) to prevent the unit from racking, nail-and-glue assembly is sufficiently strong. Quarter-inch ply-

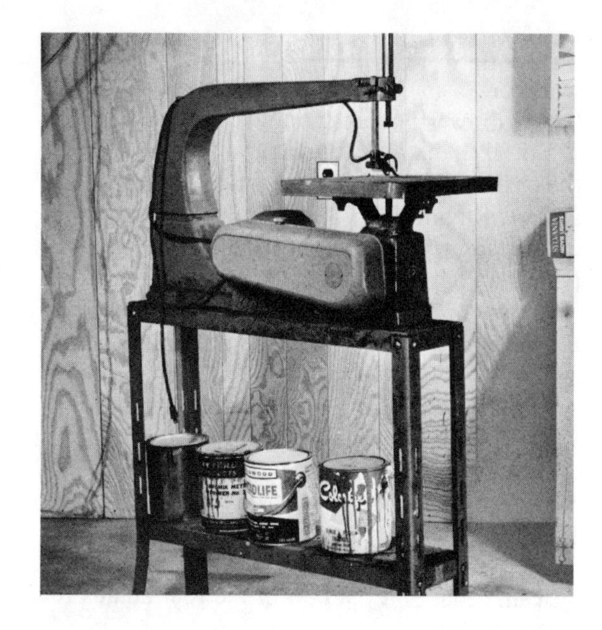

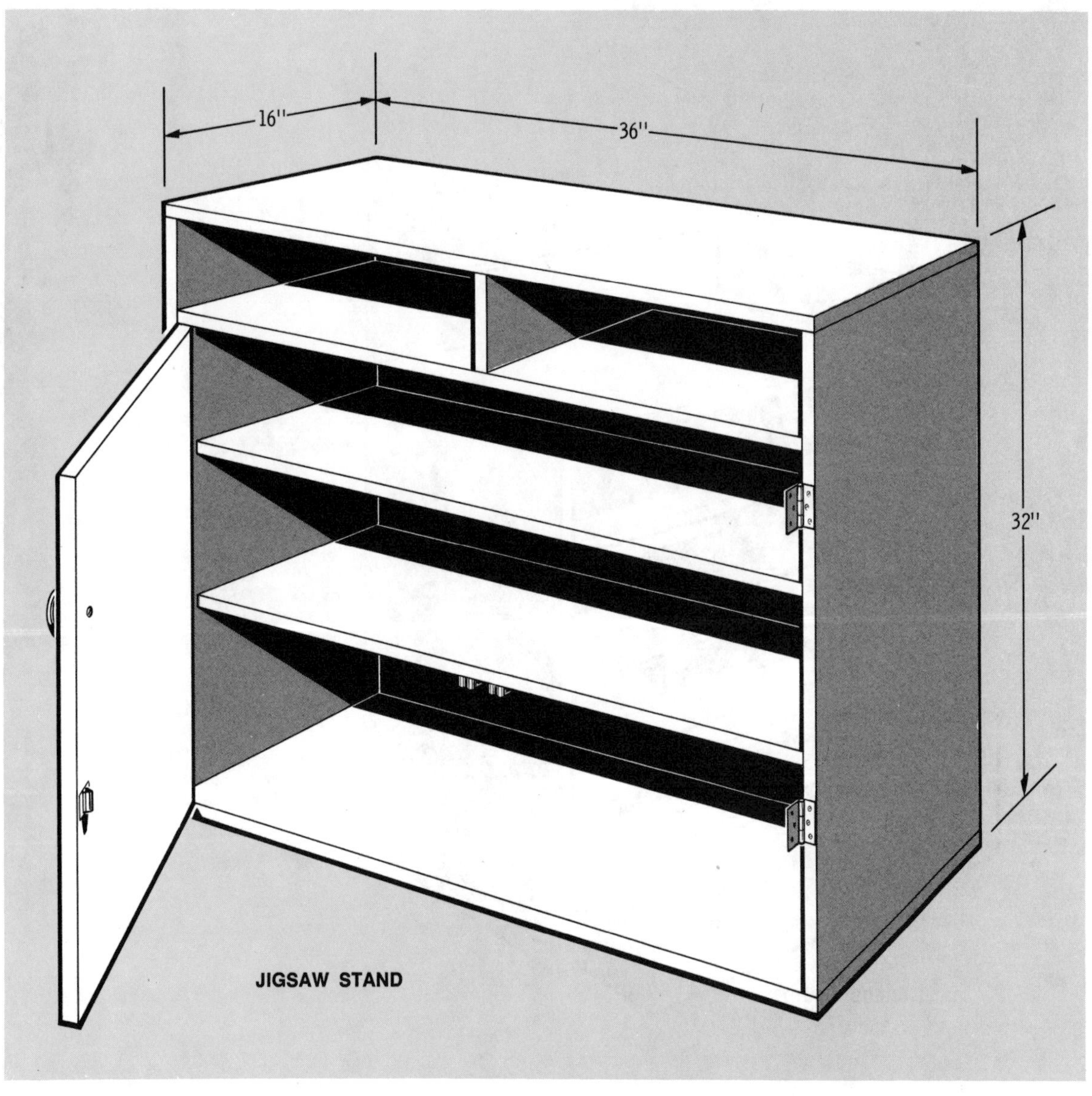

tool-cabinet designs, continued

wood or 1/8-in. hardboard work best for cabinet backs, drawer bottoms and dividers.

You'll thank yourself for going whole hog on the casters. If they are big enough (2-in. wheels) and well made, you'll roll tools around a concrete floor with ease. Cheap, small casters roll poorly and are blocked by the smallest sliver on the floor. For your guidance, the casters used on all the tools except the saw-jointer unit are Bassick No. 9706G-OC. The same casters were selected for the saw-jointer's cabinet-stand, but with a 2½-in. wheel.

The drill-press base is largely a "set" design for its use and its shape. You need a work surface beside a drill press for handy handling of the materials you use. The front-to-back depth (24 in.) makes it the best of the four stands for

HUSKY SWIVEL casters let stands roll easily over floor debris. Use sheet-metal screws to attach them.

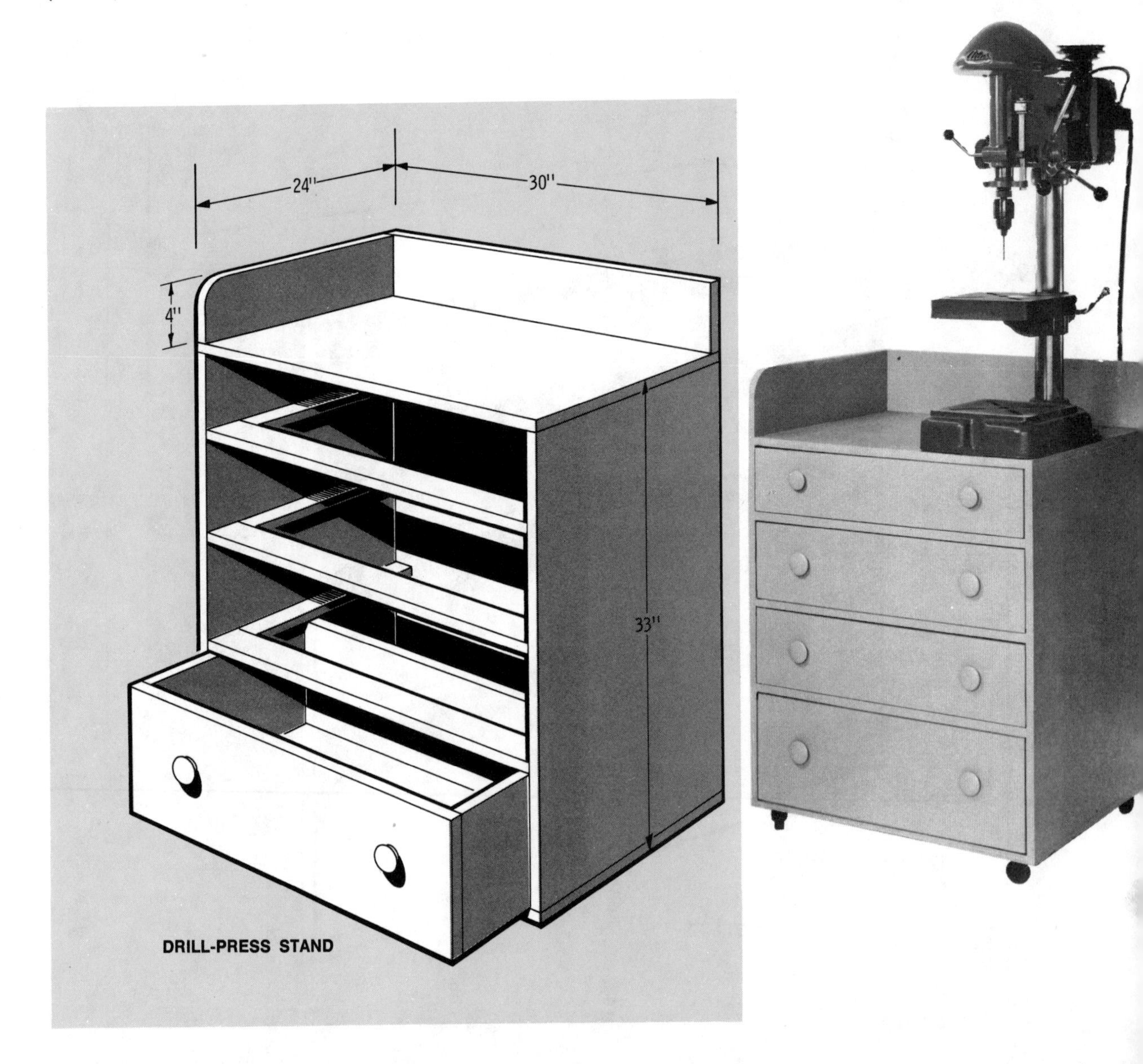

DRILL-PRESS STAND

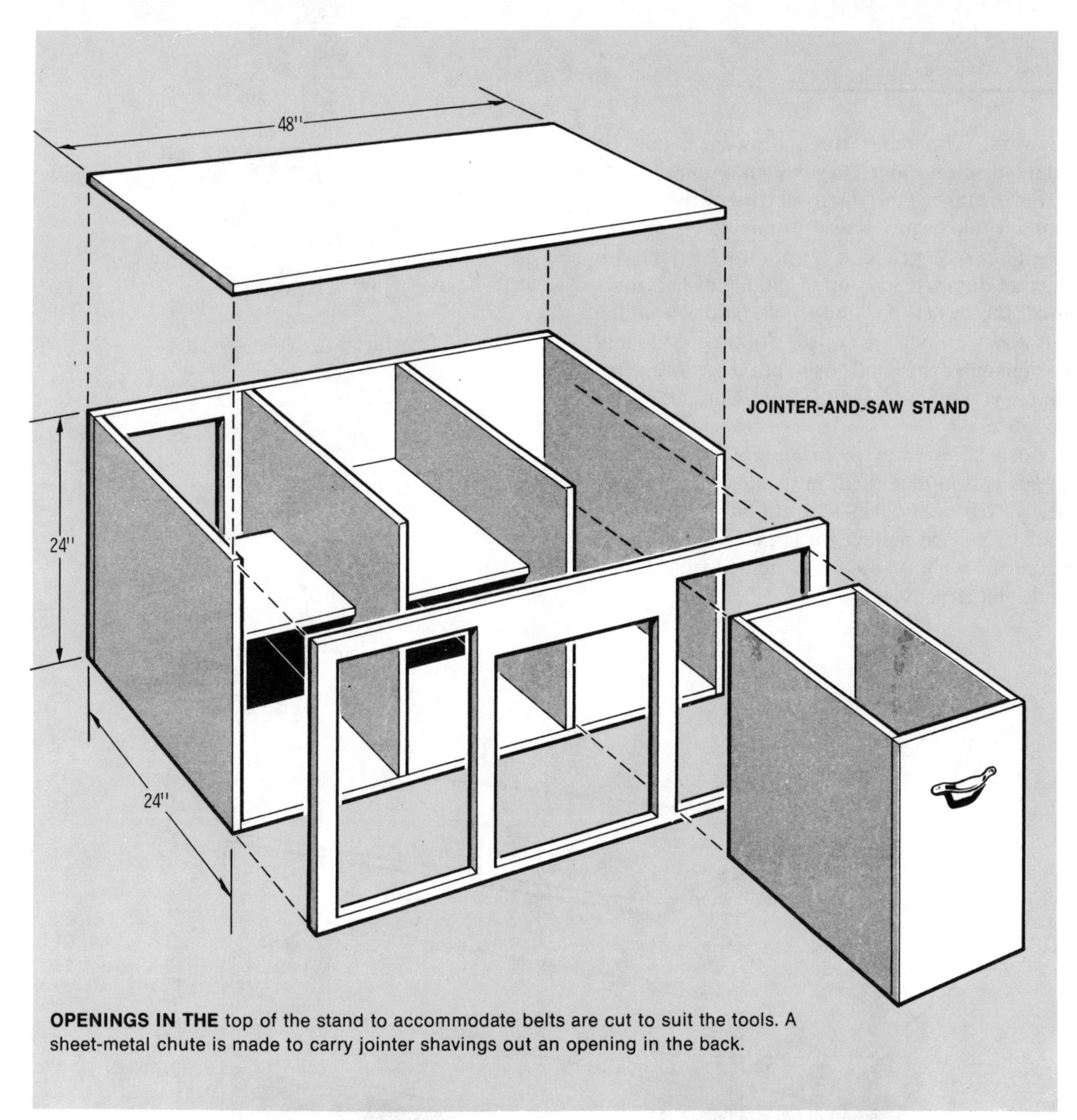

OPENINGS IN THE top of the stand to accommodate belts are cut to suit the tools. A sheet-metal chute is made to carry jointer shavings out an opening in the back.

YOUR SAW AND jointer should be side by side on a single stand. This one has storage, a sawdust bin, and a jointer chute.

JOINTER MOTOR on a hinged shelf adjusts the belt tension.

tool-cabinet designs, continued

drawers. The other three, however, can be adapted or intermixed to suit your requirements.

For instance, the open shelves of the jigsaw stand would be just as useful under the bandsaw. Or, let's say you don't want to bother with cabinet doors. Then you install plain shelf units in all the bases. As another variation, you can put doors on one side of the double-faced shelf design under the bandsaw to provide storage for things you want to shelter from workshop dust and dirt.

Got a lathe? A perfect stand for it would be a three-section modification of the jigsaw stand. Make it 5 ft. long (20 in. to a section) and the open shelves will be perfect for lathe tools. You can get at them, but they are protected from burial under lathe shavings.

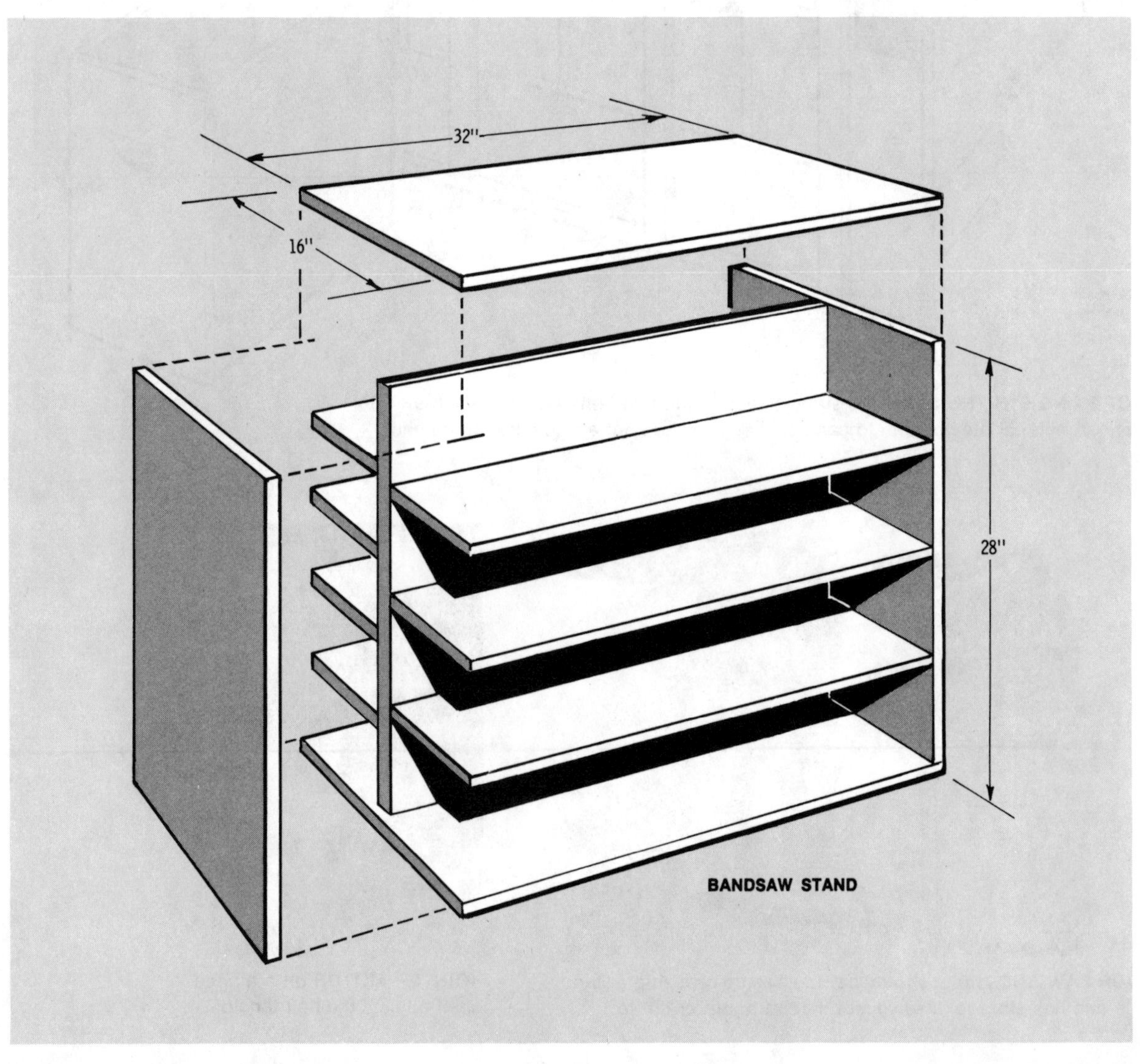

BANDSAW STAND

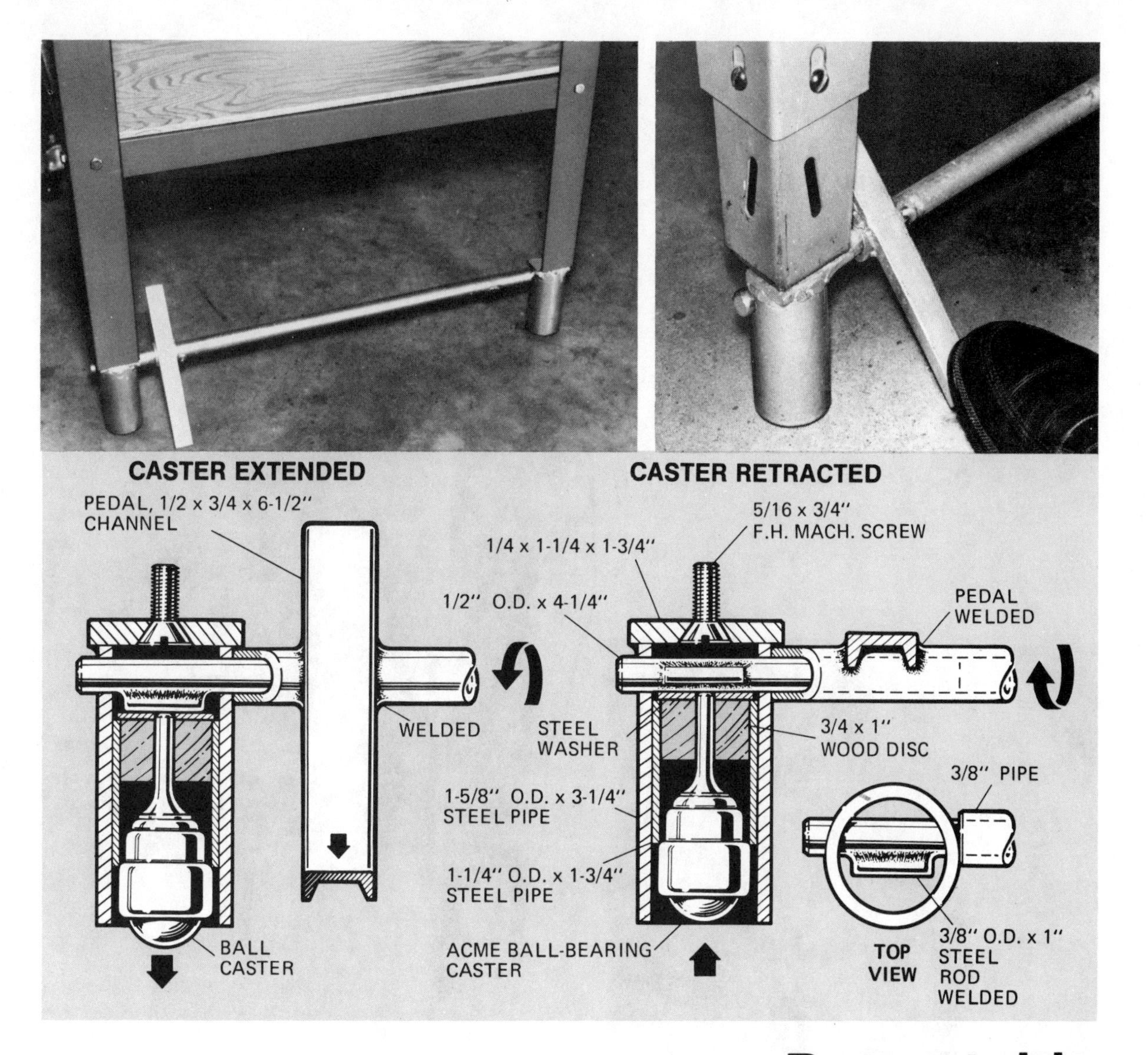

Retractable casters for your tool stands

By WILLIAM G. WAGGONER

■ TIRED OF PUSHING, shoving and groaning every time a piece of shop equipment needs moving across the room? Then picture yourself depressing a foot pedal and rolling the tool effortlessly. By making the retractable-type caster set shown in the drawings above, you can enjoy such shop convenience. When the lever is depressed, the ball casters are forced out of their sockets and locked in a ready-to-roll position. This retractable caster is easy to make—there is no machining called for, yet it's quick-acting and positive. And, as shown in the photos, one pedal activates the pair of casters. Basically, the idea is simply a fit of 1-in. pipe into 1¼-in. pipe, and the use of a 1-in.-dia. ball caster which seats neatly into the smaller pipe. The trade name of the caster used is Acme. While one set of casters is adequate for a radial or table saw it's best to have a caster on each leg of the stand to save your back.

SEE ALSO
Bandsaws . . . Bench saws . . . Drill presses . . . Motors, shop . . . Power hacksaws . . . Radial-arm saws . . . Shapers . . . Table saws . . . Workbenches . . . Workshops

Roll-away stand holds router and drill

By PAUL D. FIEBICH

Since it is on wheels, you can take this handy unit right to the job. In addition to holding a portable drill stand and router table, the cabinet features a sawdust chute and storage space

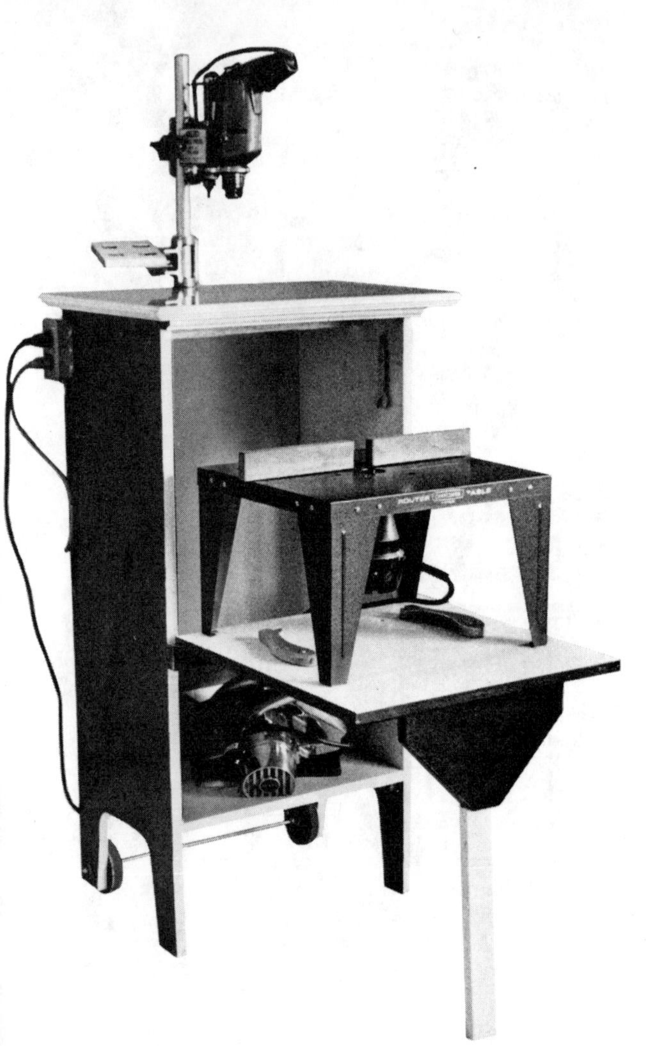

THE WHEELS on the rear legs of the unit let you roll this mini-workshop to the job or stow it away in a corner when you want it out of the way. It's just the thing for a handyman with limited space.

STEEL ROUTER table, bolted to a hinged shelf, converts router into a handy shaper. The table retracts and stores in the cabinet when you use drill.

SEE ALSO
Belt sanders . . . Circular saws, portable . . . Drills, portable . . . Pad sanders . . . Routers . . . Routers, accessories . . . Workbenches

DESIGNED SO YOU can wheel it about like a hand truck, this compact tool cabinet provides a dandy place to mount a portable-drill stand and a portable router table. What's more, there is an open shelf below where you can store a sabre saw, circular saw and finishing sander. For the man whose "workshop" consists mainly of portable electric tools, you won't find a handier setup anywhere.

Bolted to a shelf, the router table retracts into the cabinet when the shelf and supporting leg are swung upward, and a built-in sheet-metal chute funnels wood chips from the router to a catch

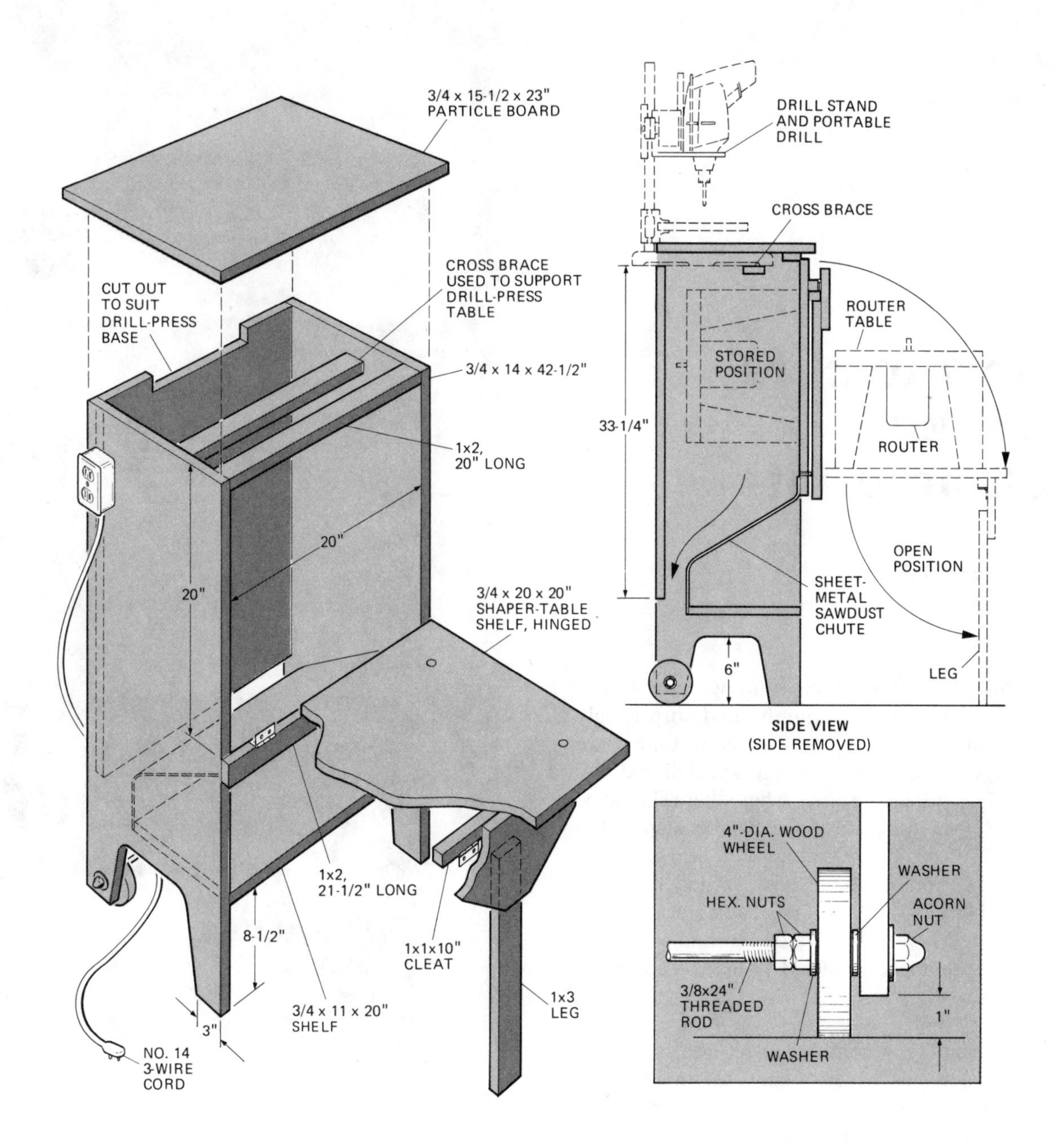

box at the rear. With the base of the drill stand anchored below the cabinet's top, the latter offers a king-size drill-press "table."

I designed the cabinet for my Shopmate drill, Sears drill stand and Sears router table, although it can be made to suit other makes of tools. While I used ¾-in.-thick particle board, the cabinet can be made of fir plywood. Both ends of the cabinet are alike and are nailed to a 20x34¼-in. back, an 11x20-in. bottom shelf and a 1x2 top rail 20 in. long. A second cross rail 20 in. down from the top supports the sheet-metal chute at the front. The 4-in. wheels and supporting ⅜-in. axle must be in place, of course, as side members are glued and nailed.

The supporting leg for the router-table shelf is hinged to a 1x1 cleat glued and screwed to the front face of the shelf, then the shelf itself is hinged to the top edge of the 1x2 cross rail.

The side-view drawing shows how the base of the drill-press stand rests in a notch cut in the back panel and is bolted to a cross brace installed between the end members of the cabinet. A surface-mounted duplex receptacle on one side of the cabinet fitted with a 6-ft. cord provides a plug.

How to cure muddy photo prints

By IVAN BERGER

■ PRINTS FROM other photographers pour across my desk each month—and surprisingly many of them, even when the contributors are professionals, are muddy, murky, dull and lifeless. There are mere grays where there should be blacks, and the whites appear to be seen in dim light through a dirty window. Yet the causes and cures of muddiness are easy to understand. I should know—in the years since I started printing (when I was 11), I've had to find out every cure in the book, because I've made most of the blunders.

The first step, of course, is to look closely at your prints. I'm convinced that the reason so many people try to sell or show off muddy work is because they're so carried away by the image of the picture itself that they can't take an objective look at how horribly that image is displayed. So take that look: A good print virtually always has at least one spot of pure, rich black, and one of pure, sparkling white to set off its range of middle tones. If you've deliberately broken this rule, fine—presumably you had a reason. But if your prints accidentally lack true whites or blacks, find out what you're doing wrong.

SEE ALSO

Darkrooms . . . Developing, photo . . . Dryers, photo . . . Enlarging, photo . . . Exposure meters . . . Lenses, photo . . . Photo hints . . . Photography

First, look at your negatives. If they don't cover the full range of tones, from a few, almost black spots of highlight to a few spots of shadow that are almost clear with a wide range of gray tones in between, you'll have trouble getting a good print.

When you take the picture, make sure you expose correctly, then follow the manufacturer's developing times and temperatures *exactly*. Adjust the exposure index setting of your light meter, setting the meter to a slightly higher than normal film speed if your films are

GOOD PRINT (far left), has a wide tonal range, from white to black and all gray tones between. Muddy prints above are caused by: (1) overexposure, underdevelopment; (2) too-low paper contrast; (3) thin negative over-exposed in printing for deeper blacks; (4) thin negative underexposed for cleaner whites; (5) thin negative "saved" as far as possible by contrasty No. 4 paper—but still a bit flat and muddy because of deficiencies in the negative.

consistently overexposed or setting it a bit lower if you normally underexpose negatives.

But most muddy prints are made from negatives that could yield better prints with better work. One of the easiest temptations to bad workmanship is to overexpose and underdevelop the print. In our impatience to see the picture, it's easy to blast a print with so much light that an image will pop into view as soon as the developer hits the paper, or to pull a print out of the developer when it begins to "look all right" under the safelight, even if the entire recommended developing time (usually about a minute) hasn't yet gone by. Unfortunately, that doesn't give the developer time to work evenly and thoroughly on the whole print. As a result, the prints are muddy and often mottled with poor highlight detail.

A second temptation—letting underexposed prints linger in the developer in hopes that they'll somehow improve—will only give you fog, stain, a lack of highlight detail, or all three at once. Never try to make up in development for a gross exposure error. If you have to change development times more than 20 or 30 seconds from the recommended time, remake the print with another exposure (stabilization printing, which gives you no leeway to fool around with processing time, is a great teacher of exposure discipline).

use the correct exposure

And make sure you have *exactly* the right exposure—often an exposure difference of only 10 or 20 percent can turn a merely adequate print into a good one, or vice versa. Your goal is a print that not only contains a full range of tones, but has all the shadow and highlight details that were in the negative. Correct paper contrast will help with this.

Overdevelopment or underdevelopment can still occur when you follow the paper manufacturer's developing-time recommendations, if your developer is at the wrong temperature or concentration. Underdevelopment (and, frequently, stains) will also occur if you try to process too many prints in a tray of developer or let it get contaminated by stop bath or fixer (refill it with fresh developer when its level drops visibly; discard the whole tray at the first sign of discoloration or sludge).

Proper agitation and inspection make a difference, too. Swishing the paper around in the developer with print tongs (preferably rubber-tipped, to prevent print scratching) or by rocking

IMPROPER INSPECTION—raising the print from the tray—lets developer run off or oxidize, causing blotchy, uneven development, contrast loss and stains. The proper technique is to hold the print just below the developer surface.

PROPER AGITATION promotes even development. Agitate the print by moving it with tongs (top), taking care not to scratch the print surface, or by rocking the tray (above)—easier with smaller trays, many of which are designed to rock easily, even on flat surfaces.

the tray will ensure that development starts and continues evenly; agitation in the stop bath means that it will stop evenly, too. And agitation in the fixing bath for just the right amount of time will ensure prints that (if properly washed) will last for years. Agitation is the right way to handle a print—but hauling it out of the developer for inspection is the wrong way; developer drains off in spots, oxidizes in others, and that's another cause of uneven development. The best way to inspect a print is in a good white light, after it's been developed and fixed, but learn, too, to compensate for the slight differences in tonality between a processed, wet print and a dry one—what you see in the fixing bath is not quite what you'll get.

If you don't work in your darkroom very often, your chemicals and paper may hang around for months before they're finally used up, and can go stale in the meantime. To prevent this, buy small quantities of paper (even though it costs less per sheet in larger packages), and refrigerate it between darkroom sessions (let it get back to room temperature before you use it).

mix just what you'll use

Your chemicals, especially developers, should be mixed up only in batches just big enough to fill the biggest tank or tray you use. Keep records of how much you use each chemical, discarding it when it's been used to its rated capacity; the lives of many film developers can be extended, though, by adding a "replenisher" after each use. Stale paper can sometimes be salvaged by adding Kodak Anti-Fog to your developer, but fresh paper will do an even better job.

Stale materials may cause stains, veiled highlights that never show pure whites, or fog that covers the whole paper, including borders. It usually prevents both proper blacks and whites from forming; in fact, the inability to get a proper black, no matter how much you expose the paper, is usually a sign of staleness.

But the inability to get a proper white is more often an effect of light fog. Fog that covers the whole paper visibly is usually caused by light leaks. Darkrooms that look dark when you first turn off the light may not be. A few small light leaks can sometimes be tolerated for printing (but never for film loading) provided none of them admits enough light to illuminate the darkroom (if you can see where you're going in the "dark," it's too light) and none shines directly on the paper. Check for enlarger light leaks, too.

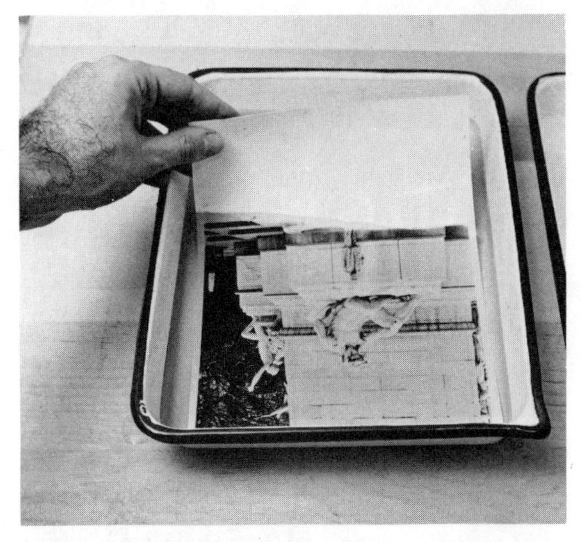

PRINTS THAT "POP UP" almost as you put them into the developer are overexposed; shortening developing time this way seems like a great time-saver, but the developing is uneven and blotchy with poor contrast.

Fog that just veils the highlights is harder to spot. Usually it comes from safelights. The easiest test is to unpack and expose a sheet of paper in complete darkness, then partially cover it with a box and turn the safelights on again. After five minutes, move the box to uncover half of the remaining area; then develop. If you can see a shadow line across the print, you have a fogging problem. Such fog can also come from light that bounces from a white easel back up to the paper emulsion.

Muddy prints are low in contrast, but not all poor contrast is due to the mud-producing errors noted above. Low-contrast subjects (often the result of shooting on a cloudy day) can explain a few "flat" prints; under or overexposed negatives that lack full tonal range will explain even more. These errors can be partially corrected (see Fig. 4) by printing on a "harder," or higher-contrast paper, such as Nos. 4, 5 or Agfa Brovira 6, just as soft papers (No. 1) can help with negatives too high in contrast. If you don't want to stock several paper grades for fear the less-used grades will go stale, use a variable contrast paper (though you'll still need graded papers for contrasts above No. 4 or so). Dust or dirt on your enlarging lens will also cut contrast, as will a cheap, low-grade lens (the difference between enlarger lenses, I've found, is less in detail resolution than in contrast). Condenser enlargers will also give a bit more contrast than diffusion-type ones.

Privacy screens get admiring glances

By ROBERT W. HOFFNER

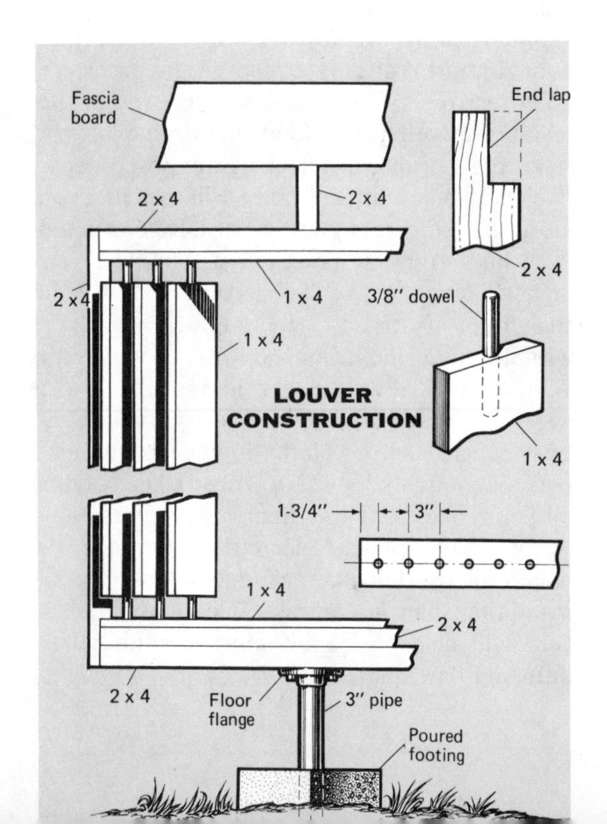

THERE WERE several reasons why my wife and I decided to add a fence to our home. For one thing, the bedroom on the southwest corner was unbearably hot every summer and, for another, we wanted privacy when entertaining on the patio. The screen we selected (above) satisfied both requisites with a bonus to boot: It features movable louvers that let cool breezes in or shut them out, as we choose.

Redwood was our choice for the project. It's good looking when installed, it weathers attractively and, most important, it is long lasting. The frame is constructed of 2 x 4s with the top and bottom rails doubled up for strength. The louvers are of nominal 1 x 4 stock with a ⅜-in. hole drilled to approximately a 1-in. depth on both ends to receive the dowels upon which they pivot.

Make certain that you extend your footings (for the posts) below the frost line in your area; a frost upheaval could twist the framing and make the louvers inoperable. The louvers can be fastened in the rear for easier operation.

By ADAM F. WOJNOWSKI

BUILT ALMOST ENTIRELY of scrap, this handsome fence (shown above) satisfies a champagne taste on a beer budget. By sizing the grille-like squares to suit the cutoffs I had on hand, the only items I had to buy were four 10-ft. 2 x 4s, nails, and the white paint I used to finish it.

I built the fence in two 8-ft. sections on the patio floor. Then as each section was completed, it was raised and fastened to the supporting posts with galvanized 10d common nails. These should be toenailed as shown in the drawing.

Before starting construction, you'll be wise to make a scale drawing of the area to be screened. Though the fence shown consists of 12-in.-sq. blocks and 6-in. stringers, the overall length of your fence could cause a change in these figures. Thus the dimensions shown in the drawing at the right should be considered merely as a starting point when you lay out your own design. By altering the dimensions to increase or decrease the size and number of the boxes, you can let in more or less light as you wish.

All of the hardware used should be of the non-rusting type. Then, whether you decide to paint or stain the wood, the handsome appearance of your fence will not be marred by weathering.

SIMPLICITY OF design gives this screen its look of elegance. It is simply squared 2x4 boxes connected with stringers 6 in. long.

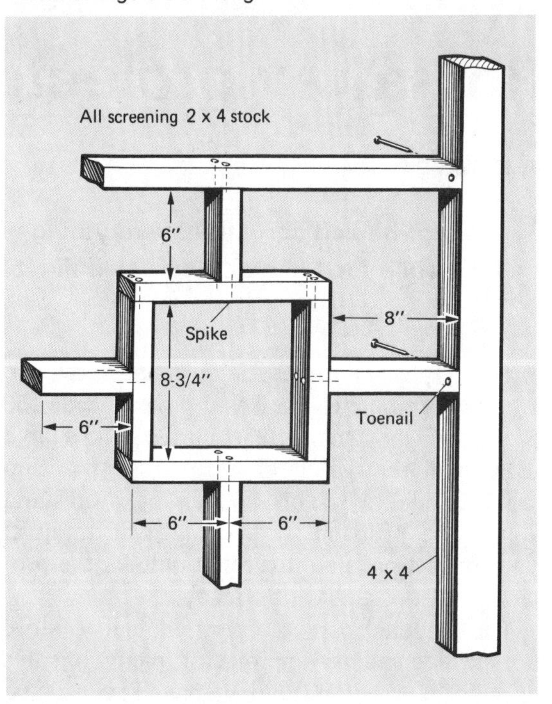

SEE ALSO

Barbecues . . . Benches, deck . . . Decks . . . Fences . . . Garden shelters . . . Gazebos . . . Patios . . . Picnic tables . . . Planters

Roll-away projector stand

By HOWARD R. CLARK

This wheeled cart stores everything you need for putting on shows and also doubles as a mobile food server. You can build it in either a modern or traditional style

SETTING UP for a slide or movie show can be a bothersome chore if you have to drag the projector out of a closetful of clutter, find a table to put it on, then go searching for those stray film reels or slide trays. This mobile projection stand solves the problem by keeping everything at your fingertips. You just roll it out, set the projector on top, and you're ready.

The wheeled cart is roomy enough to store both a slide and movie projector, plenty of trays or reels, extra editing equipment and even a tape recorder for adding sound to your presentations. The top surface puts the projector at a height of about 32 inches—a convenient working level that lets you operate it comfortably from a sitting position.

SEE ALSO
Mobile furniture . . . Photo hints . . . Photography . . . Slides, photo . . . Theaters, home

The slickest feature of all is a built-in, slope-front control panel that slides out like a drawer from one end. The panel contains three switched power outlets and a back-lighted slide viewer for checking and editing your transparencies. The outlets enable you to plug in not only the projector but additional equipment like a tape recorder and a floor or table lamp. With a lamp plugged in, you can control room illumination yourself without having to ask someone else to turn the lights on and off every few minutes.

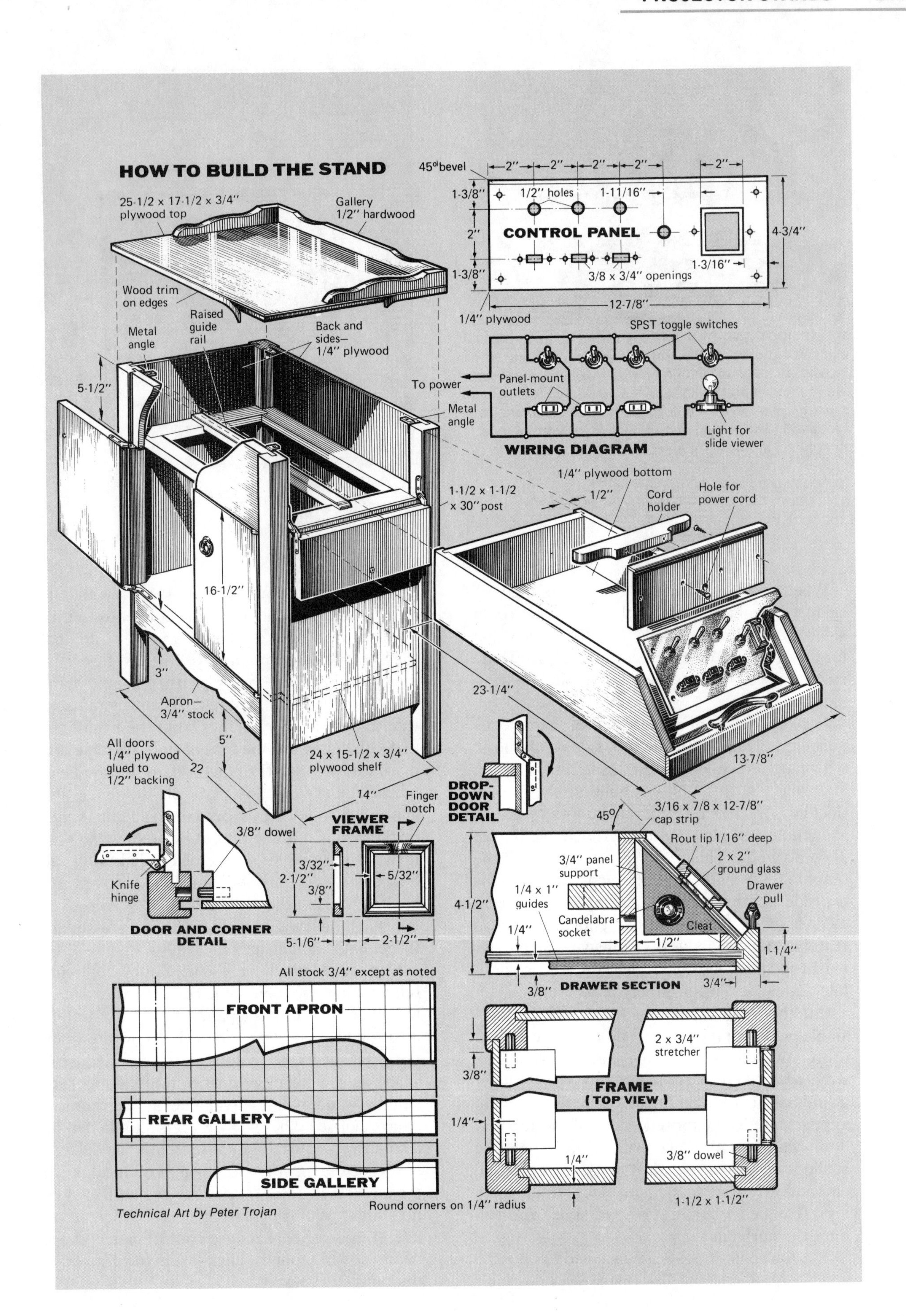

Technical Art by Peter Trojan

BASIC POST-AND-RAIL frame is shown in the photo at right. The grooves in the corner posts for back and side panels are blind, extending only part way down so they won't show where the legs are exposed. Setup for cutting these grooves on a dado head is shown above. Mark the fence to indicate blind end of post, then drop the post over blade at this point and feed it forward.

When not in use, the cart rolls out of the way against a wall and can double as a dining room sideboard, mobile snack bar or roll-around stand for a portable TV set. Decorative clear-plastic casters make good wheels since they're trim-looking.

For a rich appearance, use hardwood-veneered plywood for the top, sides and doors, with matching solid stock for the leg posts, apron and gallery strips. You can build up the ¾-inch thickness for the top, front and doors by gluing ¼-inch veneer plywood to a ½-inch backing of plain plywood. This trick will let you cut all the outer faces from the same ¼-inch sheet used for the side and back panels, saving the cost of a ¾-inch sheet. Birch is a good choice since it is readily available and less expensive than fancier hardwood plywoods, yet can be finished to simulate almost any wood tone you desire.

Cut the main doors and front panel from a single piece of plywood and do the same for the drop-down side door and the panel below it. This way, when the pieces are assembled, you'll get an unbroken flow of grain for a neat, professional appearance. The exposed edges of the top and doors can be concealed with wood tape. The scalloped edges on the apron and gallery give the cart an Early American appearance. If you have a preference for a more modern style, you can omit the curlycues.

The four corner posts are grooved to take the edges of the side and back panels for a sturdy construction. The grooves are ¼ inch wide and ⅜ inch deep and can be cut on a table saw with a dado head set to a ¼-inch width. Note that they're blind, stopping five inches from the lower ends of the posts so they won't show where the legs are exposed. To cut them accurately, measure five inches from the rim of the dado blade toward the rear of the saw table and mark this point on the fence. Align the blind end of each post with this mark on the fence and carefully lower the post onto the blade, making a pocket cut. Continue the cut by feeding the post forward to complete the groove. This way, all four posts will come out identically grooved. By hand, chisel out the rounded ends of the grooves left by the curved blade so the cuts are square throughout their length.

Use offset knife hinges so the doors will swing fully open without binding. The drop-down door that hides the control panel must be carefully positioned so it clears the drawer in the open position, but makes a snug fit when it's closed. The toggle switches and panel-mount outlets are standard radio parts available at electronics-supply houses. The slide viewer is illuminated by a small 7½-watt nightlight bulb in a candelabra socket. Note that there's a finger notch cut out at the top of the viewer frame. This makes it easy to lift slides out of the frame's recess. When not in use, the power cord for the control panel is kept neatly coiled around a cleat inside the drawer so it's out of the way.

Pick the right propeller

By JIM MARTENHOFF

YOUR PROPELLER is a pump. It moves a cone-shaped column of water, producing thrust. The water is cone-shaped because it expands as it moves away from the boat. Its diameter depends upon the diameter of the propeller. Speed of movement is determined by the speed of the propeller and its pitch.

The faster you can move that discharge cone, the faster your boat is going to go. There are, of course, a variety of factors limiting perfect performance. You can have too much pitch, for example, and turn the propeller too fast, losing bite and overspeeding your engine.

Propeller experts delve into a multitude of details when computing probable speed performance. They twiddle their slide rules and ulti-

SEE ALSO
Boats . . . Boating . . . Boat testing . . . Outboard motors

TIME A RUN over a measured course, compare the true speed to the theoretical and determine prop efficiency.

mately come up with a set of figures, but the average small-boat skipper can do the same with a lot less work. All you have to know is a simple rule of thumb and how to use it. You can stand on a dock, look at a man's boat, and tell at a glance what speed he probably makes. All you need is gear ratio and pitch.

Pitch is the big secret. This is the distance a propeller would move through the water in one revolution—like a woodscrew moving through wood—if it didn't slip. Propellers always slip, and the slippage is worked out as a percentage.

Diameter of a propeller, and its pitch, are usually stamped on the prop hub in that order. A propeller marked 16x18, for example, is one with a diameter of 16 inches and a pitch of 18. They are interrelated. If you increase the diameter of a prop to make a larger discharge cone of water, you may have to reduce the pitch.

pitch ratio

Your engine can only do so much work; diameter and pitch must share the mechanical muscle. Engineers think of the relationship as pitch ratio. This is pitch divided by diameter. That 16x18 wheel has a ratio of a bit over 1.1, and if it were an 18x16 the ratio would be under 0.9.

This is useful background, but it has already been done for you on a correctly propped craft. High-performance hulls usually call for a pitch ratio of as much as 1.5, while heavy cruisers might go down to 1.0 or 0.8. Yet you can stump

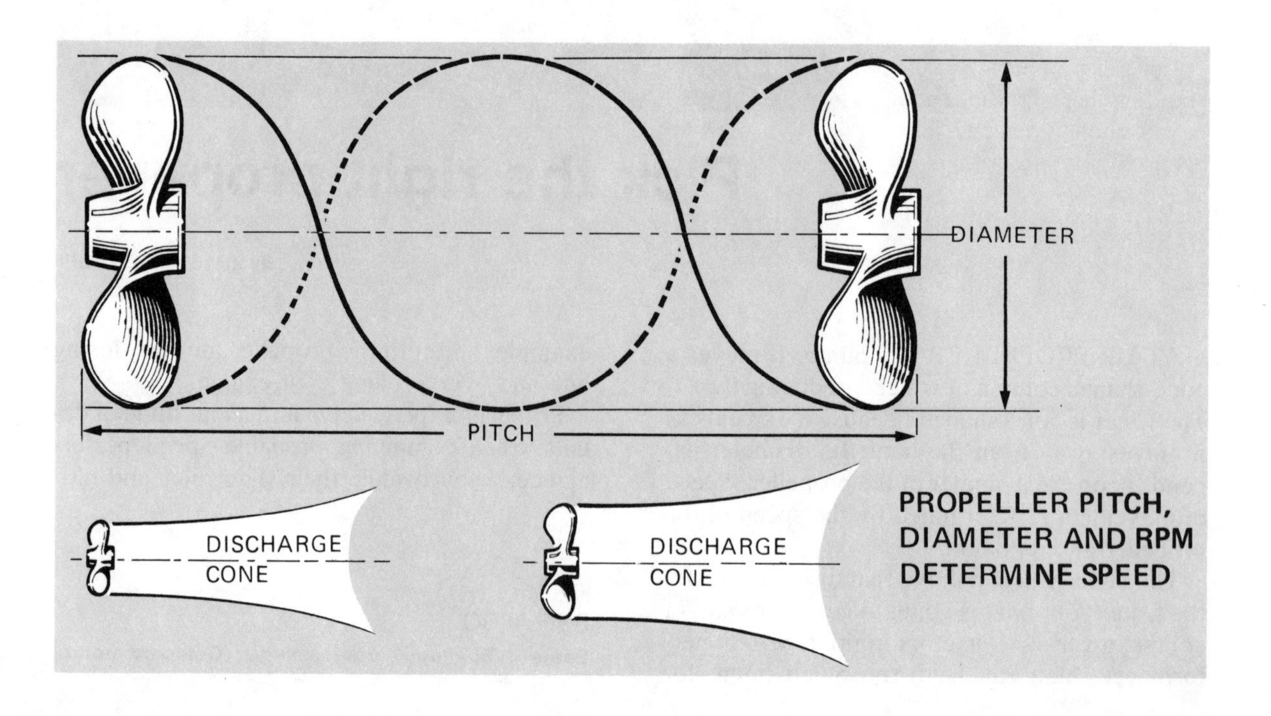

PROPELLER PITCH, DIAMETER AND RPM DETERMINE SPEED

the experts by overloading your boat or distributing weight unevenly to upset its trim. Hence the need for this know-how. If you loaded your fishing boat with a huge, heavy ice chest and other gear so that performance fell off, a little prop judgment might solve your problem.

Forget everything but pitch. Use this figure to figure your possible speed. This is the speed you would make if there were no prop slippage. Clock your boat over a measured distance and compare true speed to theoretical. The difference is "apparent slip," as the engineers put it. Slip is not an ideal way to determine efficient performance, but it's handiest if used with understanding.

You figure theoretical speed by multiplying propeller pitch in inches by shaft rpm. Note this is shaft turns, not necessarily what your tach reads. If you have a 2:1 gear reduction between engine and prop, your shaft turns at half the speed of the engine. The 5000 rpm on the tach means only 2500 shaft rpm. Engineers multiply pitch by shaft rpm, then divide by 1056 to find theoretical speed in statute miles per hour, or divide by 1216 to find knots.

This is a lot of work, so here's a trick so simple that you can often figure theoretical speed mentally, knock off expected slippage, and get true speed frequently within a mile or so of the actual figure. It never ceases to surprise friends when you can stand at a dock, listen to pitch, gear ratio and rpm figures, and then announce probable speed.

figuring speed

Here is how it works: Theoretical speed, in statute miles per hour, for each 1000 shaft turns, equals pitch minus one. That 18-inch prop we've been talking about will deliver a theoretical speed of 17 statute miles per hour for each 1000 shaft revolutions. This thumb-rule goes off only with low pitch props of 12 inches or less, or with more than 20 inches, so it fits the average small boat well.

Let's work an example. You have a 21-inch-pitch prop on a big outboard with a 2:1 gear reduction. The tach at top speed shows 5000 so the prop is turning 2500 rpm. With the minus-one rule, the 21-inch prop makes 20 mph per 1000 turns, that's 40 mph at 2000 plus another 10 mph for the last 500. Theoretical top speed is 50 statute mph, and timing shows true speed to be 37.5 mph. The lost 12.5 mph is 25-percent slip, acceptable for an outboard. For a stern drive you might expect about 20, inboards may run 15, and

SOME PROP SLIPPAGE can be corrected sometimes by testing various props and timing performance.

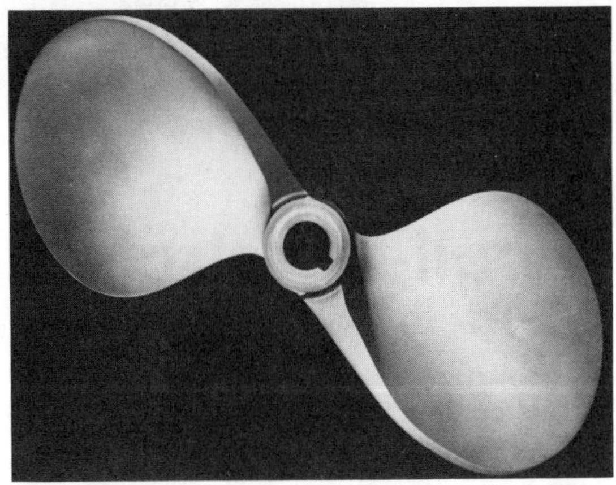

RACING PROPS, like this new titanium model from Nicson Engineering, may top 90 percent performance.

very good installations and race boats can be 10 percent or less. Heavy cruisers and houseboats may go as high as 35 percent, and hull designs will influence slip figures.

High slippage figures may indicate a propeller problem, and trying other props so that peak rpm is correct is one good way to look for increased efficiency. And efficiency is what you're after when you look for the correct prop.

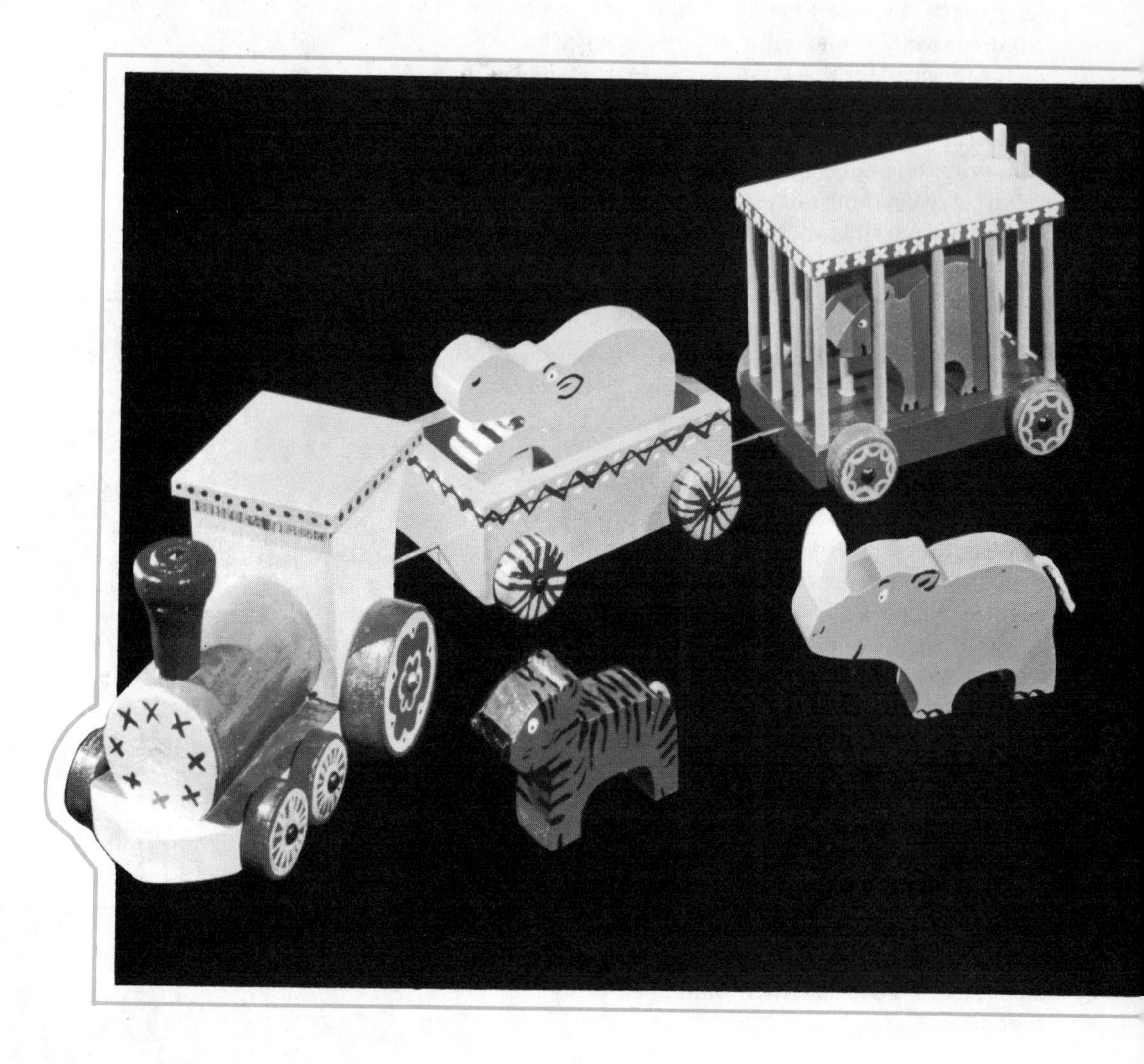

A pull-toy circus train

This colorful little circus train, built from scraps, will be the pride and joy of any young ringmaster

By ELMA and WILLARD WALTNER

SEE ALSO

Gifts, Christmas . . . Playhouses . . . Puzzles . . . Toys . . . Weekend projects

CHUGGING ALONG at the end of a string, this colorful little circus train will bring shrieks of delight from any two or three-year-old. All you'll need to buy to make the train are a few screws, screw eyes, L-hooks, a couple dowels and some *nontoxic* paint. The wood should be available in your workshop scrap box.

If you make it five cars long, the train will carry the 10 animals, each car holding two. If you own a lathe, you can quickly turn such parts as the engine's smokestack and boiler, as well as the wheels. However, if you don't have a lathe, the smokestack can be turned with your electric drill. Drill a wood block lengthwise, slip it over a bolt, tighten with a nut and chuck the end of the bolt in the drill. Cradle the drill in a vise and rig up a second block as a rest for your chisel. You

continued

can "turn" the wheels without a lathe by using a hole cutter in your drill or drill press.

Use glue and small finishing nails to assemble the cars and sand the edges smooth. In the case of the cage car, the two holes for the ½-in. "gate bars" go all the way through the roof and are 5/16 in. for a loose fit. The ends of the gate bars are pointed so they seat automatically in the holes, and ½-in. lengths of small dowel are inserted crosswise to prevent the bars from being pulled all the way out. The holes for the three center dowels, which provide stalls, are drilled in the base only. All other matching holes are spaced and drilled the same in both base and roof.

To simplify things, it's best to paint the roof and base before gluing the dowels in place. The dowels are left unpainted. Round the outer edges of the wheels with sandpaper, paint the designs on them and attach them to the wagons with roundhead wood screws so they will turn freely. The photo will serve as a guide when you paint the wagons and add the fancy designs on their roofs, sides and wheels in bright colors.

An L-hook is turned into one end of each car and a screw eye in the other; screw eyes are used at each end of the engine. The engine cab is sawed from either a solid or glued-up block.

The animals are sawed from 1 or 1⅛-in. pine with either a bandsaw or jigsaw, and ⅛-in. holes are drilled for tasseled and braided tails of yarn. For safety's sake, it's important that you use nontoxic paint and anchor the yarn tails firmly in their holes.

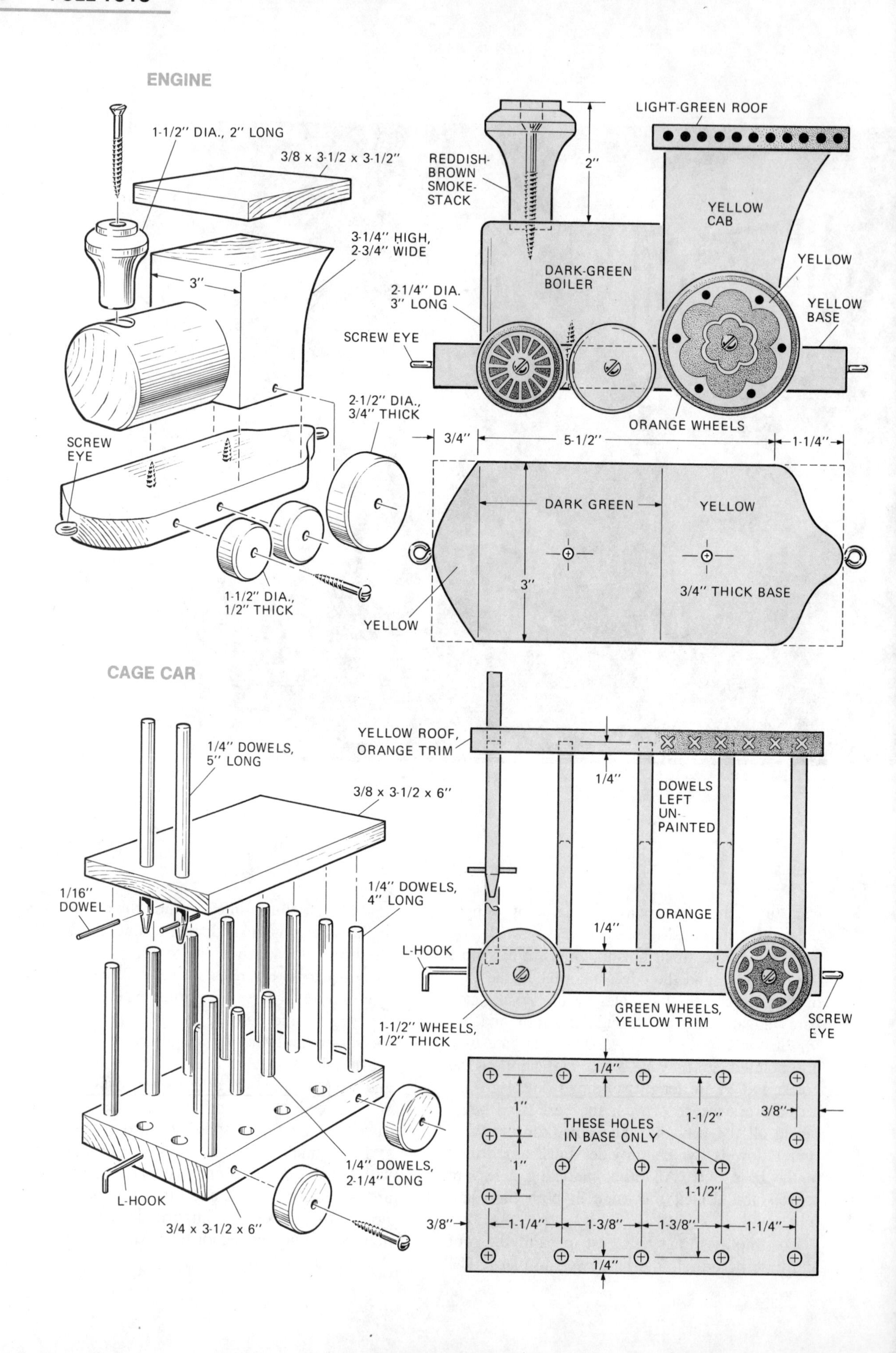
ENGINE
1-1/2" DIA., 2" LONG
3/8 x 3-1/2 x 3-1/2"
3-1/4" HIGH, 2-3/4" WIDE
3"
SCREW EYE
2-1/2" DIA., 3/4" THICK
1-1/2" DIA., 1/2" THICK
LIGHT-GREEN ROOF
REDDISH-BROWN SMOKE-STACK
2"
YELLOW CAB
DARK-GREEN BOILER
YELLOW
2-1/4" DIA. 3" LONG
YELLOW BASE
SCREW EYE
ORANGE WHEELS
3/4"
5-1/2"
1-1/4"
DARK GREEN
YELLOW
3"
3/4" THICK BASE
YELLOW
CAGE CAR
1/4" DOWELS, 5" LONG
3/8 x 3-1/2 x 6"
1/16" DOWEL
1/4" DOWELS, 4" LONG
1/4" DOWELS, 2-1/4" LONG
L-HOOK
3/4 x 3-1/2 x 6"
YELLOW ROOF, ORANGE TRIM
1/4"
DOWELS LEFT UN-PAINTED
ORANGE
1/4"
L-HOOK
1-1/2" WHEELS, 1/2" THICK
GREEN WHEELS, YELLOW TRIM
SCREW EYE
1/4"
1"
1"
THESE HOLES IN BASE ONLY
1-1/2"
3/8"
1-1/2"
3/8"
1-1/4"
1-3/8"
1-3/8"
1-1/4"
1/4"

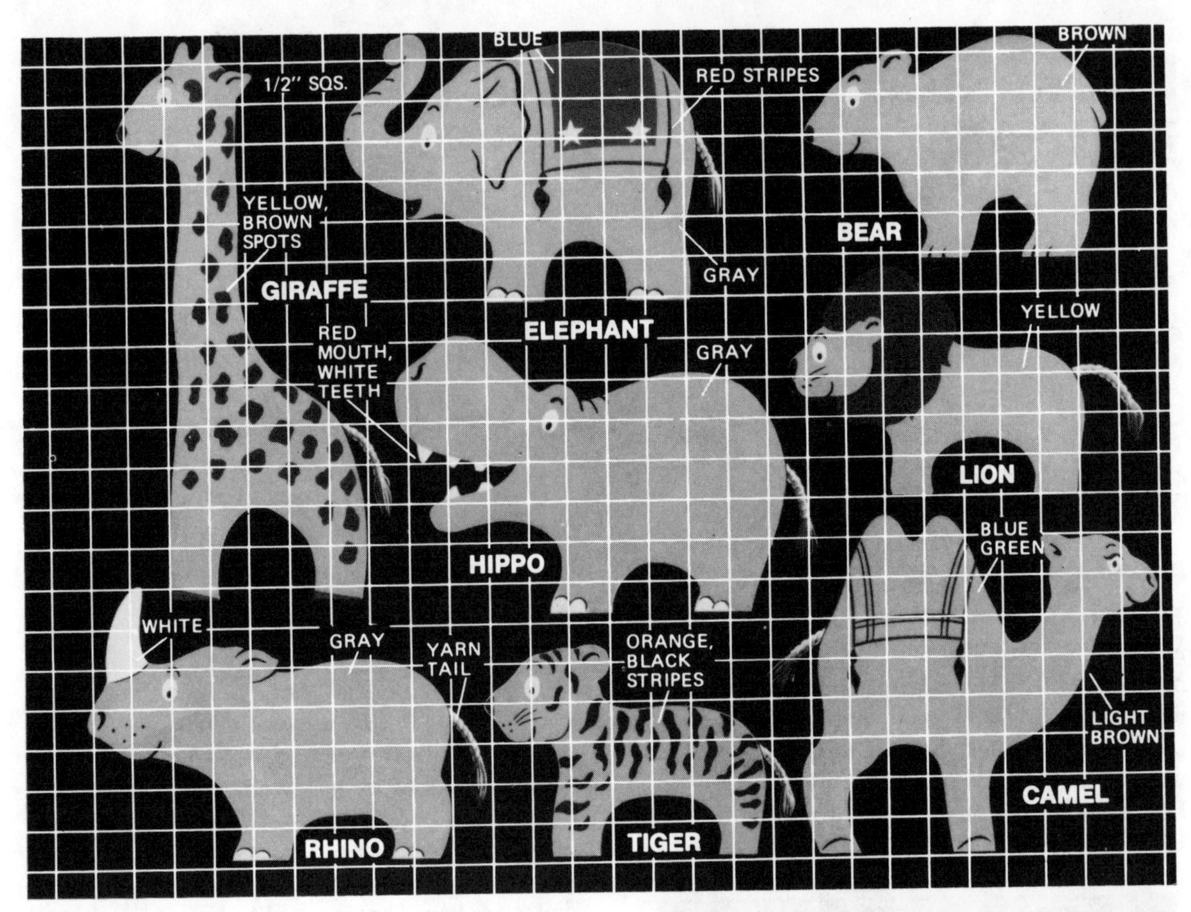
1/2" SQS.
BLUE
RED STRIPES
BROWN
YELLOW, BROWN SPOTS
GIRAFFE
GRAY
BEAR
ELEPHANT
RED MOUTH, WHITE TEETH
GRAY
YELLOW
LION
HIPPO
BLUE GREEN
WHITE
GRAY
YARN TAIL
ORANGE, BLACK STRIPES
LIGHT BROWN
CAMEL
RHINO
TIGER

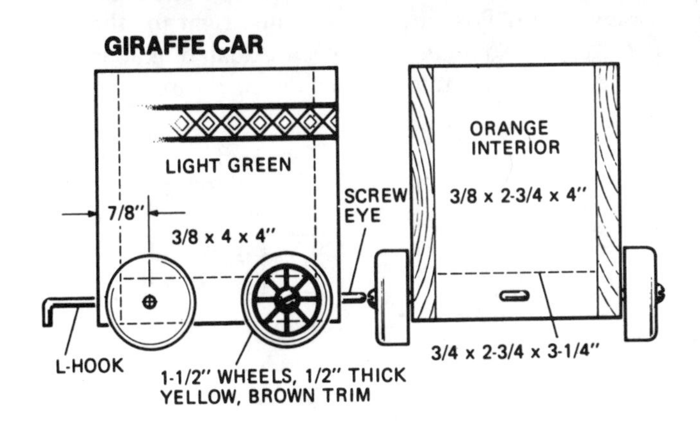
GIRAFFE CAR
LIGHT GREEN
7/8"
3/8 x 4 x 4"
SCREW EYE
ORANGE INTERIOR
3/8 x 2-3/4 x 4"
L-HOOK
1-1/2" WHEELS, 1/2" THICK
YELLOW, BROWN TRIM
3/4 x 2-3/4 x 3-1/4"

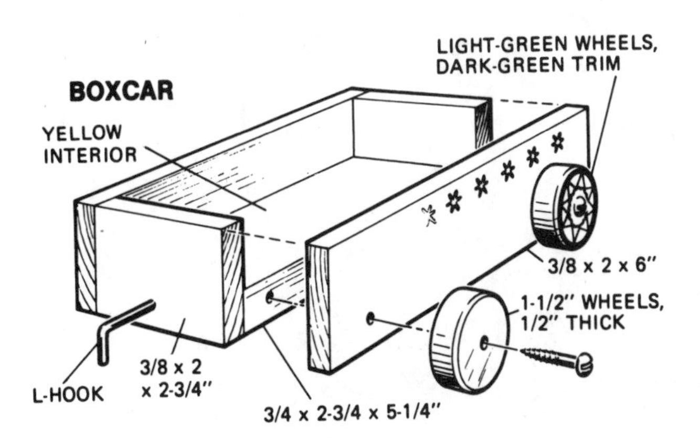
BOXCAR
LIGHT-GREEN WHEELS, DARK-GREEN TRIM
YELLOW INTERIOR
3/8 x 2 x 6"
1-1/2" WHEELS, 1/2" THICK
L-HOOK
3/8 x 2 x 2-3/4"
3/4 x 2-3/4 x 5-1/4"

Ducks and dachshunds that talk

By ELMA WALTNER

TODDLERS LIKE TOYS they can pull all around the house. If they also make a noise, so much the better. Here are a couple of animal pull toys you can make in your shop that are sure to please any toddler. Mom Duck and her kids waddle along quacking merrily and Danny Dachshund makes himself heard and waddles his hind quarters as he is pulled. Off-center wheels provide the waddle, and compression-spring necks make the heads bob. Both the ducks and the dog have the same voices. It is produced by pieces of clock spring being snapped against sounding boxes by hardwood ratchets.

The series of photos on the opposite page show all of the steps necessary in making the ducks. Notice in each case that the voice-box holes are bored before the blocks are slotted and sawed out. Postcard stock is just right for the cardboard sounding-box discs. A dab of glue is used to hold the ratchet (clacker) on the axle and

SEE ALSO
Gifts, Christmas . . . Playhouses . . . Puzzles . . . Toys . . . Weekend projects

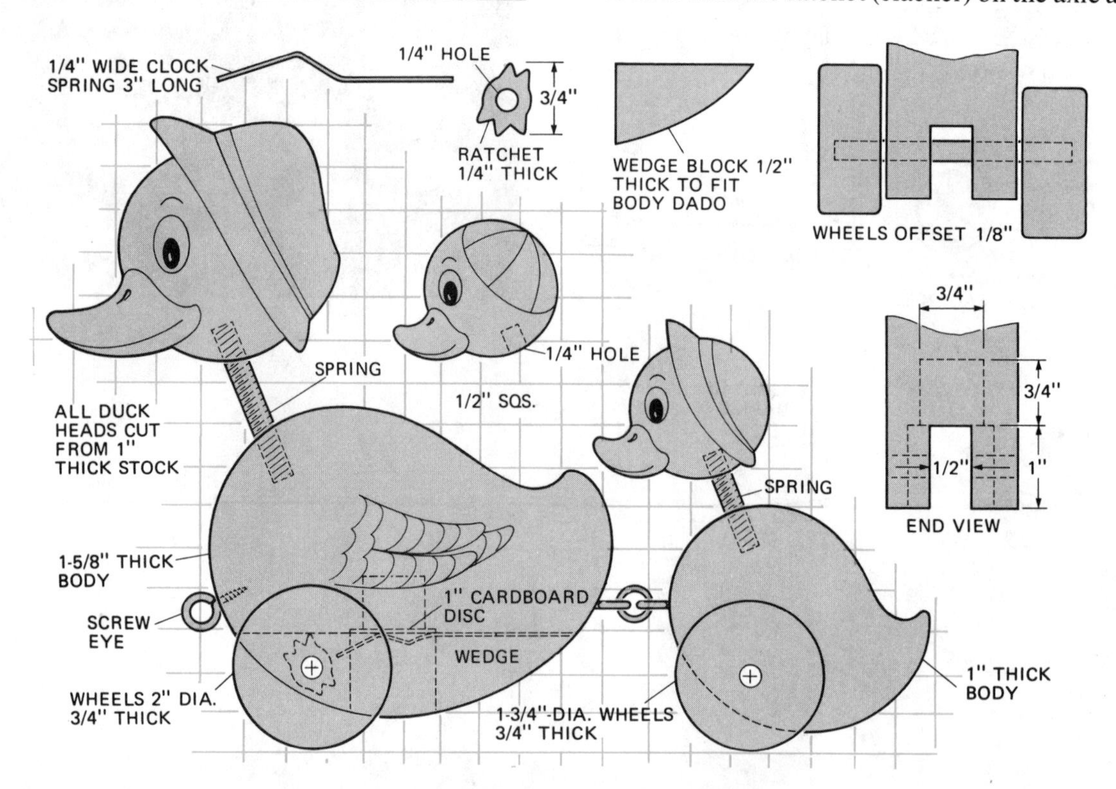

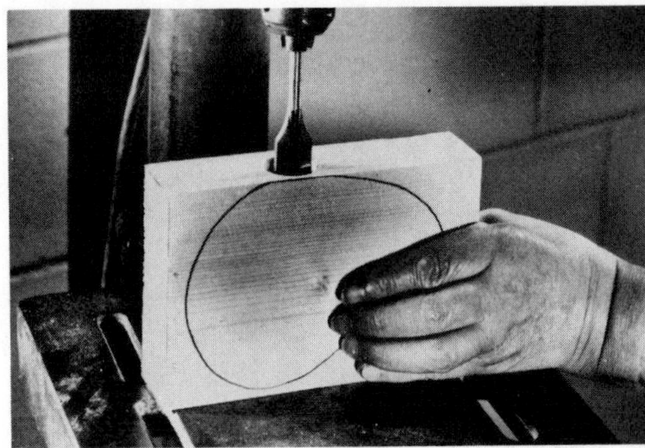
SOUNDING-BOX holes are bored in block before the body is cut out. Drill 1-in. hole first, then ¾ in.

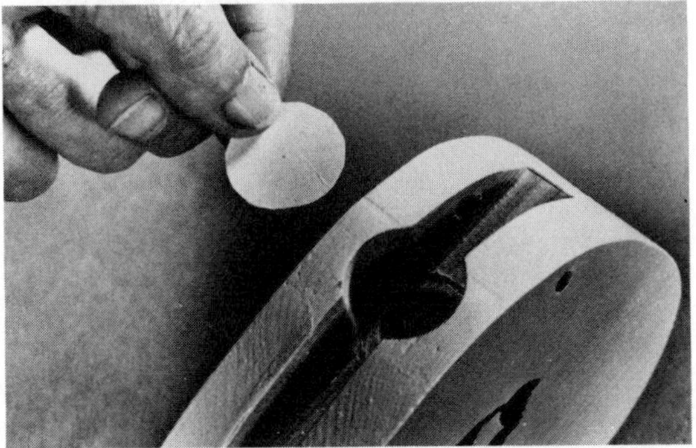
THIN CARDBOARD disc is glued to ledge formed by large hole to cover the ¾-in. sounding-box hole.

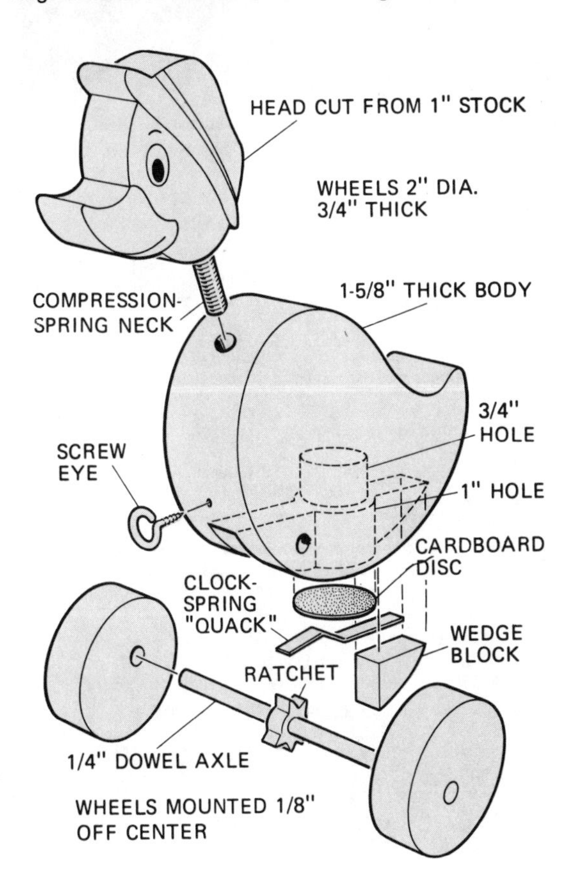

BLOCK IS passed over dado saw to form ½-inch-wide slot in bottom edge, drilled for axles then sawed.

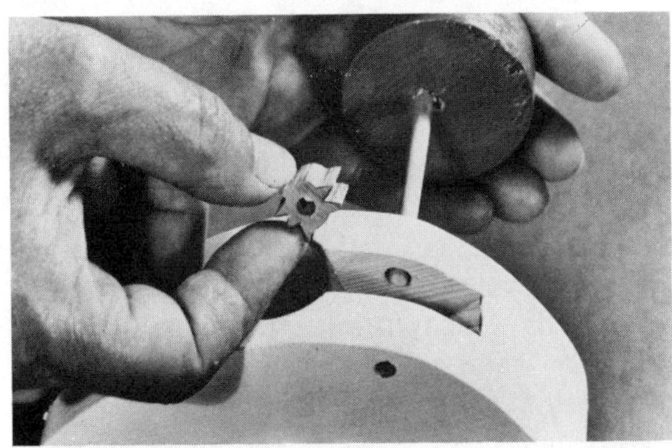
RATCHET IS SLIPPED over axle as it's passed through slot. Glue on each side holds ratchet on axle.

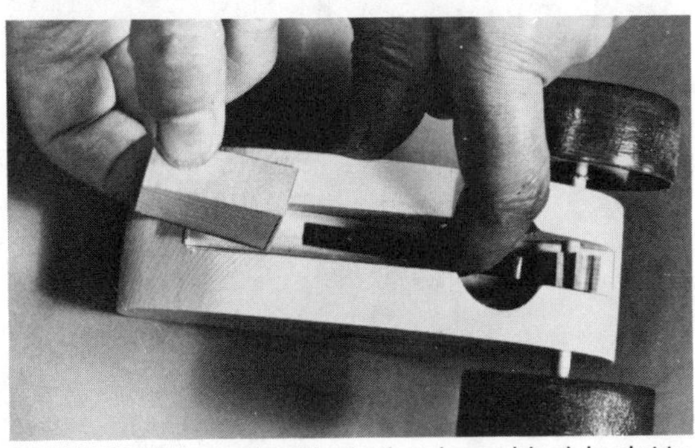
APPLY GLUE to wedge block, then insert block in slot to hold the spring against the cardboard and ratchet.

continued

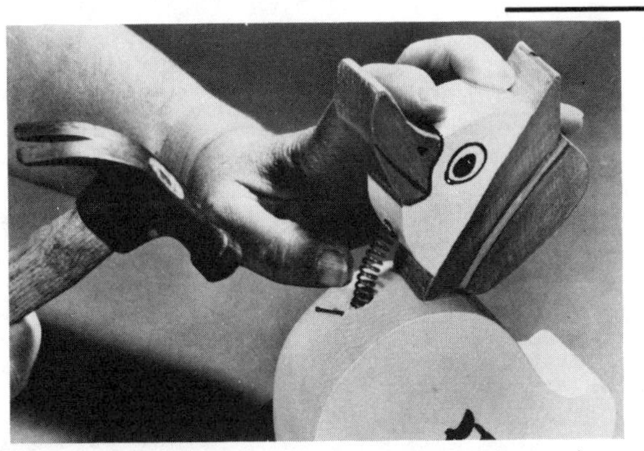
SMALL FINISHING nails, plus glue, are used to anchor neck springs in holes. Drive nails crosswise.

ATTACH EARS to head by driving nails through oversize holes in the ears, then through wooden beads.

in the center of the slot. A wedge block is inserted in the slot to hold the spring against the cardboard. Finally small finishing nails and glue are used to anchor the neck springs.

Basically, Danny is made the same way, the exception being that only his rear wheels are placed off-center. Waddle is produced by attaching his hind quarters with a nail in an oversize hole. His head is lathe-turned and then cut off at an angle to form nose and mouth.

The wheels can be cut easily from ½-inch stock with a hole cutter for either of the toys. Finally, sand all parts smooth and then paint with a nontoxic enamel.

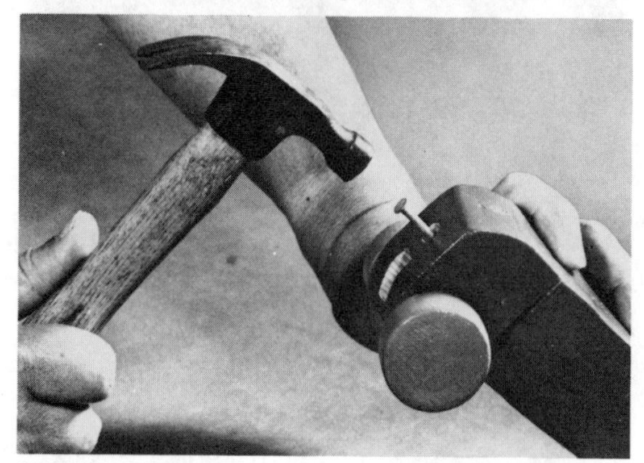

ATTACH HIND quarters to front section with washer between by driving nail through oversize hole.

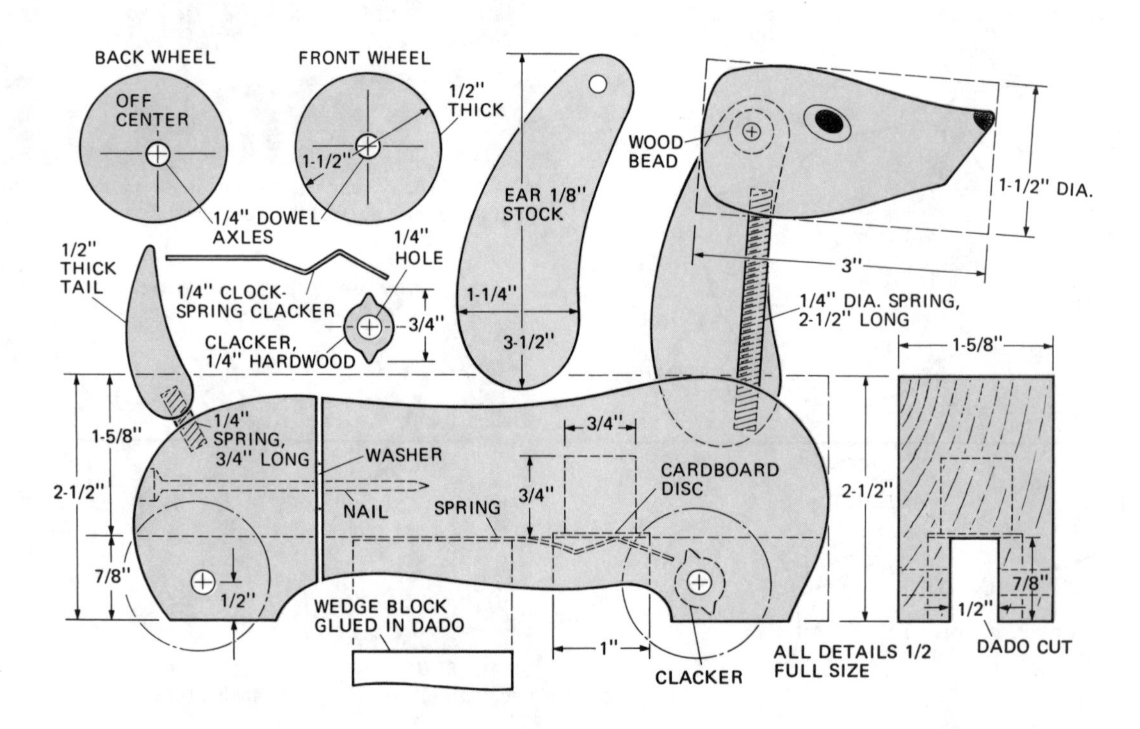

Buzzing bumblebee

By MERTON H. SLUTZ

AS THIS TOY is pulled along by a youngster, the smiling bee "buzzes" around the petal continuously, "alighting" only when the pulling stops. While sure to delight toddlers, this pull toy will make parents happy as well because the "buzzing" is silent.

As can be seen in the drawing at left, the toy is far easier to make than one would suppose when watching the finished toy in action. Parts are easy to make and assemble; no sophisticated tools, techniques or knowledge are called for in the making. In fact, the project can be completed entirely with handtools using a coping saw for shaping petals and bee, brace and bit for all necessary boring. The rest of the job calls for gluing, sawing, nailing and finish-painting with nontoxic paint.

The wheels on the toy shown were cut from ½-in.-thick plywood. If you lack a jigsaw or holesaw—either of which must be used to cut perfect circles—buy a length of 2-in.-dia. hardwood dowel, and cut off ½-in.-thick pieces like slices of bologna.

It is best to tack-assemble the toy before finishing to assure that moving parts work as they should. When satisfied, disassemble the piece, do the finish painting and permanently assemble.

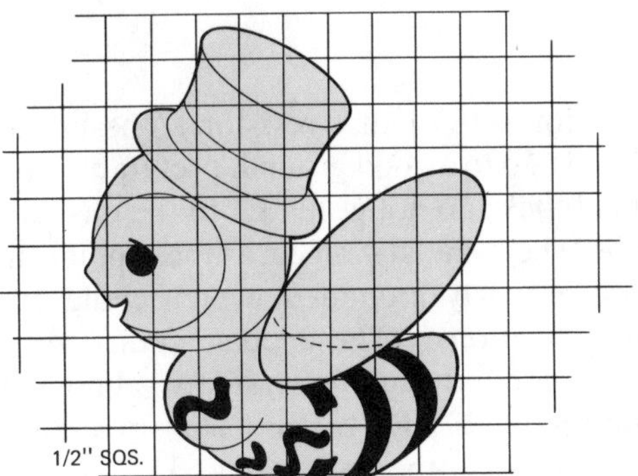

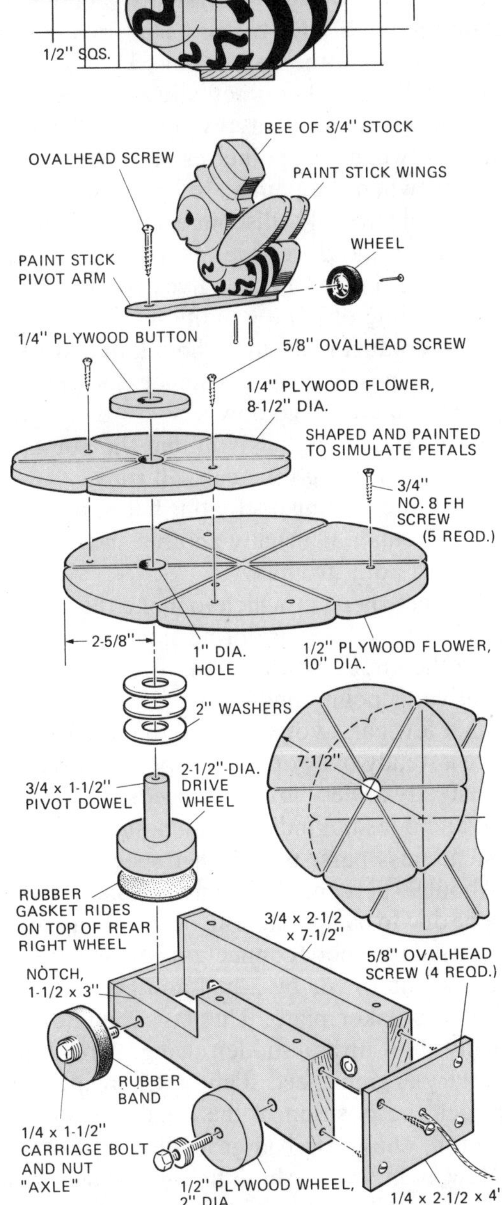

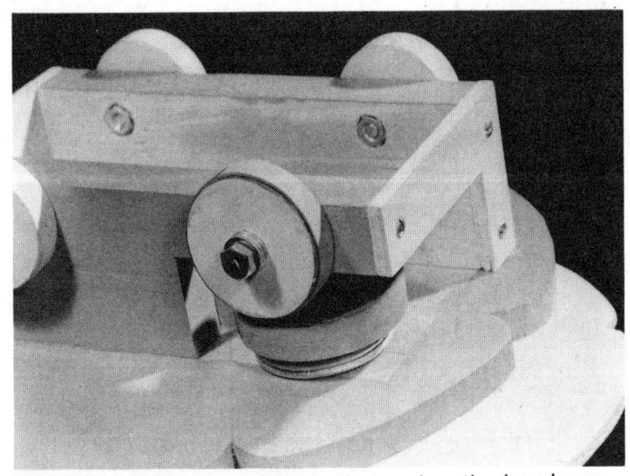

UPSIDE-DOWN view shows what makes the bee buzz—rubber gasket on drive wheel rides atop the rear wheel.

SEE ALSO
Gifts, Christmas . . . Playhouses . . . Puzzles . . . Toys . . . Weekend projects

Take your car's pulse while you drive

By A. EDWARD EVENSON

YOUR IGNITION CONTACT POINTS could well be called the heart of your car, for your engine's running depends on the steady, positive pulse of those contacts—100 million beats per year in the average eight-cylinder car.

Points are traditionally replaced at regular intervals of 10,000 to 12,000 miles. But this does little good if the points should go at 8000 miles, and is a waste of money when points are replaced that might still have another 10,000 miles of life left in them.

The trick is knowing just when points need replacing. You can tell by a visual, underhood inspection, or by checking the contacts under actual running conditions. Auto diagnostic centers perform such dynamic tests, but you can, too, with this simple, pushbutton Pulse Checker.

Circuit construction is straightforward and not too expensive. Make sure you install the diodes in their proper places and with correct polarity (see diagram). The only unusual step is adding an "OK-Bad" scale to the meter dial. Most meters allow easy disassembly and scale replacement; be careful that you don't accidentally bend the pointer. If you just mark the first tenth of the meter scale "OK," you'll be pretty close; but for a more accurate location of the scale dividing point, use the test setup shown—a voltage divider that drops a battery's 1.5 volts to about 0.22 volts. Connect the Pulse Checker's input across the 18 or 20-ohm resistor, and mark the division between the good and bad bands at the point where the meter needle comes to rest.

To hook up the Pulse Checker to your car, connect its positive lead to the primary terminal on the coil, the one that goes to the distributor. (If your car has a ballast resistor between the coil and distributor, connect the Pulse Checker to the distributor side of that resistor.) The negative lead must go to a good ground, preferably on the engine block; do not ground it to the dashboard or other sheet-metal surface, as these points may not be properly grounded, which could cause false indications. (These connections are for negative-ground ignition systems, almost universal today. If your car has a positive-ground system, reverse the connections.)

The Pulse Checker is actually a very sensitive low-voltage meter that responds to the resistance between the points as they are making contact (when the points are open, the test circuit is electrically disconnected). Since the points open and close several thousand times per minute, the Pulse Checker gives continuous average reading of point condition.

Point contact resistance should, of course, be as low as possible; as resistance goes up, coil current and output go down. So a "Bad" (high-resistance) reading tells you that the points are failing, even though the car still runs.

An erratic reading fluctuating between the OK and Bad bands is usually another indication of beginning point trouble.

The best speed at which to make the check is slightly above idle, or during slow city driving. While the circuit works at any speed, it is most sensitive to point conditions in this range.

On a few cars, you may find that the reading, while a steady okay or zero at speeds above idle, is unsteady at very low idle speeds. This is normal, and does not indicate bad points unless the unsteadiness persists at higher speeds.

About 99 percent of the time, a "Bad" reading will be due to bad points. But occasionally, it will be caused by a poor connection between the coil and distributor, or by a bad ground in the distributor breaker plate. This last condition will usually show up as a sudden change in reading as you vary engine speed slightly. Changing speed changes the position of the breaker plate, and therefore shows up bad grounding, if it exists.

New points may show high-resistance readings for a while, until their contact surfaces wear in.

SEE ALSO

Batteries, auto . . . Ignition systems, auto . . . Sparkplugs, auto . . . Tune-up, auto

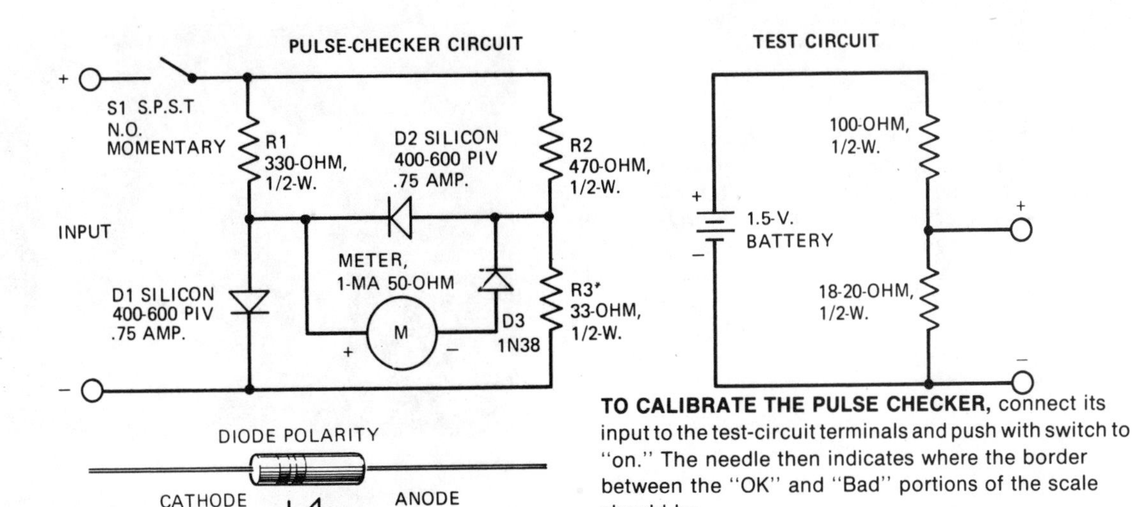

TO CALIBRATE THE PULSE CHECKER, connect its input to the test-circuit terminals and push with switch to "on." The needle then indicates where the border between the "OK" and "Bad" portions of the scale should be.

THE CIRCUIT BOARD can be mounted directly to the meter terminals. Any board and parts layout can be used.

PARTS LIST

D1, D2—Silicone diode, 400 PIV, .75-amp rating. (Radio Shack 276-1138; Lafayette 19 P 42093; Olson TR-216B)
D3—General-purpose germanium diode, 60 PIV, 5 ma. (type 1N34A; Radio Shack 276-821; Lafayette 19 P 15057; Olson TR-210B)
R1—330-ohm, 1/2-w., 10% resistor (Radio Shack 271-017; Lafayette 52 P 3061; Olson RS-009B)
R2—470-ohm, 1/2-w., 10% resistor (Radio Shack 271-019; Lafayette 52 P 3065; Olson RS-010B)
R3—33-ohm, 1/2-w., 10% resistor (Radio Shack 271-007; Lafayette 52 P 3037)
S1—S.p.s.t., normally-open pushbutton switch (Radio Shack 275-1547; Lafayette 34 P 34594; Olson SW-452B)
M—Meter, 0-1 ma., 50-100 ohm, 2½" square (Simpson) or 0-1 ma., 80-ohm, 1 13/16 x 1½" (not shown; Radio Shack 22-018; Lafayette 99 P 50528)
Misc.—Perfboard or circuit board, hookup wire, solder, aluminum for mounting bracket (optional).

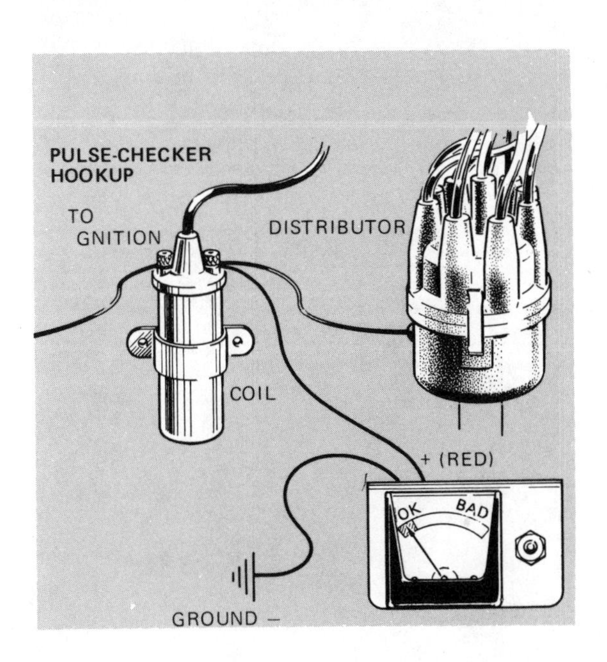

THE PULSE CHECKER indicates the condition of the ignition points. You can mount it on your dashboard, there's room, or underneath it as shown below.

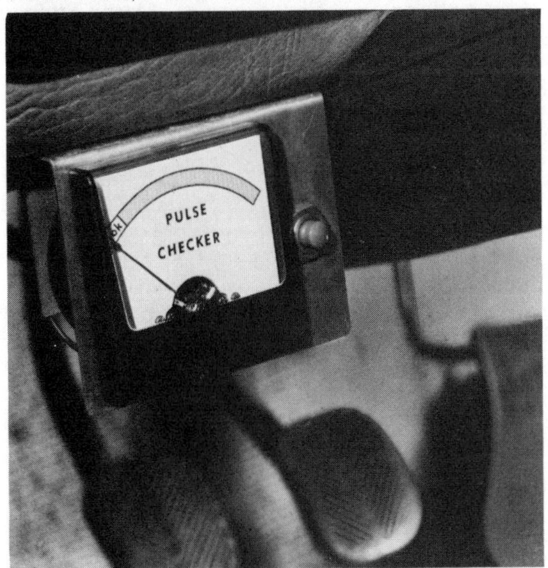

THE PLASTIC LID taken from a 2-lb. coffee can will securely grip thinwall tubing in a bench vise without damaging it in any way. Simply wrap the plastic lid around the tube or length of conduit, then bend the ends and pinch them in the jaws of a bench vise. This is especially handy when working with plated tubing that could be scratched or cracked.—*Albert Pippi.*

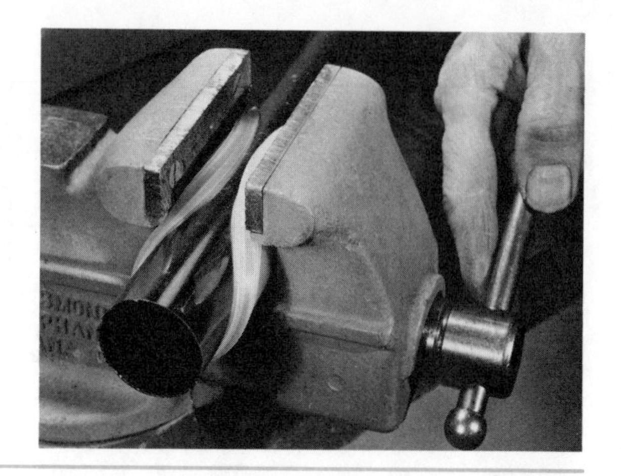

SAWDUST ACCUMULATION along the fence of your radial-arm saw can be avoided with this self-clearing device. Simply bore a row of ¾-in. holes along the edge of the front table insert. Thus when you slide the work along the fence to position it, the board automatically pushes the sawdust down through the holes to the floor. If you prefer, you can achieve the same results by making the holes in the edge of an auxiliary table and using it as shown in the photo.—*Victor Lamoy.*

THIS MINIATURE VISE will hold tiny parts while you're working on them and avoid possible damage in the knurled jaws of a conventional bench vise. First clamp the work in the jaws of a small C-clamp, then secure the backbone of the clamp in the jaws of the vise. Now you can quickly insert or remove pieces of work without removing the clamp from the vise. If you use a regular clamp with a long adjusting handle, be sure the handle will clear the vise.—*Martin Steinagle.*

A MITERBOX will support your work while you cut small pieces of wood or metal with a sabre saw. This keeps the free end of a workpiece from vibrating when you're working on the other end, a problem which arises if the work is supported in a vise. Simply set the work over the miterbox, letting the saw blade cut between the two uprights. If you don't have a suitably deep miterbox, try improvising a simple sawing jig from a length of 2 x 4 and a few pieces of scrap pine.—*Harold Miglin.*

Caulking cartridge makes a handy pump

DRAWING UP on the pump handle will suck leftover gas from a power mower when storing it for winter.

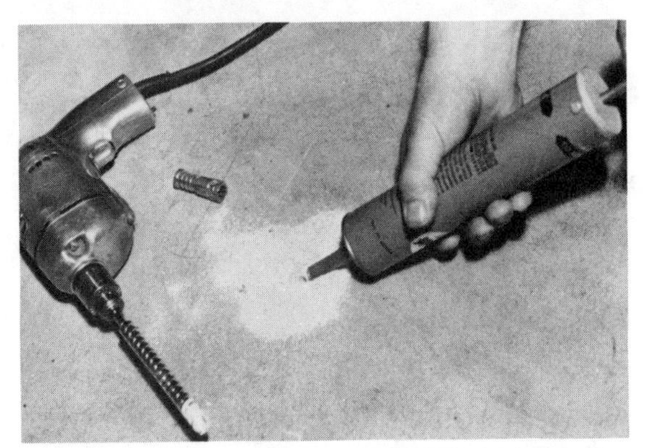

PUSHING IN on the handle causes the pump to blow a strong jet of air, fine to blow dust from a drilled hole.

THE PUMP becomes a grease gun by filling the cartridge with lubricant and squirting it out the nozzle.

By RAY SHOBERG

WHEN IT'S EMPTY, you might not think a caulking cartridge could be of much use, but that's where you're wrong. Fitted with a piston and handle it becomes a dandy little hand pump.

With it you can fill a gear case with grease, suck the gas out of a power mower when putting it away for the season or bail those last few cupfuls of water from your boat. You'll also find it handy when you need to blow chips or dust from a hole drilled in concrete.

It's simple enough to make as shown in the drawing. The piston consists of a threaded rod fitted with two plastic cups placed back to back with a plywood washer between. One of these cups is in each cartridge—it's what forces the caulking out the nozzle.

The pump works best when the cups rub firmly against the sides of the tube. By tightening the nuts a little, you can flare the cups a bit for a better fit. A drop of oil or a little grease on the cups will improve the seal and ease pumping.

When the pump is to be used only as a blow-gun, one plastic cup on the piston (with its lip toward the nozzle) is enough. For extra reach a length of plastic hose can be forced over the nozzle.

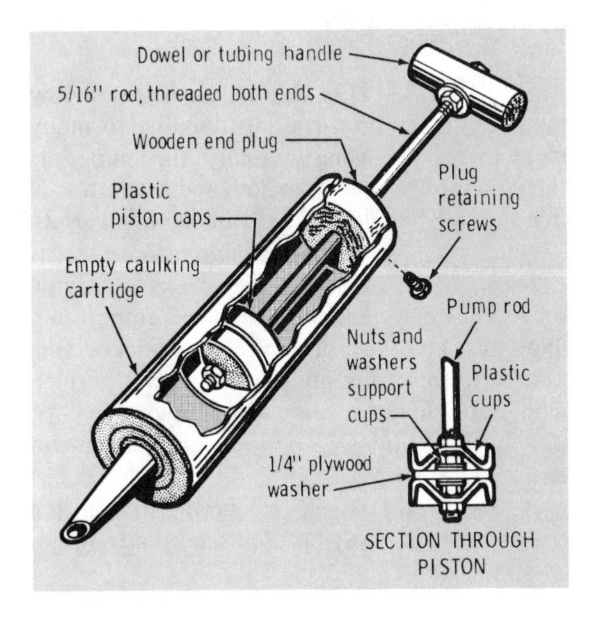

SEE ALSO

Boat accessories . . . Caulking . . . Concrete . . . Lubrication, auto . . . Mowers

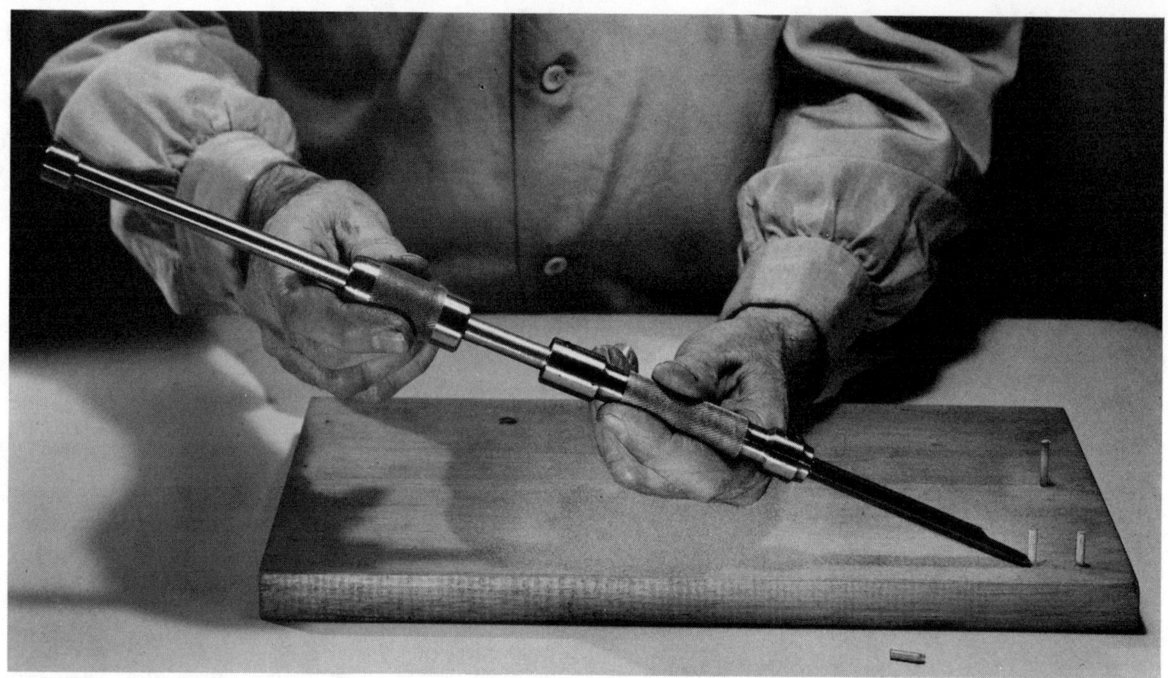

INTENDED for relatively light work, the self-hammering tool is shown here being used in a chiseling operation.

Hammer-punch holds other tools

This self-hammering toolholder is designed to take a variety of bits—everything from chisels to punches to engraving points. Here's what you need to know to turn out one for yourself on your lathe

By WALTER E. BURTON

PUNCHES WITH built-in hammers (sliding metal cylinders on a rod) are familiar to many mechanics. By using virtually the same arrangement, I went one better and made a tool that not only would handle a punch but a variety of other bits, all interchangeable.

These bits include various chisels; carving tools; center and piercing punches; embossing, dapping, chasing, or background-decorating punches; engraving points and other "percussion" attachments; and also fittings used for pulling operations, such as a cotter-pin-extracting hook.

A feature of this self-hammering tool is that the hammer is always present and ready to go.

SEE ALSO

Metal-lathe accessories . . .
Metal-lathe techniques . . . Scrapers . . .
Sharpening, tool . . . Toolboxes . . . Tools, hand . . .
Wrenches

Also, the bit can be held in precise position while the hammer operates. And, in some instances, hammer blows can be kept uniform—as by letting the hammer fall from a fixed height in punching sequences.

The "power" of such a self-hammering tool involves the characteristics of the sliding hammer. The unit illustrated was intended for relatively light work. With a typical punch in its chuck, it weighs slightly over one pound. It has a four-ounce hammer 2 in. long; other hammer sizes could be made, and used interchangeably.

The tool has four principal parts, other than the bit being used: A "chuck" that serves also as the handle or grip; a hammer; a rod on which the hammer slides, and a cap to prevent the hammer from sliding off the rod and to enable the tool to be used for pulling or extracting operations. All parts are steel.

I machined the chuck from ¾-in. rod to the shape and dimensions indicated in the drawing. The central portion was knurled for a better grip.

A ¼-20 setscrew (two could be used) locks the bit in the 5/16-in. hole in the outer end of the chuck. The opposite end of the chuck is drilled to receive the ⅜-in. hammer-guiding rod. Another ¼-20 setscrew locks this rod in its socket. The rod was drilled so the screw end penetrates it about 1/16 in. to discourage endwise shifting.

The guide rod shown is 9 in. long. This is sufficient to let the hammer travel about 6 in. In delicate work, it may travel only a fraction of an inch.

The hammer is simply a steel cylinder having a 13/32-in. longitudinal hole, which is sufficiently larger than the ⅜-in. guide rod to enable it (the hammer) to slide freely.

The guide-rod cap is secured with a ⅛-in.-diameter rivet made from unhardened drill rod (which is less likely to shear than a soft-iron rivet when you're "reverse hammering").

Chisels and other bits were made as needed, usually from drill rod or by adapting existing tools—such as a nailset, whose shank was machined to fit the chuck. A flat setscrew seat was filed on each bit. Besides discouraging burrs from interfering with bit removal, such a flat tends to prevent the bit from dropping out of the chuck if the setscrew is loosened by vibration.

After being shaped on a lathe or by filing, the bits were hardened and tempered as for similar conventional tools. But because the tool was not intended for severe service, parts of the hammer assembly were not hardened. Bit-cutting edges and points customarily are shielded, when not in use, with slip-on-caps.

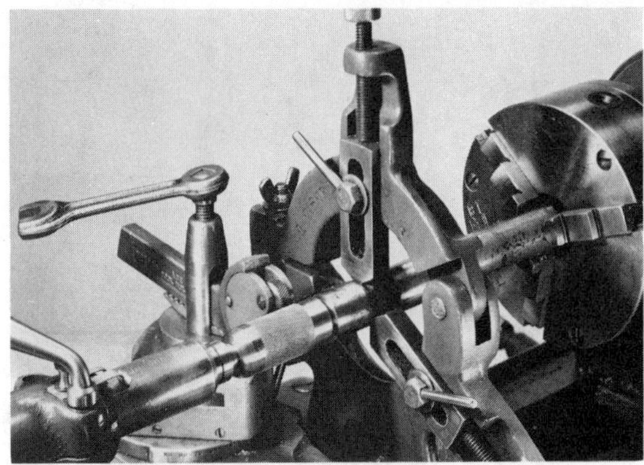

THE HAMMER is knurled while held by the steady rest. The same support is used when drilling the axial hole.

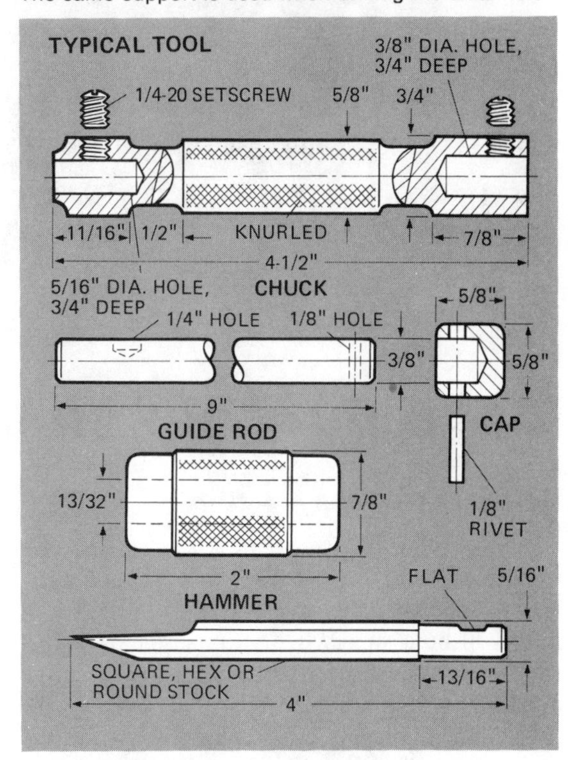

WHEN A PUNCH is inserted in the chuck, the setscrew is tightened against a flat filed on the shank of the punch.

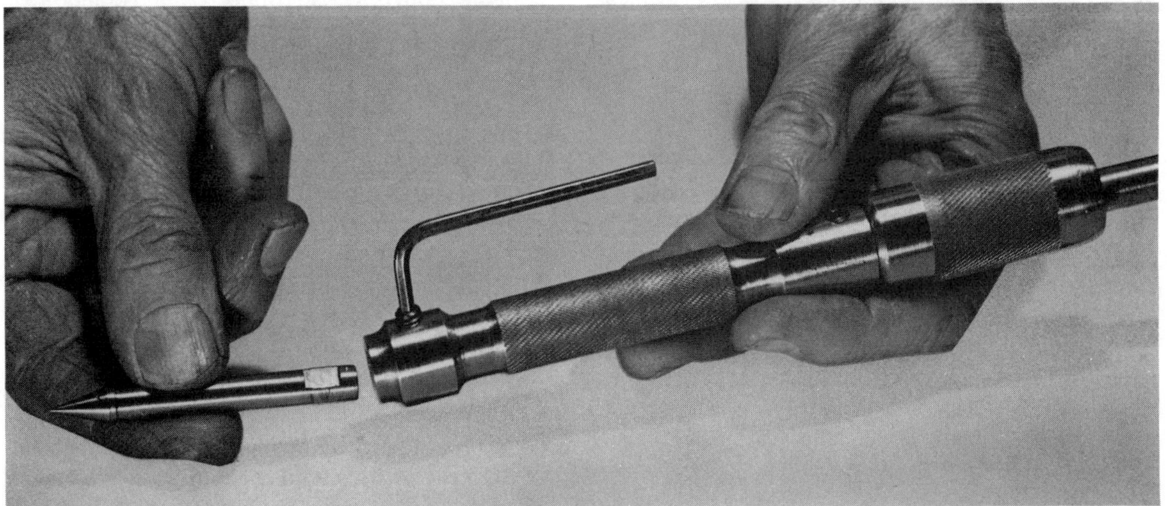

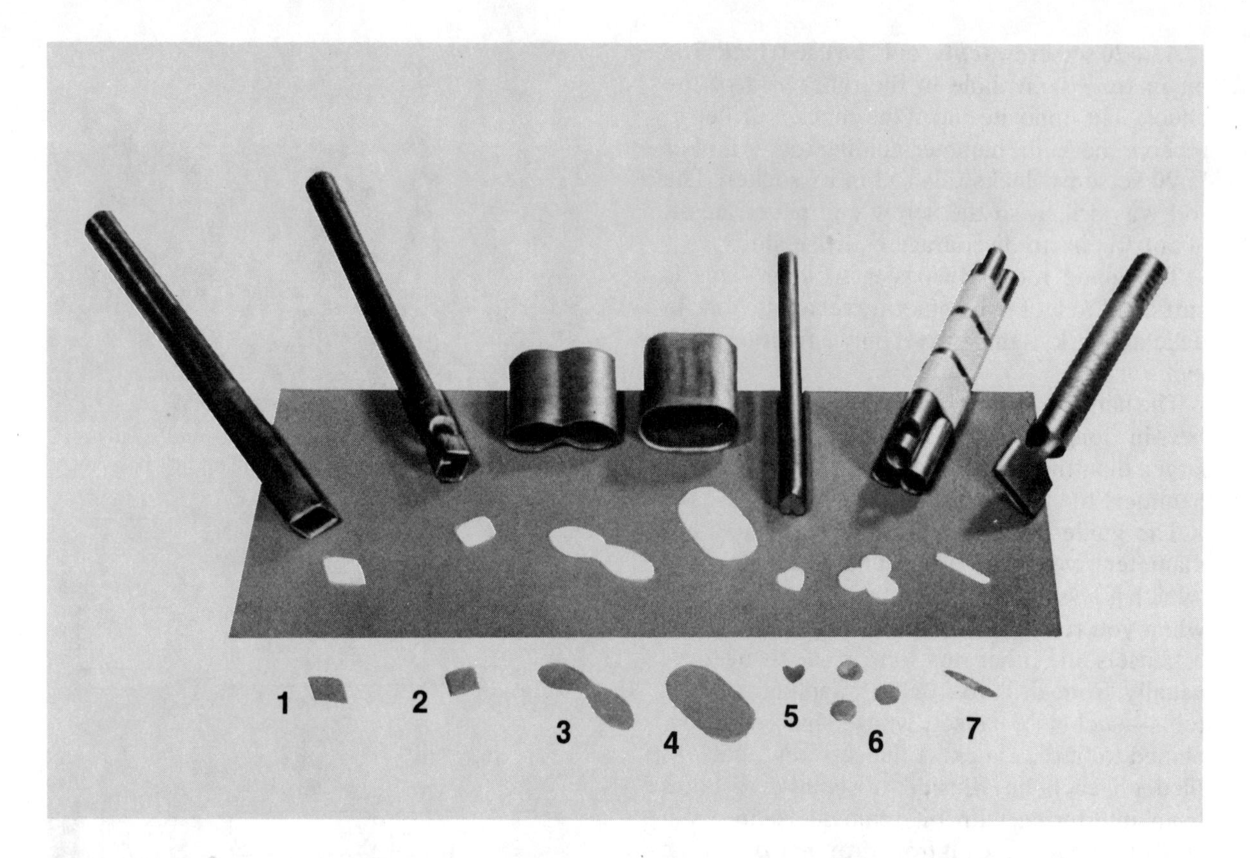

Make punches in special shapes

By WALTER E. BURTON

DECORATIVE INLAY work for tabletops, cabinets and other pieces of finely crafted furniture will be a snap when you use inexpensive, shaped punches like these. With just a whack of a hammer, or a squeeze of a press or vise, the punches will cleanly cut through thin wood veneers, as well as metal foil, cardboard, plastics, paper, rubber, fabric and even leather.

Shapes that are easy to produce include slots, squares, ovals, rectangles, diamonds, hearts, spades, clubs, triangles and polygons—and in almost any size desired. What's more, while a lathe may be helpful, you can make these punches with just a hacksaw, drill and files.

The seven punches shown above can be divided into three basic groups:

SEE ALSO
Finishes, wood . . . Inlays, cloth tape . . . Jewelry boxes . . . Marquetry . . . Sharpening, tool . . . Toolboxes . . . Tools, hand . . . Veneering . . . Wood sculpture

- Punches 3 and 4 are made of thinwall steel tubing and are short so they can be used in a press or vise. Such punches are often called cutting dies and are similar to the steel-rule dies used industrially.
- Punches 1, 2, 6 and 7 are hollow-drive punches. No. 1 was made from steel tubing, No. 2 machined from cold-rolled steel rod, and Nos. 6 and 7 from drill rod.
- Punch No. 5 was formed from a solid steel rod, shaped by filing and finished with an oilstone.

All of these punches have one thing in common: they start out as simple round shapes. Subsequently, they are squeezed, bent, filed, flared or otherwise processed to produce the desired cutting contours.

To make a hollow punch from a solid rod, first chuck the rod in a lathe (or drill) and machine one end square. Then convert a short length of the rod (usually a half inch or so) to a thinwall tube by drilling out the center of the rod. Using a round file, form one or two openings in the side of the tube to permit easy removal of the cutout pieces.

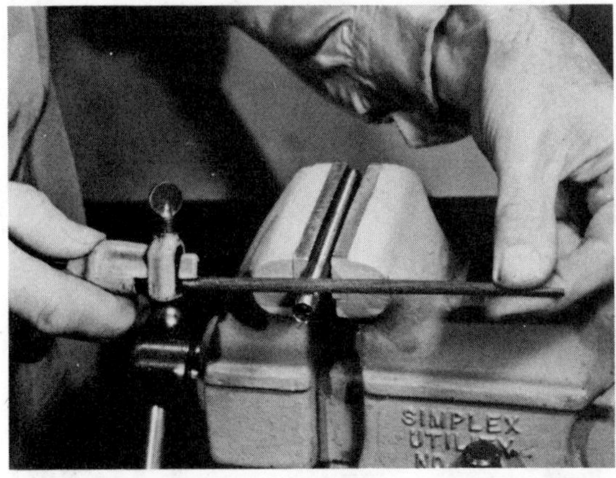

FILE ROUND NOTCHES in the side of a tubular portion cut in a solid rod. Depending on the final shape, one or two notches may be needed for removal of pieces.

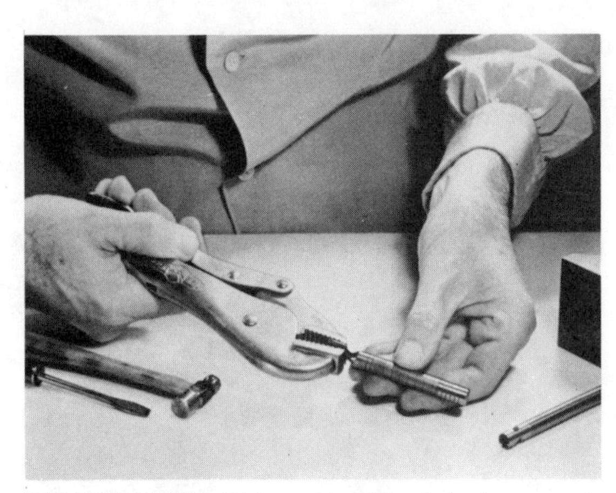

NARROW SLOTS will be cut by this particular type of punch. After annealing, flatten the hollow end to the desired degree. A vise or vise pliers will work.

Bevel the outer end of the tube to form a sharp cutting edge and then anneal the beveled edge by heating it to redness and letting it air-cool. Finally, shape the cutting edge to the desired configuration.

Punch No. 7, for example, can be shaped by squeezing the tube in a vise or a pair of pliers. Use this method with caution, however, as the simple squeezing of a tube in a vise often results in unwanted curves, much as in punch No. 3.

To make a square punch, heat the hollow end of the tube to a glowing red and immediately drive it over the square shank of a brace bit or some other square, tapered form. Tap the sides of the edges with a hammer to produce a true square.

No side opening is required for punches made of steel tubing (like that used for automobile fuel lines) because you can run a rod through the length of the tube to eject the cut pieces. When using seamed tubing, be careful not to open the seam when forming the cutting edge.

The sharp edge-bevels on a hollow punch can be formed with an inside bevel, an outside bevel, or both. An inside bevel produces clean-cut openings, while an outside bevel produces clean cutouts. A double bevel places the cutting edge in the middle of the wall and therefore produces a

THREE BASIC BEVELS will equip you with the right punch for almost any job. For the most common shop uses, double bevel is best.

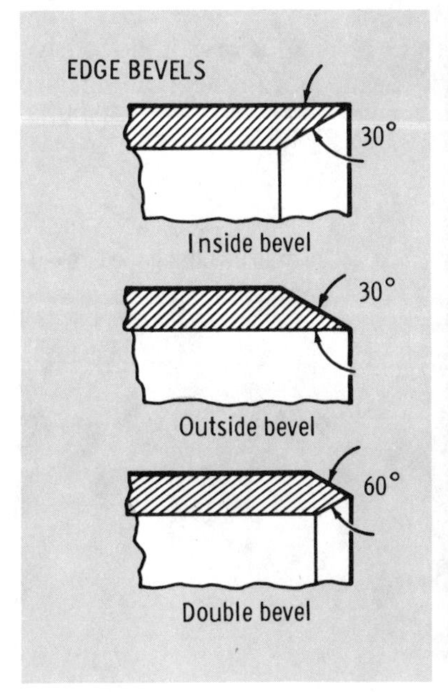

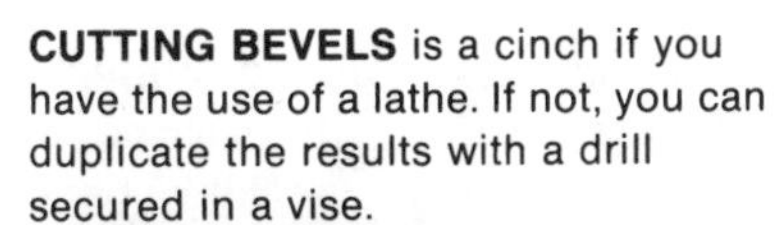

CUTTING BEVELS is a cinch if you have the use of a lathe. If not, you can duplicate the results with a drill secured in a vise.

SQUEEZING TUBES requires both practice and the use of a spacer block. Otherwise, the flat center surfaces could bend inward.

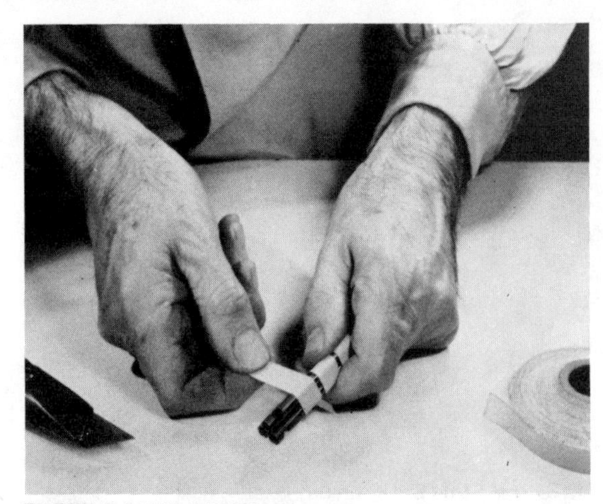

THREE ROUND PUNCHES, when taped together, will produce a cutout shaped similar to a cloverleaf. Each ganged punch must be provided with an inside bevel.

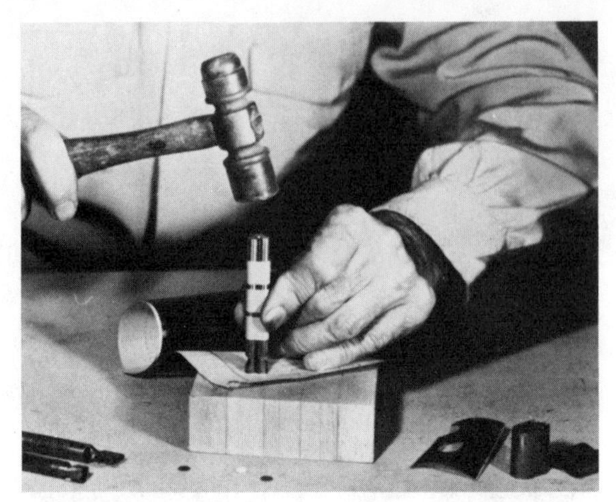

SCRAP WOOD is the most common material used to support the work being cut. Be sure, however, to have only the end grain of the wood facing the punch.

slightly distorted opening and cutout. For most uses, however, this slight distortion is of little consequence. Ganged punches (simply two or more punches bonded together by tape or other means) must always be provided with inside bevels.

When forming a punch of drill rod or any other hardenable steel, remember to harden and temper the cutting end. If in doubt as to the specific directions for working with a particular alloy, try heating the cutting end to a deep red color (in a dimly lighted room) and then plunge it into cold water. Clean off the punch so the actual color of the steel is visible and then heat it again. When it turns to a reddish-brown or purple color, plunge it into the water for a final quenching.

Punches of soft steel, such as ordinary tubing or cold-rolled rods, must be treated by case-hardening the edges, and often the head as well. After using any of the common hardening compounds (follow the directions on the package implicitly), temper the punch in the same manner as other hardenable steels.

When using any of the punches, be sure to back the material being cut with a support of wood, cardboard or hardboard. Wood should always be placed with the end grain facing the cutting edge.

SQUARE PUNCHES are simply round tubes heated and then tapped over the square, tapered end of a brace bit. Tap all four sides gently for a true square.

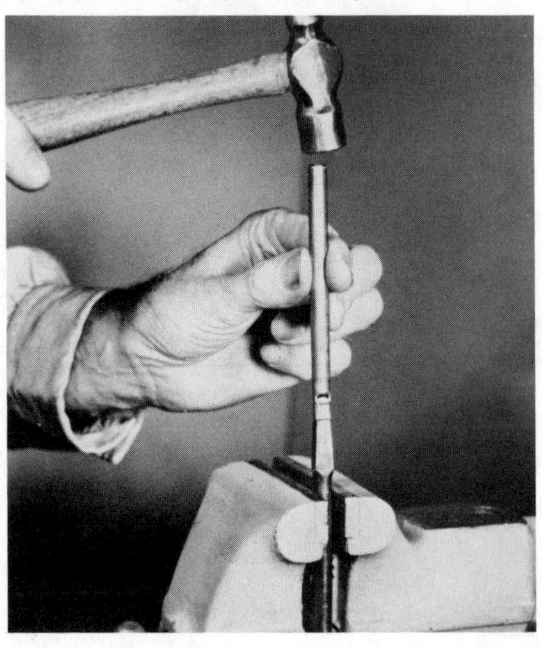

ODD-SHAPED PUNCHES can be made in many ways. A heart shape, for example, can be solid rod filed to shape, or a tube formed around a shaped dowel (inset).

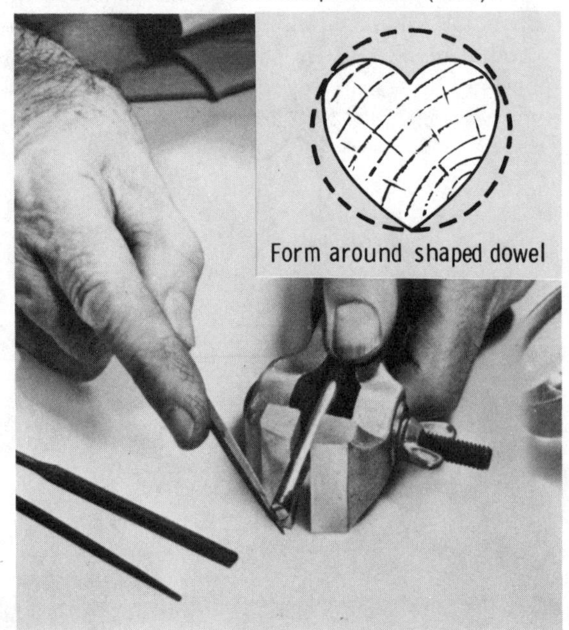

By WALTER E. BURTON

An adjustable-sleeve punch

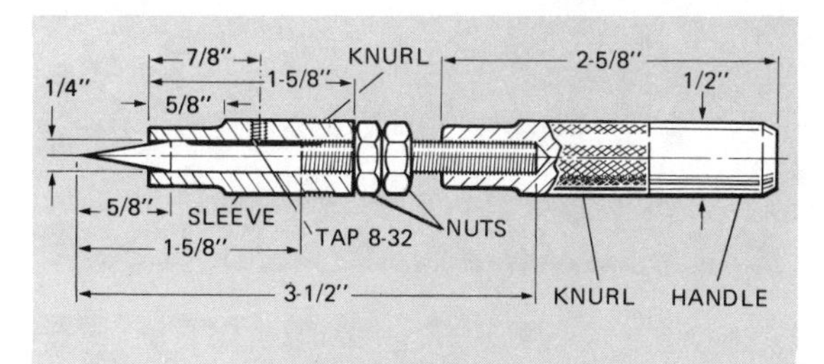

FITTED with a sliding adjustable stop to control hole size, this unique hand tool lets you punch same-size holes repeatedly in sheet material with a tap of a hammer. It will produce holes ranging from a tiny pinprick to ¼ in. dia. in lightweight aluminum, tin-can stock or cardboard when the material is supported by a wooden block. In use, the sleeve limits point penetration, and is set for depth by tightening two hex jam nuts, which limit the sleeve's upward travel.

Begin by threading a ¼-in. drill rod (¼-20 or ¼-28 thread) as shown, and trim so that a 1⅝-in. unthreaded length remains. On the unthreaded end, form the conical point. Starting about ⅛ in. from the point taper, file a flat extended to the thread for the sleeve setscrew. Then harden and temper the unthreaded section of the rod.

Make the sleeve and handle from ½-in. rod to the shape and dimensions shown. (Turning down of ends is for appearance; knurling is optional.) Both parts can also be hardened for maximum resistance to wear. At a point ⅞ in. from the sleeve's smaller end, drill and tap for the setscrew. Drill and tap an axial hole in the handle to take the pointed rod to a depth of about ¾ in.

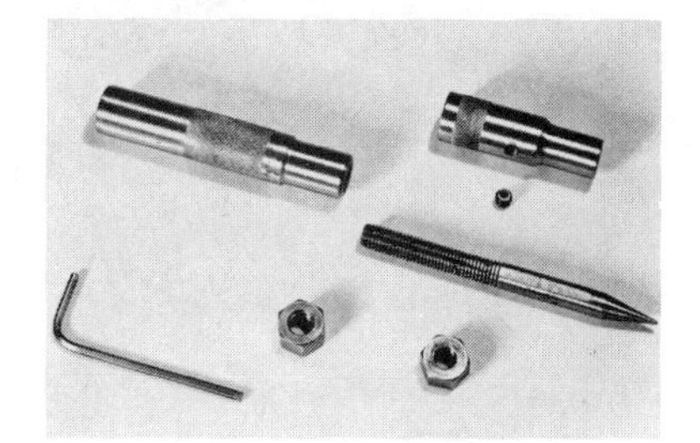

THREADING A drill rod is first step in construction of punch. Annealing the rod first may be necessary for easiest threading. Photo (top) shows the finished parts of the punch and Allen wrench used to tighten sleeve's setscrew. At top of page, sheeting being punched is supported over hole in wood block.

SEE ALSO

Sharpening, tool . . . Threading . . . Toolboxes . . . Tools, hand

18

Build a putting green from artificial turf

This synthetic turf is easy to install and durable. It's perfect for laying your own greens

IF YOU'D RATHER spend Saturdays swinging a putter than a grass whip, Lawnscape Landscaping is the material that can make your dreams come true. The decorative "carpet" has a fiber facing that closely resembles living grass both in appearance and feel. The beauty of it is that once it is installed, there's no maintenance.

Made of second-generation polypropylene that is polymerized to withstand aging and the weathering of extreme outdoor conditions, Lawnscape is a product of the Ozite Corp., 1755 Butterfield Rd., Libertyville, IL 60048. The synthetic turf is sold nationally through carpet dealers and building-supply centers that also stock installation materials. Ask their advice regarding installation in your area.

The material can be installed professionally or by a do-it-yourselfer. Since the carpet comes in 6 and 12-ft. widths, the putting greens shown here are designed to utilize those modules.

The dirt or soil subsurface of the area to be covered should be shaped and well tamped. The manufacturer recommends either 1½ in. of asphalt or concrete over the compacted base for the Lawnscape to adhere to. (This minimum thickness will vary with load requirements.) Installation directly over earth is not recommended.

The surface finish should be as smooth and nonporous as possible. Because of the latter requirement, the covered area should be pitched slightly to direct water runoff where you want it to go.

The perimeter boards (headers) can be installed as shown in the drawings (page 10) or as in the photos below. The latter method creates shiplap joints by doubling up two-bys. Start by installing the headers because these can also be used for screeding the concrete. Once they are in and secured by stakes, the earth inside can be excavated and tamped. Then the concrete is laid

SEE ALSO

Carpeting, outdoor . . . Landscaping . . . Lawns . . . Paths, garden . . . Patios . . . Playgrounds . . . Swings . . . Tennis . . . Trees . . . Yard lighting

USE A NOTCHED TROWEL to spread adhesive on the base. When it's almost dry, put down the turf.

FOR INVISIBLE seams, press Seaming Pin-Tape into the adhesive. Its barbs will hold the turf.

up to the solid header and maintained approximately ⅜ to ½ in. below the header's top edge. This measurement should be as consistent as possible to maintain a uniform grass height. You can achieve it by using a notched screed on the header boards to level the concrete. If you use asphalt instead of concrete, seal the surface and allow it to dry overnight before installing Lawnscape.

Sweep the surface clean and patch any irregularities. Spread the synthetic turf in the sun to warm it and trim the edges to be butted. Then, using a 3/32-in. notched trowel, spread Ozite AP 770 adhesive over the area of exposed width. When the adhesive barely transfers to your finger (10 to 20 minutes), the turf can be rolled onto the surface. You can assure invisible seams with Pin Tapes (see photos, page 2467). These are positioned astraddle the edge. The grass is simply tapped into place with a hammer.

Lawnscape and related material—flags, cups and instructions—come as a kit. Simply select the layout you want and order the amount of carpeting in the kit.

In addition to a putting green, you might want to consider the synthetic turf for swimming-pool aprons, patios, roof decks and the like. It's comfortable to walk on and durable.

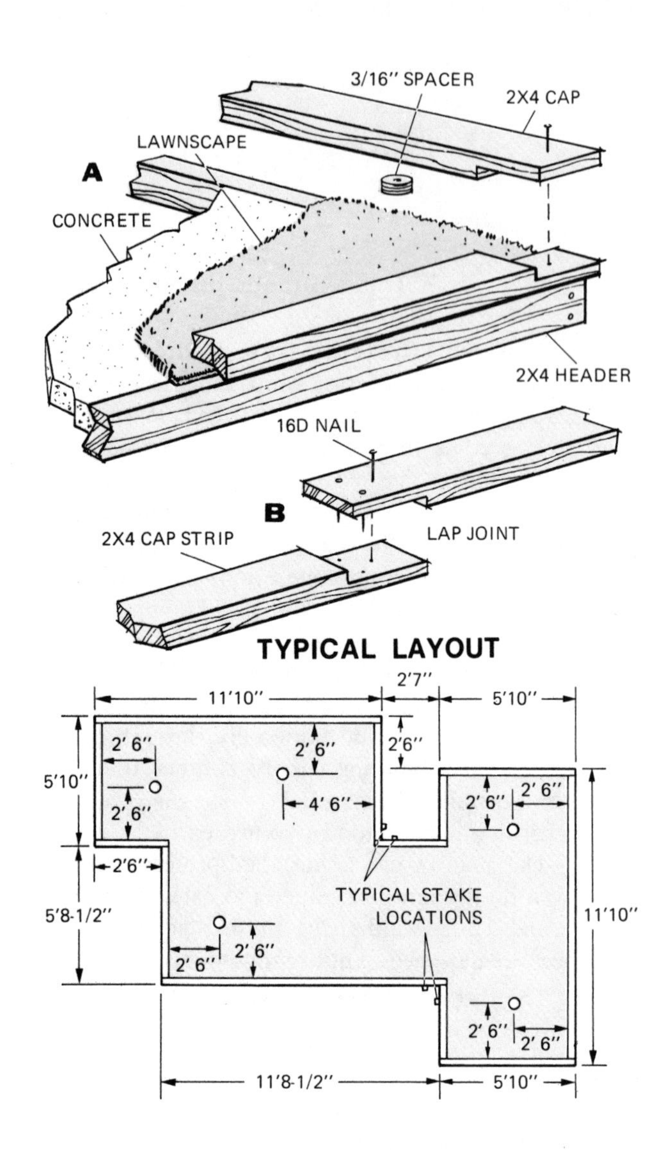

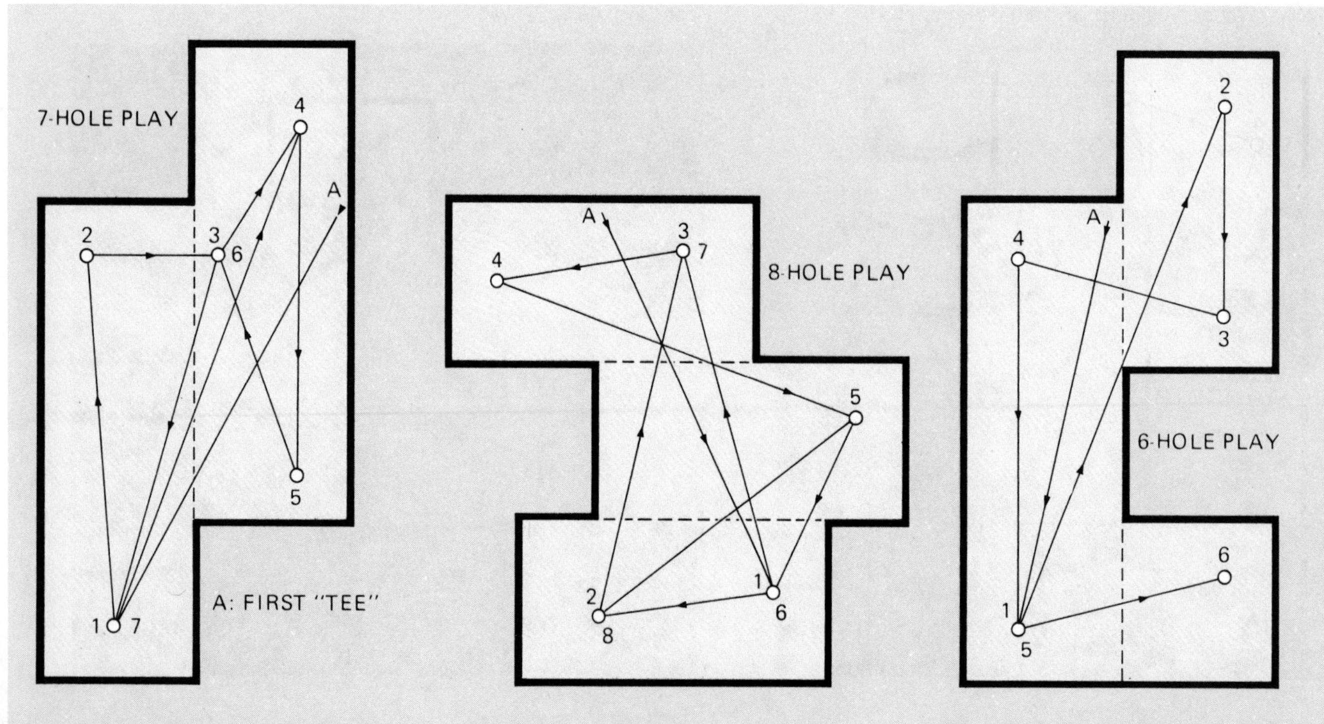

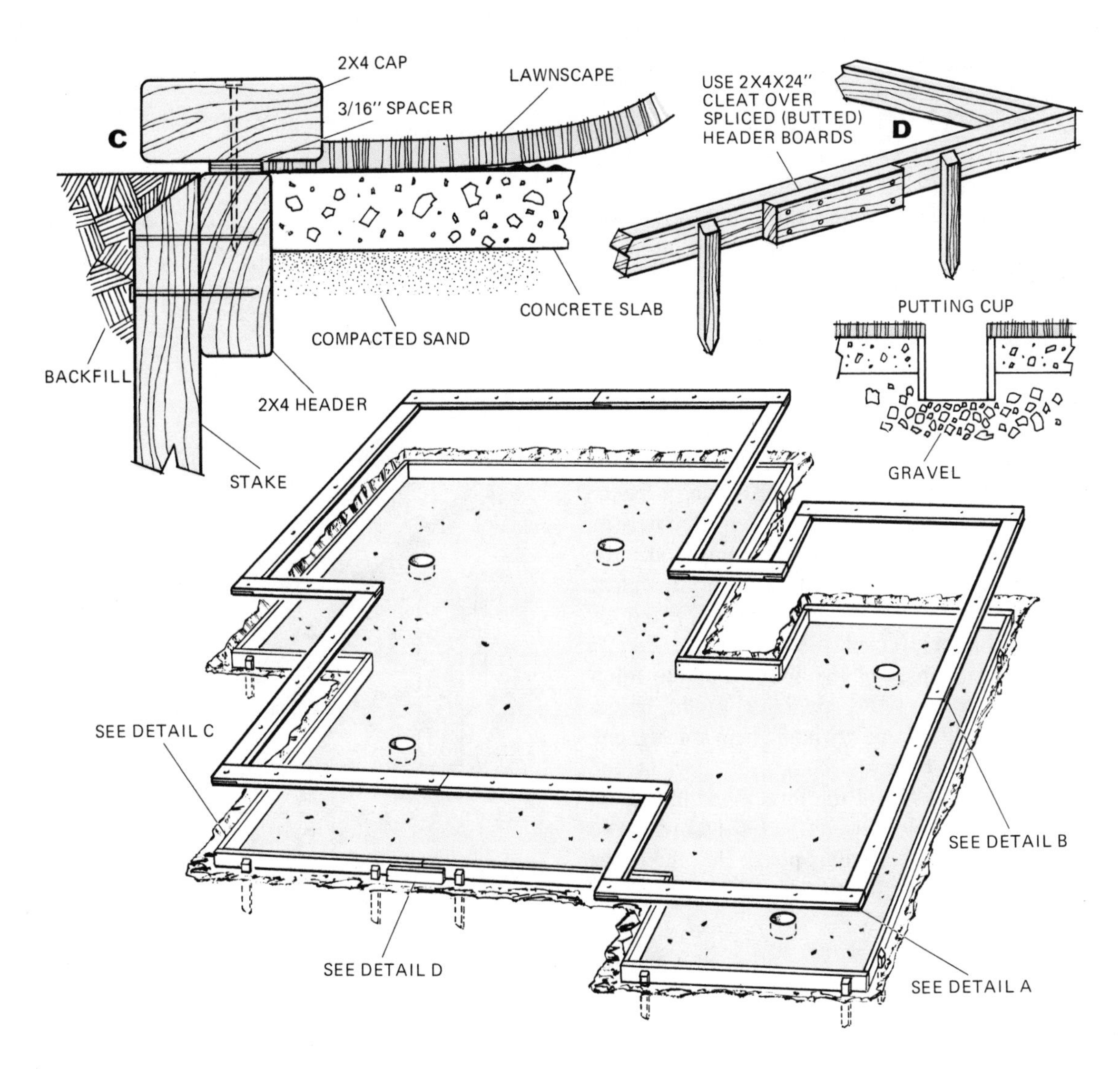
2X4 CAP
LAWNSCAPE
3/16" SPACER
C
CONCRETE SLAB
COMPACTED SAND
BACKFILL
2X4 HEADER
STAKE
USE 2X4X24" CLEAT OVER SPLICED (BUTTED) HEADER BOARDS
D
PUTTING CUP
GRAVEL
SEE DETAIL C
SEE DETAIL B
SEE DETAIL D
SEE DETAIL A

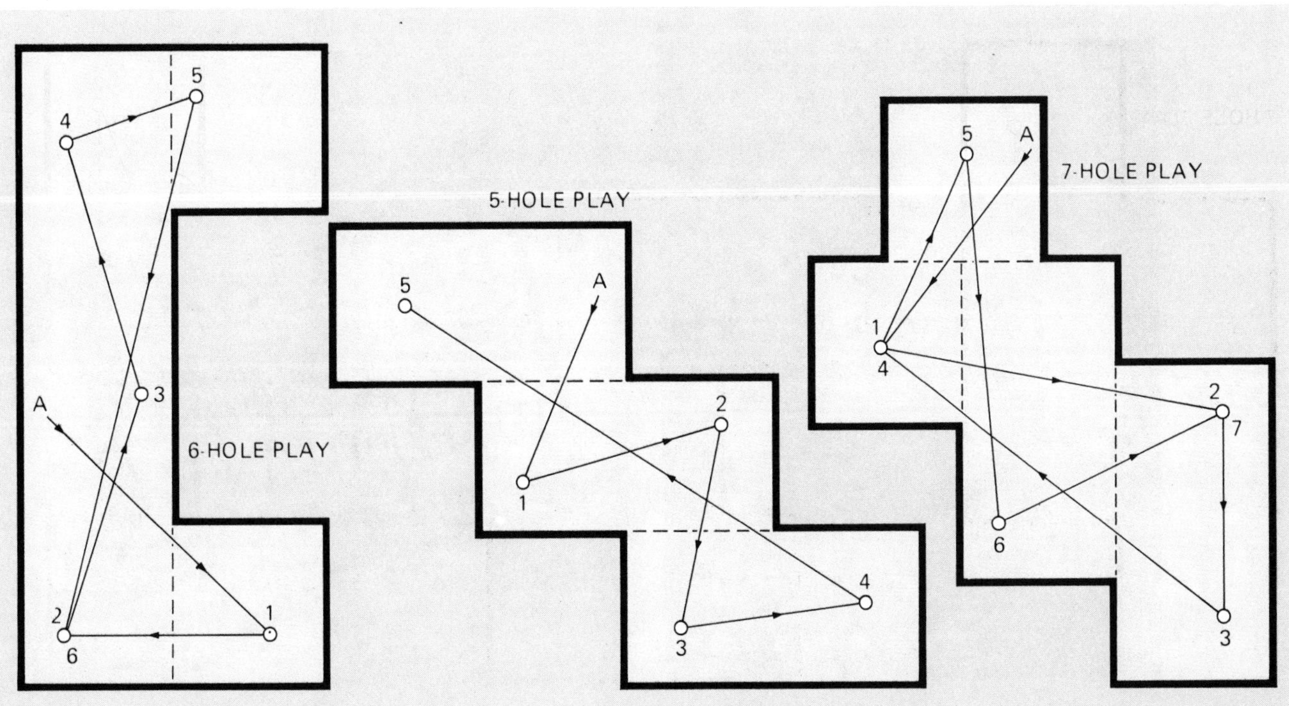
6-HOLE PLAY
5-HOLE PLAY
7-HOLE PLAY

A real puzzler

By KENNETH WELLS

WITH THIS intriguing little puzzle you can compete with yourself or friends to find the fewest moves—or shortest time—you need to reverse positions of the words "black" and "white." It's not too frustrating when you have unlimited moves; the real skill lies in your ability to effect this change in as few moves as possible.

Make the cubes first, then build the box to fit. From a strip of ¾-in. square stock saw off pieces just a little over ¾-in. long. True the cube ends square (and to length) using a bench disc sander or with a similar setup mounted on the lathe. Careful sanding is very important.

To obtain the inside length of the holder, place five cubes together, measure the overall length (it should be approximately 3¾ in.) and add 1/16 in. Measuring three of the cubes plus the tolerance gives width. Miter the sides of the holder and use masking tape to hold them during gluing. When the holder is completely dry, fit and glue in the bottom and the three fixed blocks on the bottom. The holder can be finished with two coats of sealer or shellac polish to make the cubes slide freely within the box.

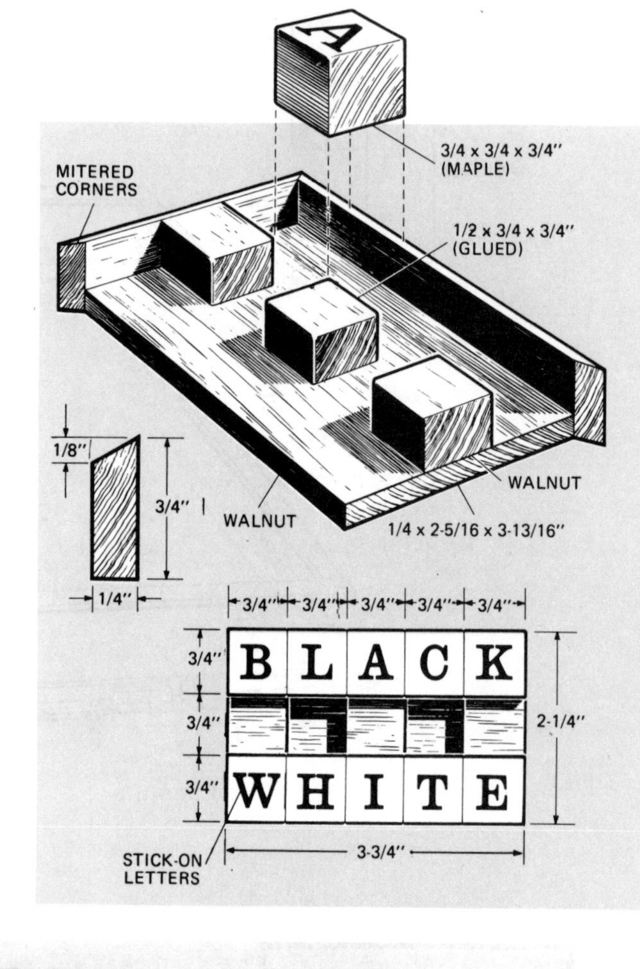

SEE ALSO

Air games . . . Chess sets . . . Cribbage boards . . . Game tables . . . Games . . . Gifts, Christmas . . . Pool tables . . . Pull toys . . . Shuffleboard tables . . . Toys . . . Weekend projects

How to use a radial-arm saw

By W. CLYDE LAMMEY

From a simple power tool for crosscutting, mitering and ripping lumber, the radial-arm saw has evolved into a nearly complete power workshop in one unit. Using accessories and a variety of setups, you can do shaping, routing, grooving, sanding, dadoing and rabbeting

A RADIAL SAW is comparable to a table saw turned upside down. The motor, arbor, controls and mountings are all *above* the table rather than *below* it.

In crosscutting and mitering operations, and also in dadoing, you move the blade or cutter to the work, rather than the work to the blade or cutter as with the table saw. The exceptions are ripping, and some operations with accessories where the work is moved to the cutter, as in grooving, rabbeting, routing and shaping.

This "upside down" saw calls for a somewhat different operating technique and an extra measure of caution in all operations. This applies even when the blade housing and guard are in position. You will notice when making that first crosscut with your new saw that the blade tends to move, or "pull," toward you as the cut progresses. You are making what experienced operators of radial saws call a "climb" cut, where the blade tends to pull itself into the work. Here you make sure of that extra measure of caution and have a firm hold on the handle with which you draw the blade forward into the workpiece; you actually offer a slight resistance to the travel of the blade into the workpiece. Otherwise the cut may be too fast for smoothness, and the blade may exit from the cut unexpectedly, possibly endangering you. This is especially true when crosscutting or mitering wide pieces of stock 2 in. or more in thickness.

The rules for safe operation of the radial saw are quite simple and should quickly become habit: (a) Before you plug in the tool, make sure the motor switch is in the "off" position. (b) Make sure before starting the motor that all control handles are tightened properly. (c) Never—repeat, *never*—permit loose pieces of stock, other objects such as end cuttings, wrenches, clamps, etc., on the table when operating the unit. (d) Never—repeat, *never*—allow your attention to wander even for a moment while the unit is in operation. (e) Always operate the unit with both the blade housing and the blade guard in position.

All the precautions can be summed up in two words—*be careful!*

The manual that comes with the saw will tell: how to set it up and operate it when making the basic cuts; how to align the blade should this be necessary; and how to arrange the table spacer boards for in and out ripping.

Some radials may come with the table already grooved and recessed. If not you can easily cut these yourself. To make the crosscut groove, raise the blade to clear, slide the carriage back as far as it will go, start the motor, and lower the blade until it cuts into the table about $^3/_{16}$ in. Then pull the blade forward as far as it will go. Cut the right and left miter grooves in the same manner, moving the arm 45 degrees to the right and left. Then raise the blade to clear, swing the arm to the 90 degree position, swing the yoke 90 degrees to the out-rip position, pull it forward as far as it will go, start the motor and lower the blade until it cuts into the table about $^3/_{16}$ in. Push it back as far as it will go, very slowly, so that it cuts a concave recess in the tabletop. The purpose of the grooves and recess, of course, is to permit the lowering of the blade below the table surface so that it will cut all the way through the stock.

SEE ALSO

Bandsaws . . . Bench saws . . . Disc sanders . . . Drill presses . . . Jigsaws . . . Motors, shop . . . Power-tool stands . . . Shapers . . . Table saws . . . Workbenches . . . Workshops

CROSSCUTTING is a basic operation on radial saw. Blade is drawn only far enough to cut through material, then returned to starting position.

WHEN SETTING up for ripping, tilt blade housing to just clear the stock, then adjust kickback arm with a block the thickness of stock to be ripped.

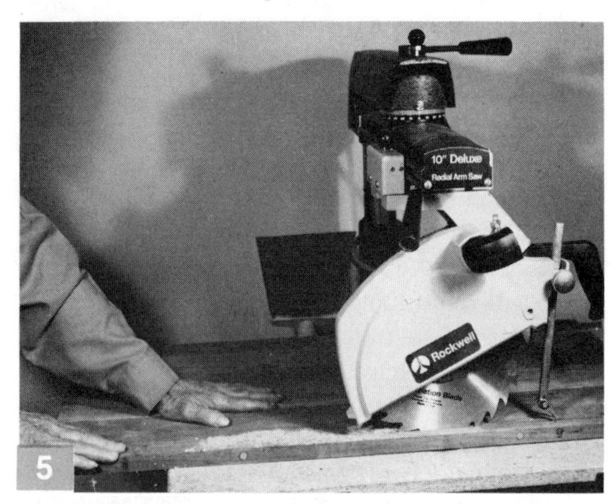

RIP CUT in relatively wide stock is common radial-saw operation. In rip cuts make sure carriage, yoke and blade housing are securely locked in place.

LEFT-HAND miter cut is perhaps less common of the two. As in all crosscutting, draw blade only far enough to cut through stock.

In making the crosscut, Fig. 1, you have a choice of left or right-hand pull. In the illustration, the left-hand pull is shown, as the longer stock is more conveniently held in the position by the right hand. If the workpiece were short, and only a small waste piece was to be removed, you could use the right-hand pull with left-hand hold. Either position is permissible, but you should know where that right or left holding hand is at all times!

When making the crosscut or the miter (either right or lefthand) don't pull the blade all the way past the stock. Stop when the waste is completely severed. This assures that when you move the blade back through the cut there is no chance that the portion of the blade coming up will catch the waste. The same is true when making the miter cuts.

Before you make a rip cut, always set the anti-kickback arm as in Fig. 2. First tilt the blade guard so that its rear edge will be about ⅛ to ¼ in. above the surface of the stock. Then, if ¾-in. stock is to be ripped, set the kickback arm with the swiveling points, or fingers, in the position shown, using a ¾-in. block. Next, if you have not already done so, set the pointers on the rip scale to the correct positions to assure ripping to the precise width desired, Fig. 3. (See your instruction manual.) In any ripping operation make sure *both yoke and carriage* are locked in position before starting the motor.

When ripping short, narrow stock as in Fig. 4, use a push stick and place the stick so that it contacts the material near the outer edge as shown. This will prevent any tendency of the workpiece to edge away from the fence. Fig. 5 shows the common procedure of ripping a long, wide workpiece. *Here the blade guard has been removed, as it has in other following illustrations, only for the sake of clarity.*

Figs. 6 and 7 show positions in cutting left and right-hand miters. The left-hand miter is the least

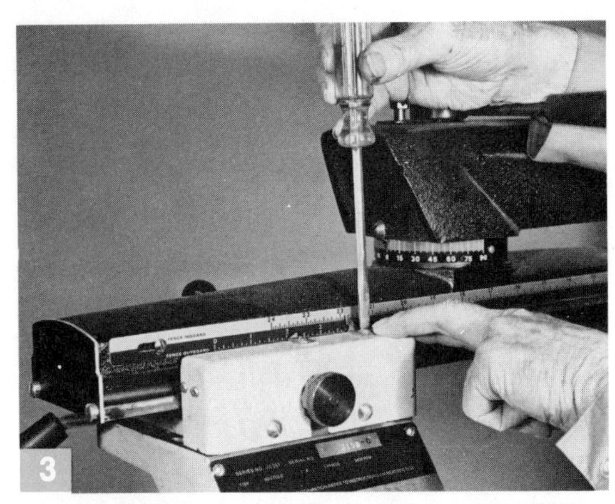

IF YOU HAVE NOT already done so, set rip-scale pointers for in and out-rip positions to assure accuracy. See instructions that come with your saw.

USE PUSH STICK when ripping short, narrow stock. Place stick near outer corner of stock to prevent it drifting away from the fence.

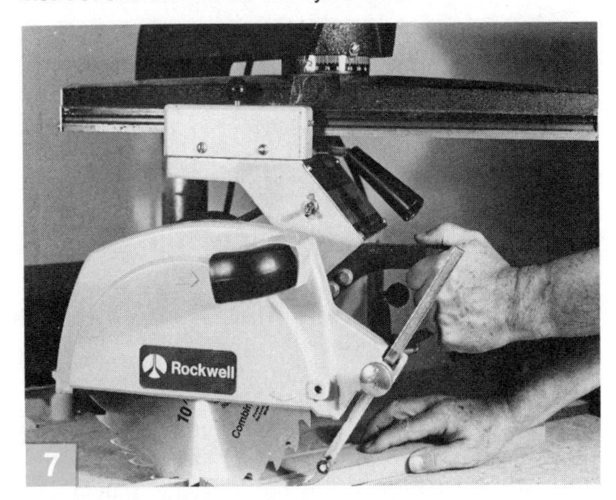

RIGHT-HAND MITER is made just opposite. After first cut, turn stock over and move to left to miter opposite end. Exception is mitering molded stock.

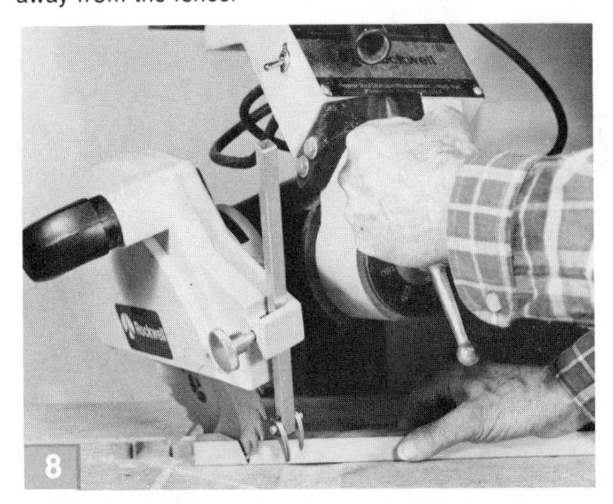

COMPOUND MITER is made by swinging the arm and tilting the blade the required number of degrees. Consult a table for proper degree setting.

used as it generally is possible to shift the stock from right to left positions after turning it over when necessary to miter both ends. The exception, of course, is mitering picture molding. The compound miter, Fig. 8, requires setting both the arm and the tilt to the required number of degrees to form the "hopper" joint. There are tables available which give the degree settings for this type of joinery on the radial-arm saw.

When you want to trim a number of small workpieces to exact length, you can clamp a stop to the fence as in Fig. 9. Make sure that the clamp is properly positioned and that it is *tight*. Remove each waste piece as it is cut only after the saw is moved back to its extreme rear position.

Your radial saw is a first-rate disc sander. You first remove the fence and substitute two ¾-in. square strips, placing these on each side of the disc as in Fig. 10. Then lower the disc through the slot thus formed as in Fig. 11. Be sure that the disc clears before starting the motor; also be sure that it just clears the fixed edge of the saw table. Use a medium to coarse grade abrasive disc for fast cutting and to avoid burning the end grain of hardwoods. Use the finer grades for finishing, and apply only light pressure to the work.

To use a drum sander, swivel the motor to the vertical position with the spindle, or arbor, down. Cut a half-round opening in the edge of each of the spacer boards, as in Fig. 12. The diameter of the opening should be about 1½ times the diameter of the drum. Leave the square spacers in position as shown in Fig. 11, but be sure that the table clamps are drawn tight so nothing can shift while sanding is being done. Be especially careful to avoid a finger or hand contacting the rotating drum; a rather painful burn can be the penalty. The same caution is necessary when using the disc. Also, in any of these operations, make sure that the yoke is

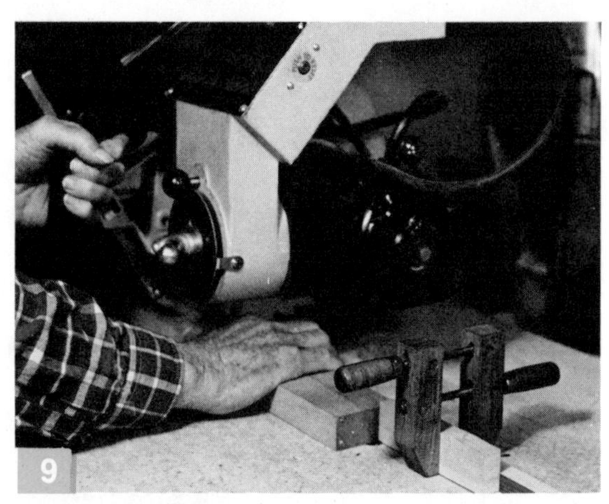

TO CUT DUPLICATE short lengths, clamp a stop to the fence and measure distance from blade to stop. Make sure that the clamp is drawn tight!

FOR DISC SANDING substitute ¾-in. strips for fence, one on each side of disc. Lower disc into opening and be sure carriage and yoke are locked.

WITH THE MOTOR still in the vertical position it's a straight router. If the groove is more than ⅛ in. in depth, cut in two or more passes.

REPLACE ROUTER CHUCK with three-knife shaper cutter and accessory spindle and you have a vertical-spindle shaper. Make the finish cut in two passes.

locked securely in position with the yoke clamp provided.

The radial is not only a useful drum and disc sander, it's a handy router, as you can see in Fig. 13. It takes only a minute to make the conversion. Leave the motor in its vertical position and replace the drum with an accessory router-bit chuck. Set the motor to the desired position to rout the groove, lock it in position, and feed the work slowly. If the groove is more than ⅛ in. deep you'll get a smoother job by cutting to the desired depth in several passes, each not more than about ⅛ in. deep.

In Fig. 14 the radial is set up as a spindle shaper, using an accessory spindle and a three-knife cutterhead of the type used on vertical-spindle shapers. The guard does not come with the accessory spindle; it's improvised from a sheet-metal disc and is not really necessary if one is cautious. In this operation it's best to make the cut in two or more passes for the smoothest work. Feed slowly in either hard or softwood; again, make sure the yoke is securely locked before starting the cut.

A quick conversion makes your radial saw a rotary planer, as in Fig. 15. Use the same two-piece fence as in shaping, change to the router-bit chuck, and fit a rotary planing head. As you can see, it does a smooth, clean job. If you must reduce the thickness of stock more than ⅛ in., make the cuts in two or more passes.

If you don't have the three-knife molding cutter pictured in Fig. 14, you can set up with the three-knife head such as that commonly used for cutting moldings on a table saw. Figs. 16 and 17 show how the setup is made, using the special guard furnished as an accessory. Notice in Fig. 17 that the motor is tilted about 5 degrees from the vertical. For this work you'll need to make the special fence, as shown in the inset detail, to obtain the necessary clearance. The molding shape is similar to that being cut in

WHEN SANDING end grain, use coarse abrasive and a light pressure to avoid "burning" stock. Don't permit hand or fingers to touch the rotating disc!

YOUR RADIAL SAW is also a drum sander. Swing motor to vertical position and cut half-round opening in spacer boards. Use ¾-in. spacers as shown.

REPLACE shaping spindle with that for router bit, insert planing head and you have a surfacer. Cuts should not exceed ⅛ in.

A MOLDING HEAD of the type used on the table saw will also work well on most radials. Here the three-knife head is being placed on the motor spindle.

Fig. 14, but of course other molding shapes can be cut with the same setup. In Fig. 18 a panel-raising cut is being made with the same setup, but using a straight knife on the cutterhead rather than the molding knife shown on the head in Fig. 16. You can also do rabbeting with this setup, tilting the motor back to the vertical position. Again the reminder: Don't forget when making any of these setups to lock the yoke firmly in place so that it cannot slide forward or back. And be just as certain that all controls are tight before starting the motor.

Figs. 19 and 20 show dadoing and grooving with a carbide-tipped cutter of the "wobble" type; the width of cut is adjusted by movable "washers" that form the hub. It's a simple gadget easily adjusted for various groove widths, and cuts extremely smoothly on both hard and soft woods. Notice in Fig. 20 that the blade housing has been tilted back so that the rear edge just clears the surface of the stock, as in the ripping cut with the saw blade; also that the kickback arm has been adjusted for ¾-in. stock.

In Fig. 21 the same type of head pictured in Fig. 20 is being used to make spaced dado cuts in a dentil molding. Here the cuts are spaced by means of a heavy pencil line on the table; if you need greater accuracy, make the special fence in the detail having a fixed stop, the stop entering each successive cut as you move the stock after making the first dado cut.

In ordinary shop work you'll not often be called upon to make a uniform bend in stock. In case you need to make such a bend, Fig. 22 and the insert detail show how it can be done. Once you get the spacing of the successive cuts, as in the detail, mark the location of the cuts on one face of the workpiece and then set the saw blade to cut within about ⅛ in. less than the thickness of the stock. Should it be necessary to hold the workpiece in the curved position until application, Fig. 21, place a few drops of glue in each

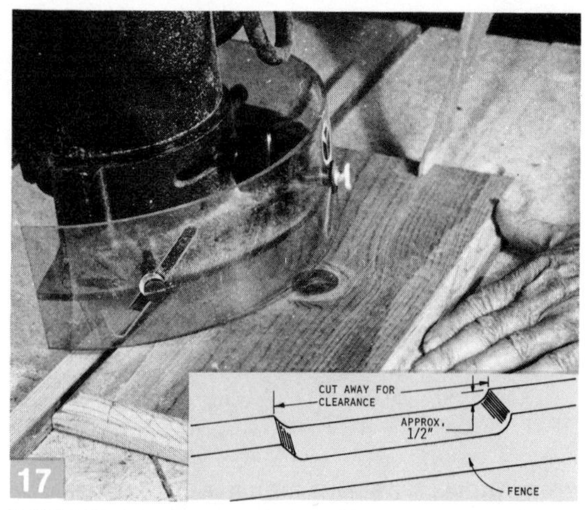

USING HEAD pictured in Fig. 16 and accessory guard permits doing a range of shaping work. When workpieces are small use push stick.

HERE'S A panel-raising job being done with the same head shown in Fig. 16, using a straight cutter. The motor is tilted and the same guard is used.

GROOVES are cut with the same head, the setup made as in ripping cuts. It's well to test for depth on waste stock to assure accuracy. Use the push stick.

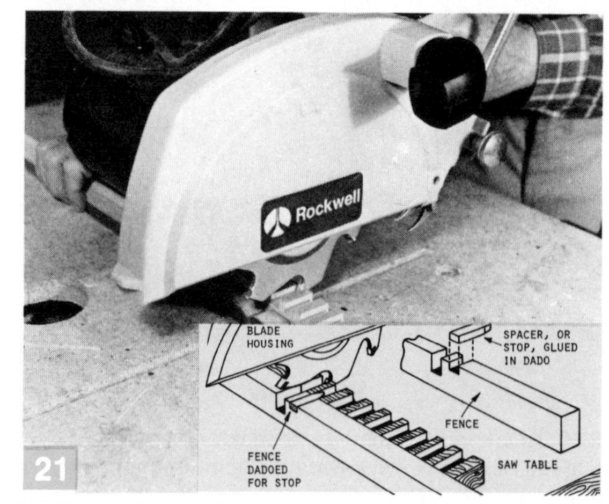

IN MAKING a dentil molding the cuts are simply spaced dadoes. For precise accuracy you can make the special fence shown in the insert detail.

JOINING NARROW pieces to build up to a given width is usually done by doweling but the pros generally prefer to cut a glue joint on the meeting edges.

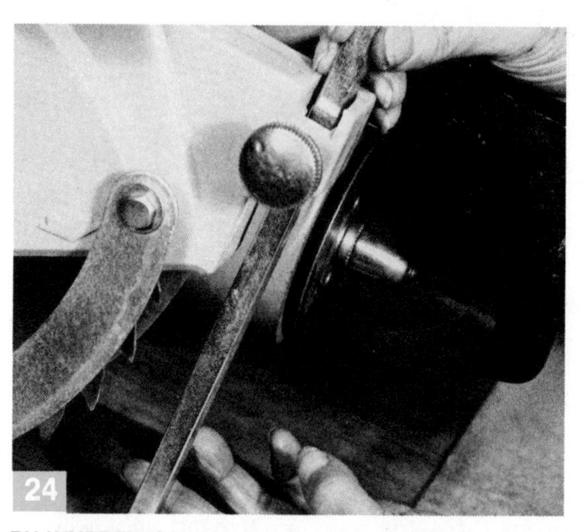

BY INVERTING the kickback arm in its opening in the housing it can form an additional blade guard for added safety when making repetitive cuts.

CUT DADOES from ¼ to ¾ in. with grooving head of the "wobble" type. Adjustments for width are made by rotating washers that form hub.

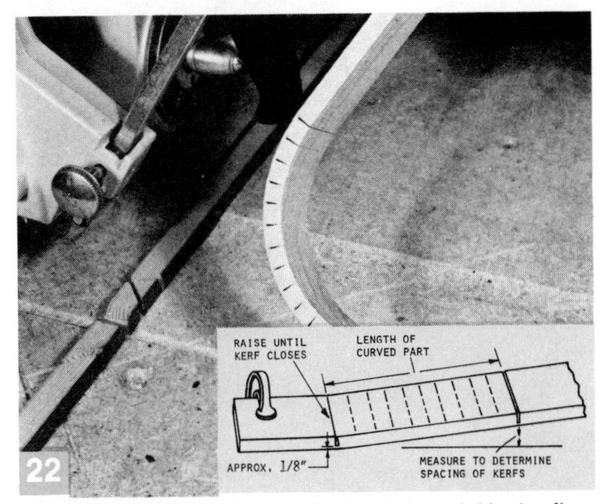

IT'S NOT OFTEN you'll need to bend material by kerfing but the photo and inset detail show how it can be done. Space the kerfs accurately.

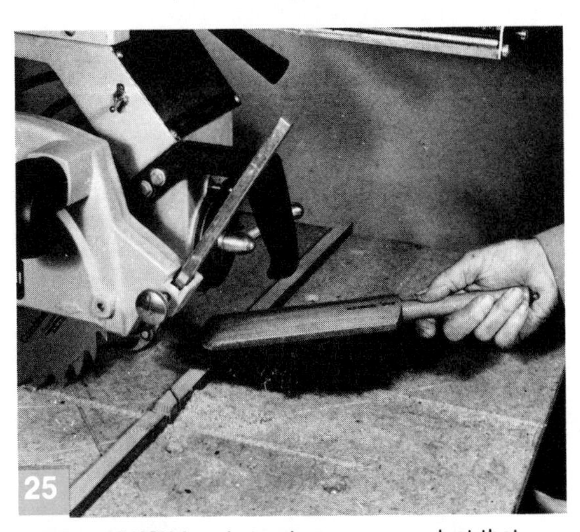

KEEP A BRUSH handy to clear away sawdust that tends to collect in front of the fence. It can cause inaccuracies and may be an operating hazard.

kerf, bend to the full curve and hold in place with clamps until the glue has set.

Home woodworkers generally join pieces edge-to-edge with dowels where it is necessary to build up to a given width with narrow pieces. Many pros prefer to cut glue joints on both edges of the joining pieces. This is easily done on the radial saw by using a three-knife glue-joint cutter and the same molding cutter accessory arbor as that pictured in Fig. 14; also the same two-piece fence. In this job you have to be especially careful to set the cutter to the precise height to cut accurately so that the joining pieces will fit together without any offset at the joining edges. It's best to check the setting by making test cuts on waste stock.

The kickback arm can provide additional guarding of the blade in some operations, such as making a series of repetitive crosscuts. Invert it in its opening and then slide it down so that the end just clears the surface of the stock being cut, as in Fig. 24. In this position it could, conceivably, prevent fingers of even a hand contacting the spinning blade. Make sure that the holding screw is tight and also be sure to replace the arm correctly when changing it back to its original position. On most radials you will have to remove the blade housing to make this change either way.

It's well to check the blade guard occasionally to make sure that all parts, such as the bolts holding the curved parts and the spacer at the back, are properly tightened. Any such metal parts that chance to come loose while the saw is in operation might be caught by the blade and thrown with dangerous force.

a necessary precaution

A final and very necessary precaution is pictured in Fig. 25. Keep a brush handy to clear away sawdust that tends to collect in front of the fence. It not only can cause inaccurate work, but can also be a hazard. It may be a cause of the blade binding suddenly due to the stock being inadvertantly tilted. This may stall the motor, damage the material or even cause an injury. And cautious operators who don't wear glasses always wear industrial goggles or a face shield to protect their eyes.

There are, of course, other operations than those shown which can be done on a radial saw, such as novelty cuts, crosshatching with dado cuts and the like.

In any case, a radial saw is one of the most versatile of all shop tools.

A fine cabinet for your radial-arm saw

By HARRY WICKS

This unique cabinet, which you can build in your shop, makes use of that wasted space beneath your radial saw— no matter what brand or size of saw you own

SEE ALSO
Drawers . . . Motors, shop . . . Power-tool stands . . .
Storage ideas . . . Workbenches . . . Workshops

THIS CABINET for a radial saw was designed to provide a convenient, attractive and easy-to-keep-clean storage unit that will hold the accessories you need for your saw. This particular cabinet fits beneath Sears' 12-in. radial saw. However, the overall size can be easily altered to fit any make of radial saw.

To make cleanup a simple chore, we covered all exposed parts of the cabinet with Johns-Manville Melamite (plastic laminate). For appearance and eye-relief, we used avocado and white. Admittedly, the laminate is a luxury, but the thought of never having to repaint a dirt-smeared cabinet more than justified the cash outlay. However, if you prefer, the cabinet can simply be painted with an enamel.

How it's built. Constructed of ¾-in. A-D plywood, the box is actually symmetrical—with one exception: The top, bottom and sides are edge rabbeted to receive the ¼-in. hardboard back. Similarly, drawer slides at the back are set in for the back. All edges are flush.

When laying out your cabinet, take all dimensions directly from your radial saw. Then, if any dimensions vary from those shown in the drawing, simply mark the changes right on the drawing and custom-build your cabinet to suit your saw. Also, the dimensions shown do not allow for the laminate, so make certain that you make such allowance if you plan to cover your cabinet.

Also, when laying out your cabinet—and before doing any cutting, rabbeting, or dadoing—double check exact location of the four drawers at the front. If you've altered the cabinet dimensions, drawer depths must be adjusted accordingly.

The drawers. The amount of drawer space that the cabinet provides surprised me when we finished the project. In fact, there was more storage space than I needed for my radial-saw accessories, so I used the bottom drawer for table-saw items. And for the first time in 20 years I have all those items in one convenient spot.

For future flexibility, I decided simply to butt-join all divider/partitions. I used ½-in. pine, gluing and nailing them in place after positioning the various accessories in each drawer. Should my requirements ever change, it will be easy to knock out the old dividers and install new ones

BASIC CONSTRUCTION is symmetrical. The unit can be sectioned into identical quarters with one exception: Back edges of the sides are edge-rabbeted and drawer slides are let in ¼ in. to receive hardboard back. The ends are fitted with perforated board.

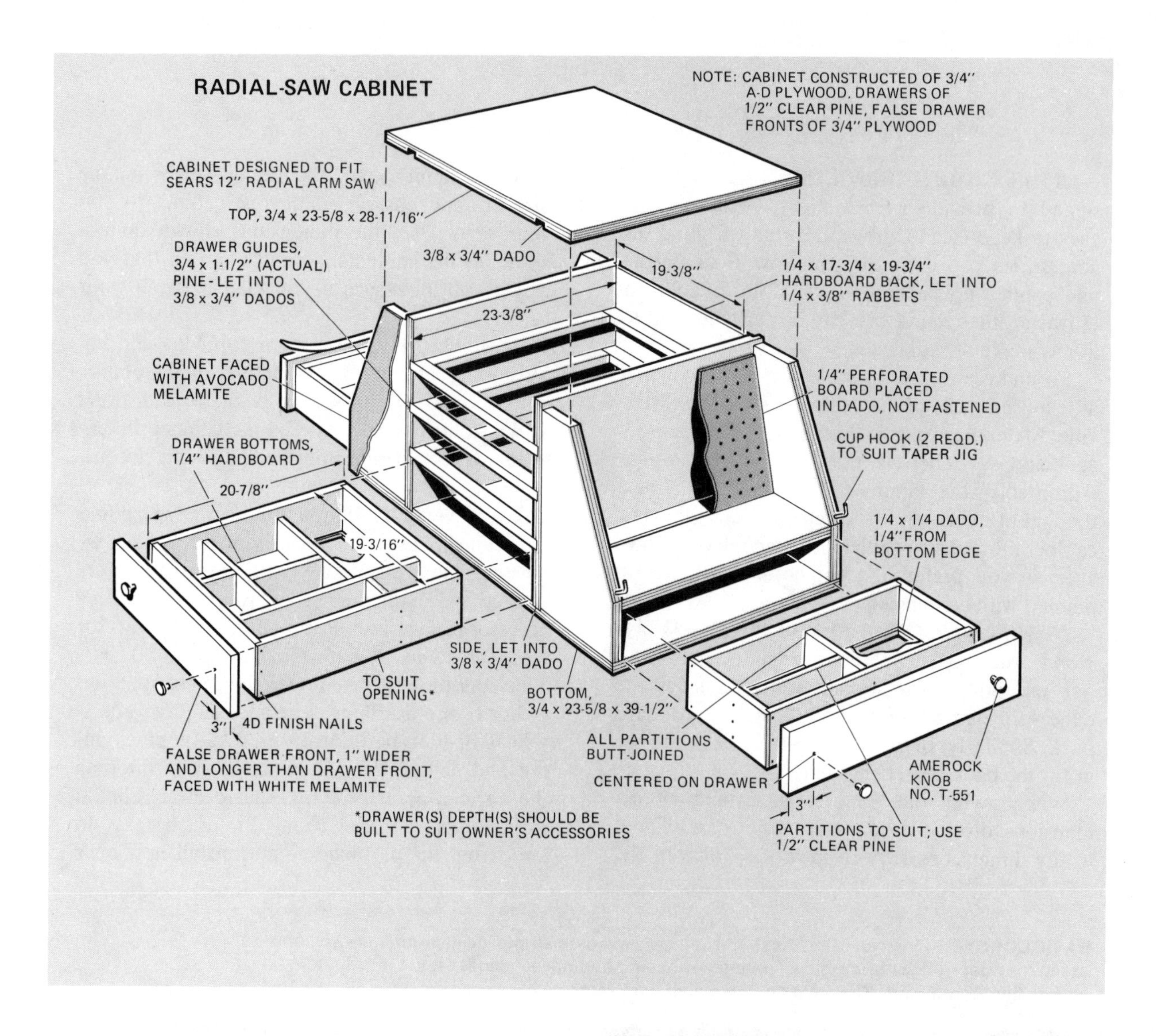

saw accessory cabinet, continued

where I want them. Location of accessories in the drawers is a matter of personal taste and working habits. I laid them all on the workbench and then, based upon frequency of use, placed them in the drawers.

The cabinet ends. Since there was space at both ends I installed a pair of shallow drawers. They are extremely handy for small items such as pencils, tape measures, dividers and the like—which seem to have a way of getting lost in the shuffle when left on the workbench. The perforated board was left brown (as it comes) and given two coats of McCloskey Heirloom varnish.

THE ACCESSORY cabinet sits on the base (below) and the whole assembly rides on casters.

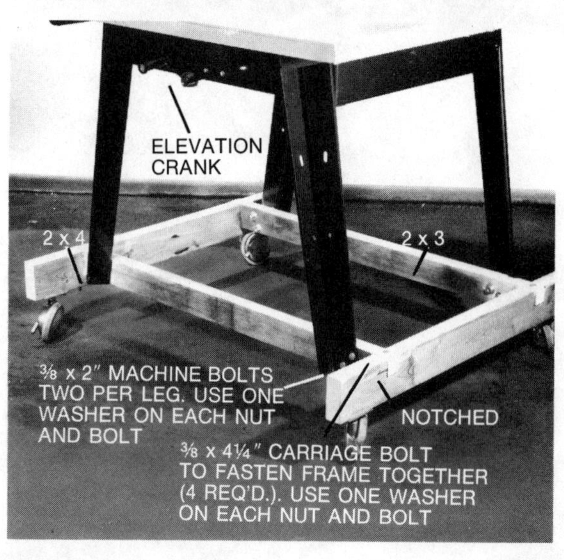

Flexible drawer layouts

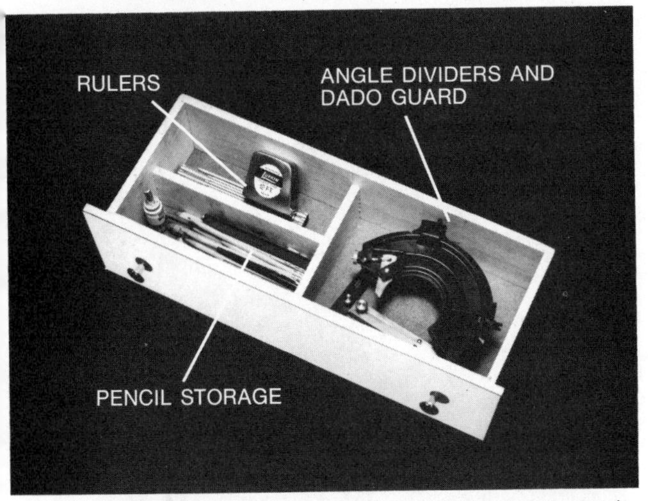

THE END drawer is shallow, ideal for frequently used items such as a tape measure and pencils.

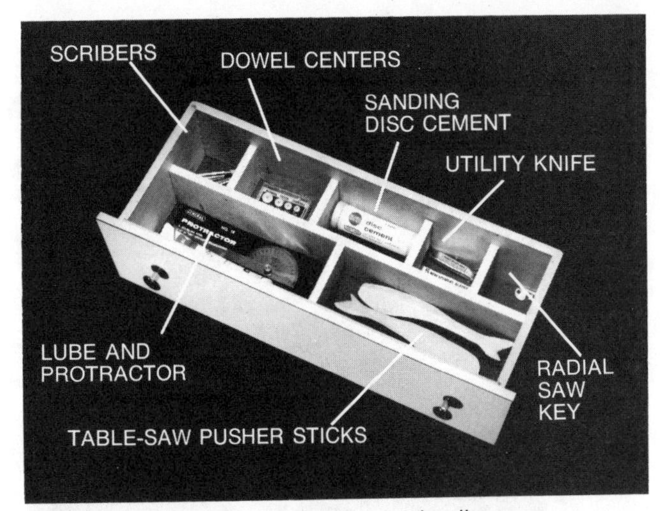

DRAWER at the other end holds more miscellaneous equipment, including the table-saw push sticks.

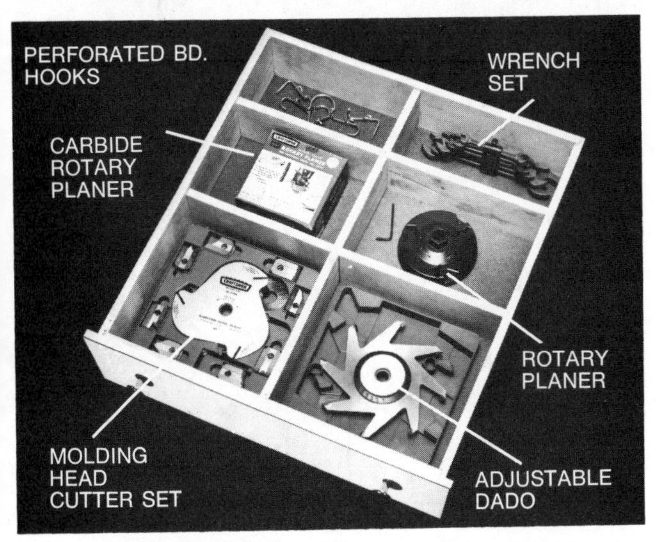

TOP FRONT drawer gets the most-used accessories plus such small items as the wrench set and hooks.

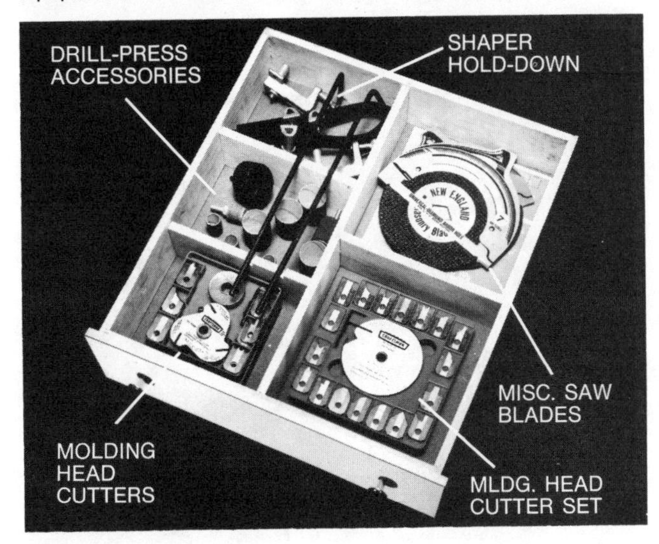

SECOND-DRAWER items are those used less often—for masonry- and metal-cutting blades, for example.

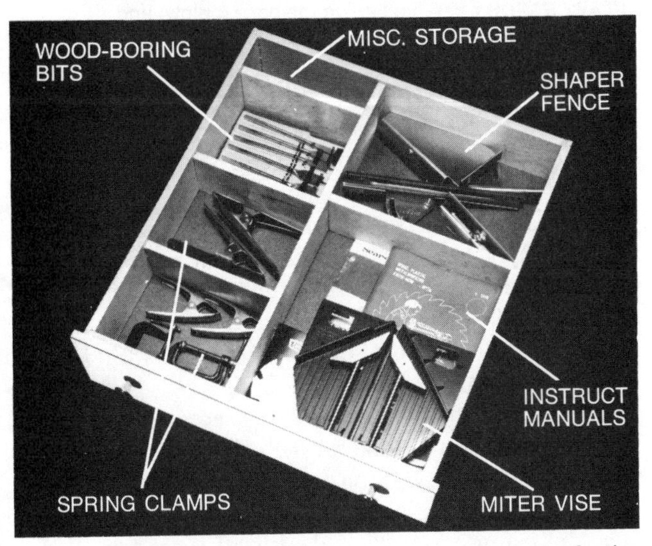

THE THIRD drawer concentrates the accessories for the saw's conversion to use as a drill press.

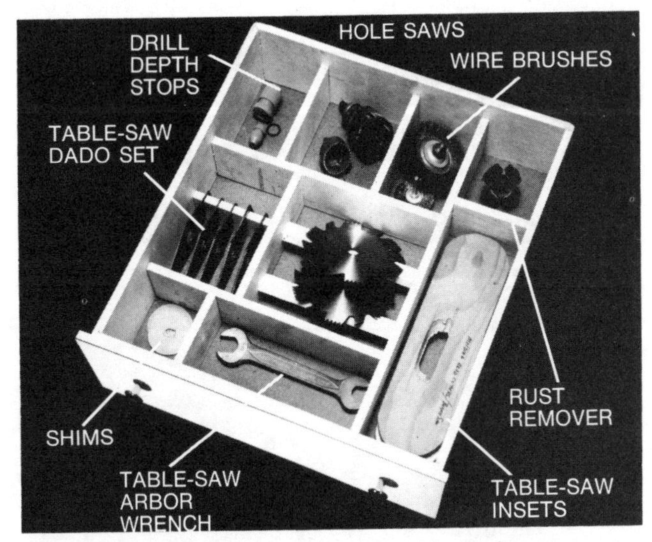

BOTTOM DRAWER keeps the bulk of the table-saw items together in one organized collection.

Removable perforated panels

SAW BLADES hang on a removable ½-in. dowel in the left end of the cabinet with separators.

PERFORATED boards aren't fastened permanently in place, but rest in dadoes as in the top sketch.

THE DOWEL'S block must be located with care; your blades' size will dictate its proper position.

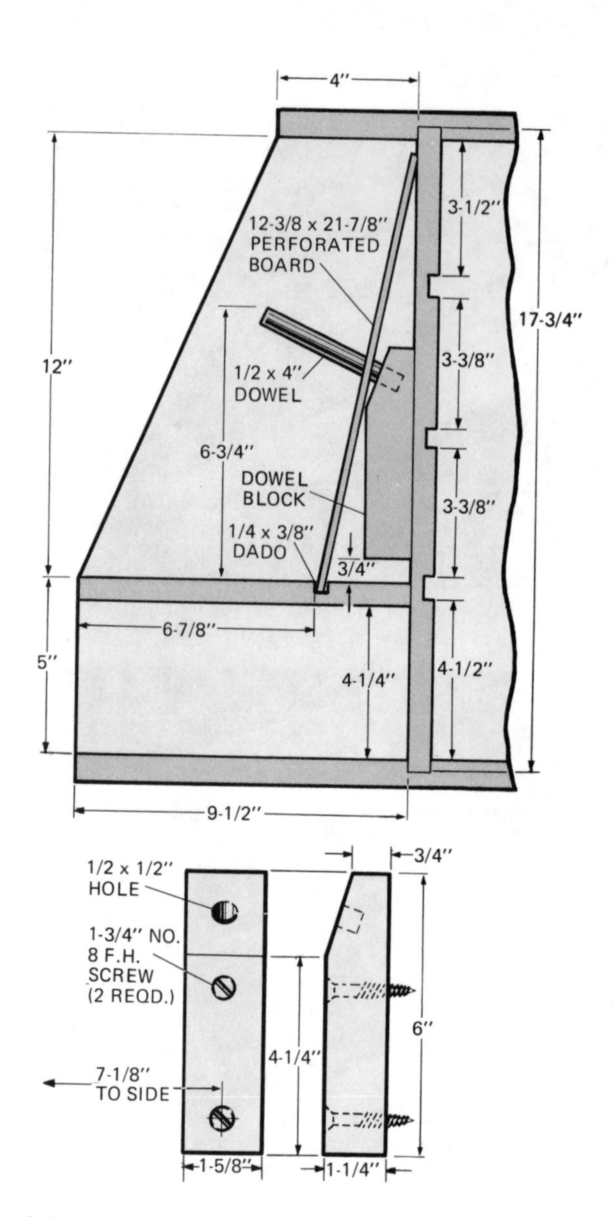

My feeling here was that if I painted them, dirt and smudge marks would inevitably appear and I would be constantly repainting.

The radial-saw blades are hung on a removable ½-in. dowel (see the sketch above). It's good shop practice to use spacers between the blades to keep them from dulling one another. (I used 6-in.-dia. circles cut from hardboard.)

The reason both perforated ends are removable is simply one of cleanliness. From time to time, the boards can be lifted out and the dust removed with a vacuum cleaner. To keep sawdust out of the drawers, the back is fitted with ¼-in. hardboard.

Even if the number of radial-saw accessories you currently own is limited, the cabinet shown will be a welcome addition to your shop. While in the process of building your accessory collection, you can use that valuable drawer space for almost any kind of storage.

Never try to work on a radial-arm saw that doesn't have a level table. To make simple leveling jacks you can use carriage bolts and nuts

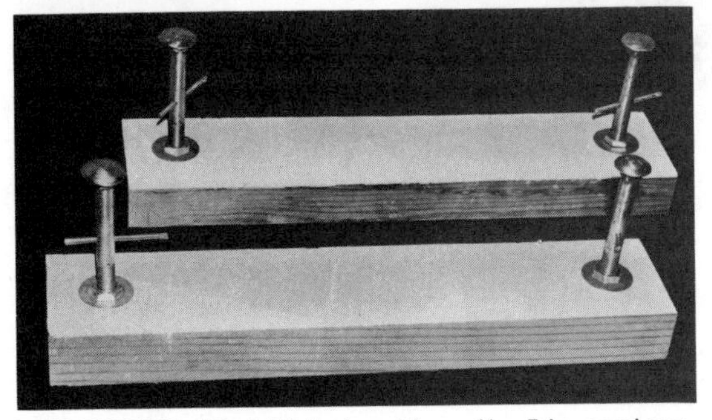

TWO PIECES of 2x4 (18 in. long) have ½ x 5-in. carriage bolts turned into holes at the ends and locked in place with nuts and washers. The cross handles in the bolts are simply nails—optional but handy.

Jacks quickly level a radial-saw table

By WILLIAM WAGGONER

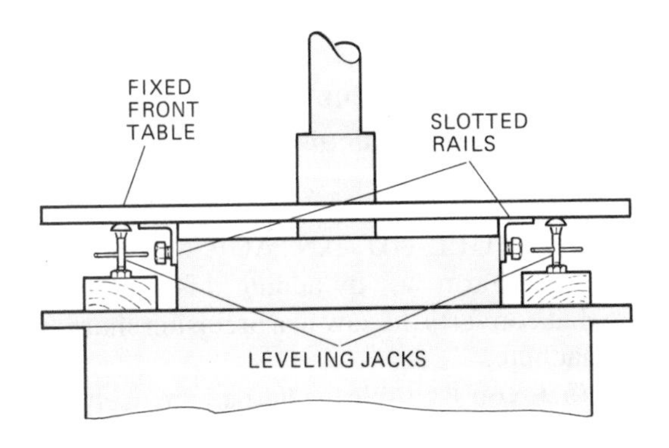

THE IMPORTANCE of a perfectly level table is obvious in the case of a radial-arm saw. If the fixed table runs "down-hill," rabbets and dadoes will run downhill and vary in thickness from one end to the other. Only when the table surface is level with the saw's overarm will the saw cut rabbets and dadoes right on the button.

I find the best way to check the table on my DeWalt saw is with these leveling jacks. To use them you loosen the four bolts that hold the slotted rails, set the jacks in place as in the drawing, lock the motor in a vertical position and then move the motor and arm over the entire surface. When the motor shaft lightly touches the surface at all points, the table will be level. A slight turn of the jacks will correct any variance.

SEE ALSO
Power-tool stands . . . Workbenches . . . Workshops

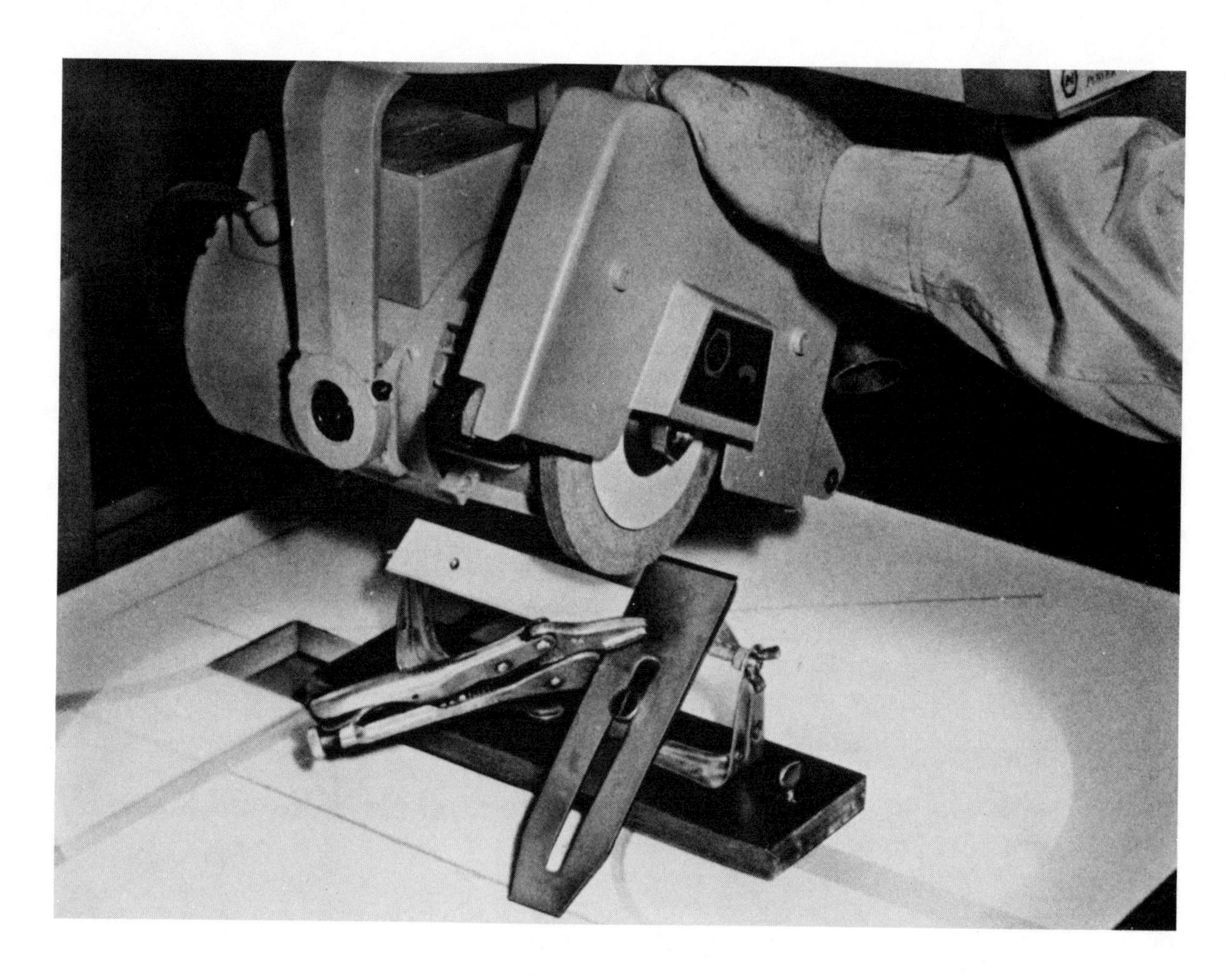

How to sharpen tools on your radial-arm saw

By WILLIAM G. WAGGONER

By building this little jig and putting an emery wheel on your radial-arm saw you can sharpen practically any tool around the house with a high degree of precision

■ TAKE FULL ADVANTAGE of your versatile radial-arm saw by adding this simple fixture that converts the saw to a precision sharpening machine.

With it, you'll be able to sharpen precisely just about any tool around your home, shop or garden, including hollow-ground chisels, plane irons, jointer and planer knives, wood bits, hedge trimmers, tin snips and other cutting tools.

SEE ALSO
Abrasives . . . Grinding wheels . . .
Power-tool stands . . . Sharpening, tool . . .
Workbenches . . . Workshops

As shown on the opposite page, the threaded studs welded to the angle iron are headless ¼-20 bolts 2 in. long, with about ½ in. of the threaded portions protruding at each end of the angle iron.

To insure alignment of the bolts with each other and with the holes in the shelf brackets, lay a section of ¾-in. angle on the inside of the 1¼-in. angle and position the bolts on the step formed by the smaller angle. Clamp the two pieces in place and tack-weld the bolts to the 1¼-in. angle. Remove the length of ¾-in. angle and complete the welding.

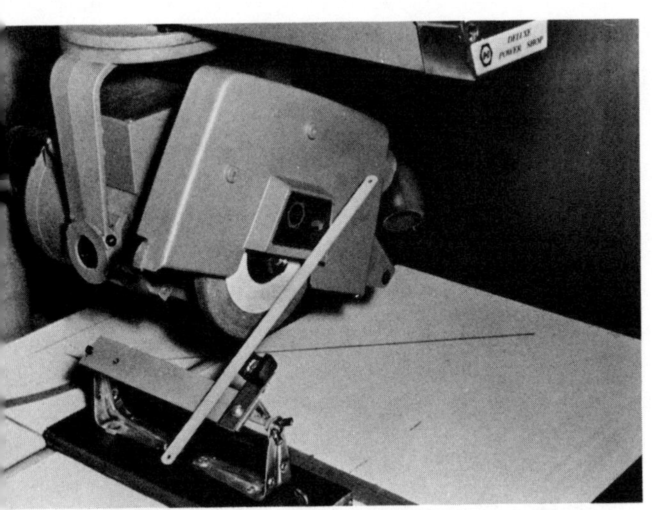

CORRECT POSITION of the angle iron is indicated when hacksaw blade falls slightly below the wheel arbor.

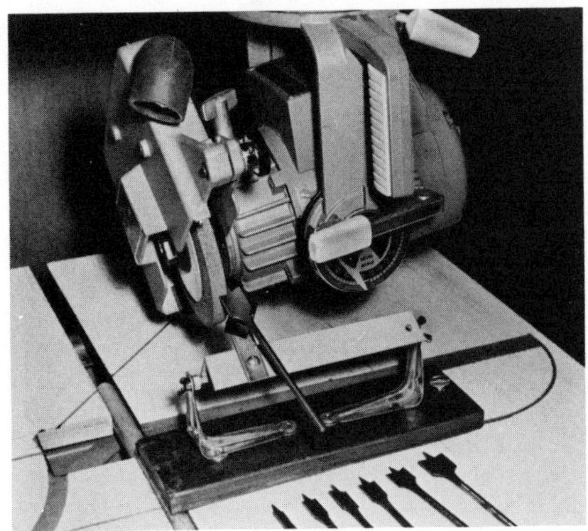

WING-TYPE wood bits are among many precision-ground tools you can resharpen quickly and accurately.

If necessary, enlarge the holes in the shelf brackets by reaming or drilling, then mount them on the bed of ¾-in. plywood. Note that two ¼-in. washers are placed under the bracket at the end of the bed fitted with the length of ¾-in. dowel. At the other end of the bed, a ¼-20 thumb-screw and Teenut are used to permit adjustment of the bed for slight angles or bevels.

The magnetic toolrest assembly consists of a 1-in. horseshoe magnet fitted to a 2½-in. length of ⅛ x ¾-in. flat iron. For light sharpening operations, the work can be held by the magnet alone, but for heavier sharpening chores, be sure to clamp the work firmly to the angle iron.

A 100-grit, 6-in.-dia. emery wheel is used on the radial saw. Because the sharpening is always done under the wheel, you can see exactly what you're doing, especially since there is no toolrest, wheel guard or motor housing in the way.

To get the proper plane for sharpening, lay a straightedge, such as a hacksaw blade, on the magnet and adjust the angle iron so the straightedge is slightly below the wheel arbor. Lock in this position. This procedure also provides the correct relief clearance.

Occasionally you'll find it necessary to dress the emery wheel precisely, using a diamond-tipped wheel dresser. Lock the dresser to the angle iron and position it so that it is at a "drag" position in relation to the wheel's rotation. This will also prevent the dresser from gouging pieces out of the wheel.

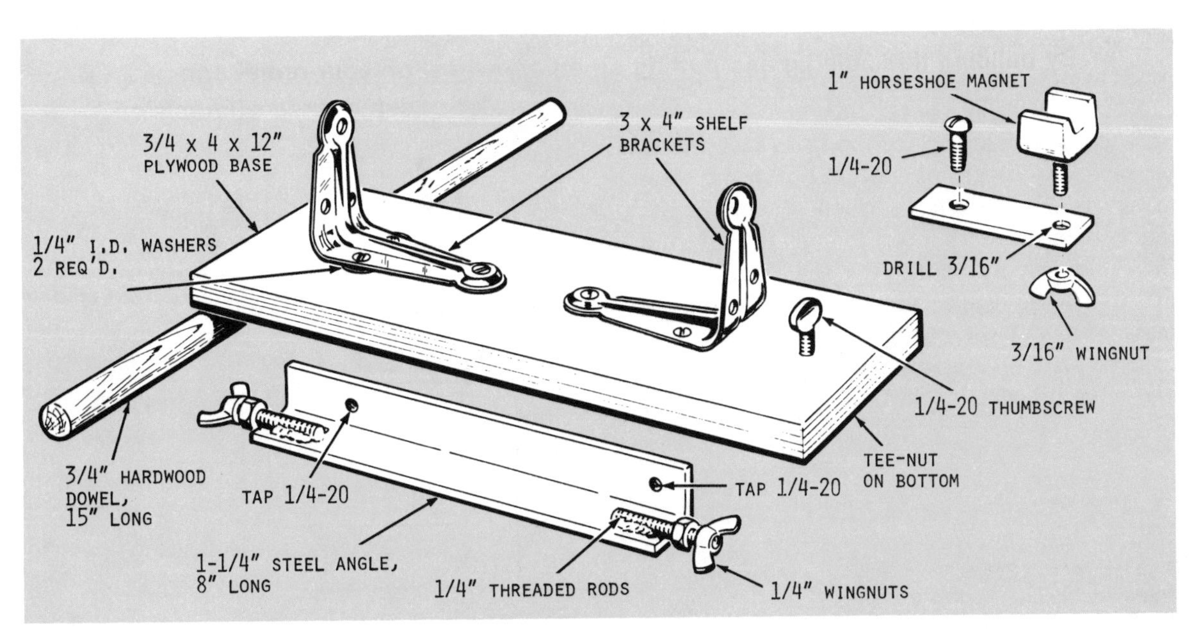

Stretch your radial's crosscut capacity

By WILLIAM G. WAGGONER

YOU CAN ADD several inches to the crosscut limit of your radial-arm saw when you next replace the protective covering on the saw table. Simply make the replacement with two ⅜-in.-thick plywood pieces with space left between them to suit your table-saw miter gauge. Locate this groove space on one side of the 45° bevel position of your saw, and you'll add crosscut capacity for straight bevel cuts.

To use the setup, place the saw fence in the back position, lock the saw and push the wide material into the blade. When it reaches the fence, hold the work intact, unlock the saw and finish the cut by pulling the saw through the material in the regular manner. You'll be able to make your cut without moving the fence from front to back on each cut, turning the motor on and off or "jiggling" a partial cut into the blade.

HOW IT WORKS: Fence is placed in back position, saw locked and work pushed into blade (top drawing). Work is held and blade pulled through to complete cut.

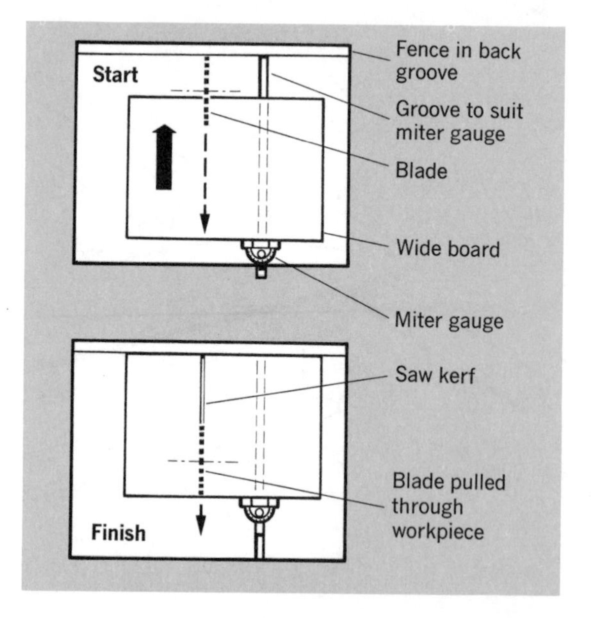

SEE ALSO
Bench saws . . . Power-tool stands . . . Table saws . . . Workbenches . . . Workshops

Table extensions for a radial saw

By R. S. HEDIN

SEE ALSO

Bench saws . . . Power-tool stands . . . Table saws . . . Workbenches . . . Workshops

DOUBLED-UP ½-in. plywood was used in these fold-down extensions to match the original table's thickness. You can shim the hinges if necessary.

WHEN YOU'RE CUTTING long boards, the weight of the outboard section often makes the sawing operation a dangerous one. To avoid an accident under those conditions, a radial-saw table may be rigged with a pair of fold-down extensions. With proper support under those extra-long workpieces, cutting is a snap.

The extensions shown were made of plywood built up to match table thickness. Hinged to the saw table, they drop down when not needed, yet automatically engage when raised into position.

To fasten them to the saw table, lay a long board across and clamp the extensions to it. Use wood screws to attach them, and, if necessary, shim under the hinges to make the extensions flush with the tabletop. Notice in the drawing that the supports are offset 2 inches so that they pass each other when in the folded position.

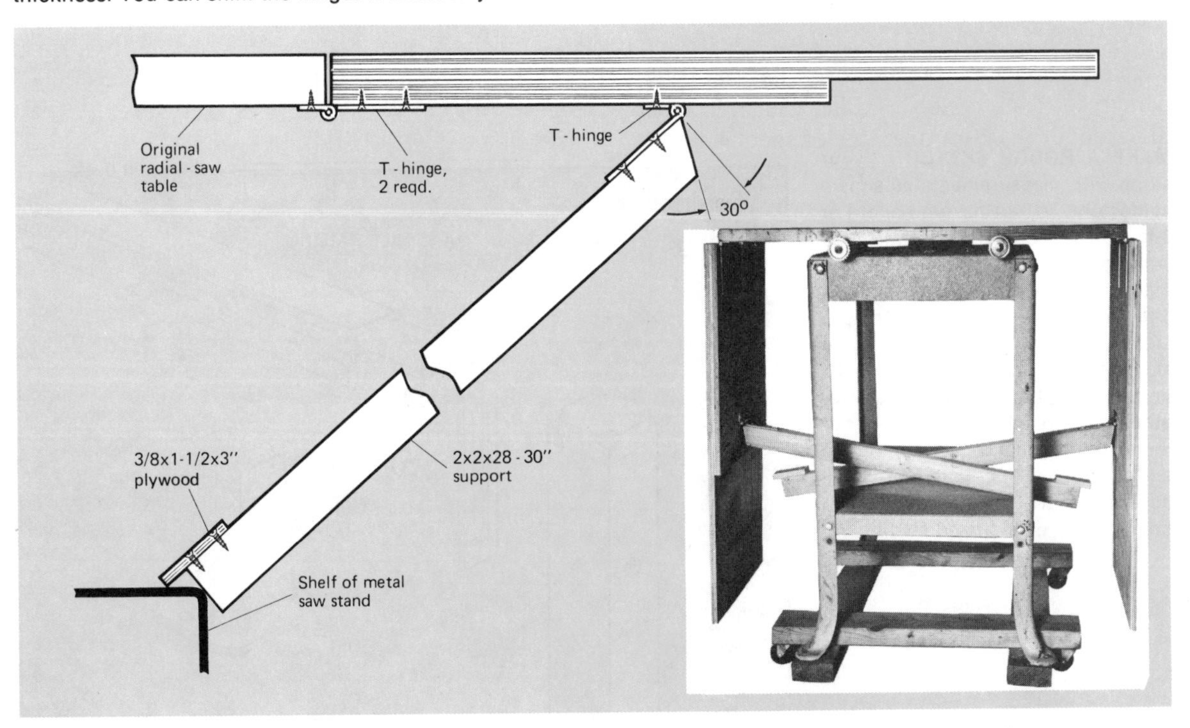

NEWEL POSTS are used for the end posts, corner posts and intermediate posts. The number required is determined by the overall size of the stoop. A stoop that is the same width as the steps generally requires four posts. A stoop wider than the steps can require as many as six or more posts. Posts are anchored to the masonry stoop and steps by flanges that are attached with expansion bolts inserted in predrilled holes. A concrete bit is used to drill the holes for the bolts.

AFTER THE NEWEL POSTS are in place, preassembled, adjustable rail sections are marked for length. Here in order to maintain uniform spacing of spindles, excess length is cut from each end of the upper and lower rails. To cut the rails, you'll need a hacksaw. A vise is handy for holding the rails while they are being cut. Any burred edges should be smoothed with a file so connectors insert easily. Railings are usually installed 31 in. high and even with the tops of the new posts.

How to install wrought-iron railings

MAKE A ROUGH SKETCH of your stoop with measurements as shown at the right. To find the number of 4 or 6-ft. rail sections you'll need, measure from the house to the edge of the platform. To determine whether a 4 or 6-ft. rail section is needed for the steps, measure the length of the stairs, top to bottom as shown. To find the number of newel posts required, figure one for each corner of the platform and one each for the top and bottom of the stairs. If railings consist of more than one section, add one post for each added section.

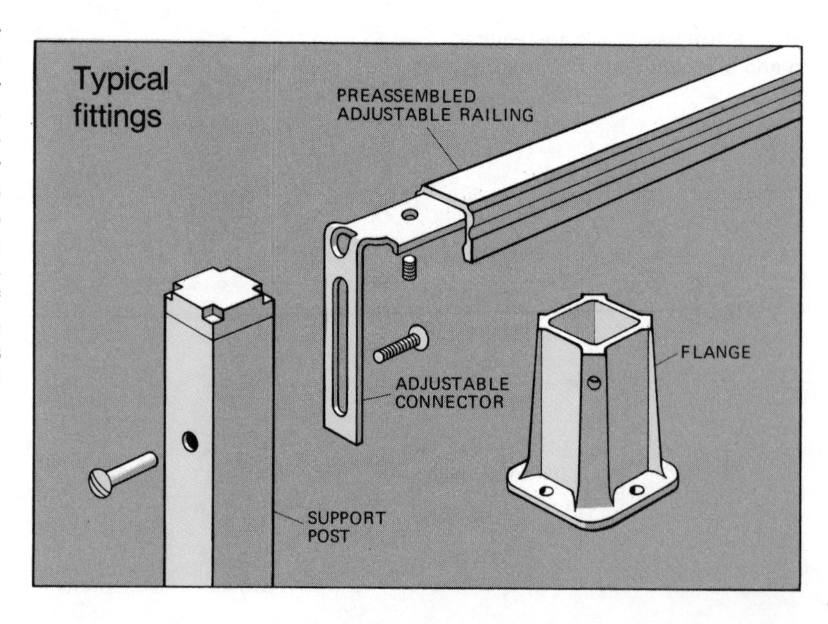

RAIL SECTIONS are attached to newel posts with adjustable connectors that require no drilling. Each connector slides inside the upper and lower rails and is tightened by a setscrew. Rail sections come in 4 and 6-ft. lengths and require support posts between sections. The same connectors attach the sections to the house. Before drilling holes, be sure to level the railing. If it's to be attached to wood, use regular screws; if to masonry, bolts in expansion anchors.

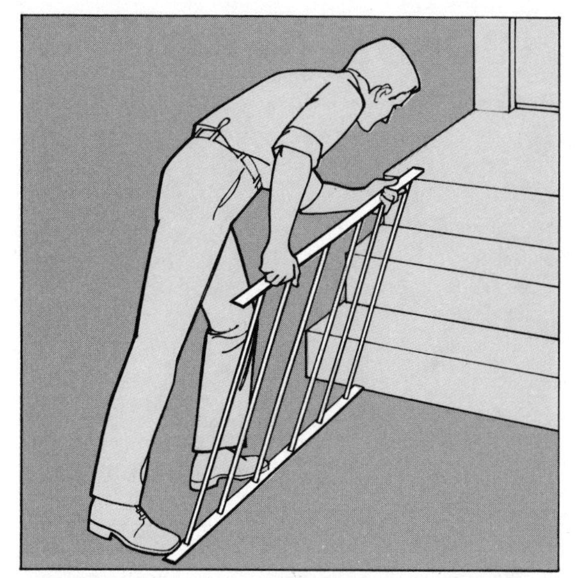

PREASSEMBLED RAIL SECTIONS adjust to any stair slope. To bend, put foot on the lower rail and push forward on the top rail to suit the stair pitch. Spindles are generally electrically fused to top and bottom rails to make the railing stronger than welded ironwork. Connectors are bent to the same angles as the rail section to join the section to the top and bottom newel posts. Extra wrought-iron scrolls, called lamb's tongue and finial, are available for the bottom newel post.

SEE ALSO

Basement stairwell . . . Concrete . . . Decks . . . Measurements . . . Patios . . . Spiral stairs . . . Stairs . . . Steps

ONLY FOUR basic parts are required to add a wrought-iron railing to any porch or stoop—rail section, support post, adjustable connector and flange. Support (newel) posts are 1¼ in. square, 35 and 48 in. high. Posts fit into flanges, which are attached with setscrews; flanges are anchored to wood or masonry with screws or expansion bolts. Adjustable connectors join rail sections to posts like an Erector set. Complete railings are made up of 4 and 6-ft. sections, joined end to end with a post between.

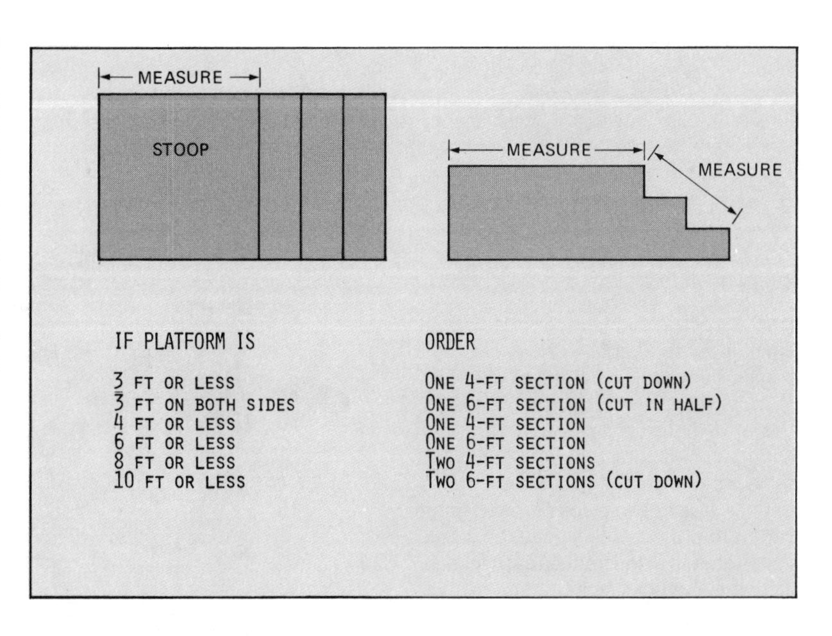

IF PLATFORM IS	ORDER
3 FT OR LESS	ONE 4-FT SECTION (CUT DOWN)
3 FT ON BOTH SIDES	ONE 6-FT SECTION (CUT IN HALF)
4 FT OR LESS	ONE 4-FT SECTION
6 FT OR LESS	ONE 6-FT SECTION
8 FT OR LESS	TWO 4-FT SECTIONS
10 FT OR LESS	TWO 6-FT SECTIONS (CUT DOWN)

Rocker 'car pit'

By GENE ROGERS

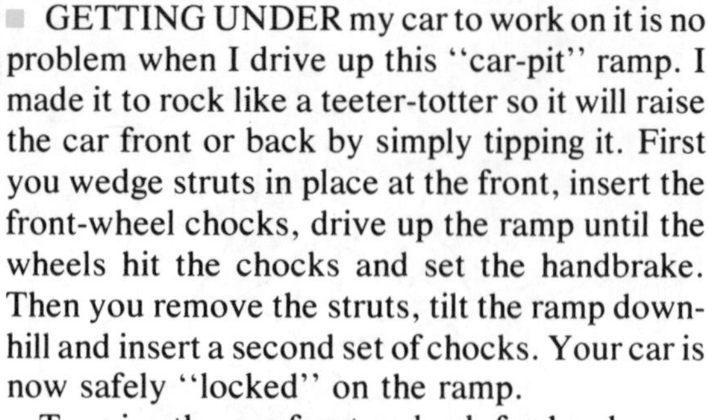

GETTING UNDER my car to work on it is no problem when I drive up this "car-pit" ramp. I made it to rock like a teeter-totter so it will raise the car front or back by simply tipping it. First you wedge struts in place at the front, insert the front-wheel chocks, drive up the ramp until the wheels hit the chocks and set the handbrake. Then you remove the struts, tilt the ramp downhill and insert a second set of chocks. Your car is now safely "locked" on the ramp.

To raise the car front or back for headroom, you merely lift up on the bumpers. To gain full access to the underside of the car, you insert struts at each end of the ramp to support it level. The ramp can be dismantled for storing by using bolts to attach the 2x4 tiepiece.

ROCKER RAMP will support the car uphill, downhill or on the level. Front-wheel chocks keep car from rolling, though for safety be sure to put it in gear and set the handbrake. The ramp will safely support up to 3000 lbs. and is made basically for compact cars.

SEE ALSO

Autos, body care . . . Autos, repair . . . Brakes, auto . . . Lubrication, auto . . . Tune-up, auto . . . Wheels, auto

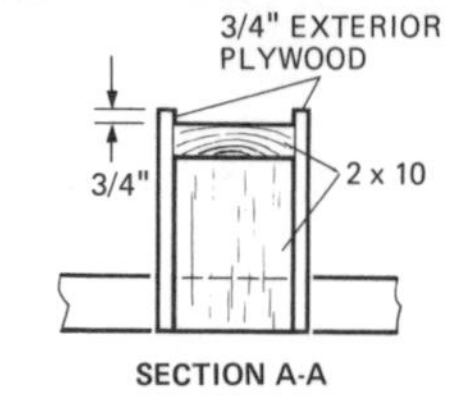

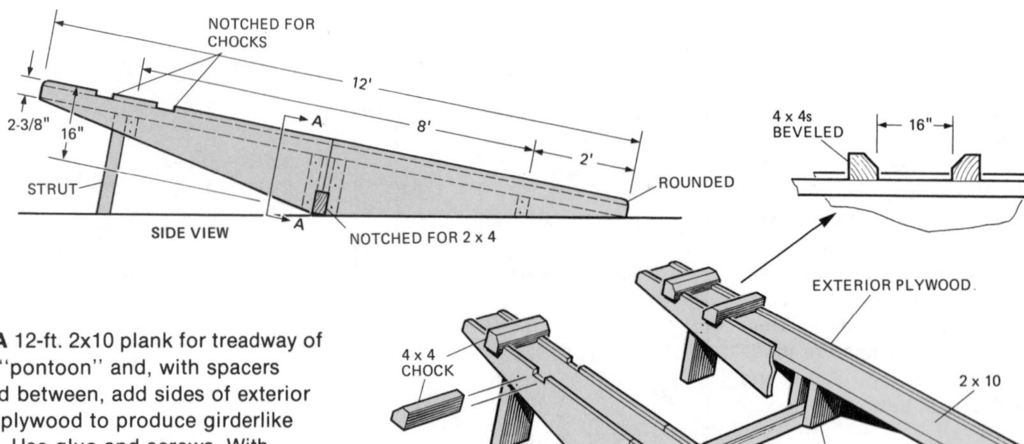

USE A 12-ft. 2x10 plank for treadway of each "pontoon" and, with spacers placed between, add sides of exterior ¾-in. plywood to produce girderlike beam. Use glue and screws. With economical cutting, you can get four sides from less than two 4x8 sheets. Each side is in two pieces, butted at the center to project ¾ in. above the plank, then notched at the front ends to receive 4x4 wheel chocks 16 in. apart.

How to troubleshoot your electric range

YOUR ELECTRIC RANGE is one of the simplest appliances in the house—it's really just heating elements and their controls. Although it uses 230-v. power, it's no more difficult to troubleshoot than a 115-v. appliance, so long as you show the respect you always should for the potential danger of electricity. And while the controls used on ranges have become increasingly sophisticated over the years, their basic principles have not changed.

Most electric ranges have four surface elements, two large ones and two smaller ones. The large elements can have a wattage of 2100 to 2600 w., while smaller ones range from 1150 to 1500 w. Older surface elements consisted of an open coil of wire fitted into a ceramic block. Elements of this type are rarely seen today, except on hotplates, as they burn out easily. They have been replaced by hermetically sealed elements. This element has a Nichrome resistance wire embedded in an insulating powder, usually magnesium oxide, housed in D-shaped stainless-steel tubing. The insulating powder keeps the resistance wire from touching the tubing sheath.

A surface element has either one or two resistance elements and two or four connections. For these connections, one of three types of terminal—banana, knuckle or screw-on—is used. These terminal types are shown below. A terminal block used with the surface element provides a positive connection point between element and switch wiring. Terminal blocks are usually attached to the underside of the cooktop with a screw. Screw-on terminals have, instead of a terminal block, a glass or ceramic covering over terminal ends to prevent shorting. Problems that can arise with surface elements are shorting, breaks in Nichrome wire and pitted or corroded terminals; terminal blocks are also subject to corrosion and pitting, and to damage from internal arcing.

Surface switches are used to regulate the amount of heat produced by surface elements.

SEE ALSO
Appliance centers . . . Electrical wiring . . . Freezers . . . Garbage disposers . . . Kitchens . . . Mixers, food . . . Oven hoods . . . Refrigerators . . . Toasters . . . Trash compactors

SURFACE-ELEMENT ASSEMBLY

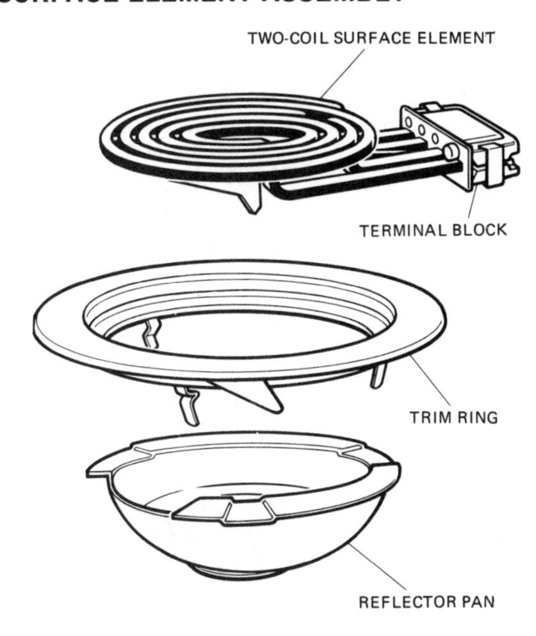

SURFACE-ELEMENT CONNECTIONS

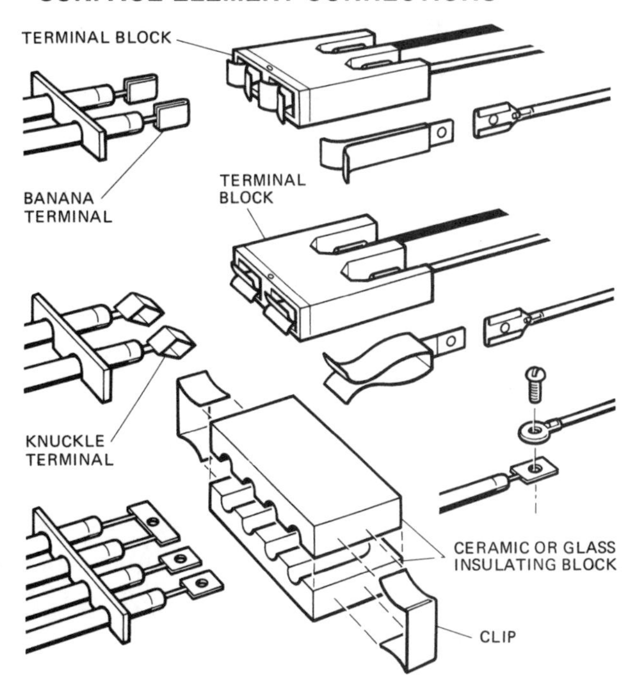

THERMOSTAT COMPONENTS

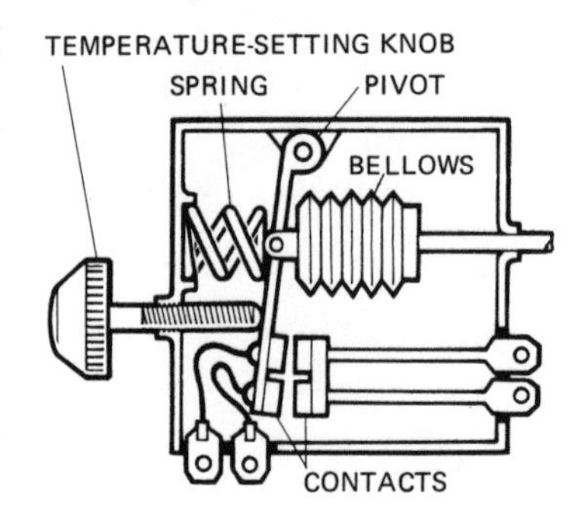

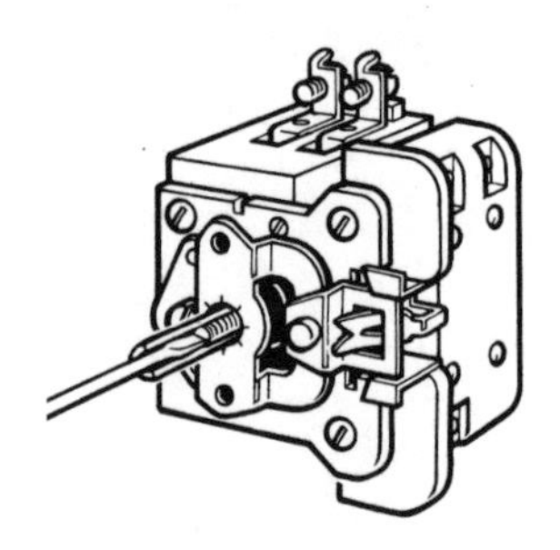

THERMOSTAT CALIBRATION POINTS

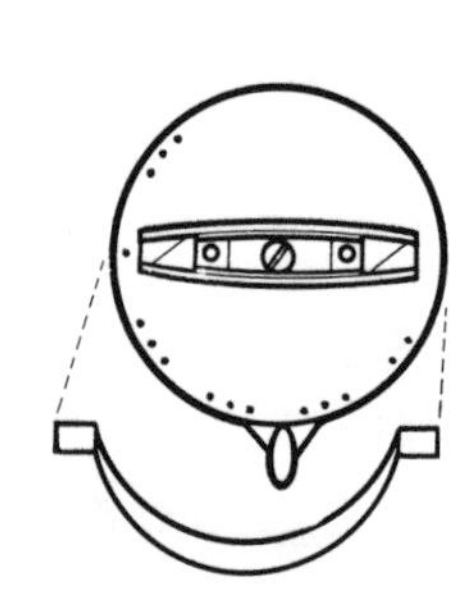

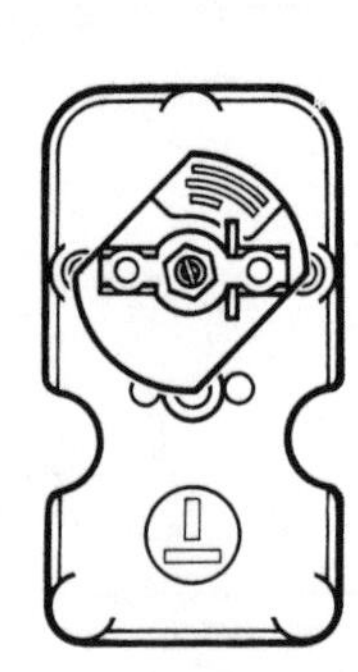

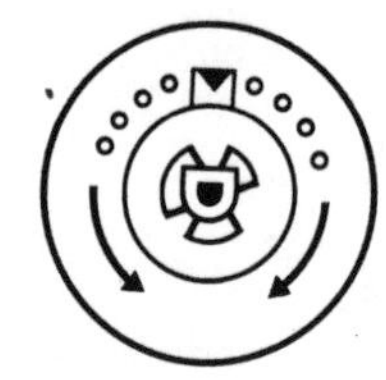

Oven does not heat

POSSIBLE CAUSES	WHAT TO TRY
1. Fuse blown or circuit breaker tripped.	Replace fuse or reset circuit breaker. If blowing or tripping is repeated, disconnect the power and check for shorts.
2. Automatic timer set improperly	Make sure timer is in "manual" position for everyday cooking. Refer to manufacturer's instructions.
3. Automatic timer defective.	Check timer for defective motor or contacts (see clock-timer discussion on page 2495). If gears are bound or broken, repair or replace timer.
4. Selector switch set improperly	Make sure that selector switch is set for type of cooking desired.
5. Thermostat defective.	Place voltmeter across thermostat input terminals; reading should be 230 v. Loosen bake element in oven and pull it forward a fraction of an inch to make terminals accessible; turn thermostat on and check voltage across bake-element terminals; reading should be 230 v. Otherwise, thermostat is defective and must be replaced. Check thermostat's broil operation the same way.
6. Element(s) defective.	Inspect bake and broil elements for breaks or cracks. Check elements one at a time as described above; if voltage is present but element does not heat, replace it.
7. Wires loose or shorted.	Disconnect power, check wiring for breaks or charring. Replace damaged wires. Be sure connections are tight.

Oven temperatures are uneven

POSSIBLE CAUSES	WHAT TO TRY
1. Thermostat out of calibration.	Check oven temperature with an accurate mercury thermometer. Recalibrate thermostat according to the maker's instructions.
2. Door gaskets defective.	Open oven door and inspect sealing gaskets; replace any that are worn, cracked or flat.
3. Door fit uneven.	Check door alignment; if adjustment is needed, loosen door-hinge screws, realign door, then retighten the screws. Check door springs, too; adjust for equal tension if necessary.

SEVEN-HEAT SWITCH OPERATION

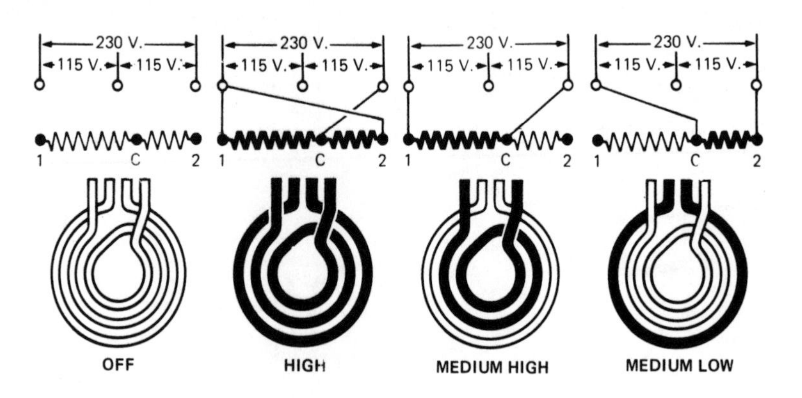

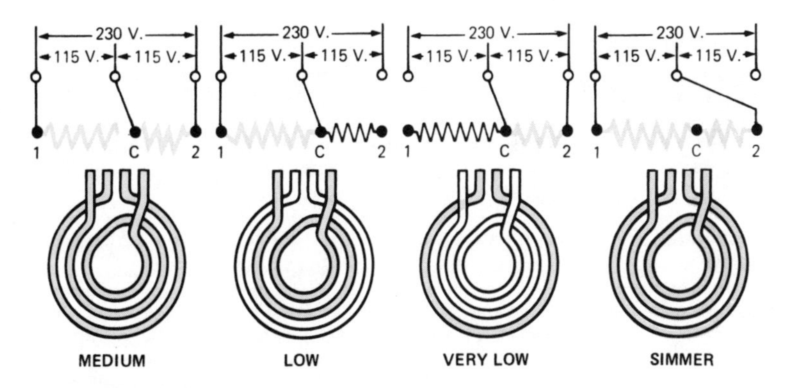

Oven does not shut off

POSSIBLE CAUSES	WHAT TO TRY
1. Thermostat defective.	Disconnect power, pull bake element (see first chart) and set thermostat in "off" position; reconnect power and check voltage across element terminals. If 230 v. is present, replace thermostat.
2. Automatic timer defective.	Set timer on "automatic," turn clock by hand until it clicks to the "off" position; there should now be no voltage to the thermostat. If there is voltage present, repair or replace the timer.

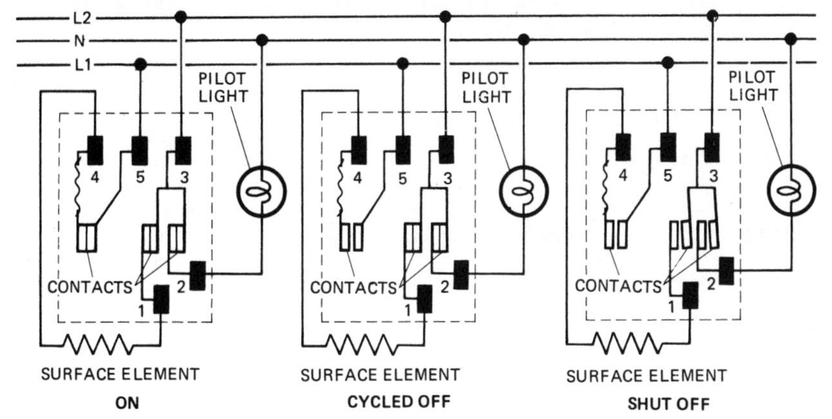

Timer does not operate properly

POSSIBLE CAUSES	WHAT TO TRY
1. Timer set incorrectly.	Refer to the manufacturer's instructions for correct settings.
2. Loose connection.	Disconnect power, tighten all loose connections, then reconnect power.
3. Motor defective.	Disconnect power, remove timer motor and test it directly with 115-v. power. If drive gear does not turn, replace the motor.
4. Blown fuse.	Inspect 15-amp. fuse behind control panel; replace if blown. If new fuse blows, disconnect power and check timer for shorts (see clock-timer discussion, page 2495).
5. Gears worn, stripped or broken.	Inspect clock gears in timer; if any are visibly worn, broken or stripped, repair or replace timer. If gears are jammed, try to free them with silicone spray or a TV-tuner cleaner.
6. Contacts defective.	Make voltage checks on timer as explained on page 2495.

SELF-CLEANING OVEN COMPONENTS

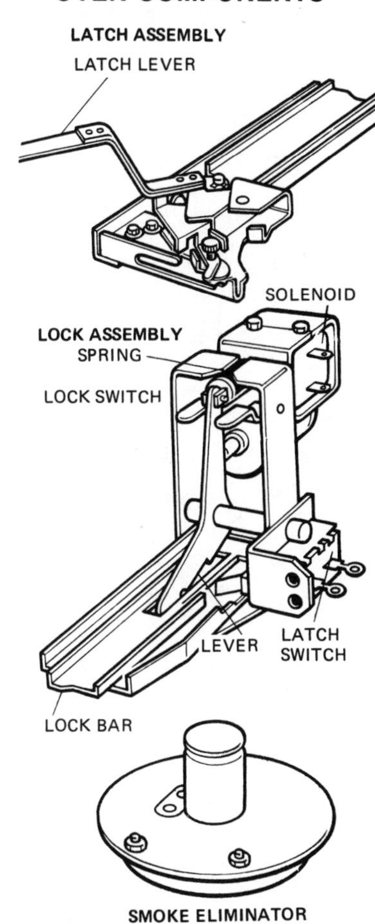

INFINITE-HEAT SWITCH

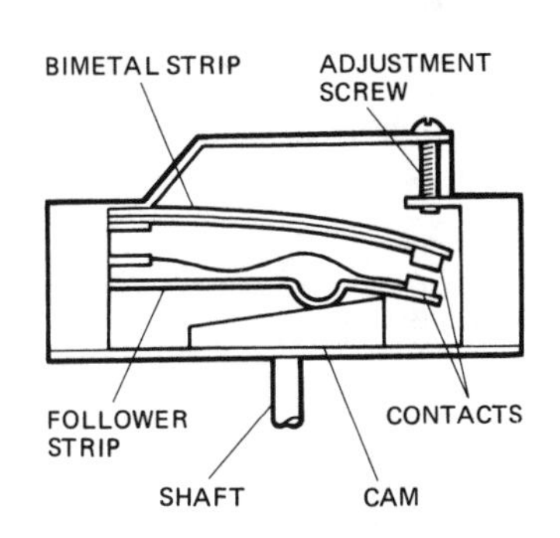

OVEN ELEMENTS

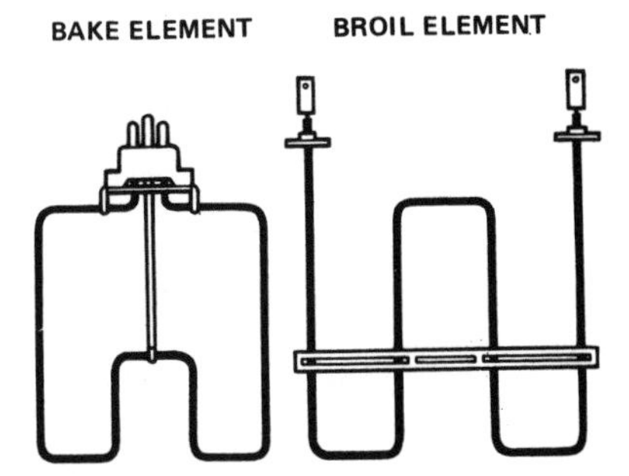

DOOR-HINGE ASSEMBLY

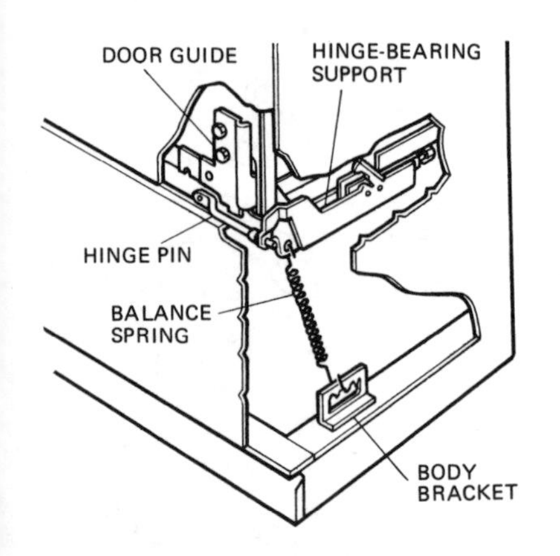

FLUID SENSING BULB

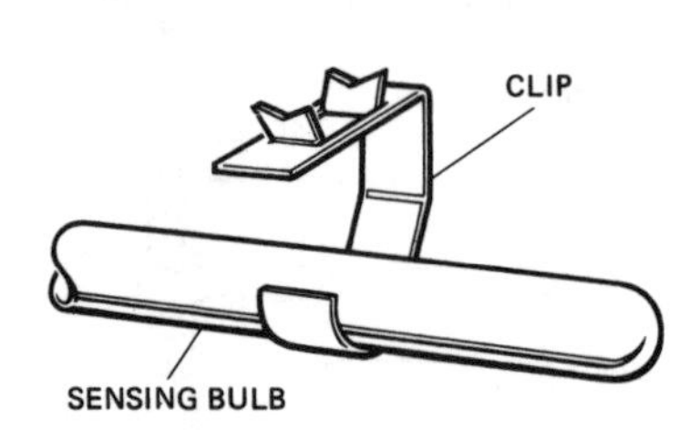

Surface unit does not heat

POSSIBLE CAUSES	WHAT TO TRY
1. Fuse blown or circuit breaker.	Replace fuse or reset circuit breaker. If blowing or tripping is repeated, disconnect the power and check for shorts.
2. Connection loose or shorted.	Disconnect power, tighten any loose connections and replace any charred wiring, reconnect power.
3. Switch defective.	Place voltmeter across switch's input terminals (usually labeled L1 and L2); reading should be 230 v. Turn switch on and place voltmeter across output terminals (to surface element); reading should be 230 v. Replace switch if you do not get these readings.
4. Terminal block defective.	Disconnect power. Inspect inside of terminal block. If it is charred or broken, replace it. If it is pitted or dirty, try to clean it with a contact file; replace it if this cannot be done.
5. Surface element defective.	If element is the plug-in type, unplug it and then plug it into one of the sockets into which the element is known to work; if it does not heat there, replace it. If element is the screw-on type, pull it forward, turn switch on and place voltmenter across surface-element terminals; reading should be 230 v. If voltage is present and element does not heat, replace it. Any replacement element must be of same size and wattage as the original and have the same type of terminals.

Oven door drops down or pops open

POSSIBLE CAUSES	WHAT TO TRY
1. Door out of alignment.	Loosen door-hinge screws, realign door and retighten screws. Check to make sure range is level.
2. Hinge pin worn or loose.	Disassemble door, inspect hinge pins, replace them if worn or broken—an 8d nail can sometimes be used.
3. Hinge worn.	Hinge worn: replace hinge if edges are worn.
4. Spring broken.	Open door slightly. If it fails to spring closed or drops easily, a broken spring is likely. Inspect springs; if one is broken, replace both.
5. Roller bearing broken.	If door is hard to open or close, a bearing is broken. Replace both.

Oven drips water or sweats

POSSIBLE CAUSES	WHAT TO TRY
1. Oven preheated improperly.	Preheat oven with door open at first stop.
2. Oven temperature too high.	Use an accurate mercury thermometer to check on calibration of oven thermostat.
3. Door not sealing.	Check door alignment and condition of the door gaskets; realign door if necessary (see chart, "Oven temperatures are uneven," page 2492). Replace any worn, cracked or flat gaskets.
4. Oven vent clogged.	Inspect oven vents for obstructions and clear them. If the oven uses a filter clean or replace it.

Oven lamp does not light

POSSIBLE CAUSES	WHAT TO TRY
1. Bulb loose or defective.	Tighten bulb in socket. If it still does not work, replace it with a new *appliance* bulb.
2. Switch defective.	Disconnect power, disconnect both leads to switch, place a continuity tester across both switch leads and turn on the switch. There should be a reading of continuity. Turn the switch off. There should be no reading. Replace the switch if you do not get correct readings.
3. Bad contact in socket.	Disconnect power and remove bulb from socket. With finger or blade of a small screwdriver, bend the center socket contact outward a fraction of an inch. Replace bulb and reconnect power.

AUTOMATIC TIMER

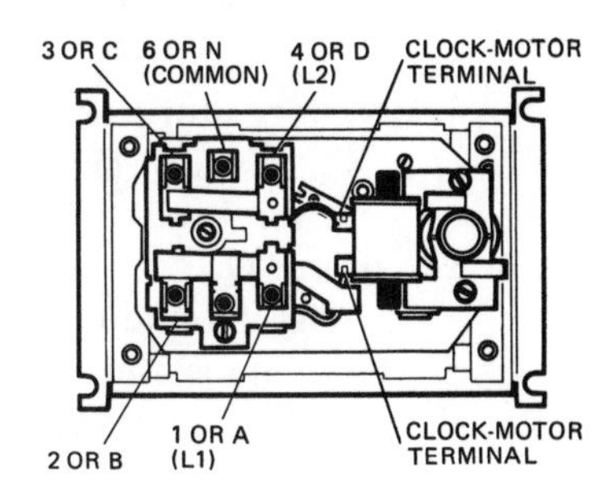

TESTING AUTOMATIC TIMERS: Motor: voltage across terminals 1 and 6 should be 115; if not, check for blown 15-amp. fuse behind panel; if fuse is good, see whether motor drive wheel is turning; if not, replace motor. Switch: voltage across 1 and 4 should be 230, as across 2 and 3 with timer set on manual and when the timer has turned the oven on in automatic operation. If these voltage readings are not obtained, the timer must be repaired or replaced.

No heat for cleaning (self-cleaning ovens)

POSSIBLE CAUSES	WHAT TO TRY
1. Controls set improperly.	Refer to manufacturer's instructions for setting controls for cleaning cycle; after setting controls, wait a minute to determine whether they are working.
2. Fuse blown or circuit breaker tripped.	Replace fuse or reset circuit breaker; if blowing or tripping is repeated, disconnect the power, check for shorts.
3. Thermostat defective.	See chart "Oven does not heat" (page 2492).
4. Door unlocked.	Inspect door for firm seat against oven, make sure latch is all the way over in locked position; if not, check both door and locking mechanism for alignment.

Cleaning is incomplete (self-cleaning ovens)

POSSIBLE CAUSES	WHAT TO TRY
1. Controls set improperly.	See chart "No heat for cleaning."
2. Cleaning time short.	See maker's instructions on length of cleaning time.
3. Oven elements defective.	See chart "Oven does not heat" (page 2492).
4. Line voltage low.	Check voltage at terminal block at rear of range; it should be within 10 percent of 230 v. If it is lower than 207 v., call local power company.
5. Smoke eliminator defective.	Disconnect power, locate smoke eliminator and disconnect its leads; then place continuity tester across eliminator terminals. Replace eliminator if there is no reading or if there are visible breaks in its mesh screen.

continued

The switches most commonly used are the step switch and the infinite-heat switch. The step type is a rotary or pushbutton switch that provides a choice of from five to seven different heats (wattages) by connecting the resistances in the surface element in parallel, in series, or singly to either 230-v. or 115-v. current. Typical wattages for a seven-heat switch could be 212, 287, 500, 850, 1150, 2000 and 3000. Operation of a seven-heat switch is shown schematically on page 2492.

The infinite-heat switch, which provides a continuous range of settings between "high" and "off," uses an internal bimetal strip, which is anchored at one end and has a switch contact at the other end. As current passes through the bimetal and heats it, it curls up and away from the cam-follower strip that carries the switch's other contact. The position of the cam determines how long the element will be on before the bending bimetal breaks contact and cycles the element off. In its extreme position—the "high" setting—the cam holds the contacts together without cycling.

Like surface switches, oven controls vary. Some ovens have only a thermostat, while others also have a selector switch and automatic clock. The selector switch is used where a range has more than one oven or there is more than one function for the thermostat to perform, or it can determine which oven elements are supplied with current and whether they are connected in series or in parallel.

The thermostat that regulates oven temperature has a fluid-filled sensing bulb, similar to the bulb at the end of a thermometer, suspended within the oven. Expansion of the fluid with increasing temperature activates a bellows in the thermostat that forces contacts apart, cutting off current to oven elements and cycling the oven off; reduced oven temperature and contraction of fluid bring the contacts together again, cycling the oven back on. The thermostat's control knob varies tension between contacts.

checking oven thermostat

Thermostat calibration can be checked by putting a mercury (not bimetal) thermometer in the oven and setting the thermostat at 400° F. Let the oven cycle three or four times, then check the temperature; if it is more than 15° F. above or below the thermostat setting, the thermostat requires recalibration. Calibration instructions are usually stamped on the thermostat, but if none can be found, assume that a quarter turn equals 25° F. Turn the calibration screw in either direction, then observe the result. Check calibration annually, more often if the oven gets unusually heavy use. (A source of calibration thermometers is Charles Connolly Distributing Co., 41 River Rd., North Arlington, NJ 07032.)

Construction of oven elements is similar to that of surface elements. The broil element usually has two resistances, with a maximum of 3000 w; the bake element is a single resistance rated at about 2500 w. Elements are fastened to the oven's rear wall, but can usually be lowered or lifted slightly.

A range clock may be fully automatic or nothing more than a clock with a buzzer timer. The fully automatic timer is connected to the oven controls.

self-cleaning ovens

Electric self-cleaning ovens use temperatures of 850° to 1000° F. to decompose oven soil. The process, called pyrolysis, leaves only a loose ash that is easily removed. The self-cleaning oven has more insulation, heavier body metal, larger and more durable controls and a number of safety features.

The cleaning cycle uses the oven thermostat, a bias circuit and door-locking circuit. The bias circuit lets the thermostat run in the higher temperature range required for pyrolysis. The door-locking circuit assures positive locking of the oven door at temperatures over 550° F. and keeps the cleaning cycle from starting if the door is not locked; this circuit is essential for safety, as a rush of air mixing with carbonized soil at high temperature could cause an explosion.

The self-cleaning cycle also involves a cooling fan that circulates air in and around the oven liner and, usually, a smoke eliminator, a device that promotes the decomposition of smoke.

Setup sequence for cleaning and duration of cleaning vary among manufacturers. The appearance of the soil remaining at the end of a cleaning cycle indicates cleaning effectiveness. If it is brown and soft, no cleaning has taken place; if it is dark brown, cleaning has been incomplete. Loose gray ash indicates complete cleaning.

Continuous-cleaning ovens require none of the extra circuits and safety devices self-cleaning ovens do. They differ from ordinary noncleaning ovens only in the porcelain with which they are lined. This is somewhat porous, and allows fat spatters to spread out and then decompose at normal cooking temperatures.

METRIC CONVERSION

Conversion factors can be carried so far they become impractical. In cases below where an entry is exact it is followed by an asterisk (*). Where considerable rounding off has taken place, the entry is followed by a + or a - sign.

CUSTOMARY TO METRIC

Linear Measure

inches	millimeters
1/16	1.5875*
1/8	3.2
3/16	4.8
1/4	6.35*
5/16	7.9
3/8	9.5
7/16	11.1
1/2	12.7*
9/16	14.3
5/8	15.9
11/16	17.5
3/4	19.05*
13/16	20.6
7/8	22.2
15/16	23.8
1	25.4*

inches	centimeters
1	2.54*
2	5.1
3	7.6
4	10.2
5	12.7*
6	15.2
7	17.8
8	20.3
9	22.9
10	25.4*
11	27.9
12	30.5

feet	centimeters	meters
1	30.48*	.3048*
2	61	.61
3	91	.91
4	122	1.22
5	152	1.52
6	183	1.83
7	213	2.13
8	244	2.44
9	274	2.74
10	305	3.05
50	1524*	15.24*
100	3048*	30.48*

1 yard = .9144* meters

1 rod = 5.0292* meters

1 mile = 1.6 kilometers

1 nautical mile = 1.852* kilometers

Fluid Measure

(Milliliters [ml] and cubic centimeters [cc or cu cm] are equivalent, but it is customary to use milliliters for liquids.)

1 cu in = 16.39 ml

1 fl oz = 29.6 ml

1 cup = 237 ml

1 pint = 473 ml

1 quart = 946 ml
= .946 liters

1 gallon = 3785 ml
= 3.785 liters

Formula (exact):
fluid ounces × 29.573 529 562 5* = milliliters

Weights

ounces	grams
1	28.3
2	56.7
3	85
4	113
5	142
6	170
7	198
8	227
9	255
10	283
11	312
12	340
13	369
14	397
15	425
16	454

Formula (exact):
ounces × 28.349 523 125* = grams

pounds	kilograms
1	.45
2	.9
3	1.4
4	1.8
5	2.3
6	2.7
7	3.2
8	3.6
9	4.1
10	4.5

1 short ton (2000 lbs) = 907 kilograms (kg)

Formula (exact):
pounds × .453 592 37* = kilograms

Volume

1 cu in = 16.39 cubic centimeters (cc)

1 cu ft = 28 316.7 cc

1 bushel = 35 239.1 cc

1 peck = 8 809.8 cc

Area

1 sq in = 6.45 sq cm

1 sq ft = 929 sq cm
= .093 sq meters

1 sq yd = .84 sq meters

1 acre = 4 046.9 sq meters
= .404 7 hectares

1 sq mile = 2 589 988 sq meters
= 259 hectares
= 2.589 9 sq kilometers

Kitchen Measure

1 teaspoon = 4.93 milliliters (ml)

1 Tablespoon = 14.79 milliliters (ml)

Miscellaneous

1 British thermal unit (Btu) (mean)
= 1 055.9 joules

1 calorie (mean) = 4.19 joules

1 horsepower = 745.7 watts
= .75 kilowatts

caliber (diameter of a firearm's bore in hundredths of an inch)
= .254 millimeters (mm)

1 atmosphere pressure = 101 325* pascals (newtons per sq meter)

1 pound per square inch (psi) = 6 895 pascals

1 pound per square foot = 47.9 pascals

1 knot = 1.85 kilometers per hour

25 miles per hour = 40.2 kilometers per hour

50 miles per hour = 80.5 kilometers per hour

75 miles per hour = 120.7 kilometers per hour

PIPE FITTINGS

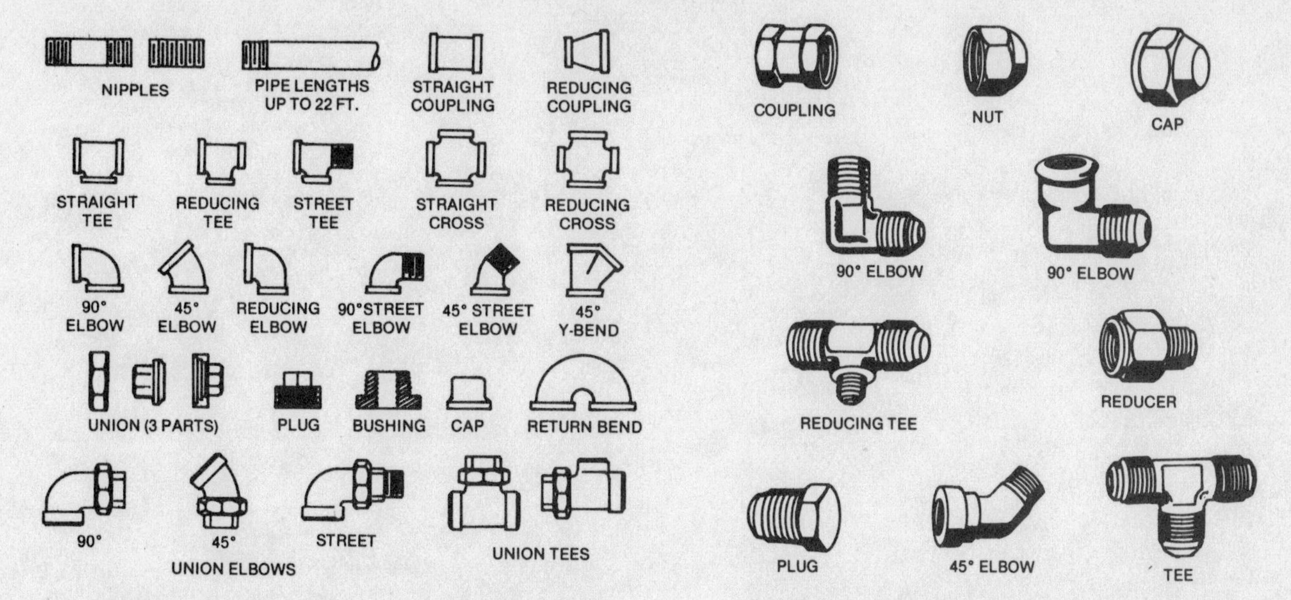

Here are the common steel pipe fittings. Nipples are simply short lengths of pipe threaded on both ends. Reducing fittings join two different sizes of pipe.

Compression fittings of the flared-tube type are the easiest for the novice to handle when working with copper tubing.

STANDARD STEEL PIPE (All Dimensions in Inches)					
Nominal Size	Outside Diameter	Inside Diameter	Nominal Size	Outside Diameter	Inside Diameter
1/8	0.405	0.269	1	1.315	1.049
1/4	0.540	0.364	1 1/4	1.660	1.380
3/8	0.675	0.493	1 1/2	1.900	1.610
1/2	0.840	0.622	2	2.375	2.067
3/4	1.050	0.824	2 1/2	2.875	2.469

SQUARE MEASURE

144 sq in = 1 sq ft
9 sq ft = 1 sq yd
272.25 sq ft = 1 sq rod
160 sq rods = 1 acre

VOLUME MEASURE

1728 cu in = 1 cu ft
27 cu ft = 1 cu yd

MEASURES OF CAPACITY

1 cup = 8 fl oz
2 cups = 1 pint
2 pints = 1 quart
4 quarts = 1 gallon
2 gallons = 1 peck
4 pecks = 1 bushel

WOOD SCREWS

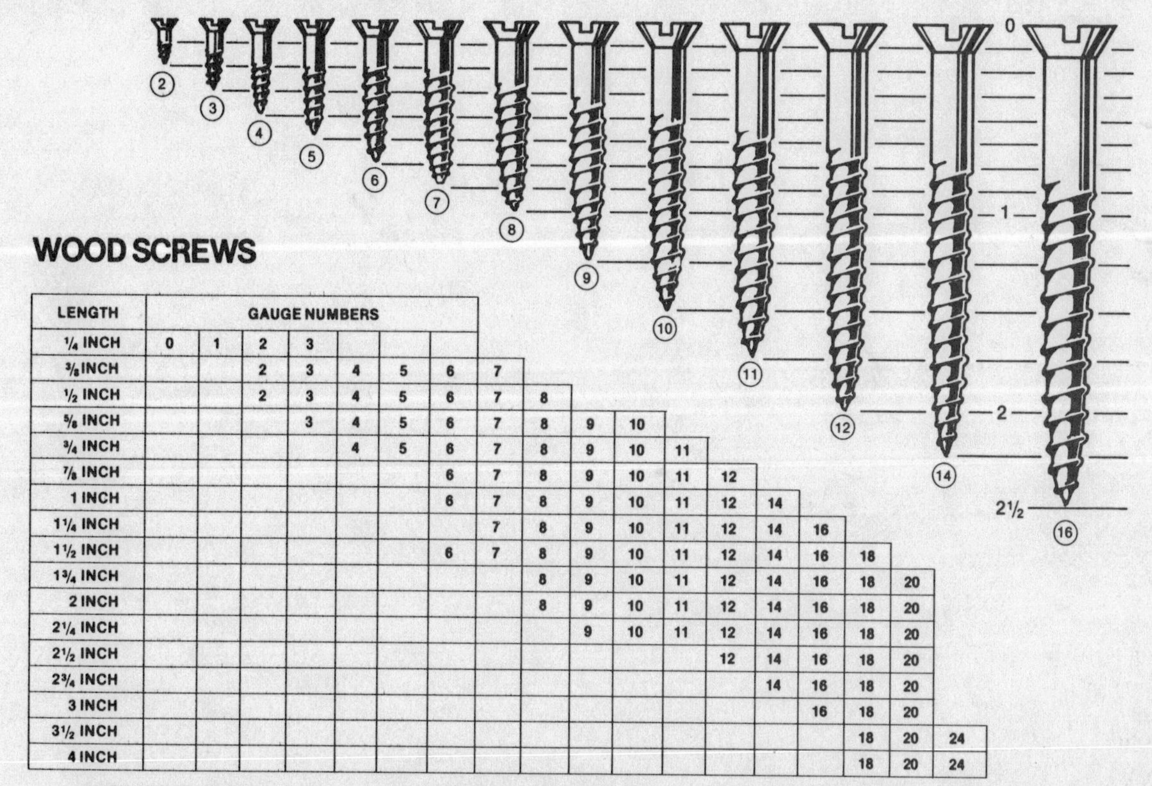

LENGTH	GAUGE NUMBERS																
1/4 INCH	0	1	2	3													
3/8 INCH			2	3	4	5	6	7									
1/2 INCH			2	3	4	5	6	7	8								
5/8 INCH				3	4	5	6	7	8	9	10						
3/4 INCH					4	5	6	7	8	9	10	11					
7/8 INCH							6	7	8	9	10	11	12				
1 INCH							6	7	8	9	10	11	12	14			
1 1/4 INCH								7	8	9	10	11	12	14	16		
1 1/2 INCH							6	7	8	9	10	11	12	14	16	18	
1 3/4 INCH									8	9	10	11	12	14	16	18	20
2 INCH									8	9	10	11	12	14	16	18	20
2 1/4 INCH										9	10	11	12	14	16	18	20
2 1/2 INCH													12	14	16	18	20
2 3/4 INCH														14	16	18	20
3 INCH															16	18	20
3 1/2 INCH																18	20	24
4 INCH																18	20	24

WHEN YOU BUY SCREWS, SPECIFY (1) LENGTH, (2) GAUGE NUMBER, (3) TYPE OF HEAD—FLAT, ROUND, OR OVAL, (4) MATERIAL—STEEL, BRASS, BRONZE, ETC., (5) FINISH—BRIGHT, STEEL BLUED, CADMIUM, NICKEL, OR CHROMIUM PLATED.